THE REJECT

FORDHAM UNIVERSITY PRESS   NEW YORK 2015

COMMONALITIES
Timothy C. Campbell, series editor

THE REJECT

Community, Politics, and Religion
after the Subject

IRVING GOH

THIS BOOK IS MADE POSSIBLE BY A COLLABORATIVE GRANT
FROM THE ANDREW W. MELLON FOUNDATION.

Fordham University Press has no responsibility for the persistence
or accuracy of URLs for external or third-party Internet websites re-
ferred to in this publication and does not guarantee that any content
on such websites is, or will remain, accurate or appropriate.

Fordham University Press also publishes its books in a variety of
electronic formats. Some content that appears in print may not be
available in electronic books.

Library of Congress Cataloging-in-Publication Data

Goh, Irving.
  The reject : community, politics, and religion after the subject /
Irving Goh. — First edition.
      pages cm. — (Commonalities)
  Includes bibliographical references and index.
  ISBN 978-0-8232-6268-7 (cloth : alk. paper)
  ISBN 978-0-8232-6269-4 (pbk. : alk. paper)
  1. Rejection (Psychology) 2. Outcasts. I. Title.
  BF575.R35G64 2014
  126—dc23

                                        2014017789

Printed in the United States of America

17 16 15   5 4 3 2 1

First edition

CONTENTS

PREFACE: A BOOK FOR EVERYONE

This book is for everyone. As a book on the *reject*, it speaks for everyone. After all, each of us, at some point of our lives, has been a *reject* in one way or another. In the context of our academic lives, we have had our journal submissions, job applications, fellowship applications, grant applications, and book proposals rejected. Outside that professional life, we have experienced no less being *rejects* in our everyday lives, for example, being rejected in love. In both our professional and everyday lives, then, we have indeed been *rejects* in the face of certain communities, organizations, institutions, working groups, and social circles. We must, however, keep in mind that we have not been mere passive *rejects*. We have also, in our turns, actively exercised the force of rejection against others: we ourselves have rejected submissions in our reviews; we have considered a job applicant not to be a "good fit" for the department when we sit on search committees; we have rejected the amorous advances of others, disdained a gesture of friendship from another, excluded certain people from our circles, and so on. Some of us have even turned the force of rejection on ourselves. We do that when we turn back on a belief or philosophy that we have been holding on so firmly or practicing so rigorously for so long in our lives. We do that when we disdain our previous lifestyles and embrace a different one, such as it is manifested, for example, in the moment of epiphany when a meat-eater declares that he or she has decided to become a vegan. We do that too when we undergo religious conversions, rejecting one religious faith for another, or when we seek to be so-called atheists and attempt to free ourselves entirely from religion. In more despairing situations, some have even rejected an entire existence in the form of suicide. In any case, whether we reject ourselves, or we reject others, or others reject us, we will have lived through the figure of the *reject*.

It has to be said, though, that while we are admittedly quick to label others *rejects*, especially in negative terms, we tend not to acknowledge the *reject* in us. In that sense, so long as we do not recognize ourselves as *rejects*, this book is also a book for no one. Things are slowly changing for the better, however. Without yet explicitly articulating the term *reject*, we have begun to rethink *rejects* in ways whereby we no longer shun, discriminate, or even persecute them. For example, in contemporary intellectual discourses in the academic world, particularly in the fields of continental philosophy, literature, and cultural studies, we are now beginning to highlight the significance of disabled beings and animals in transforming the ways we view and interact with the world, while previously such entities were not considered worthy of critical discussions in almost every discipline. Today, we not only talk about them under the rubric of "posthuman" discourse, but we also have fields such as Critical Animal Studies and Critical Disability Studies. In other words, we are, in the academic world, gradually celebrating *rejects*. We seem to do likewise in certain domains of everyday life: Is the *reject* not celebrated in the world of popular culture when a series such as *Glee*—essentially a story about a bunch of high-school *rejects* who eventually rise above the rest through their show-choir endeavors—has been a hit on both American and global television networks? Other recent television series such as *The Big Bang Theory* and *New Girl*, likewise centered around, and sympathetic to, *rejects*, have also found similar success. And in the Occupy movement of 2011, do we not declare ourselves *rejects* as well when we claim to be the 99%, that is to say, the 99% rejected of the riches enjoyed by the 1% because of unequal wealth distribution?

In this early part of the twenty-first century, it seems like the times call for the articulation of the *reject*, and we will have to articulate that in a critically comprehensive manner. That is to say, we must not elicit the *reject* only in other disabled beings or animals, while we stand apart from the term and talk about it from afar, as if immune to it. Instead, what is required of us is to not refrain from recognizing the *rejects* in ourselves, and we must do this not only in moments of revolutionary fervor (as is the case of the Occupy movement) but also in moments of thoughtful, analytic meditations. The articulation of the *reject*, as a figure that *all of us* undeniably or even irreducibly assume at some point in time in our lives, is the task of this book.

As will become evident, this book proceeds by way of contemporary French thought, and in that regard, the narrative will unfold, unfortunately or fortunately, in a register more somber than this Preface. The choice of the philosophical register is due to the scholarly basis or motivation of this book, which has contemporary French thought precisely as its point of departure, and I explicate this is in the Introduction. But let me add here that there is perhaps no better starting point than contemporary French thought for the story of the *reject*, since, more than others, French philosophers associated with that line of thought, which is also known as "structuralism" and/or "poststructuralism," have largely been regarded as *rejects* by academic and cultural institutions in both France and abroad. Indeed, "structuralism" had to begin outside of institutional walls in France in the early 1960s. It gained some momentum just before the eventful May of 1968 and no doubt made some inroads into academic institutions around that time. However, it had by then taken on a conservative, if not reactionary, disposition and was rejected by those who desired a more open and dynamic mode of thinking. This led to the development of "poststructuralism" in the post-1968 era, but French academia and culture seemed to be ready to be done with "structuralism." "Poststructuralism" eventually found its home in Anglo-American universities in the 1980s. Regrettably, that hospitality has waned, as large pockets of the academy in the United States seem more eager to pronounce the "death" of contemporary French thought instead. Things do not seem to be improving for the epigones, as French academia continues to relegate "structuralism" and/or "poststructuralism" to a forgotten moment in the history of French philosophy. Hence, we find scholars such as Catherine Malabou (a former student of Derrida, who also, at the *rencontre* on the occasion of the publication of her *Changer de différence* in 2009, has said that she does not want to be the heir of Derridean deconstruction), Éric Alliez (a former student of Deleuze), and Frédéric Neyrat (a former student of Jean-Luc Nancy), seeking to further their respective careers in Anglo-American universities. Given the story of "structuralism" and/or "poststructuralism" as very much a story of *rejects*, it seems only apt to begin this story of the *reject* precisely with contemporary French thought.

Having its basis in contemporary French thought does not mean that this book is limited by it. It looks toward a wider horizon, as it seeks to work out a theory of the *reject*, and a theory must resonate with other more general experiences or empirical phenomena so as to suggest possible applications in those instances. In the course of the narrative, then, this book will also elucidate the philosophical, ethical, and political potentialities of the *reject* and their implications for the contemporary world, particularly with regard to our world of network-centric sociality, our "postsecular" situation, our post-9/11 world where radical politics seems impossible, and our "posthuman" condition. I have no doubt that those potentialities can have further implications for fields of inquiries such as Gender and Sexuality Studies, Animal Studies, Disabilities Studies, Trauma Studies, and Critical Race Studies. An exploration into the specific stakes of the *reject* for each of those fields of study, however, is beyond the scope and expertise of this work. There are also surely aesthetic implications of the *reject*, especially literary ones, and I acknowledge the numerous candidates for the *reject* in literature here: Shakespeare's Shylock, Lear, Hamlet, Caliban, and Prospero; Melville's Ahab, Ishmael, and some would say Bartleby, though I contest this claim in the chapter on politics; Dostoevsky's Raskolnikov and the underground man; almost all of Kafka's characters including Gregor Samsa; Ellison's invisible man; Blanchot's Thomas the Obscure; Beckett's dramatic personae, and the list goes on. These literary characters have definitely been studied and analyzed in their names or according to categories with which they are typically associated, if not typecast, but not yet in terms of their status as *rejects*. That, again, is beyond the scope of this book and must be left as another story for another book. I would prefer a book such as the present one to be written first, which, as said, works out a theory of the *reject*, and after which we can have the rhetorical tools to articulate and explicate the adventures, literary or otherwise, of the *reject*.

In short, the book's main concern is to argue that the *reject* is a critical figure of thought for the contemporary world, and that one must therefore articulate it without further hesitation or reservation. Before going further, it should be said here that foregrounding the *reject* will not have as its tenor or horizon a self-negating or self-deprecating anguish, which one tends to associate with the *reject* in its previous invocations. As it will be revealed in this book, articulating or theorizing the *reject*, including the *reject* that is each of us, is nothing but an affirmative gesture. To reiterate, the following pages follow a philosophical contour, and all philosophy, according to Nietzsche, is very much autobiographical. I would not deny that a philosophy of the *reject* is in many ways my autobiography. However, it is not just my autobiography. It is also *our* autobiography, and that is why this book is a book for everyone. In that respect, I hope this book will be a modest beginning for other stories of other *rejects* to come, stories that will also be written, surely, by others.

ACKNOWLEDGMENTS

First and foremost, I thank the late Helen Tartar for believing in this project and for seeing it through as a book with Fordham University Press. It is with immense regret that she is no longer around to see this book in print. She could have, actually, if only I had not been unwell for the whole of 2013, which left me unable to do much, hence delaying the delivery of the final manuscript. Helen's warmth, kindness, patience, and generosity were such that she told me then not to worry about the book but to get well first, constantly sending me encouraging notes and what she called "positive energies." I wish I could have sent her those energies in return when she needed them. With Helen's passing, I have lost not only a great editor and mentor, but also a dear friend and guardian angel. At Fordham University Press, I am also grateful to Thomas Lay for all his editorial assistance, and Alex Giardino at the Modern Language Initiative for her meticulous copyediting. This book would not have been possible too without all the amazing teachers that I have had. I am therefore indebted to Ryan Bishop, Verena Andermatt Conley, Jonathan Culler, Werner Hamacher, Ian James, Dominick LaCapra, Timothy Murray, Jean-Luc Nancy, Frédéric Neyrat, John WP Phillips, Geoff Waite, and Samuel Weber. Dominick LaCapra and Timothy Murray also made possible a fellowship at the Society for the Humanities at Cornell in 2012–13, allowing me to finalize the manuscript, so I give further thanks to them. I owe gratitude too to my readers Philip Armstrong and Gregg Lambert, whose comments and suggestions only helped improve the manuscript. My project also benefited from conversations with Isabelle Alfandary, Marc Crépon, Priyanka Deshmukh, Évelyne Grossman, and François Noudelmann during several visits to Paris, and I extend my appreciation to them. I also had wonderful discussions on the book's topic with Eduardo Cadava and Daniel Heller-Roazen at Princeton, and I thank them for that. I have shared ideas of this project with my students at Cornell, particularly those who attended my seminars "Friendship, Love, and Community," "Thinking the Post-Secular," and "Touching Literature"; I appreciate their taking interest in the *reject*. At Ithaca, I certainly do not forget Sue Besemer, Anh Ngọc Dủỏng, Củỏng Hủỏng, Qủốc Con Lủu, Eddy Quach, Helen Quach, and Khôn Vinh Quach, all of whom had made sure that I was eating and living well while writing. Parts of this project were also written in Singapore, and I am grateful to Lionel Wee and the Department of English Language and Literature at the National University of Singapore for providing me office space during those times, which greatly facilitated the completion of the manuscript. I also thank the late Arthur Yap, who always believed in me and for whom this work comes too late, and his wonderful sisters Fanny, Alice, and Jenny, who always keep me in their prayers. Heartfelt thanks go to Ying-Ying Tan, who accepts me for who I am, *reject* or not.

Portions of this manuscript have appeared in other forms as journal articles: "The Question of Community in Deleuze and Guattari" I & II in *symplokē* 14 (2007) and *symplokē* 15 (2008); "Rejecting Friendship: Toward a Radical Reading of Derrida's *Politics of Friendship* for Today" in *Cultural Critique* 79 (2011); "Becoming-Animal: Transversal Politics" in *diacritics* 39(2) (2009, which appeared in 2012); and, "Posthuman Auto-Rejects: From Bacterial Life to *Clinamen*" in *Subjectivity* 5 (2012). I thank the University of Nebraska Press, the University of Minnesota Press, Johns Hopkins University Press, and Palgrave Macmillan for the kind permission to reprint versions of those materials here.

THE REJECT

1

INTRODUCTION

Let's Drop the Subject

> Everything seems [. . .] to point to the necessity, not of a 'return to the subject' [. . .] but on the contrary, of a move forward toward someone—some one—else in its place [. . .].
>
> —JEAN-LUC NANCY[1]

> There is never for anyone the Subject [. . .].
>
> —JACQUES DERRIDA[2]

This present work in many ways responds to the spirit of our times, that is to say, the early twenty-first century. The philosophical motivation for this work, however, has a slightly longer history, as it comes from the question Jean-Luc Nancy posed in 1986: *Qui vient après le sujet,* or *who comes after the subject?*[3] Given the date of Nancy's question, it might seem at first glance an anachronism, if not (better), an untimely gesture, for a work today to revisit that question almost thirty years later. There is, however, as with all things untimely, a certain necessity in addressing that question again. I will elucidate that necessity in a while, but I would first like to recall that Nancy's question comes in the wake of the dissolution, or even the "liquidation," of the *subject*. As Nancy says, his question comes after "the critique or the deconstruction of subjectivity," which, according to him, "is to be considered one of the great motifs of contemporary philosophical work in France [. . .]."[4] The *subject*, to put it in a very simple and admittedly unjust manner here, is that category or figure of thought that has served the humanist aspiration to ascertain Man's holistic presence in the world, including helping Man convince himself of his unparalleled ability to think in apparently rational terms. Man in this case, however, is typically, or rather limitedly, "the average adult-white-heterosexual-European-male-speaking a standard language."[5] It tends to be the case too that those certainties of presence and capacity to rationalize will be taken to be the foundation of that male *subject*, from which he will proceed to assume a position of power or even sovereignty. There, presuming his point of view as the only true one worthy to be disseminated to the rest of the world, he takes it that the perspectives of others can be ignored or even negated.[6] As it can be imagined today, in light of the decades of feminist and postcolonial discourses, any thought or discourse predicated on the male, authoritarian, and Eurocentric *subject* will prove nothing less than problematic. In fact, by the time of Nancy's question, intellectual discourses, especially those inclined toward contemporary French thought, and no less aware of the voices coming from feminist and postcolonial discourses, will have launched an extensive critique of the *subject*, not only to expose the fiction of its certainty, foundation, and sovereignty, but also to recognize and affirm the existence and perspectives of others, especially female others, nonhuman others, and those not in a position of power.[7]

The deconstruction of the *subject* that has begun with contemporary French thought has led to an archival explosion of works that continue the critique or the problematizing of the *subject*, an archive that continues to grow today. In that respect, one could continue to tarry with such critique or deconstruction of the *subject* to further elicit the intricate and complex problems in deploying the *subject*. Otherwise, one could, as Gilles Deleuze says in his response to Nancy, "construct new functions and discover new fields that make [the *subject*] useless or inadequate," which Deleuze considers to be the "better" strategy.[8] Or, as is Jacques Derrida's suggestion to Nancy, one could free oneself from "the necessity to keep at all cost the word *subject*, especially if the context and the conventions of discourse risk reintroducing what is precisely in question."[9] Keeping the term *subject*, as Derrida finds in the "decentered," "lost," or "fading" *subject* in Jacques Lacan,[10] in the *subject* of "interpellation" in Louis Althusser, or in Michel Foucault's author-*subject* as an effect of discourse-networks surrounding the intellectual and economic production of texts, seemed only to have "placed the subject behind them."[11] In other words, in Lacan, Althusser, and Foucault, "the subject is perhaps reinterpreted, resituated, re-inscribed; it is certainly not 'liquidated.'"[12] One needs "a passage beyond," therefore, "an annulation" [*péremption*] of all tarrying with the *subject*.[13] For Derrida, this "passage beyond" is the postulation of a "who" that "responds even before the [subjective] power to formulate a question, that is responsible without autonomy, before and in view of all possible autonomy of the who-subject [*qui-sujet*]," a "who" that "is perhaps no longer a grammatical derivation [*ne relève peut-être plus de la grammaire*], not even of a relative or interrogative pronoun that always returns to the grammatical function of the subject."[14] Derrida would also posit this "who" in terms of a "differing and deferring singularity" [*singularité différante*],[15] while Deleuze would postulate "pre-individual singularities and non-personal individuations," whose constantly mobile "emissions [. . .] constitute a transcendental field without a subject."[16] In any case, Derrida will say that for any such "passage beyond," or to "overhaul [*refondre*], if not to refound [*refonder*] in a rigorous fashion, a discourse on the 'subject,' on what would take the place (or replace the place [*remplacera la place*]) of the subject,"[17] one must pass through "the experience of a deconstruction [of the subject]."[18] In passing through this experience, Derrida will continue to say later, "it always seemed to me that it was better, once the way was inaugurated, to forget a little the word [*subject*]."[19] He will be precise to state that it is not, however, a total oblivion of the *subject* that is involved here: "Not to forget it—it is unforgettable, but to move it, to subject it to the laws of a context such that it no longer dominates from the center."[20]

Most of the responses to Nancy (aside from Derrida's, Deleuze's, and also Blanchot's, which proposed to think the figure of children), however, would only reveal a resistance to articulate a figure of thought other than the *subject*.[21] They either stay with the *subject*—which are the responses of Alain Badiou, Jacques Rancière, Gérard Granel, and Mikkel Borch-Jacobsen, or else add to the *subject* predicates that have been previously left out in its earlier foundation—as in Étienne Balibar's response, where he argues for the supplementing of the *subject* with the attribute of citizenship, henceforth calling for the thought of the *citizen subject*. In my view, these responses, which remained with the *subject*, have been somewhat inadequate in the sense that they did not match the radical contour or promise of Nancy's question. The articulation of a category or figure of thought otherwise of the *subject* remains lacking in them. It could even be said that what they had done, consciously or not, was to discourage, or even *reject*, the coming to presence of a figure of thought other than the *subject*. In any case, we have yet to generate a response that is adequate, radical or not, to Nancy's question, and this is why we still need to go back to Nancy's question and attempt at that more adequate response. That is the endeavor of this present work.

In a way, responding adequately to the question of "who comes after the subject" is perhaps also the unfinished business of contemporary French thought. In other words, despite all the desires of naysayers to have done with contemporary French thought, and despite their claims to be witnessing the "deaths" of "French Theory" over the past decades, we are not done yet with contemporary French thought.[22] To be sure, providing an adequate response in no way looks toward that seemingly imminent closure of contemporary French thought. As I will suggest in this present work, articulating finally (but not once and for all—since I do not mean at all that there is only one adequate response to Nancy's question) the figure of thought that "comes after the subject" can show "French Theory" to have relevance to the contemporary world, if not future applications for it. I believe Cary Wolfe shares this view in his *What Is Posthumanism?*, as he suggests there that the future of "posthumanism" or "posthuman" discourse can take a leaf precisely from contemporary French thought's question of "who comes after the subject," taking as its point of departure a working through of that question.[23] Contemporary "posthuman" discourse is certainly not the only benefiting party here. Putting contemporary French thought in dialogue with the contemporary world, via the articulation of a figure otherwise of the *subject*, can in turn ensure the maintenance or even futures of contemporary French thought, since contemporary demands and contexts can encourage contemporary French thought to push further its radical horizons, or go beyond its limits. Hence, instead of prematurely and unjustifiably declaring the end of "French Theory," one could say: *la pensée française contemporaine, encore un effort!*

The other reason why we need to readdress Nancy's question of "who comes after the subject," perhaps more urgently this time, is because, despite the extensive work done by contemporary French thought and by other intellectual discourses elsewhere in unveiling the problems of predicating thought on the *subject*, we are witnessing the marked rise or even resurrection of the *subject*, albeit in a different form. This has been evident as Anglo-American scholars, since the last decade or so, joined by French intellectuals more recently, have begun not only focusing their attention on the work of Badiou but also celebrating it. Badiou was one of Nancy's respondents and one of those who remained faithful to the category of the *subject*. But that is only Badiou being consistent with his early political *Théorie du sujet* (1982), which predates his response to Nancy. Badiou never loses sight of the *subject*, as he develops his theory of the *subject* in the more philosophical *L'Être et l'événement* (1988) and *Logique des mondes* (2006). Returning lately to more political tracts such as *L'Hypothèse communiste* (2009) and *Le Réveil de l'histoire* (2011), he has only reaffirmed the *subject*, or even intensified it by calling for the militant *subject* of the event. No doubt, Badiou would claim that his *subject* is radically different from all other *subjects*, which have been based on, or rather mutated from, Descartes's "self-supposing" or "self-positioning" *ego sum*.[24] However, I would say that Badiou's *subject* is still haunted by similar problems related to the classical *subject*. The main problem—and I discuss this in greater detail in Chapter 3 on the "postsecular"—is that it still tends to take on a sovereign, imperialistic contour, which in turn risks violently negating others who have no claims, or have no wish to lay claim, to this *subject*. In any case, the resurrection of the *subject* via Badiou's philosophy, which undeniably brings with it similar or even worse problems associated with the *subject*, is not insignificant and cannot be ignored. In the face of such a return of the *subject*, one can surely respond with an incisive critique. But one can also respond by going back to Nancy's question and respond without hesitation with a figure of thought that can counter the *subject* (and such a response is surely no less a critique, albeit an oblique one).

Responding to Nancy's question with a figure of thought other than the *subject* is the strategy of this present work. To reiterate, I will not tarry with the *subject* here. Neither will I tarry with texts that continue to problematize the *subject*.[25] And even though I have mentioned Badiou's work, and I will critique it in the chapter on the "postsecular," I will not, in general, tarry with the more problematic texts that continue to refer, if not return, to the *subject*. These texts are usually written not just "by those who would like to think that nothing has happened, and that there is nothing new to be thought, except maybe variations or modifications of the subject,"[26] but also by those who choose to believe that the *subject*, in a different form from its classical manifestation, might be useful for their causes. The latter set of texts tends to belong, ironically, to the fields of feminist and postcolonial studies, which have been instrumental in critiquing the *subject*.[27] With regard to those texts, I do not assume a position whereby I claim an expertise to deny the usefulness of the *subject* for their authors. Nonetheless, I do believe that their causes can be pursued with other figures of thought, which would allow their discourses to avoid the trappings of the *subject*, or else avoid the risk of the problematic *subject* compromising their causes. Both Hélène Cixous and Catherine Clément, whom I discuss respectively in the chapters on the "postsecular," and on friendship, love, and community, have indeed shown how that can be done, as they remarkably do not take recourse to the *subject* in their conceptualization of the feminine. If they mention it, it is only to critique it and to move feminist discourse away from such a figure of thought.[28] In any case, texts that problematize the *subject*, texts that bracket out the problems of the *subject*, and texts that claim to find some uses of the *subject* will always continue to be written and to proliferate. In contrast to them, I seek to "construct new functions" that are not those of the *subject*, to "forget a little" the *subject*, to "no longer speak of it,"[29] even though I do keep in mind that what follows from my gesture is not detached from the deconstruction of the *subject*. In that sense, I do not seek so much "to write *over*" [*écrire 'sur'*],[30] or even "overwrite" the *subject*, but rather to inscribe *under* the *subject* another concept, another "who." That is to say, I do not mean at all to totally erase, *reject*, or even obliterate the *subject*. I follow Nancy here, when he cautions that "that which obliterates is nihilism—itself an implicit form of the metaphysics of the subject (self-presence of that which knows itself as the dissolution of its own difference)."[31] It is time, even though it is already untimely, to drop the *subject*, to gesture toward "that to which one can no longer allot the grammar of the subject nor, therefore, to be clear, allot the word 'subject.'"[32]

"BEFORE/AFTER THE SUBJECT": THE REJECT

To the supposition of a subject, must one still suppose something else? From the moment one has begun to make a supposition, why not suppose further, if not up to the point of a de-supposition [*dé-supposition*]?

—JEAN-LUC NANCY[33]

Let's drop the subject then, or else "de-suppose" the *subject*, without further hesitation. To the question of "who comes after the subject," I respond here by saying: the *reject*. The *reject*, as I would like to conceptualize it here, is constituted by three turns. The first turn concerns the *reject* as it is conventionally understood: a passive figure targeted to be denied, denigrated, negated, disregarded, disposed of, abandoned, banished, or even exiled. The *reject* is not always passive, however. In its turn, it can actively express a force of rejection in retaliation to the external forces acting against it. The *reject* can in fact also be the one who *first* rejects things and people around it with a force so overwhelming that it is only *subsequently* rendered a *reject* by those around it. Whichever the case, the active force of rejection constitutes the second turn of the *reject*. The third turn concerns the *reject*'s turning of the force of rejection around on itself, and this is where one may speak of the *auto-reject*. Now, auto-rejection is not something nihilistic (I recall Nancy's remark, cited above, that nihilism belongs to the order of the *subject*). The *auto-reject* does not reject itself so as to let itself precipitate into an anguishing abyss of abjection, at which point everything falls hopelessly into absolute ruin. Rather, the *auto-reject* puts in place an auto-rejection in order not to hypostasize itself on a particular thought or disposition.[34] In this way, it is always able to think (itself) anew constantly and to be always open to what arrives to thought and to itself, which arrives not only from the future but also from the past.[35] Auto-rejection involves creative regeneration, therefore, and not, I repeat, self-annihilation.

These three turns are certainly not mutually exclusive. Instead, they turn on one another constantly. What I argue a theory of the *reject* should underscore, though, is the third turn of the *auto-reject*. The *auto-reject* is a critical turn in many ways, and let it be said at the outset that this turn not only sets the *reject* apart from the *subject*, but also affirms the theory of the *reject* as a question of ethics before everything else. Given these stakes, let me explicate a little further this particular turn, beginning with the actual difficulty in adopting the disposition of the *auto-reject*. I consider it relatively easy to see oneself as a passive *reject*, especially when one is placed, if not when one places oneself, in a victim position. It is also relatively easy to position oneself as an active *reject*, projecting a force of rejection against anything. It is not so easy, however, to think of oneself in terms of an *auto-reject*, to regard oneself as a *reject* by oneself. It actually requires immense humility for an *auto-reject* to rethink or reassess its existing thought or disposition *and* see to its complete abandonment.[36] This goes beyond auto-critique because, in auto-critique, one might change one's strategy or means, but the horizon or end in sight remains largely the same. In auto-rejection, on the contrary, one does not just deviate from one's original trajectory or strategies, but the horizon changes too. The *auto-reject*, in rejecting itself, seeks other means *and* other ends (if any intended end ever comes to an end). Giving up all that one has prepared and gathered for oneself, and giving up the position on which one has begun to ground or found oneself with all that one has gathered: that is what the *subject* is unable or reluctant to do. The *auto-reject*, meanwhile, detaches or frees itself from such gathering and (self-) positioning.

Where auto-rejection becomes a question of ethics is when the *auto-reject* rejects itself by specifically keeping in mind that there is always the possibility that one is a *reject* in the eyes of others. In doing so, one likewise rethinks and modulates one's thoughts, actions, and behavior, but this time in order to make sure that they do not compromise those of others. Sometimes, this might involve a shift or a sidestepping to an adjacent space; at other times, it involves an adoption of an entirely other mode of *being*, which might also mean once again the renunciation of one's previous thought, actions, and behavior, and hence freeing the *reject* in another instance from any hypostasis of thought and action. The additional ethical force comes from the fact that all this stems from the affirmation and respect of others. This is especially so when the shift or sidestepping to an adjacent space further requires that the *auto-reject* respect the other's desire to not fill the space left by the *auto-reject*. In that respect, the *auto-reject* rejects in itself the demand for the other to arrive. It recognizes that it is always possible that the other rejects coming to presence, that is to say, rejecting appearing in the presence of the *auto-reject*. The *auto-reject* in this case rejects any false presumption of having the prerogative to demand that the other disclose itself, hence circumventing any move to appropriate the other and its predicates, as the *subject* is wont to do. To reiterate, the *auto-reject*, unlike the *subject*, has no interest in accumulating for itself predicates that might contribute to its foundation; it has no interest in totalizing everything, including elements outside of itself, within its grasp and control, not to mention that it has no interest either in whatsoever foundation of itself. It has no "madness" of the *subject* for "the unconditional surveillance of everything that could undermine its absolute exception [or sovereignty] [. . .]."[37]

In the sidestepping of the *auto-reject*, which is tantamount to leaving the other free to come *and/ or not to come, and go*, I would even wager that this is perhaps "another possibility" of being "responsible without autonomy" according to Derrida.[38] For Derrida, that possibility is "neither subjective nor human,"[39] for it does not assume, but rather renounces any autonomy or power to question "who comes," abandoning even any call to the other to come within its space and claiming to provide hospitality to the other.[40] I will try to make all these clearer in the following chapters. In the next chapter on friendship, love, and community, I also speak of side-stepping in terms of *walking away*, and I elucidate that in relation to the writings of Clément and Luce Irigaray. But here, I would like to emphasize that *walking away* does not constitute the absolute characteristic, gesture, or strategy of the *auto-reject*: the *auto-reject* does not make *walking away* its necessary condition. I recall that the second turn of the active *reject* (which is always at work, as said, simultaneously with the first and third turns) will require the *reject*, in certain situations, to stay and repel forces that are denigrating it. Yet, as I will argue in the chapter on politics, even in these situations, the *reject* must be open to the option of *walking away*, especially when life, not just its own but also that of others, is in danger. *Walking away* in this case does not entail the total abdication of its cause and goal. Rather, it is a means of surviving or continuing to live, in order to construct other strategies that can reach its aims in life-affirming ways.

The *auto-reject*, besides bearing an ethical force, is also critical in preventing any return to the *subject*. That regression is what the *reject* admittedly risks through its second turn, especially when its active force of rejection goes unchecked. In that case, the *reject* can appear to be not so much different from the *subject*, given the *subject*'s tendency to pride itself on its power to negate others in both cognitive and material terms.[41] Auto-rejection, which can moderate the active force of rejection, then prevents the regressive precipitation of the *reject* into the *subject*. The *auto-reject* can also save the *reject*, especially the passive *reject*, from sinking into a condition of the *abject* figure. According to Julia Kristeva's theorization in *Pouvoirs de l'horreur* (1980), the *abject*, with all that is improper, dirty, disdained, and despised that accompanies it, can also be a figure that challenges or throws into upheaval the *subject*, which thinks itself to be proper, or to be in an elevated position, and pure, if not immune to all things base. However, Kristeva's figure of the *abject* is also one that comes after experiencing a debasing master-slave relation. The *abject* does not forget that painful history of being subjugated, if not of being a passive *reject*, and is caught up in that traumatic memory, which also means that it remains ineluctably entangled in a master-slave relation. This is why Kristeva says right at the beginning of her text that the *abject* "does not cease to defy its master."[42] As I see it, that signals, however, a certain inability to walk away from its subjugated situation. The movement from a passive *reject* to *abject* then only seems to be an incessant work of mourning with respect to its strife with its (past) master and, consequently, perhaps marks its inability to embark on a new, liberated or liberating trajectory. The *auto-reject*, it is hoped, will be able to have done with mourning its previous subjugated condition, to be indifferent to its (past) master, and to create another trajectory of life for itself. To be sure, I am not saying that the *walking away* of the *auto-reject* here puts in place an absolute forgetfulness of a traumatic past. Rather, it is a demonstration of its ability to not burden itself eternally with a traumatic memory or a past master. The difficulty of *walking away* in this case is acknowledged, and I recognize it especially in the *reject* as embodied by the victim of Nazi concentration camps in the following chapter, with reference to the writings of Jean Améry and Robert Antelme.

Auto-rejection, in all, despite being a difficult aspect of the *reject*, is instrumental in countering any return of the *subject*, in freeing the *reject* from an *abject* condition, and in opening the *reject* to another ethics, "another possibility" of being "responsible without autonomy," which still affirms and respects the other and its differences. A theory of the *reject* must therefore always task itself to put in place the *auto-reject*, no matter how difficult it is, to foreground it even, when everything hinges too fixedly either on the active or the passive *reject*. Besides, even though one *reject* is different from another in its condition of being a passive *reject*— differently rejected by different external forces, or different in being an active *reject*—rejecting in different ways different targets, it is via the *auto-reject*, that is to say, whether one is capable of auto-rejection or not, and according to ways and degrees that one rejects oneself, that each *reject* distinguishes itself from another. I recall furthermore that the *auto-reject* is more inclined to free itself from any fixed predicates than to gather them, upon which it can conjure up some foundation of itself. In that respect, it will always be difficult to reduce *rejects* into some sort of common or similar *rejects*, unlike the case of the *subject*, whose predicates of self-supposition, self-positioning, self-representation, consciousness, unitariness, and mastery allow one to speak of *subjects* in somewhat homogeneous terms, if not *a Subject* for all *subjects*. In other words, *the reject* is in fact a misnomer, since there are always *rejects* rather than *a reject* or *the reject*. The phrase *the reject*, at best, is but shorthand for a theory that seeks to articulate and affirm a figure of thought that would give expression to the multiplicity of heterogeneous *rejects*.

Before going on, one could at this point pose the question of violence in relation to the *reject*, given what has been said above about the *reject*'s *walking away*, its counteracting the *subject*, and its wrestling itself from any abjection. I have to concede here, though, that the topic of violence is too huge and vast to be adequately covered in this present work. All I am able to say here is that there is no doubt violence in the *reject*, and we will see this, in the course of this work, through its figurations as the one who breaks away from all figurations of community, the friend who leaves town, the one who regards the friend with fatigue and distrust, the syncopic lover, the nomadic war machine, the one who counteracts existing "postsecular" violence, and as becoming-animal. The *reject* does not claim any indemnity from violence, nor seek to be untainted or untouched by it. It could be said that the *reject* certainly keeps in mind what Slavoj Žižek calls "systemic violence,"[43] which is the violence inherent in all ideologies or structures (for example, capitalism) that are imposed upon others, and which results in real and/or symbolic violence against others in terms of denigrating them within that ideology or structure, or else expelling them from it to the point of denying them any means of, or even right to, existence. However, instead of an immediate abdication to that violence, or what Žižek calls an immediate "doing nothing," which he also advocates, the *reject* acts. It acts via its second turn of active rejection, which can constitute a counterviolence against external "systemic violence." In other words (and I borrow the words of Simon Critchley here, who critiques Žižek's gesture of "doing nothing" as a form of hypocrisy that fails to recognize its own "dream of divine violence, cruelty, and force"), in resisting "systemic violence," which can amount to "an ethics and politics of nonviolence," the *reject* "cannot exclude the possibility of acts of violence."[44]

As I have suggested earlier, and I will explicate it further especially in the politics chapter, violence in the *reject* will not be pursued to the point of a fight-to-the-death with its adversary. Nihilistic violence that leads to complete destruction, I repeat, is the path of the *subject* and not of the *reject*. I cannot emphasize enough that for the *reject*, the question of life or existing is of utmost critical importance. Whenever it senses that life (not only its own but also of those around it, including even that of its adversary) is threatened, it modulates its active, violent force. This is where the *auto-reject* and its *walking away* comes in, in order to preserve life. In that regard, it is willing to sacrifice the means or trajectories by which it achieves its objectives (and I make another confession here that the topic of sacrifice is again too huge to be dealt with in this work). It might even sacrifice its objective. It will not, however, sacrifice life. In that respect, the *reject* is in accordance with Nancy's philosophy of existing as "unsacrifice-able."[45] *Walking away*, to be sure, is not innocent with regard to violence. *Walking away* can constitute some form of symbolic violence on at least two counts: it is firstly a serious affront to the other who demands the *reject* to stay its ground and fight it out till the end; and it is no less a violence to the *reject* itself when it abandons its stance and initial strategies and/or objectives (which might not be a bad thing in the end, since it short-circuits all possibilities of the *reject* becoming-*subject*). In either case (but perhaps more so in the first), there is no less a "systemic violence" in the *auto-reject*, and the *reject* recognizes that, which is also a recognition of the "objective violence of the world, a violence where we are perpetrators and not just innocent bystanders."[46] *Walking away* is also perhaps when "doing nothing is the most violent thing do to,"[47] but, again, it is violent only in order to prevent further violence against life.

The recognition of "objective violence" does not need to leave the *reject* with violence as its remaining thought. In that regard, it might be help-ful to speak of the *reject* in terms of precarity. The *reject*, when it stays its active force of rejection, or when it *walks away*, also exposes itself to a state of precarity, especially when the other refuses any offering of peace but pursues, if not intensifies, the course of violence. According to Judith Butler, precarity is the condition of having one's "unbearable vulnerability [. . .] exposed."[48] It is not necessarily a passive state, though. The aware-ness of one's "injurability" can be a "cause for fear and for mourning," but it can also "lead straightaway to military violence and retribution."[49] Butler argues that one does not need to go down the latter path. Instead, precarity can be an occasion for reflecting on the violent consequences of one's previous actions and on the further violence one can generate should one pursue retaliatory trajectories. As Butler says, "To be injured means that one has the chance to reflect upon injury, to find out the mechanisms of its distribution, to find out who else suffers from permeable borders, unexpected violence, dispossession, and fear, and in what ways."[50] In other words, it is in critically reflecting on the condition of precarity, which is also to be attuned to the "constant tension between the fear of undergoing violence and the fear of inflicting violence," that we can be on the way of "arresting cycles of violence to produce less violent outcomes."[51] This is what the *auto-reject* does when it abandons its means of active rejection and its hypostasis on any disposition or thought, the complete projection of which might come at the cost of compromising others and their views. Or, as in the case of Antelme, it takes place when the victim of Nazi concentration camp chooses to abandon all physical, violent vengeance against the Nazi torturers and those who come after, so as to stop the cycle of human violence against other humans. Antelme makes clear, though, that the abandonment of vengeance does not mean giving up writing about the horrific experiences of being tortured, a mode of writing that can bear the (violent) force of constantly reminding the perpetrators his or her cruelty and of making postwar Germany face up to its Nazi past and not forget it.[52]

THE REJECT IN CONTEMPORARY FRENCH THOUGHT

I will now leave aside any further discussion of violence and return to the task at hand, which is to articulate the figure of the *reject*. In responding to Nancy's question of "who comes after the subject" with the *reject*, I would like to clarify that the *reject* is not of my conjuration. In other words, when I respond to Nancy's question with the *reject*, I am, in a certain way, responding "without autonomy." I might have articulated the term or the name *reject*, or I might even be outlining a possible theory of the *reject*. However, I would say that the *reject*, either as a figure or a gesture, has always subtended philosophy. The *reject* can even be said to be already with philosophy right at its beginning, that is to say, with Plato. Socrates, Plato's philosophical "conceptual persona," to borrow Deleuze and Guattari's term in *Qu'est-ce que la philosophie?*, practices a dialectical method that first proceeds by eliciting from others what they claim to be concepts, following which, he systematically rejects almost all of them. Nothing is spared at the end. As Deleuze and Guattari put it in *Qu'est-ce que la philosophie?*, everyone is vanquished at the end of the philosophical feast, save Socrates, the soliloquy bird, hovering above and surveying the destroyed terrain of the philosophical banquet. According to Deleuze and Guattari, then, Socrates is not really interested in dialogues, a view also shared by Derrida.[53] Socrates certainly does not escape the force of rejection himself. The *Apologia* stands as a testimony of Socrates being a *reject* in the eyes of Athens' moral authorities. Socrates's (mis)teachings of Athenian youths to deviate from, or even reject, the conventional ways of learning set by those authorities can no longer be tolerated, so the authorities put him on trial for corrupting the education of Athens' youths. The *Apologia* goes further: it shows Socrates turning the force of rejection against himself, that is, an auto-rejection on Socrates's part, albeit an auto-nihilistic one here, when he declares that he would rather choose suicide than submit to the injunction by the Athenian tribunal to stop thinking. One could say that auto-rejection in Socrates extends to the *Phaedo* too, but this time without any tinge of auto-nihilism. This occurs when one witnesses Socrates there reflecting on poetry in relation to the immortality of the soul. One knows, however, that poetry is the art of writing that Socrates famously denounces in the *Republic*. In reconsidering what he has previously rejected, one could say that toward the end of his life, Socrates is beginning to doubt, and therefore also (auto-)reject, what he has previously insisted on in his philosophy.

The *reject* traverses philosophy no less after Socrates/Plato.[54] In fact, it can be said that the force of rejection is very much a philosophical constant. Without going into details, it is almost evident that each philosophy tends to reject the one before. Before Descartes constructed the *ego*, or rather *ego sum*, from the act of thinking (*cogito*), Descartes would first declare his rejection of the thought-systems that have come before him. Centuries later, Hegel rejected Kant and Fichte. Then in the twentieth century, Deleuze rejected Hegel. A little later, Badiou rejected Deleuze, Derrida, Nancy, and other "poststructuralist" thinkers. The story goes on.[55] Given this trajectory of the *reject*, the *reject* can even be considered to come, as Nancy puts it, "before/after the subject."[56] It is obviously impossible for this present work to cover all the *rejects* in Western philosophy, so it will only concern itself with eliciting and elucidating the figure of the *reject* that has subtended contemporary French thought. In a similar vein, it will not be able to cover every contemporary French philosopher (not to mention that this work does not proceed by having each chapter devoted to a singular philosopher). This book will focus on the writings of Derrida, Deleuze, and Cixous, and I pay particular attention to these thinkers not just because they (Derrida and Deleuze) were respondents to Nancy's question,[57] or that in their quest to depart from the *subject*, they have constructed radical conceptual figures such as the friend who leaves town (Derrida), the *homo tantum* (Deleuze), the blind or myopic figure (Cixous), or the messianic figure "without messianism" (Derrida), all of which are (pre)figurations of the *reject*, as I will show. More importantly, they have gone further to make thought approach the animal—a figure of the *reject* no doubt for a long time in intellectual discourses, via the motifs of *animots* (Cixous and Derrida), *divinanimalité* (Derrida), animal-messiah (Cixous), and the becoming-animal (Deleuze). Such figuration and approach can enable contemporary French thought to make critical interventions in the questions of (1) forming ethical relations beyond existing conceptualizations of friendship, love, and community; (2) a "postsecular" future that sees to a more peaceful coexistence between secularity and religiosity; (3) a "democracy-to-come" that goes beyond anthropocentric and anthropologic limits, and (4) a "posthuman" future without the acculturation, taming, or reining in of others and their radical differences.

Each of the above questions will frame each chapter of this book. In taking on those questions, there will also be turns to the works of Irigaray, Badiou, Balibar, and Rancière, only to show how the *reject* so nascent there is ultimately suppressed by the reconceptualization of the *subject* by these thinkers. It is also with respect to those questions that discussions of other contemporary French thinkers, whose writings inscribe no less the *reject*, however, have to be regrettably left aside. These include Blanchot, Bataille, Lévinas, Lyotard, and Foucault. Certainly, the *reject* can be read in Blanchot's "neutral" or his philosophy of writing [*écriture*], and in Bataille's "unproductive expenditure," and I do not fail to acknowledge in the chapter on friendship, love, and community how the *reject* in Blanchot and Bataille contributes to the aspiration for radical forms of relations that would play out in Nancy, Derrida, Clément, and Deleuze. The *reject* can also be read in Lévinas's work on faciality [*visage*] or being "outside-the-subject" [*hors sujet*], or in Lyotard's "inhuman" [*l'inhumain*] that escapes all representability or his notion of the "postmodern" that does not contribute to any sensible communication and therefore has to be dropped. It can also even be read in Foucault's turn away from the *subject* in his last lectures beginning with *La Naissance de la biopolitique*, where the *subject* is recognized as very much a trap in the sense that its constitution serves the biopolitical function of identifying it either as an obedient political *subject* or a deviant to be eradicated. This would lead to *L'Herméneutique du sujet*, where Foucault would posit the notion of a "form of life" that goes beyond the *subject* and its trappings, not to mention his much earlier lectures on *Les Anormaux*, where he turns to social outcasts that could expose and critique biopolitics' reductive mechanisms against life. However, I am bracketing out any real discussion of these thinkers, because I do not find the *reject* in Blanchot, Bataille, Lévinas, Lyotard, Foucault, and other contemporary French thinkers to have as far-reaching implications specifically for the contemporary question of the animal and for "postsecular" and "posthuman" concerns as the *reject* in Derrida, Deleuze, and Cixous, hence my focus on these three thinkers here. To be precise, it will not be a homogeneous figure of the *reject* that is at work in Derrida, Deleuze, and Cixous. Once again, the different degrees and force of the *auto-reject* will be the distinguishing feature that sets each *reject* in each thinker apart from another.

I certainly have not forgotten Nancy when I said I would turn my thoughts particularly to Derrida, Deleuze, and Cixous in this present work. No doubt, one might not find as much close readings of Nancy's texts in the following chapters as of Derrida's, Deleuze's, and Cixous's. However, as it will be evident at the beginning of each chapter, Nancy's writings will always form some sort of guiding thought, constantly leading this work toward a thought "without subject," as Nancy would say. Furthermore, I do return to his writings on abandonment in this work's Conclusion. Let it be said here, though, that the *reject* is no less nascent in Nancy in his deconstruction of the *subject*. Right from his early *Ego sum* (1979), the *subject*, according to Nancy, conjures, re-presents, and posits itself from the Cartesian enunciation of *ego sum* or "I am." In other words, the *subject* exists only in, or as, the linguistic articulation of *ego sum*: "The *pure* subject is 'I' who in enunciating enunciates himself" [*le sujet* pur *est je qui s'énonce énonçant*].[58] However, this *subject* can never fully capture the sense of the actual, existing, corporal body that says "I." There is certainly a presence to that body, but Nancy will also say elsewhere that "presence precedes and succeeds itself always, [. . .] and has for its essence *passing* the moment it is there, and more precisely, to be there only in passing and in effacing at that instant the present that it is."[59] The body, coming into presence at each instance, ex-isting in existence always, is then each time different from what the *subject* (pre)supposes it to be. Or, as Nancy puts it, "In the passage, what passes, each time, is a singularity,"[60] which constantly differs, at each time, from the fixed, singular image that the *subject* (pre)supposes for itself. The (enunciation of the) *subject* is never adequate to the presenc-ing or existing of the corporeal body. Given that the enunciated "I" "is distinct from my body (as I am a thing that thinks)," saying *ego sum* then does not entail any "positive knowledge of the nature of [the] substance" that is the thinking body.[61] To persist in thinking oneself as a *subject*, or in believing in the fable of a "complete and veritable *being*" [*l'être véritable et entier*] in *ego sum*, one only alienates, if not *rejects*, oneself from any true relation with one's true corporeal existing: "Saying *I* does not indicate some distinct *thing*, does not posit a distinct substance, but produces the distinction with everything (and with every *judgment* on the reality and/ or the true of a thing). I entrench myself [further in the fictionalizing of myself as a *subject*] or cut myself off from myself [*je me retranche*], and I separate myself from myself [*me distingue*]: it is the *I* that sets *me* apart [me *distingue*], and entrenches *me* or cuts *me* off [me *retranche*]."[62] In other words, the *subject*, in enunciating itself, always rejects the existing, corporeal body that it seeks to locate and identify; vice versa, the corporeal body, in its coming to presence in *différance* or in difference/ deference at each instant, always rejects the *subject* that enunciates it either too early or too late. Ultimately, "I must renounce defining [the *subject*]."[63] This is because, after all, the instantiation of a *subject* always only involves a certain (auto-)rejection: "That which enunciates itself," as Nancy argues, also "denounces itself."[64]

Nancy returns to the deconstruction of the *subject* again in the essay "Ipso facto cogitans et demens." This time, he further observes that *ego sum* says more than "I am": the verbal form of *sum* already includes the first-person pronoun in question in the enunciation, "without the need of an additional pronoun," and so *ego*, which "announces the subject of the *sum*," is only "a superfluous pronoun."[65] In other words, *ego sum* literally says, "I, I am," and the enunciation of *ego* instantiates the *subject* that seeks to establish or reaffirm the first-person pronoun in *sum*. However, the superfluity of *ego* only betrays the fact that *ego*, in its manifestation as an enunciation as *sum*, that is to say, as a linguistic articulation, has already disseminated itself to an outside beyond the control of both the *ego* and the speaking body: in *ego sum*, "I present myself outside and consequently I stray. I stray 'me': I expose it and I exile it outside of its dwelling [*demeure*]."[66] In other words, the *subject*, as it announces itself superfluously in *ego*, is again a *reject*, this time before the first-person pronoun inscribed in *sum*, since it never finds the latter, and thus is not only "alone" but also always "remains abandoned."[67] In short, it can be said that what unfolds from Nancy's deconstruction of the *subject* is some form of a *reject*. As Nancy puts it, the *subject* after all "knows itself not to be itself."[68]

"UNE MAUVAISE IDÉE DE LANGAGE"?

In this present work, I focus on eliciting and elucidating the *reject* in Derrida, Deleuze, and Cixous. I am also, in doing so, no doubt suggesting that the emergence or stirrings of the *reject* is rather marked in contemporary French thought. The entrenched questioning and critique of the *subject* in contemporary French thought, which began with early French structuralism and to which the respective philosophies of Derrida, Deleuze, and Cixous are closely linked, can be said to play a major role in that.[69] Yet, one could still ask: If the *reject* subtends the thoughts or writings of contemporary French thinkers, why is it that these thinkers have never themselves articulated the figure of the *reject*, even though some of their contemporaries have thought of other -*jects* in the hope of surpassing the *subject*, such as the aforementioned *abject* of Kristeva, Jean Baudrillard's *object* that thinks us, and the *traject* of Paul Virilio? One possible response may be that this figure has always lived out a condition under which it is made to be true to its name, that is to say, present but denied from coming to presence, hence the reticence even from contemporary French thinkers with regard to the articulation of this figure. The more precise response, however, would be that the French language does not possess a term that French thinkers could deploy in order to articulate the *reject* as I have sensed it from my reading of contemporary French thought and which I outline in this work, that is, the *reject* in all its senses of a passive, active, and auto-*reject*. The French language certainly has *rejet* to signify rejection, but one does not say *rejet* in French to mean a figure of thought, a "conceptual personage," a person, or a thing, as one says *sujet* for the *subject*, *objet* for the *object*, *abject* for the *abject*, or even *trajet* for the *traject*.

The closest the French language comes to articulating something of a *reject* is *rejeté* or perhaps *rebut*, which is commonly translated into English as trash or waste. *Rejeté* and *rebut*, however, are not adequate for the sense of the *reject* that is at stake here, since they point too much to the passive condition of being thrown out or being disposed of. They do not capture the sense of active rejection that the *reject* also bears, and neither do they suggest in the least that critical aspect of the *reject* as *auto-reject*. The verb form of the French *rejeter*, though, might point to auto-rejection as I understand it, that is, as creative regeneration, for one could morphologically separate *rejeter* into *re-* and *jeter*, where *jeter*, which means to throw or to launch, is modified by the *re-* prefix, which signifies the act of repeating. So, in rewriting *rejeter* as *re-jeter*, one may signal to the event of a re-launching, of throwing oneself again, or of re-beginning. But in fact, even without resorting to creative morphological rewritings, the French *rejet*, when used in the context of botany, can also signify the sense of re-beginning or re-birth, since, in that context, *rejet* names the new growth, an offshoot, springing forth from an existing stem of a plant. *Rejet* in that sense no doubt resonates with the sense of regeneration in the *auto-reject*.

It remains, nevertheless, that the French language in general does not admit *rejet* into its lexicon as a figure of thought in the likes of *sujet*, *objet*, *abject*, and *trajet*. In that respect, I also remember well Nancy's response to me when I first brought up the question of the *reject* with him sometime in 2009. As I proposed to him the idea of "*le 'rejet' en tant qu'une figure de la pensée*" or the *reject* as a figure of thought, Nancy, very politely and gently, as is characteristic of him always, expressed his suspicion that my *rejet* might just be *une mauvaise idée de langage*, a bad wordplay. To be sure, he has had no major disagreement with what the *reject* is about conceptually, but as a matter of language, to think *rejet* as a figure of thought is a move with which he cannot quite agree. I could certainly let this incommensurability between the English language, which calls with ease the *reject* anyone who is denigrated or abandoned, and the French language, which resists, if not considers impossible, the use of *rejet* to describe such a person, be the amicable "dissensus" between us. But I could also make an appeal, which I would prefer to do, not only to Nancy but also to the French language, to be open to the possibility of accommodating *rejet* as a figure of thought, or for the French language to open itself to the sense of *rejet* as a figure of thought. Put another way, and to borrow Nancy's term from the title of his first volume on the deconstruction of Christianity, I would make an appeal for the "dis-closure" [*déclosion*] in the French language in order for it to welcome, to receive, what it has always considered impossible.[70] To let arrive that which is impossible, is that not also an event according to Derrida, or more precisely, the event according to Badiou, since Badiou's event concerns the affirmation of the coming to presence of what has been previously denounced (by dominant powers, dominant discourses, and majority groups) as "inexistent" (which is surely some form of the *reject*)? To receive the event, or for the "dis-closure," of *le "rejet" en tant qu'une figure de la pensée*: that is my modest plea to the French language and to Nancy. Or else, I would like to think that *le "rejet" en tant qu'une figure de la pensée* resounds within or beneath the French language as its silence (Derrida), its stammering (Deleuze), its murmuring or (animal) grunting [*borborygmes*] (Nancy), its *animot* (Derrida, Cixous), its countersignature (Derrida again), its *écriture feminine* (Cixous), or even its syncope (Clément).

Having made the appeal for the French language to open itself to *le "rejet"en tant qu'une figure de la pensée*, one could in fact reconsider the absence of a French equivalent for the English *reject* and argue that that absence might in fact be advantageous to the present endeavor to articulate the *reject* as a theory, which should entail that the *reject* resonates with a general condition of being that transcends both temporal limits and spatial boundaries instituted by national frontiers. In the absence of a French equivalent to the English *reject*, one can never claim that the *reject* is strictly or uniquely a French conceptualization (despite its marked emergence in contemporary French thought, as I argue in this work), as one might claim the *subject* to be when one attributes the thinking of the *sujet* to Descartes (even though he does not mobilize that term), if not claim it to be German when one points to the transcendental *Subjekt* in Kant or the *Subjekt* of Spirit or Absolute Knowledge in Hegel. The German language, I add here, also has no similar term for the *reject* as it has for the *subject*. Instead, it has *Ausgestoßene* (for the *reject* in terms of a person) or *Ausschuss* (for a thing). And while the French has *rejeter* as a verb for the act of rejecting, the German has *ablehnen*, *abweisen*, *verweigern*, and *zurückweisen*. Meanwhile, in Italian, there is *reietto* to mean *reject* in terms of a figure or person. In any case, given the French and German cases (and I am sure it also occurs in other languages where there is no equivalent for the *reject* to refer to a figure of thought or person), I would like to think that the *reject*, in contrast to the *subject* either as the French *sujet* or German *Subjekt*, knows no national boundaries. (It also knows no epochal delimitations, to which the *subject* seems to have been subjected when Heidegger proclaimed in

Nietzsche the end of metaphysics, which is also the end of a metaphysics of the *subject*, and announced *Dasein* in place of the *subject* that is capable of comprehensively re-presenting himself and the world to himself.) The *reject* is more common than being Anglo-American, French, German, or Italian, more common than being a phenomenon of a particular time period. I will even say that the *reject* is also more common, without it ever having to have proclaimed or to proclaim to form some sort of common, than the common that is formed by the contemporary multitude according to Michael Hardt and Antonio Negri.[71] I return to the question of the *reject* in relation to "being-in-common," which is effectively being *uncommon*, in the Conclusion.

THE REJECT NOW

We live, more than ever perhaps, in an age of *rejects*. The *reject* gradually fills the thoughts of our time, as we come to acknowledge the *reject* to be a general condition of contemporary *being*. Just to underscore again what was said in the Preface, there is an increasing turn to, and even celebration, of the *reject* today, as one takes into account the growing archive of works on topics such as animal lives and disabled beings, "subjects" that used to be neglected or even rejected (especially the topic of nonhuman animals) in dominant intellectual discourse just decades ago. On that note, and as a way to close this Introduction, I would just like to highlight here Zygmunt Bauman's work of 2004. Inspired by the work of the Italian philosopher Giorgio Agamben on the *homo sacer*, which is undoubtedly very much a figure of the *reject*, Bauman would speak of "wasted lives" or lives that are considered to be like trash in the eyes of global capital in our contemporary world. According to Bauman:

> The production of 'human waste,' or more correctly wasted humans (the 'excessive' and 'redundant,' that is the populations of those who either could not or were not wished to be recognized or allowed to stay), is an inevitable outcome of modernization, and an inseparable accompaniment of modernity. It is an inescapable side-effect of *order-building* (each order casts some parts of the extant population as 'out of place,' 'unfit' or 'undesirable') and of *economic progress* (that cannot proceed without degrading and devaluing the previously effective modes of

'making a living' and therefore cannot but deprive their practitioners of their livelihood).[72]

He goes on later: "To be 'redundant' means to be supernumerary, unneeded, of no use [. . .]. To be declared redundant means to have been disposed of *because of being disposable* [. . .]. 'Redundancy' shares its semantic space with 'rejects,' 'wastrels,' 'garbage,' 'refuse'—with *waste*."[73] As Bauman notes too, one cannot, however, simply make these *rejects* disappear in "the waste yard, the rubbish heap."[74] The rubbish heap grows too, and around the world, there is also the sense that there is not only not enough space in these heaps for wasted *rejects*, but also not enough space for such heaps. Here, the space of rubbish heaps is also a subject of rejection.

Yet the over-spilling of more "wasted lives" would become unstoppable with the global financial crisis that begun in 2007. The increasing phenomenon of "wasted lives" would explode into the Occupy movements in late 2011, not only in cities in the United States but also in major cities around the world. Through Occupy, the sense or even the fact that *we* are almost all *rejects* ourselves will be forcefully acknowledged, as declared by the movement's slogan of "we are the 99%," that is to say, the 99% *rejected* of the wealth enjoyed by the 1% due to unequal economic distribution. In the course of the movement and in its aftermath, we have also begun *rejecting* the questionable financial and banking practices that have produced that economic inequality. The *reject*, though, is more than a mere product or remnant of the economic machine. As I will underscore in the chapter on politics, it is also a political and existential condition, as experienced by illegal immigrants, refugees, stateless people, the *sans papiers* in France, the *Roms* in Europe, or in a more "eventful" way, by what Badiou calls the "inexistents" in their massive uprisings during the Arab Spring of 2011. But back to the question of the *reject* in relation to "wasted lives": as I have suggested earlier, and as I will also further explicate in the rest of this work, a theory of the *reject* goes beyond the recognition of passive "wasted lives." Like Jacob Rogozinki and Michel Surya's work on *le rebut humain* or "human trash," it can also offer passive *rejects* or "wasted lives" a way to think beyond their condition as "a destiny," to think themselves otherwise than being hopelessly "vanquished," but incite them to "strategies of resistance against [their] being-put-to-waste [*mise-au-rebut*]."[75] Or else, and I stress again the role of the *auto-reject* here, a theory of the *reject* can encourage them to see beyond the anguishing limits of their condition, or even make light of them, and pursue another trajectory of thought or living that frees them from their "vanquished" condition.[76]

Without delay then, we need a theory of the *reject*, and we need to articulate or elucidate the stakes of such a theory. The following chapters, therefore, will be engaged in eliciting the figure of the *reject*, if not a nascent theory of the *reject*, from concepts that primarily preoccupy contemporary French thought—concepts such as community and friendship, "religion without religion," and democracy. At the same time, they will also situate the *reject* according to contemporary French thought in more current contexts, for example, the explosion of social media platforms such as Facebook and Twitter, the "postsecular" condition, the apparent impasse in radical political thought in the post-9/11 "democratic" world, and the contemporary "posthuman" interests in animal and bacterial life and system theories. In engaging with these contemporary contexts, the aim would be, on the one hand, to show how the *reject* according to contemporary French thought can make a critical intervention in these contexts, or else how the *reject* is in the process of positing another ethics, another "religion without religion," and another politics, all "without the *subject*." On the other hand, the aim would also be to consider how current developments in the questions of community and friendship, religion, and politics can refine or redefine a theory of the *reject*, thereby pushing contemporary French thought beyond its existing horizons or limits.

2

(AFTER) FRIENDSHIP, LOVE, AND COMMUNITY

Let me begin eliciting the *reject* from within concepts that almost every contemporary French thinker from Bataille to Badiou more recently has been invested in: the related or interrelated concepts of friendship, love, and community. I will demonstrate in the following pages that the *reject* underlies contemporary French thought in its engagement with these concepts. Put another way, I will show that what is nascent, or at work, in these thinkers' "obsession"[1] with these concepts is the subterranean inscription of the *reject*, and I argue that such implicit mobilization of the *reject* has served the purpose of radicalizing those concepts, giving them new and future trajectories beyond the limits imposed by past and present understanding. I venture to say too that unveiling or articulating the *reject* today can further broaden those radical horizons already opened up by contemporary French thought. In that case, merely eliciting the *reject* from within concepts will not be enough. Instead, one needs to take into account contemporary thinking *and* practices of friendship, love, and community and to ask if the *reject* can make any critical intervention there. That is perhaps the real task or challenge of theorizing the *reject* today: not just to elicit it from within safe textual boundaries and elucidate it "on paper," but also to contextualize it amidst the irreducible and undeniable fact of existing with others in the real world. In fact, the contextualization within *both* textual and empirical domains of friendship, love, and community is indispensable to a theory of the *reject*, since the *reject* does not, and cannot, exist on its own in absolute terms. There is, after all, no *reject* without others rejecting it (or without it rejecting others), so it is senseless or meaningless to theorize the *reject* or to even think about the *reject* while claiming it to be absolutely singular without others. The fact of existing with others, or to exist amid the existence of others, cannot be denied in the thinking of the *reject*. That is to say too that the existence of real others is always at stake in the *reject*'s relation to the thinking of friendship, love, and community, if not the thought of existing with others constitutes the ethical dimension of a theory of the *reject*.

One can reformulate the above as follows: in taking into account the reality, or fact, of community, a theory of the *reject* places itself in a kind of limit-situation whereby it inquires into the way the *reject*, which might seem to set itself apart or be set apart from others, nevertheless negotiates with others in the world. It asks how the *reject* can coexist with others in friendship, love, and community, or more precisely, how it traces its trajectory without negating the existence and difference of others. In the course of such inquiry, one would have to ask: How does the *reject* function in relation to friendship, love, and community? What role does it play there, and how does it play itself out? Does one, or should one, transform one's thinking of friendship, love, and community, as one takes into account the *reject*, especially when one also re-cognizes oneself as a *reject*? Is it possible to think a friendship, love, or community of, and for, *rejects*? Are these concepts still relevant, or even possible, with the *reject*? And can the *reject* even be the figure of thought for a critical rethinking of contemporary friendship, love, and community? These are some of the questions that inform this present chapter as it situates the *reject* in relation to friendship, love, and community. Let it be said at the outset that if the *reject*, at first glance, gives the impression that it makes the thinking of friendship, love, or community almost impossible, its sense of anticommunity, antifriendship, or antilove is not in view of nihilistic or destructive ends. Instead, as it will become clear in this chapter, any semblances of anticommunity, antifriendship, or antilove that the *reject* seems to project is but the critical refusal to allow existing understandings of love, friendship, and community to limit the ways it negotiates relations with others. Besides, as said in the Introduction, nihilistic or destructive ends are usually the result of an overprojection of the second turn of the active *reject*, something that is too easy to accomplish and more characteristic of the supposed sovereign *subject*, which is always too keen to negate others in order to serve its own ends. A theory of the *reject*, as I am articulating in this work, must not allow that force to overassert itself; instead, it will be more critical to put in effect the third turn of the *auto-reject*, which keeps in check that second turn of the active *reject*, and I will explicate in due course the ethical and political stakes in doing so. In any case, in articulating the *reject* in relation to the concepts of friendship, love, and community, the aim is to keep open the radical horizons that contemporary French thought has introduced to those concepts *and* to allow something other to inflect those very same radicalizations. In that sense, thinking the *reject* in relation to friendship, love, and community looks toward a new ethics of being in, or "being-with," as Nancy would say following Heidegger, the world. This ethics is one that always modulates itself, at every instant, as different beings come into contact with one another at each time.

In addition to the above considerations, the quest to think the *reject* in relation to friendship, love, and community also stems from Nancy's call to think of a "community *without subject*."[2] To be sure, Nancy was not the first to posit a "community without subject." Bataille, before Nancy, had already put forth a thought of community where the subject undergoes a dissolution. This is particularly evident in *L'Expérience intérieure*, which can be said to be Bataille's critique of the appropriation and determination of everything, including the thought of community, by knowledge, especially Hegelian, dialectic absolute knowledge. Under the latter, everything is claimed to be knowable or to develop within the limits of speculative knowledge, while those that resist such determination are relegated to the shadows of the night, to which one can remain blind. Put another way, everything in Hegelian dialectical knowledge is reduced to the possible, which is to say too that everything is at an impasse, since things cannot play out in ways unthought of by speculative knowledge. In Bataille's analysis, this impasse arises out of the *subject* and "its will to knowledge."[3] This *subject* experiences only "limited existence,"[4] where everything transpires according to the determinations of the *subject* and *object*, that is, within the confines of either the one as possessor of another, or the other as possessed by another.[5] In that case, one forgets the "ecstasy"—to use Bataille's word in *L'Expérience intérieure*, of being immersed in "human existence"[6] as in an ocean—another of Bataille's imagery,[7] where, should one wish to retain the terms *subject* and *object*, there will only be a *subject* without knowledge [*sujet non-savoir*], and an unknown or unknowable *object* [*objet l'inconnu*].[8] Bataille calls this immersion "communication," which is not just something before and beyond all intelligible, linguistic discourse, and which may therefore include silence too.[9] It is also the fact of existence of one and the other, before and beyond all construction of one and the other as *subject* or *object*. Simply put, it is the fact of existing with the other who is already there and/or the other who is to come. It is existence where "there is no longer subject=object, but 'gaping opening' [*brèche béante*] between one and the other; and in this gap, subject and object are dissolved. There is passage, communication, but not from one to the other: *one* and *the other* have lost distinct existence."[10] It is in this sense that Bataille will say, "existence is communication," and "communication" in this sense is also, for Bataille, "the sense of a community."[11] If it is not already evident, this sense of community proceeds, in Bataille's terms, via the "contestation,"[12] or even rejection, of the categories of *subject* and *object*, and consequently, of all knowledge, or of what is claimed to be known and knowable.

Bataille's "contestation" assumes various forms. In addition to the aforementioned ecstasy, it also includes laughter, poetry, sacrifice, anguish [*l'angoisse*], hopelessness [*le désespoir*], and unproductive expenditure [*la dépense*]. Nancy's thoughts on community are clearly indebted to Bataille, and Nancy duly acknowledges this in *La Communauté désœuvrée*. However, Nancy makes a break with Bataille in refraining from resorting to radical, anguishing measures that tend toward extreme ends such as sacrificial unproductive expenditure, where the thought of community freed from all present forms or understanding can be found only in the day after the apocalypse, after the ruin without remainder of everything, that is to say, after the absolute loss of the sacrificial victim, the executioner of the sacrifice, the witnesses of the sacrifice, and the very structure of sacrifice itself. For Nancy, that thought of community does not depend on such apocalyptic messianism as a necessary condition. In fact, one could say that for Nancy, *there is*, always already, such a community or such a thought of community, if not community tout court, except that it has been smothered by the teleologic quests for communitarian fusion, communion, closed finality or identity, and even totality, based on the determination of either a singular, sovereign *subject* or a collective of likeminded *subjects*.[13] Nancy would even go further to argue that community is not just beyond "the immanence of a subject," it is also "originary or ontological."[14] In other words, the existence of every entity, especially of every singularity before its constitution as a *subject* or individual, already articulates community, so long as one recognizes that this existence always already situates itself beside or among the existence of other entities. It is through this recognition that the Heideggerian *Being* or *Dasein*, or even *Mitsein* or *being-with* [*être-avec*], must be rearticulated or refined in Nancy's philosophy as giving exposition to community, or even simply "*as community*"[15]: there is the exposition of community through the co-presence, or what Nancy calls *comparution*, of *beings*.[16] Such existence as always already community is a fact of existence that is shared by all *beings*, a sharing that makes each of us, according to Nancy, *being-in-common* [*être-en-commun*], a commonality that must not be confused with the idea that each *being* is homogeneous to the next: "being is *in* common, without ever being common."[17] Given the prepositions that Nancy mobilizes in the thinking of *being*, from "with" [*avec*] to "in" [*en*], or to "to" [*à*] in Nancy's more recent rephrasing of *being* as *being-to* or *être-à*,[18] one could also say that *being* for Nancy is always *prepositional being*, which is to say, *being* is always pre-positioned toward community before it positions itself as a *subject*. *Being*, in short, for Nancy, is always (already) existing and moving among other entities; or, *being* is always approaching another community in the movement of its existence in the world. All this has nothing to do with the work or project of a *subject* or individual. Instead, it is but "the passion of community,"[19] which escapes all determination of a *subject* or individual.

It is at this point where one finds a force of rejection in Nancy's thought on community, which is articulated in terms of *désœuvrement* or unworking, that is to say, the undoing of all subjective work or project that seeks the constitution of a defined or definable community. *Désœuvrement* is also put in simpler terms as "resistance," or more precisely as "infinite resistance," to anything that seeks to render community as complete(d), absolute, defined, or accomplished.[20] It is with such a force of rejection that community affirms that it is always *there*, that it "never disappears" in the face of all the works and projects *on* a supposed perfectible community.[21] Nancy would also be precise to say that the "passion of community" is vigilant to *unwork itself* as well, or to *(auto-)reject* itself as I would say, when community is on the verge of establishing itself as a hypostasis or foundation: the "passion of community" must be "incompletion" [*inachèvement*] itself, "an activity constantly unworked, unworking" [*à nouveau, une activité désœuvrée, désœuvrante*].[22] Given the forces of rejection and auto-rejection of community, which see to its infinite affirmation in finitely differential terms at each different time, it does not mean that all we have to do is simply say that *there is* community. Rather, the task for us is to precisely expose that fact of community that remains, despite, or after, the rejection of all the work of the *subject*: there is always the fact of community that remains when entities or singularities depart and occupy a different space, space being that which all beings continue to share irreducibly in one way or another *in common*. In Nancy's words, that is "the task of exposing the inexposable 'in'" of *being-in-common*, the "in" where we are all thrown or "abandoned" (and therefore in a way *rejected*) to be "first [...] received, perceived, felt, touched, managed, desired, *rejected* [my emphasis], called, named, communicated."[23] The question, as I see it then, is: Which figure of thought can be adequate to this task of "exposing the inexposable 'in,'" of keeping open the thought of community even when we are "rejected" in this "in," while maintaining the *désœuvrement* of community at the same time? For Nancy, this figure of thought is clearly not the *subject*, since, as he states right at the beginning of *La Communauté désœuvrée*, it is that "which is *not* [my emphasis] a subject [that] opens and opens itself instantaneously onto a community."[24] Would the *reject* be this figure of thought then, the *reject* that is no less "rejected" in the "in" of *being-in-common*? Would it be the *reject* that also risks not being counted in what Nancy calls the "community of the arrived" [*communauté d'arrivée*],[25] since it has departed or is departing, henceforth constituting (without any conscious intention) a community of the departing or departed, if not a community of the *rejected* [*communauté de rejeté*], or even what Bataille calls "the community of those who have no community"?

At this point, I would like to note that the Italian thinker Giorgio Agamben in *The Coming Community* has indeed taken up Nancy's challenge to think of "a community without presupposition and without subjects."[26] In place of the *subject*, Agamben proposes the singularity of "whatever being."[27] According to Agamben, the force of "whatever," or *quodlibet*, frees a being from all binding to a class or set, from all determination of having this or that predicate or property, which would allow it to assume a definable form or identity—and one might elicit some sort of (*auto-*)*reject* here. "Whatever" or *quodlibet* is just the very force of being, the force of "being *such as it is*,"[28] or—and Agamben comes close to Nancy's rhetoric here—its very exposure or "its own taking-place" before anything else.[29] In Nancy's terms, such "taking-place" would be the very presence of being itself, before it articulates itself and before it works out a relation with others around it. For Agamben, an example of "whatever being" would be the example itself, which speaks of and for itself, but whose very articulation "holds for all cases of the same type" as well, speaking "for each of them and serv[ing] for all" at the same time.[30] "Neither particular nor universal" in this case, "the example is a singular object that presents itself as such, that *shows* its singularity."[31] The ipseity of the *subject* or subjectivity, with its predicates that define its distinction from others, is evacuated here. In the example's articulation of itself, in making itself "purely linguistic being," the example can also be said to take on a contour of the *auto-reject* in terms of rejecting any ground of substance, or rejecting thinking its substance as a ground of subjective certitude, for "the proper place of the example is always beside itself [in the linguistic articulation of itself as example], in the empty space in which its undefinable and unforgettable life unfolds."[32] (In that case, it can be said too that the example sidesteps all appellation to subjectivity or subjecthood according to Althusser's theory of the *subject,* even though it is "defined [...] by being-called.")[33] But this *auto-reject* has a force of rejection on its own too: by force of its "exemplary being," that is to say, by articulating what it has in common with others—*and* reserving a singularity and hence difference for itself at the same time—the example or "whatever being" as "the Most Common" undoes all forms of community delimited by the notions of class, properties, predicates, or identities, shared more or less in common by its members.[34] According to Agamben, "Whatever singularities cannot form a *societas* because they do not possess any identity to vindicate nor any bond of belonging for which to seek recognition."[35] This *auto-reject* then "cuts off any real community," and that is "the impotent omnivalence of whatever being."[36] Yet, that is not to say that "whatever beings" are anticommunity in a nihilistic sense, or that they resist all senses of community. On the contrary, their "impotent omnivalence" would mean that "whatever beings," through the fact that they exist alongside one another, "form a community without affirming an identity," that is, "an absolutely unrepresentable community," or one could say, *whatever* community, no matter how transient such a community may be in finite temporality.[37] They are examples that testify to the fact that "humans co-belong," before and beyond all circumscription of community, "without any representable condition of belonging."[38]

To go further in positing the *reject* in relation to community in Agamben would require further discussions on the problematic questions of Agamben's *homo sacer*, bare life, the state of exception, and the open.[39] However, the basis of this work, as said, is contemporary French thought, so I will now take leave of Agamben's work and return to the question of the *reject* in contemporary French thoughts' engagement with the concepts of community, love, and friendship. This chapter will focus on those concepts in the works of Derrida and Deleuze, with momentary diversions to the writings of Clément and Irigaray. Both Derrida's and Deleuze's engagements with those concepts tend toward a forceful exposition of the figure of the *reject*. That is not to say, however, that their thoughts on friendship, love, and community, in relation to the *reject*, are not problematic. The contrary is true in fact. For example, there is, on the one hand, the unequivocal rejection of community in Derrida: in *A Taste for the Secret*, Derrida acknowledges, "if I have always hesitated to use [the] word [community], it is because too often the word 'community' resounds with the 'common' [*commun*], the as-one [*comme-un*]";[40] toward the end of his *Politiques de l'amitié*, he reflects on "why the word 'community' (avowable or unavowable, inoperative or not)—why I have never been able to write it, on my own initiative and in my name, as it were. Why? Where does my reticence come from?"[41] On the other hand, with regard to friendship, it is not quite clear how far Derrida goes in rejecting it. As for Deleuze, the distrust and rejection of friendship are almost precise, but his position on community can be ambiguous when he seems to disdain it while advocating the concept of nomadology, which undeniably retains some sense of community, since nomads, from which nomadology is derived, do form some sort of group or community. These ambiguous oscillations between (rejecting) friendship and community constitute an interesting problematic, and hence the focus on Derrida and Deleuze here in order to explicate that problematic.[42] The more critical motivation to focus on Derrida and Deleuze, however, is the context of the rising dominance or hegemony of teletechnologies and digital modes of communication from which Deleuze and Derrida launch their respective rejections of existing community and friendship. That technological context is certainly not distant from our present network-culture.[43] The implication here is that if Derrida and Deleuze show how ideologically corrupt friendship and community are within such context, and if one can elicit the workings of the *reject* in their philosophical critiques of such friendship and community, (re) reading Derrida and Deleuze today could give us the philosophical force to mobilize the *reject* to likewise combat our contemporary network-centric *doxā* of friendship, love, and community. That (re)reading constitutes the endeavor of the following pages.

DESIRING AN "UNTIMELY BEING-ALONE": DERRIDA'S *POLITIQUES DE L'AMITIÉ* FOR TODAY

I begin with Derrida's philosophy of friendship, particularly in *Politiques de l'amitié*, before moving on to Deleuze's negotiation with the question of community. The *reject* is very much at the center of Derrida's philosophy of friendship, and it results from Derrida's "deconstructive" reading of several friendship texts in the history of philosophy. I have earlier mentioned that the cultural context, that is, the burgeoning teletechnological culture, in which the writing and publication of *Politiques de l'amitié* is undeniably situated, could also serve to motivate the thinking of the *reject* in friendship. Derrida certainly does not really foreground this context in *Politiques de l'amitié*. As evident in the book's title, Derrida is more inclined to posit the political implications of his philosophy of friendship. However, given that Derrida has already published *L'Autre cap* (1991) and *Spectres de Marx* (1993), both of which take into account the rising hegemony of teletechnological culture, that culture surely forms an implicit backdrop to *Politiques de l'amitié*. That cultural context, as said too, is not something with which we have made a radical break; in fact, we may be at the height of it. I reiterate therefore that elucidating both Derrida's philosophy of friendship where the *reject* is at work *and* the intertwined, implicit critique of teletechnological culture that further motivates the need for the *reject* can have critical import for our times. Before going into Derrida's philosophy of friendship, then, some notes on that teletechnological culture, a context that is no doubt shared and further elaborated by Deleuze, are first in order.

By the late 1980s, Deleuze was already distrusting of communicative sociability and societies, especially those predicated on teletechnologies. They are of suspect firstly because they contribute little to creating concepts in the true philosophical sense. Secondly, they are oftentimes complicit in perpetuating the capitalist ideology underlying the very teletechnological apparatuses on which they base themselves and which they also disseminate. Such sociability or societies only encourage the production and subsequent selling of newer communicative apparatuses, as they buy into those teletechnologies wholesale without critical resistance. The situation degenerates, according to Deleuze, when these modes of sociability also buy into the illusion, offered by the industries driving those productions, that they are actively and creatively collaborating with those industries to articulate new "concepts" through information and communicative technics.[44] When "instant communication" via "cybernetics and computers" was quickly developing into a universal condition of sociability by the 1990s, Deleuze announced the arrival of "societies of control" where communicative sociability or societies built upon teletechnologies are but the expression of capitalism's hegemony in digital format.[45]

This hegemony was no less discerned by Derrida around the same time, recognizing it in all forms of media technics like "[the] news, the press, tele-communications, techno-tele-discursivity, techno-tele-iconicity."[46] Derrida will point out that the increasing "homogeneity of a medium, of the norms of discussion, and of discursive models," such as the unstoppable shift to network-based communications, is a testimony to the "instituted hegemonies" [hégémonies constituées] of "the new effects of capitalism (within unprecedented techno-social structures)."[47] According to Derrida, too, all existing dominant modes of communication and discourse are always already products or determinations of a veiled capitalist mechanism, which has already evaluated their (speculated) profitability "in the supermarkets of culture."[48] With Derrida's analysis, one can perhaps speak of "evaluation societies" to complement Deleuze's "societies of control." And just as users of teletechnological communications in "control societies" are never the ones in control, neither are those in "evaluation societies" autonomously evaluating their preferred modes of communication. And while users in "societies of control" do not create any real concepts, those in "evaluation societies" are neither engaged in the Nietzschean transvaluation of existing modes of thoughts and practices. In the face of the growing hegemony of "continuous control and instantaneous communication" or of a dominant mode of communicative sociability,[49] there is to be no philosophical compromise for both Deleuze and Derrida. One must respond with a critical stance against "societies of control" or "evaluation societies." For Derrida, "it is necessary that we learn to detect, in order to resist new forms of cultural takeover."[50] Deleuze, adopting a more radical position, will call for "a hijacking of speech" or the creation of "vacuoles of non-communication, circuit-breakers, to escape control."[51]

In our present early twenty-first century, it is clear that "societies of control" or "evaluation societies" are no longer imminent phenomena. It is not the case, however, that we have freed ourselves from them today. Rather, we find ourselves deeply implicated in such societies, as they have established themselves as an undeniable reality. Today, they are fortifying themselves stronger than ever behind the global expanse of digital social networks such as Facebook and Twitter. These are apparatuses that not only enable communicative sociability to be redefined by the overexposure of real-time messages and images incessantly exchanged and disseminated via digital platforms; they also enable users to maintain and augment an archive of almost all the friends they have had by creating digital links to an ever-expanding social network. Here, friendship is clearly the "concept" that digital social networks are claiming to redefine or "create." However, what results is but the perversion of friendship, turning it into a mere "gregarious" buzz where one "defin[es] 'friend' simply as [anyone] who communicates a wish to be one."[52] Such friendship clearly glosses over all the difficulties involved in critically reflecting on what friendship is or how it comes about: it refuses what Blanchot calls the "slow work of time" that the thought and practice of friendship require.[53] In the Deleuzian analysis, such friendship would also mean that the (philosophical) concept of friendship is in the process of being appropriated and corrupted by those digital apparatuses. There is also no doubt that digital social networks are determining themselves to be the universal if not dominant (discursive) norm, condition, medium, model, and even law of friendship today.[54] Furthermore, that a capitalist machine of "continuous control and instant communication" continues to motivate and drive this hegemonic dimension of digital network sociability is evident when the re-"conceptualization" and dissemination of friendship through networks or even *as* networks serve only to promote the development, proliferation, and selling of all sorts of network technics and services, feeding what Deleuze calls "capitalism's supreme thought" of marketing.[55] The "concept" of friendship proclaimed by digital social networks, then, is no less corrupt than the mode of communicative sociability that Deleuze has analyzed in the late 1980s and early 1990s. And users of contemporary social networks— caught up in, or bought into the friendship archive fever and the ecstasy of hyper-gregariousness that digital social networks offer—are equally complicit in sustaining capitalist ideology and its network apparatuses.[56]

Given the global scope of digital social networks today, one could say that "societies of control" or "evaluation societies" have "upgraded" into an empire of networks or a network empire.[57] What remains, then, of the Deleuzian and Derridean philosophical imperative to resist the hegemony of capitalist information and communication technics in the face of this network empire? With regard to that question, I will not be so concerned with the critical import of Deleuze's philosophy for today, since several contemporary theorists have also already developed Deleuzian responses and critiques against the network empire.[58] Having said that, those responses and critiques neither necessarily presuppose nor entail any thorough understanding of friendship and community according to Deleuze, so I will return to that topic after the treatment of Derrida's philosophy of friendship. For the moment, I will be concerned rather with the potentiality of Derrida's philosophy today to break with, or to "be *unequal*" to,[59] the dominant and universalizing "concept" and communicative norm of friendship as disseminated by digital social networks. Can Derrida's philosophy wrest the concept of friendship back from its ideological appropriation by digital social networks or the network empire, as Deleuze did with the concept of the concept?[60] One may indeed say that this question is raised in an untimely fashion, since Derrida in 1994 has already published his work on friendship in *Politiques de l'amitié*. In short, *Politiques de l'amitié* exposes the illusion of any friendship predicated on counting one's number of friends and on a foundation of similitude in terms of personality traits, habits, and likes and dislikes. It critiques such friendship as ultimately narcissistic, devoid of any critical attention to the absolute difference if not otherness of the friend. In the wake of *Politiques de l'amitié*, network-centric friendship comes across as nothing but an immense philosophical let-down: to reiterate, its fever for friendship archive is borne largely by an anxiety to make a spectacle of one's ability, as the hyperlinking technics of digital social networks allow, to possess and acquire a massive number of friends; friends here are usually similar to oneself, betraying the fact that network-centric friendship hardly displays any regard for the dissimilar friend. But even before questioning network-centric friendship's openness to the other who is different or dissimilar, it is already difficult to speak of its genuine interest or sincerity in truly knowing—in the most basic sense—even the hyperlinked friend.[61] Given that there is no stopping the technological drive that will enhance and further proliferate current digital social networks, nor the global dissemination of the *doxā* that this contemporary hyper-gregariousness is the true condition of friendship today, can a return to *Politiques de l'amitié* allow one to "write and think, in particular as regards friendship, against great numbers"?[62] Once again, the question is an untimely one, but untimeliness, according to philosophers from Nietzsche to Deleuze, Derrida, and Agamben,[63] is but the proper philosophical response to what *today* or the *contemporary* is. According to Derrida, philosophy's critical engagement with *today* is an opening of the contemporary as the "non-contemporaneity with itself of the living present,"[64] in contradistinction, for example, to the hegemonic determination of contemporaneous ideological technics; it is, in short, to "consider other rhythms and other trajectories."[65] The purpose of an untimely rereading of *Politiques de l'amitié* here would not only be about eliciting the *reject*, but also, in relation to the contemporary appropriation of the concept of friendship, to "consider other rhythms and trajectories" in the thinking of friendship, and "not to let oneself be fascinated by [the] quantitative immediacy" of network-centric friendship.[66]

At this point, one may wonder if Bernard Stiegler's work on *technē*, which is not just technology but also technics in the sense of the know-how or art of invention and craftsmanship (which could also include craftiness), as opposed to *epistēmē* or theoretical knowledge, can critically contribute to the discussion at hand. According to Stiegler, philosophy has always been preoccupied with the pursuit of *epistēmē* while refusing to acknowledge that *technē* is ineluctably implicated in the question of *being*. Stiegler argues that the relation between *technē* and *being* lies in the double fault of Epimetheus and Prometheus with regard to the creation of man in Greek mythology, the first being Epimetheus's forgetting of man when he tasked himself to distribute survival skills to every mortal creature, which is then supplemented by the second fault committed by Prometheus, who, in trying to repair the damage done by Epimetheus, steals fire from the gods and gives it to man so that man can be equipped with the crafts of civilization. Stiegler's endeavor, then, as articulated in *La Technique et le temps*, is to return thought to that forgotten mode of *being*, of "technical existing" [*l'étant technique*]. In that sense, Stiegler's work has its basis in something of a *reject* in the eyes of epistemic philosophy, which is reinforced by his sympathy for Epimetheus, whom he observes to be "not only *forgetful*, the figure of essential thoughtlessness [...]," but "also the *forgotten*," or in short, the "excluded" of metaphysics and thought.[67] This is not the space to enter into any real discussion of Stiegler's philosophy, but I would just like to highlight here that the question of the *reject* seems to be relegated to oblivion in Stiegler's writings on network culture. On the one hand, Stiegler is no doubt critical of network-centric sociality or friendship. He has no illusions that "friends" in digital social networks are not really friends [*familiers*] "but rather addressees and vectors" of one's "'reputation' [created] by the *network effect of network*, which demands that 'friends' of my 'friends' be my 'friends.'"[68] He even compares the subscription to those social network platforms, which will allow one to claim to be a "friend" hyperlinked to an entire network of "friends," but which first requires the declaration of one's personal data and then the public declaration of his or her subscription, to an act of interpellation, that is, what one does when summoned by the police.[69]

On the other hand, Stiegler also proposes to look at things another way. "And yet ... and yet," he says, "perhaps friendship always involves some public, if not explicit, declaration, precisely in the manner by which it is very often the source from which a social network is effectively formed, which can be extremely restrained, and in some way, an intimate publicity [*publicité intime*] [...]."[70] Here, Stiegler argues that the notion of a social network is not a (new) product of early twenty-first-century digital teletechnology, but something that has already been inscribed in Aristotle's *philia*. According to Stiegler's reading, *philia* is "the most precious good" because it is the "power [*pouvoir*] to form solidarities, which constitute relational interconnections [*trames*], which is to say, *social networks* precisely."[71] In that sense, social networks need not be seen as contrary to friendship but constitutive of it. The question, then, for Stiegler, is how one makes use of contemporary social networks. He believes that if they are "intelligently put to work by communities and networks of collective understanding [*intelligence*]," they can lead to "the emergence of twenty-first century processes of psychic, collective, and technical individuation, which would effectively become relational without antagonism [*relationnellement paisible*], or kind [*bienveillant*], founded on a new benevolence (or good will)."[72] This is possible in Stiegler's view because digital social networks are predicated as well on some sort of writing system, in contrast to other audiovisual media such as television, which, according to Stiegler, reduce the spectator to a mere, passive audience without any platform to express his or her opinion. Digital network platforms, even the most minimal Twitter feed, call for some writing on the part of its user. Following any inscription that is henceforth disseminated and shared within the network, there is the "process of transindividuation," through which all the hyperlinked "friends" may recognize the singularity of each "friend," allowing them to "therefore co-individualize socially."[73] It is in this light that Stiegler considers social networks as "a stage in a process of grammatization, which leads to the *grammatization of social relations* themselves and as such."[74]

Given what I have said earlier about digital social networks, I do think that it still remains to be seen if such a media platform can have the potentiality to support the thought and/or practice of friendship that is not tied to marketing purposes or capitalist ideology. In that regard, I do not disagree with Stiegler's endeavor "to invent the future of social networks, *in* and *with* social networks, as long as we are capable of attaining an understanding [*intelligence*] of these networks that are at once technological and social, and an understanding whereby these sociotechnological networks could become *agents of* [transindividual] *reflexivity*."[75] What I find problematic is Stiegler's take on *philia*, which forms the basis and horizon of his thoughts on digital social networks. Stiegler strictly abides by a reading of Aristotelian *philia* as essentially a "centripetal social energy," which entails that it holds the promise of "an endurance of the social link" [*une durabilité du lien social*].[76] Stiegler seeks the fulfillment of that promise, as he argues that *philia* must lead to—and this is also what he believes *philia* in digital social networks can attain—a milieu where everyone is associated [*un milieu associé*].[77] That means that Stiegler's *philia* does not allow for those who have no wish to be part of, or stand apart from, that milieu: it barely entertains the thought of relations that are "unequal" or "non-contemporaneous" to existing forms of *philia* (for example, network-centric friendship and sociality), the thought of a transient *whatever* community,[78] the thought of a community of the departing or the departed, or the thought of an "inoperative" community. Very likely, Stiegler would view negatively any figure of thought that posits such relations in terms of an unproductive death-drive [*pulsion*] that leads to the undoing of social ties. In other words, despite Stiegler's sympathy for Epimetheus the *reject*, he hardly allows any consideration of other figures of the *reject* when it comes to the thought of friendship and community.

Let me return, then, to Derrida's *Politiques de l'amitié* to "consider other rhythms and trajectories" that seek to sidestep and resist the hegemony of hyper-gregarious network-centric friendship. In contrast to Stiegler's notion of an associative *philia*, *Politiques de l'amitié* builds explicitly on Nietzsche's call for an antigregarious solitariness. In *Beyond Good and Evil*, Nietzsche has written, "We are born, sworn, jealous friends of *solitude*, our own deepest, most midnightly, noon-likely solitude. This is the type of people we are, we free spirits! and perhaps you are something of this yourselves, *you* who are approaching? you *new* philosophers?"[79] In other words, according to Nietzsche, the future philosopher, or new philosophy, arrives by way of articulating a certain solitariness within communitarian space and by disseminating it within that same space. The future philosopher, who is "not exactly the most communicative spirit," and who is also a sort of *reject* as I will explicate later, yearns for such a space so as to stand apart from the rest of the world. From there, he or she will be able to critique the world's *doxā*, dominant values, and norms of communicative discourse, and subsequently create new values and concepts, and new modes of articulation befitting those new values and concepts (and this is why he or she is a jealous friend of solitude). With the saturation of the contemporary world by digital social networks, the arrival of the future philosopher/*reject* seems to be at risk today. And should the future philosopher/*reject* have the chance to arrive, the same saturation would also make him or her more jealous than ever of solitude, since solitary spaces are almost effectively precluded or closed off now. Rereading *Politiques de l'amitié* today would also entail staking a claim for the Nietzschean force of thought, to insist on a chance for a future new philosophy or new philosopher/*reject*, *and* on the chance for the emergence of a solitary, if not antigregarious, or even anticommunitarian space amid the contemporary swarming of friendship networks.[80] That would in a way constitute the politics of friendship today, a politics of *Politiques de l'amitié* also, through which one creates a syncope (I will return to this later) to disrupt, displace, if not short-circuit, or even hack, the dissemination of the network-centric "concept" of friendship and the capitalist network empire behind it. To be sure, this will be politics strictly in a philosophical sense, which is to say, politics as a question of *reading*, arising from a specific mode of reading a particular text or concept, and resisting a prevalent *doxā*.[81] In other words, if contemporary philosophical discourse on friendship were to project a political force, I would argue that it must (first) put forth a reading that unveils and demolishes the simulacral "concept" of friendship of digital social networks.[82] A rereading of *Politiques de l'amitié* would serve that end, and it must be done with a view to posit, in a *sustained* manner, the disturbing truth that underlies *Politiques de l'amitié*, which is the radical truth that there is no such thing as friendship. As my following critique of Derrida will show, Derrida ultimately does not see that rejection of friendship to its end. Instead, Derrida will seem to retreat from that trajectory. However, to reiterate, if *Politiques de l'amitié* is to have critical force today against contemporary hyper-gregariousness, and for the chance for a Nietzschean solitary space to emerge, it is necessary that a reading of *Politiques de l'amitié* today sustains that rejection of friendship. That can be done by eliciting the figure of the *reject* from within *Politiques de l'amitié*; once that figure is elicited, one must not repress or veil it again, but affirm it and articulate it in every discourse of friendship.

I HAVE ENOUGH OF YOU, MY FRIEND, FOR NOW

That *Politiques de l'amitié* articulates a force of rejection against friendship *in friendship* itself is not missed by several readers.[83] That is made clear, after all, right at the beginning of *Politiques de l'amitié*, where Derrida puts forth without reserve the disturbing truth that there is no such thing as friendship or that friendship is impossible. There, Derrida brings to surface the unsayable or "nothing sayable" (*PA*, 17/ *PF*, 1) that subtends all friendships,[84] and this "nothing sayable" is but the Nietzschean "murderous truth" (*PA*, 72/ *PF*, 54) that "there are no more friends" (*PA*, 71/ *PF*, 53). In other words, friendship, if there is such a thing, is always already rent by a projective rejection of friendship. If there remains an appearance of friendship, it is only because the silence of the "nothing sayable" is maintained by those who continue to seek friendship, a silence constituting an "illusion" (*PA*, 72/ *PF*, 53) or simulacrum of friendship, kept "between friends, on the subject of friends, so as to not speak the truth, a murderous truth" (*PA*, 72/ *PF*, 54, trans. modified).

Derrida certainly has no interest in further repressing that "nothing sayable" of friendship that rejects friendship. Instead, he makes it the task of *Politiques de l'amitié* to unconceal that dark thought of antifriendship at the very heart of both friendship and a line of friendship texts in the history of philosophy. Before going into that, one could add that the "nothing sayable" of friendship also concerns those irreducible occasions when one friend quietly thinks, in an about-turn of friendship, *I have enough of you, my friend, for now* (and I note that this takes place even in the absence of quarrel between friends). However, for fear of murdering what they have between themselves, friends, in their respective secret reserves of thought, have not dared to say it. Yet, so long as this moment of refusing friendship remains irreducible, it will always throw any notion of friendship into disarray: it will always present itself as some sort of contradiction to, or in, friendship, an impasse or aporia that any thought of friendship must always stand before. It is also perhaps that which underlies Nietzsche's antigregariousness or rejection of friendship, since what unfolds from the Nietzschean "nothing sayable" or "murderous truth," according to Derrida, is the fact that "solitude is irremediable and [therefore] friendship impossible" (*PA*, 72/ *PF*, 54), or that we all desire ultimately, at some point, an "untimely being-alone" [*être-seul intempestif*] (*PA*, 73/ *PF*, 55). This fact of "an untimely being-alone" may also be articulated in terms of an irreducible anticommunity (albeit without any sense of nihilism, as I explicate in the subsequent section on Deleuze) and therefore perhaps antifriendship reserve of every individual, the undeniable desire at times to depart from, walk away from, or leave aside the friend. If the task of *Politiques de l'amitié* is to foreground and maintain the murderous "nothing sayable" of friendship in order to destabilize the amicable concept of friendship in the history of philosophy and at present, one must not further repress that irreducible thought of antifriendship, but foreground it without reserve. The question, then, is how to articulate and insist on such an exposition, a question to which I will return later.

As *Politiques de l'amitié* demonstrates, the history of philosophy of friendship before Nietzsche lacks the will to unveil the inherent rejection of friendship in friendship itself. Derrida's deconstructive critique of the friendship texts of Cicero and Aristotle then functions to bring them to terms with that repressed truth and force of rejection. With Cicero and Aristotle, Derrida shows that what ultimately overturns friendship in their texts is not only a narcissistic ipseity that essentially supplants any genuine or sincere thinking of the friend, but that this narcissism at the same time involves a perverse looking forward to death in friendship, which only implies a looking forward to a physical breakage in friendship. For Cicero, "virtuous friendship" concerns the work of illuminating the exemplary character of the self by the friend, and this is the narcissistic part of friendship. The worse part is that seeking this "virtuous friendship" is actually predicated on a speculation of the death of the self: one looks forward to the death of the self, the absolute (physical) separation of the self from the friend, because it is only then that the friend's work of mourning, whereby the friend remembers and embellishes the life and work of the self, can possibly be set into motion.

In Aristotle, one deals not with the death of oneself but the death of the other, that is, the beloved friend. Here, the death of the other or the friend is structured around the preeminence of loving or to-love, which Derrida will refer to as *l'aimance* ("lovence," according to George Collins's translation), over being-loved. In Derrida's analysis, that death is inscribed by rendering the beloved or being-loved not only an object of *l'aimance* but also *an object* through *l'aimance*. As Derrida writes of Aristotle's *aimance*: "If we trusted the categories of subject and object [in friendship], we would say in this logic that friendship (philía) is first accessible on the side of its subject, who thinks and lives it, not on the side of its object, who can be loved or lovable without in any way relating himself to the sentiment of which, precisely, he remains the object" (*PA*, 26/ *PF*, 9–10, trans. modified). Such reification of the beloved friend announces his or her death, even though the beloved friend is not yet dying or dead, because *l'aimance* of the one who loves or befriends proceeds and survives (or *sur-vivre*, as Derrida would say, which is to outlive all mortality) regardless if the object-other knows, receives, or responds to this *aimance*. In that regard, the other can be presumed to be inanimate or else already dead. Here is Derrida again, reading Aristotle: "One cannot love without living and without knowing that one loves, but one can still love the deceased or the inanimate who then knows nothing of it. It is even through the possibility of loving the deceased that a certain lovence comes to be decided" (*PA*, 26–27/ *PF*, 10, trans. modified). In short, the beloved-friend is really secondary in this scheme of friendship of *l'aimance*. What matters more is the perfectibility of a narcissistic giving of friendship or *l'aimance* on the part of the self, while one can almost be care-less about whether the other is living. According to Derrida, the rejection of friendship in Aristotelian friendship operates in such a way that it "plunges the friend, before mourning, into mourning" and "weeps death before death" (*PA*, 31/ *PF*, 14). Hence,

Aristotle's *aimance* would only be the "grieved act of loving" (*PA*, 31/ *PF*, 14), or a "grieving survival" [*survivance endeuillée*] (*PA*, 32/ *PF*, 15). The narcissism and work of mourning in friendship in both Cicero and Aristotle render any thought of friendship nothing but a "*post mortem* discourse" (*PA*, 21/ *PF*, 5), a projection of an end of friendship, of which Derrida will not hesitate to suggest how tiresome such scene of friendship is. As Derrida chides, "Who does not abhor this theater? Who would not see therein the repetition of a disdainful and ridiculous staging, the putting to death of friendship itself?" (*PA*, 21/ *PF*, 5).[85]

FRIENDS, OR REJECTS

Once the essential tear in the thought of friendship—ruptured by Nietzsche and auto-deconstructed in Aristotle and Cicero—is unveiled, the point, according to Derrida, is not to weave a suture over this terrifying rent: "so be it, since it is so; and keep it intact in memory, never forget it" (*PA*, 44/ *PF*, 27). In other words, one must always give exposition to the force of rejection of friendship, always make an exposé of that rejection, articulate that "murderous truth" of an irreducible antifriendship that is already shared between friends. One must plunge friendship into that impasse or abyss and let it dwell there, especially when anything resembling friendship is at the brink of (re)founding itself. In short, there must be no rapprochement. It must be admitted, however, that articulating this force of rejection is a difficult task. Its exposition or exposé tends to be further repressed and forgotten especially in the cacophony of contemporary hyper-gregariousness. In order to maintain a constant affront against any form of gregariousness, and also against any rapprochement with regard to the rejection of friendship, I argue that raising the figure of the *reject* in friendship would be instrumental. In relation to friendship, a figure of the *reject* would not only be the solitary one, the one who stands apart from friendship, but also the one who raises the impasse or abyss of friendship before friendship, raising it before the other *and* against him- or herself, constantly plunging friendship into that abyss. This figure of the *reject* does not stand outside the history of philosophy of friendship, but rather subtends that history. It traverses *Politiques de l'amitié* too, and it is in this sense that one can regard *Politiques de l'amitié* not only as a book about the rejection of friendship but also a book about *rejects*.

The figure of the *reject* already inheres in Aristotle. This *reject* is the being-loved that is unbearable to Aristotle, rejected from Aristotle's theater of "perfect friendship" because he or she knows nothing, does nothing, and says nothing, or in short, does not reciprocate. In Aristotle's perspective, this *reject* is insensible to the *aimance* of the loving friend. In Derrida's nuanced reading of Aristotle's take on the rejected being-loved, he would posit the following reflection: "*Being loved—what does that mean? Nothing, perhaps* [. . .]" (*PA*, 26/ *PF*, 9).[86] At first glance, the apparently judgmental "nothing" gives the impression that Derrida here is speaking in Aristotle's voice. But the "perhaps" that enjoins almost immediately disrupts, if not overturns, the Aristotelian judgment of the beloved as an insignificant "nothing" or mere *reject*. In other words, that "perhaps" would recall the Nietzschean "nothing sayable" that announces the "murderous truth" of an essential rejection of friendship within friendship itself: the being-loved as *reject* or "nothing"—the being-loved as *meaning-nothing* or *being-nothing*—then comes to unveil itself as the violent "nothing sayable" of murderous friendship, therefore. The being-loved, previously a targeted or passive *reject*, now becomes a figure that potentially bears the active force of rejection of friendship, precisely through his or her silence, inaction, and nonresponse. One is now uncertain if the being-loved, in his or her secret silence, is not in fact consciously *rejecting* acknowledging and responding to the *aimance* of friendship. In other words, this *reject* may already be putting in place, furtively but in an active manner, the "murderous truth" of rejecting friendship, through his or her nonresponse. If this is indeed the secret potentiality of the being-loved as *reject*, perhaps it is this figure that one should turn to today, rather than to denigrate it as Aristotle does, so as to locate a force of rejection that can strike out against the contemporary *doxā* of hyper-gregariousness.

The *reject* also figures in Nietzsche's thought of friendship, particularly in his conception of the "new philosophers." The *reject* in Nietzsche, unlike Aristotle's, is an explicitly active figure, which is to say that it is probably this figure that initiates any act of rejection. According to Derrida, these "new philosophers" reject coming to presence and reject all proximity, resemblance, access, or links to friendship or any communitarian structure. These *rejects* are "inaccessible friends, friends who are alone because they are incomparable and without common measure, reciprocity or equality, therefore, without a horizon of recognition" (*PA*, 53/ *PF*, 35). They are "the uncompromising friends of solitary singularity" who "love only in cutting ties" [*se délier*] (*PA*, 54/ *PF*, 35). However, that does not mean that Nietzsche's *reject* will be free from being a target of rejection. It will not be surprising that from the moment these "new philosophers" declare their rejection of any form of human alliances, they will very quickly become targets of rejection themselves, for even today, such anticommunitarian spirit remains as unbearable as articulating the irreducible thought of anti-friendship between friends.[87] But again, perhaps it is precisely because this Nietzschean *reject* bears or articulates something so radically displacing or disruptive against friendship that only the exposition of this figure can posit a shock to the entire network-centric system of simulacral friendship and, in that process, short-circuit or undo that system.

There is the figure of the *reject* in Derrida too. Derrida, however, does not make his *reject* articulate the irreducible thought of antifriendship. Instead, he makes that enunciation unfold through or from the other. In other words, the other is rendered an active figure of rejection, while the self becomes the passive target of that rejection. The other must become, like Nietzsche's *reject* or the "new philosopher," the figure that actively rejects friendship. Meanwhile, the self renders him- or herself like Aristotle's *reject*, that is, the beloved friend, which is a target of rejection of friendship. In that sense, one could say that Derrida's *reject* plays out, in an inverse manner, both the Nietzschean *reject* that forcefully initiates a refusal of all ties with other humans *and* the passive beloved friend whom Aristotle rejects but who may be coyly or implicitly rejecting friendship in his or her nonreciprocity. There are indeed two figures of the *reject* here, and Derrida sets up this scene of *rejects* for us: this scene takes place "as if I were calling someone, over the telephone for example, saying to him or her, in sum: I don't want you to wait for my call and become forever dependent upon it; go take a walk [*va te promener*], be free not to answer. And to prove it, the next time I call you, don't answer, or I won't see you again. If you answer my call, it's all over" (*PA*, 198/ *PF*, 174, trans. modified).[88]

For Derrida, making oneself a *reject* in the sense of a passive target, if not an *auto-reject*, is as critical as actively rejecting friendship. One can perhaps understand Derrida's rendering oneself a *reject* as a preemptive measure against lapsing into the all-too-human weakness for some sense of amicability or gregariousness. That is to say, it is only by reminding oneself that one is a *reject* in friendship, by redirecting the abyssal force of rejection against oneself—a traumatic gesture no doubt for some—can one resist or discourage oneself from any rapprochement with the other. For Derrida, it is also by making oneself a *reject* that one learns to respect the distance of the other, to respect the other as free in him- or herself, without any need for him or her to approach, speak, respond, or disclose any information about him- or herself. It is as a *reject* in this manner that I learn that "I must [. . .] leave the other to come [. . .]"—*and go*, I will add, "free in his movement, out of reach of my will or desire, beyond my very intention" (*PA*, 198/ *PF*, 174). Derrida will always remind us that there is the other who will arrive from the future. But I add again that there is always also the other who does *not* want to arrive, and does not arrive, before our presence (and it is in this respect that I argue that one must not only think of what Nancy calls *la communauté d'arrivée* or "the community of the arrived [or arrivants]" but also a community of the departed or departing—*la communauté d'écarté*). Only by rendering myself a *reject*, because the other rejects responding to me, that I will begin to learn to accede to the "desire to renounce desire" (*PA*, 198/ *PF*, 174) for any amicability or gregariousness. It is in this way that I will not forget the force of rejection in friendship, not forget that the irreducible thought of antifriendship is equally desired and shared by the other. This is how I will not forget the "murderous truth" of friendship, the truth that we are all *rejects* in friendship. As *rejects* in or before friendship, each and every one of us will have the right to refuse to respond, or even the right to walk away, silently, without explanation, and there will be neither rapprochement nor reproach. This is what has to be kept in mind at every instance of thinking about friendship, whether at the level of intellectual discourse or in the practice of everyday life.

At this point, I would like to add that even though Nietzsche's thought of the new philosopher seems close to my *reject*, there is hardly in Nietzsche that force of auto-rejection that leaves a place for the nonresponse, if not the walking away, of the other, and this is perhaps where the (*auto-*)*reject* differentiates itself from Nietzsche's *reject*. I have earlier quoted a passage from Nietzsche's *Beyond Good and Evil*, where Nietzsche senses the imminence of the "new philosophers" and *hails* them. There is no walking away here: Nietzsche does not walk away from their approaching, and he does not tell the new philosophers to disperse, or to be "free in [their] movement, out of reach of [his] will or desire, beyond [his] very intention," as Derrida tells the other. In fact, the address or call to the new philosophers—and

Derrida says that Nietzsche makes a "teleiopoetic or telephonic call to philosophers of a new genre" (*PA*, 53/ *PF*, 34, trans. modified)—is made in
expectation that they "follow" Nietzsche and other like-minded "free spirits,"[89] rather than to *not* respond or "take a walk" as in Derrida's scenario.
This following would seem to precipitate, despite the respective solitudes
of Nietzsche and the new philosophers, into some sort of communitarian
gathering, which is in fact already presupposed by the "we" that Nietzsche
uses to address the new philosophers. One wonders if, between Nietzsche
and the new philosophers, the "murderous truth" of friendship has been
smoothed out, as if Nietzsche and the new philosophers are now somewhat immune or exceptional to the irreducible thought of antifriendship.
Perhaps one could defend Nietzsche by saying that it is precisely because
of an acknowledgment of that dark thought of friendship that Nietzsche
and the new philosophers will come to recognize among themselves a
"we." Nonetheless, I would say that Nietzsche's "we" precariously betrays
a certain readiness to abandon his deepest solitude and those of the new
philosophers, articulating instead a looking forward to some sort of rapprochement among them.[90] The *auto-reject*, by contrast, always keeps in
mind the irreducible thought of antifriendship before the other, regardless
if the other is a new philosopher, and ceaselessly insists on the rejection
of any slightest sense of rapprochement. I have said that what is at stake
with regard to the contemporary condition of friendship is also the chance
for the arrival of the new philosopher and his or her space of solitariness,
but I state that it is the *possibility* of his or her irruption within the contemporary world saturated by digital social networks that one must seek.
Thinking how that chance may be created does not constitute hailing the
arrival of the new philosopher; it does not demand that he or she responds,
or that he or she joins me in this present endeavor. This is where I depart
from Nietzsche, therefore. But I now return to further explicate Derrida's
thinking of friendship; the Nietzschean problematic arises in Derrida too.

DERRIDA'S *NOUVELLE AIMANCE*

Is Derrida's *auto-reject* courageous or radical enough to walk away, so as
to put in effect a veritable rupture, breakage, or rejection of friendship?
Or does this *auto-reject* remain at the borders of an abyssal or already-
rent friendship, hoping and waiting for a rapprochement or even suture,

like what Nietzsche does before the new philosophers? To be sure, Derrida never considers such a gesture as walking away: walking away is not Derrida's strategy, not only in thinking about friendship but also in all his other concepts such as hospitality and democracy-to-come. The Derridean strategy, as is well-known, is *attendre sans s'attendre,* or waiting-without-expecting, as Derrida writes in *Foi et savoir* and other places. My quarrel with this waiting-without-expecting is that it indirectly sets up a demand for the other to arrive. In other words, it inadvertently gives rise to a situation where the other, who has no desire or intention at all to arrive in the first place, but because of some sense of ethical responsibility or obligation to respond, posed (or even imposed upon) undeniably by the presence of the one who awaits, comes under pressure to (re)approach. One can see this even in Derrida's scenario where the other is instructed not to respond to the call made by the self: the self might be programming for him- or herself a kind of waiting-without-expectation, but the fact that the other is instructed to not pick up the phone, in other words, that the other is made to know that the self nonetheless is in some way waiting for (though claiming not to expect) some form of response, might ultimately compel the other to call back some time later. As I see it, this is how Derrida's stakes for a future radical relation based on a nonresponse by the other unfortunately risk failing in a way reminiscent of Nietzsche's case with the new philosophers. In this case, in *attendre sans s'attendre,* an imminent rapprochement or even a suture over all theaters of friendship ironically begins to emerge as a promising or even possible, realizable horizon in Derrida's thinking about friendship, resurrecting the very thing that Derrida's deconstructive critique of Cicero and Aristotle seeks to reject.

I would also say that what adds to Derrida's hesitation to walk away from friendship is the notion of *l'aimance.* As pointed out earlier, *l'aimance* is a term Derrida reads in(to) Aristotle's philosophy of "perfect friendship." Derrida disagrees with such an *aimance* because it is essentially and ultimately a narcissistic loving in friendship that looks forward to the death of the friend. Nevertheless, Derrida is enchanted by the leitmotif of *l'aimance* and seeks to maintain it in his thinking about friendship. It is with *l'aimance,* however, that Derrida's thought on friendship makes an about-turn from its radical trajectory and takes on instead a limited contour, if not a reactionary swerve. This is because *l'aimance,* functioning as a supplementary leitmotif of *attendre sans s'attendre,* will make Derrida hold on to some amicable notion at the point where he could have walked away from friendship, or where the rejection of friendship could have been carried out completely. It is as such that one must problematize Derrida's *aimance*, in order for Derrida's "deconstruction" of friendship to counteract the dominance or hegemony of network-centric friendship today.

In a way, Derrida's *nouvelle aimance* is a recuperation of *l'aimance* after its violent appropriation by Aristotle and Nietzsche. Derrida's critique of the respective *aimances* of Aristotle and Nietzsche concerns the renunciation of *l'amour*. Aristotle's thinking of a "perfect friendship" will reach a point where he will say that "loving seems to be the characteristic virtue of friends" or that "friendship depends more on loving."[91] As Derrida observes, this "loving," or *aimance,* arrives via a denigration of amorous love. Indeed, Aristotle makes the claim that a "perfect friendship" of loving is "permanent" or "an enduring thing," while amorous love lacks this quality of everlastingness.[92] It is from such a critique of love that Aristotle proceeds to set up the preeminence of "loving" in friendship's *aimance* over *l'amour*. With regard to Nietzsche's *aimance,* Derrida locates it in Nietzsche's "new philosophers," identifying them as those "who love lovence" (*PA,* 54/ *PF,* 35). As in Aristotle's case, Nietzsche's *aimance* will be of a force greater than the love of *l'amour*, "a love *more loving than love*" (*PA,* 83/ *PF,* 64, my emphasis), where all forms of friendship will be ruptured, leaving only "disappropriation" or "infinite distance" between the "new philosophers" (*PA,* 84/ *PF,* 65). At this point, I would postulate that it is not difficult to deduce that Nietzsche's *aimance* here, in excess of *l'amour*, as Derrida reads it, guarantees the rejection and nonrapprochement of friendship and is therefore a potential force against any form of gregariousness.[93] Derrida does not follow through with this force of Nietzsche's *aimance,* however, and this does not come as a surprise, given that Derrida, as already evident in his reading of Aristotle's *aimance,* is disagreeable with any *aimance* that denigrates *l'amour*, as is the case of Nietzsche's.

The supersession in Nietzsche and Aristotle of *l'amour*—the very concept from which *l'aimance* is derived, since it undoubtedly bears some sense of loving—constitutes Derrida's critique of their respective *aimances*. In place of the latter, Derrida rethinks, if not countersigns, *l'aimance* by reaffirming in it a sense of *l'amour*. In contradistinction to Nietzsche and Aristotle, Derrida claims that there is always love at the beginning, at the heart, and at the end of thinking about friendship. Of *Politiques de l'amitié,*

Derrida will after all say, "J'aimerais croire que ce livre traite avant tout de l'amour," or "I would like to believe that this book concerns love before anything else."[94] This love clearly will not be the simultaneously appropriative and negating *aimance* of Nietzsche and Aristotle, an *aimance* that leaves the amorous love of *l'amour* as a rejected remnant. Instead, Derrida reinstates love as constitutive of *l'aimance*: one arrives at *l'aimance* only when *l'amour* undertakes a certain movement or crossing, a crossing of love to friendship.[95] In more precise terms, it is, according to Derrida, through the passage of a *devenir-amitié de l'amour* or "becoming-friendship of love" that one is granted a glimpse of "a new form of 'lovence'" or *nouvelle aimance* (*PA*, 85/ *PF*, 66). One gets only a "glimpse" of this *aimance* because one can suppose that Derrida's *nouvelle aimance* is of an ephemeral quality. After all, Derrida posits his *nouvelle aimance* in terms of a momentary or transitory experience, something that happens once in time and that is all: "Perhaps one day, here or there, one never knows, something may happen between two people who are in love, and who will love each other with love (is it still the right word?) of the sort that friendship, *just once*, perhaps, for the first time (another *perhaps*), once and only once, therefore for the first and last time (perhaps, perhaps), will become the correct name, the right and just name [...]" (*PA*, 85/ *PF*, 66, trans. modified). Evidently, there is no walking away (from friendship) here in Derrida's *aimance*. There is, instead, an indubitable *attendre sans s'attendre* for a "friendship," which "will become the correct name, the right and just name" of a relation beyond all conceptualizations of friendship in the history of philosophy.[96]

I certainly do not disagree with the question of a crossing of love. In fact, as I will explicate later, a passage through love will be necessary for any thought that seeks to see through to its end the rejection of friendship. The problem I have with Derrida's *aimance* is that in speaking so lovingly of *l'aimance*, it very quickly resurrects an all-too-hopeful promise or possible horizon of "friendship" at the end of this crossing of love. I would argue that this possibility is undeniable even though Derrida would claim this "friendship" to be absolutely different from all present ideas of friendship: "a friendship which will never be reduced to the desire or the potentiality [*puissance*] of friendship" (*PA*, 35/ *PF*, 17), or a "dream of friendship which goes beyond [the] proximity of the congeneric double" (*PA*, 12/ *PF*, viii). But I would ask: Why stay with the term "friendship"? Why (re)call or (re) name "friendship" as the horizon of *l'aimance*? By holding on to that name of "friendship," does it not risk a nostalgic maelstrom that will pull everything that is absolutely new and different in this *aimance* back to what has been known as "friendship," and hence override the alterity proper to *l'aimance*? Derrida might attempt time and again to qualify this "friendship" at the end of the crossing of love as wholly different from any present conception of friendship, but do not the qualifications only betray a rather weak or precarious faith in a future relation that resembles nothing that we have at present? Worse, do not the same qualifications risk betraying an irresistible yearning for friendship as we always know it, a symptom that seems to have manifested itself surreptitiously when Derrida hands over the articulating of *I have enough of you, my friend, for now* to the other, rather than declaring it oneself? With this horizon of "friendship," how truly is the other "free in his movement, out of reach of my will or desire, beyond my intention"? Why not leave whatever happens with *l'aimance* an open term, an unnameable event, leaving it as something that has yet no name, leaving it—so as to be true and just to the eventness of *l'aimance*— to be named only in the future, such that it does not in any anterior fashion recall or threaten to recall an already existing concept? Why not therefore completely reject the name of "friendship" (which is different from rejecting tout court that future relation that resembles nothing that we have at present)? Derrida himself has in fact considered this option, asking of the event of *l'aimance*: "How to name an event? For this love that would take place only once would be the only possible event: as an impossible event" (*PA*, 85/ *PF*, 66, trans. modified). Yet Derrida nonetheless takes recourse to the name of "friendship."[97]

One could say then that the renaming of "friendship" as the possible horizon of *l'aimance* risks undermining the radicality of Derrida's deconstructive critique of the history of philosophy of friendship. Consequently, it also becomes somewhat unconvincing when in relation to *l'aimance*, Derrida says, "I am saying nothing, then, that can be said or is sayable" (*PA*, 89/ *PF*, 70), especially when this "nothing sayable," as discussed earlier, is nothing but the "murderous truth" between friends—the truth that a force of rejection underlies all friendships, or that friends are all *rejects* in and before friendship. With the naming of "friendship" as the horizon of *l'aimance*, I believe that Derrida's force of thought does not quite match up to his reading of a Nietzschean wager in an "infinite distance" or an "uncompromising [. . .] solitary singularity" at the heart of the "nothing sayable" or "murderous truth" of friendship. The hope for a becoming-friendship of love only reveals a hesitation in Derrida's *aimance* at the threshold of a complete rupture with friendship. Put another way, the passion to recuperate *l'amour* back into *l'aimance* has seemingly made Derrida give in to an amicable reflex, or reflex of amicability, in what has been so far a radical critique or rejection of friendship. A fully articulated "nothing sayable" of friendship remains wanting in Derrida, therefore. In the face of hyper-gregarious digital social networks that are swarming the contemporary world and which severely threaten the solitary space from which the new philosopher will arrive, one cannot entertain the above risks in any contemporary rereading of *Politiques de l'amitié*. The rejection of friendship subtending *Politiques de l'amitié* must be put forth unequivocally today, without leaving any slightest possibility or chance to resurrect that concept or even name of "friendship" that *Politiques de l'amitié* has so far critiqued.

To prevent the return of friendship as one has always known it or expects it to be, perhaps one must go further in problematizing Derrida's *aimance*. Derrida's *aimance* might occur only once, for a moment, or "just once, [. . .] once and only once, [. . .] for the first and last time," but it does not really say that everything would be renounced, or to put it more positively, rebegin, after that "once." In other words, there would be the risk of resting with this "once"—and that would still keep to the sense of being "the first and the last time"—and making it the foundation for a future relation or friendship, which then risks compromising the *eventness* of a further future relation that is not only "a friendship which goes beyond [the] proximity of the congeneric double" but also exceeds the name of "friendship." If *l'aimance* is something really ephemeral, something that occurs "just once" without it settling down to become a norm or condition that would determine and regulate future events of relations, then it certainly must learn to walk away, especially from friendship. What characterizes the ephemeral after all is its dispersion.[98] Playing on the French *aimant*, which can mean (1) the person immersed in *l'aimance*, (2) the adjective "loving," and also (3) magnet, Samuel Weber has interpreted *l'aimance* as something of a magnetic quality, related to the force that draws magnets together.[99] But I would add that the same magnets, when they have the same poles facing each other, will experience the force of repulsion when they try to come together. This repulsion is not, however, an immediate reaction: one can feel, even though this sensation is admittedly very minute and lasts only for an almost imperceptible duration, an undeniable attraction drawing these magnets together before a force-field is generated between them to prevent them from approaching. If one wants to retain the term *l'aimance*, I would then like to think of it in terms of this nuanced force of attraction-then-repulsion that develops when two magnets of the same pole encounter each other. In other words, there must be in *l'aimance* a walking away from any recalling or even renaming of friendship, a walking away even from any *attendre sans s'attendre*. To reiterate: *Politiques de l'amitié*, in the face of the *doxā* of contemporary hyper-gregariousness, cannot afford any regressive or reactionary reflex that risks reinstating a possibility of friendship. Otherwise, it might even seem that it gives sanction to that *doxā*. *L'aimance* cannot compromise the radical rejection of friendship. To that end, one must perhaps bring *l'aimance* to a point where it does not dare go or dwell: that would be the abyss of love, or to wit, to be deep in love.

SYNCOPIC LOVE, OR WALKING AWAY: CLÉMENT AND IRIGARAY

I do not dispute the crossing or movement of love that Derrida puts to work in *l'aimance*. In fact, I think it necessary that such a crossing takes place, but only so as to arrive at the "murderous truth" of the rejection of friendship, rather than to invoke the possibility of another form of amicability, no matter if one tries time and again to claim that this new amicability will go beyond all present forms of friendship. That is to say that I do think that Derrida's *aimance*, which reinstates *l'amour* and initiates its movement or crossing, can be a critical force against any form of gregariousness. Except, contrary to the hopeful trajectory that Derrida gives to *l'aimance*, where the optimistic horizon would be the becoming-friendship of love, one must dare to think that love does not fully succeed in the crossing toward friendship. One must dare to think that love will fail friendship, precisely in that crossing. With love, there is the chance that there will be no deliverance to a future friendship. Otherwise, the crossing of love could bring about a syncope of friendship: love will suffocate, choke, smother, sink, or drown out all possibilities of friendship as we know it. In that case, love's syncopic operation will bring to surface the suffocating silence of the "nothing sayable" of friendship, the "murderous truth" between friends that "solitude is irremediable and friendship impossible." Perhaps it is with love then that the force of rejection of friendship comes to the fore affirmatively. For *l'aimance* to combat the contemporary *doxā* of hyper-gregariousness, one must henceforth follow where love in *l'aimance* leads, which is to say, sinking to the depths of love with *l'aimance*, rather than to strive toward "friendship."

At this point, the discourse of Catherine Clément, who speaks of syncope as the promise of a new mode of thought, might help further elucidate the syncopic experience of love. Clément's syncope bears in mind the pathological experience of a loss of consciousness, and she pays particular attention to the crossing from that syncope to the return of consciousness. What fascinates her about syncope is the duration involved in this syncope *before* consciousness is regained. For her, this duration is reminiscent of the musical notion of syncopation, a time-lag or "a note lag[ging] behind,"[100] which she argues to give place to a whole new dimension of thought and experience. Clément goes further to say that it is imperative to remain a little with that time-lag, to dwell within that abyss, so as to experience the "radical surprise [where] one remains effectively syncopated."[101] Whatever is new lies in that time-lag. In that sense, one must learn to survive not only the syncope but also what comes after it, for everything will not be the same anymore: any return to a prior state of reciprocal relation is lost forever in the syncopic experience of love.[102] According to Clément, "From syncope, just as from love; no one returns the same as when he left: he will not come back as he was at the beginning, he will never be the same. He will be 'dis-similar' [. . .]. It is the impossible return to the same."[103] Out of the syncope of love, there is no rapprochement, no return to love's previous conditions or stability. In other words, should there be a future love born out of syncope, there will be no reciprocity that is often expected or worked toward in love. As Clément writes, "Love will never be reciprocal, between a man and a woman," "and syncope will be the effect of such a perfect technique."[104] Keeping in mind this current work's endeavor to move away from the *subject*, I underscore that Clément's syncopic love is also where the *subject* "no longer exists," or, what remains in syncope is a "Subject Undone" [*Sujet Défait*].[105]

Syncopic experience or the syncopic disruption of the amorous *subject* can also be found in Nancy's thinking of love.[106] According to Nancy, "The moment there is love, the least act of love, the least spark [*éclat*], there is the ontological fissure [*fente*] that traverses and disjoins the elements of the subject [. . .]."[107] This is because, for the amorous *subject* who not only says *I* but also *I love you*, the *I* in the latter enunciation "is posited only in being exposed to *you*."[108] In that exposition, Nancy argues, the *I* "does not return, and consequently, something of *I* is definitively lost or dissociated in his or her act of loving."[109] Of course, the *subject* recovers him- or herself in due course, just as Clément's lover does after his or her syncopic experience of love. However, once the declaration of love is made, or once the *subject* experiences the syncope of love, he or she will not return the same: "*I* return no doubt [. . .], but *I* return broken [*brisé*] [. . .]."[110] For Nancy, the condition of being broken in fact endures throughout the experience of love,[111] and this is not simply because, despite the declaration of love, there is always "the risk that the other does not love me, or else I do not keep my promise of my love,"[112] but rather the possibility of other loves, or the possibility that either the beloved or the *I* will refuse or renounce this love and find another one, constitutes the very condition of love that the lover will experience and have to learn to accept. "Love in the singular and taken [*pris*] absolutely," as Nancy says, "is perhaps only the indefinite abundance of all possible loves, and the abandonment to their dissemination, or even to the disorder of its fragmentations [*éclats*]."[113] In other words, love will always come and go: it is an "incessant coming-and-going,"[114] and in that sense, one may say that love is pure movement. It is that very movement of love—which will always render at least one party a *reject* in love—that breaks the heart. A broken heart, however, according to Nancy, must not signal the end of the world for the jilted lover or the *reject* in love: it does not need to be a tragic or teary affair.[115] Instead, it must be seen potentially as an exposition or opening to another love, "another movement of love."[116] That is why there must be no suture to the condition of brokenness [*brisure*], or even to any breakup, in love. Rather, one must always keep it open, and partake in the "rhythm of the division [*partition*] of being" or the "syncope of the sharing [*partage*] of singularity" in endless love, which is to say, love's multiplicity.[117]

What Nancy and Clément each suggest is that there is really nothing to fear of love's syncope. In the syncope of love, there is certainly always the risk not only of losing oneself but also the beloved, or in short, an existing love. That never marks the end of love, since, in the wake of syncope, there is always the possibility of another love, of another experience of love, which in turn is possible only if one has allowed oneself to undergo love's syncope to emerge as an *other*, now open to another thought, articulation, and encounter of love unlike any existing one. So, to return to Derrida's *aimance*, if there is to be *l'amour* there, it is the syncopic experience of love in which *l'aimance* must dare to dwell. *L'aimance* then will be a love whose crossing does not return to a previous amorous state, a love that breaks with any future reciprocity. More importantly, it rejects all present forms and the name of friendship. In this *aimance*, parties are walking away: someone, or both *aimants*, would have walked away from a past love, and someone will also be walking away from a future possible return to love or friendship. One can perhaps say that all are, once again, *rejects* in *l'aimance*. In a way, the syncopic experience of solitary love is not foreign to Derrida's *aimance* in *Politiques de l'amitié*. I believe that it potentially lies in the references to night, darkness, shadows, or obscurity that Derrida attaches to his notion of a future friendship of *l'aimance*.[118] But I would reiterate that one must be willing to dwell, if not get lost, in those dark syncopic spaces, and Derrida does not retreat from them indeed. As he says, "J'aime y risquer des pas, j'aime aussi m'y perdre, le temps de m'y perdre" [I like to risk steps there; I also like to lose myself there, and the time of losing myself there].[119] Losing oneself in syncopic spaces, as I would say, and as Clément's and Nancy's respective elucidation of syncope have suggested, is nothing short of experiencing oneself as an *auto-reject*. Nietzsche's "deepest, most midnightly [...] solitude," wherein lies the "nothing sayable" of friendship, is no doubt another syncopic space, provided one does not commit the Nietzschean lapse of proclaiming a "we" that will hail the other into some sort of rapprochement. In a time of hyper-gregariousness, a time and space where the chance of the arrival of the Nietzschean solitary new philosopher or philosophy is at risk, one must learn to love getting lost in the syncopic experience of solitary love, without casting out a name such as "friendship," or an address such as "we," as a possible lifeline out of the abyss and darkness of syncope. One must learn how to walk away from any buoy marked with "friendship." One must always remember to reject "friendship," or remind oneself that one is always a *reject* in and of friendship. And that is perhaps "the most impossible"—and I would add, necessary—"declaration of love" (*PA*, 198/ *PF*, 174).

I would now like to return to the idea of dispersion as discussed with regard to *l'aimance*. I have said that dispersion is akin to walking away (or even taking a walk in Derrida's scenario of friendship between *rejects*), and I would like to highlight here that for Luce Irigaray, walking away is also something to be affirmed in love or in any relation between beings.[120] In her recent *Sharing the World*, Irigaray argues that an encounter between two beings—and for Irigaray, it is typically two beings of different sexes—is initiated especially by an "intimacy" that lies within the female.[121] It is this "intimacy" that draws the (male) other to her, which in turn gives her a sense of presence. As Irigaray makes clear, there is no necessity for physical contact in this "intimacy," or for physical contact to bring the encounter between the two further, since "intimacy" is already a haptic event in itself, making the (male) other feel that "the tactile nature of the environment [. . .] [has] changed."[122] According to Irigaray, "intimacy" affects a material change in the air, which engenders a "gesture" in the (male) other—"the gesture of going with respect and reverence" toward the female being.[123] This approach between the two must be meticulous to not see to the subordination of the female by the male, and it is at this point that Irigaray insists on a certain walking away by each party in this approach. In *Sharing the World*, Irigaray calls this walking away a "[coming] back home,"[124] and in *The Way of Love*, the "step back."[125] In this walking away, or *step back home*, what is at stake is "self-affection," which, according to Irigaray in *Sharing the World*, is the preservation of the female's subjectivity or the integrity of the female *subject*. This is to ensure that her constitution and mode of presentation, based on her own desires or what she deems proper to herself, are not lost or erased in the encounter with the (male) other. The female *subject* must get back in touch with herself so as to not abdicate or submit her differences to those of the (male) other, and for Irigaray, walking away serves that purpose.

As evident, Irigaray keeps to the *subject* as a category of thought. This is somewhat surprising, given that her work in general involves a sustained critique of the male *subject*'s denigration and marginalization of the other and the other's difference. In not calling for the dissolution of the *subject*, she deviates rather significantly from the common move made in "poststructuralist" discourse. It is perhaps out of respect for difference—which would include the male *subject*'s difference—that Irigaray lets the (male) *subject* be and not seek his dissolution. It is more certain, though, that if Irigaray refrains from any negating critique of the male *subject*, it is because she recognizes the fact that humanity is essentially or originarily constituted by *two subjects*, one male and the other female, and that humanity cannot proceed without one or the other *subject*. For Irigaray, the future or perpetuation of humanity will always require at least these *two* male and female *subjects*. However, as Irigaray recognizes throughout her work, the female *subject* has always been repressed or oppressed in the world. Irigaray makes the militant call then—while letting be the male *subject*—for the articulation and affirmation of the *autonomous female subject*: she who is not only irreducibly different, but also free from all determination by the male *subject*.

This is perhaps where one may understand Irigaray's motivation in maintaining the category of the *subject* in her discourse: not at all to take recourse to, or further promote, the thinking of the male *subject*, but to let emerge another *subject*—the *female subject*, to serve as a counterpoint to the male *subject*. In keeping with the category of the *subject* this way, Irigaray nonetheless effects a change in the conceptual terrain of subjectivity: in *Sharing the World*, she argues that with the affirmation of the female *subject*, we move from a "vertical transcendentalism" where the world is reduced to the determination of the male *subject*, to a "horizontal transcendentalism" where the world is shared equally by the two male and female *subjects* without one subjugating the other. It is with "horizontal transcendentalism" that the autonomous female *subject* comes into presence in her own terms. As Irigaray argues, the recognition of the female *subject* in a "horizontal transcendentalism" is how one begins to acknowledge and respect the differences of each and every one of us in the world. Consequently, walking away in the encounter between two *subjects* serves to reaffirm that the female *subject* is perfectly capable of establishing her *subjecthood* or subjectivity by herself, or on her own terms, and is not dependent on another, especially the male *subject*.

To be sure, walking away and the subsequent process of "self-affection" apply to the other (male) *subject* too. The latter must no less maintain his identity and difference in his own terms. Walking away then ensures that there is no fusion or assimilation in the encounter, where one risks identifying with the other, or where one's identity and difference are appropriated or neutralized by the other. In walking away, the *subjecthood* proper to one and the other, that is to say, the subjectivity of the female *subject* and that of the male *subject*, are kept intact. However, I would argue that thinking with the *subject*, even if it is with the radically different female *subject*, puts the question of difference at risk, even in the event of having walked away. After walking away, it is not the case, as Irigaray underscores, that subsequent encounters are precluded. On the contrary, future meetings are desirable. Walking away, to put it differently, is then the process or steps to allow subsequent encounters to take place, encounters that involve constant negotiations that recognize and respect the differences of others, or in short, constant negotiations that put in effect coexisting with others. But what happens when the other refuses the following encounter? Irigaray is certainly aware of this possibility and does not deny its occurrence. As she writes, the duration between the initial "gesture" and future meetings always rests "on pain of the encounter no longer taking place."[126] Should that take place, it is always possible that the one who is rejected of a subsequent encounter sinks into a self-berating abyss of abjectness, feeling that he or she is inherently or ultimately unworthy of recognition by the other. Here, the recourse to the rhetoric of the *subject* might prove critical as it lifts this imploded self from such an abyss. "Self-affection" in this instance becomes a reminder for the self that he or she is a *subject* in his or her own right, exercising his or her freedom to exist in the world in his or her own difference, and is independent of how he or she is perceived by the other, independent of whether the other wants to meet him or her (again).

However, the certitude or reascertaining of the self, granted by the rhetoric of the *subject*, might go the other extreme. Some sort of disappointment, if not resentment, with regard to recognizing and respecting the differences of others or being in touch with others, might grow. To shield him- or herself from the confidence-shattering rejection by others, the *subject*, through his or her defensive mechanism, subsequently might be inclined or tempted to recreate an insular ipseity, risking the closure of the openness to others and their differences. It is as such that staying with the *subject* risks threatening all endeavors to be in touch with the difference of others. Besides, the assertion (or reassertion) of the sovereign certitude and constitution of the *subject* does not arise only from its reaction to a rejection of a future meeting. In fact, it follows from any foundation of the *subject*, as has been the case since Descartes. This would also be the case for Irigaray, as she stays with the *subject*, and this is evident especially in her *Entre orient et occident*. There, she makes the claim that it is through a certain mode of breathing, particularly that which is practiced in yoga, that humanity will finally recognize the equal existence and freedom of one and the other, and that humanity will thence begin to solve its problems. However, I would argue that an unconscious slippage into some sort of subjective sovereignty, typically projected by the male *subject*, occurs when Irigaray claims that only the female *subject* knows how to breathe properly in the sense of knowing how to share breath, or that only female breath holds the reserve of a life-affirming and regenerative breath and hence the promise of the future of the world. Now, if Irigaray has critiqued Sartre for his claim that it is the masculine caress that grants the caressed (female) other a sense of subjectivity, one could similarly critique Irigaray's argument for its implication that it is the breath of the female *subject* that grants the future possibility of the male *subject*. Certainly, Irigaray has stated that it is not her intention to create "a reversal of power" between male and female *subjects*.[127] However, her rhetoric there in general, especially the rhetoric of the *subject*, nonetheless inclines toward privileging the female *subject*, giving it preeminence over other *subjects*. With the rhetoric of the *subject*, it is always difficult to avoid a certain denigration of (male or female) others *subject*, hence risking the undoing of the entire project of coexistence, or the recognition and respect, of differences.

This is why I am arguing for the *reject*, which may be critical in avoiding those risks in Irigaray's notion of walking away. In accepting the condition of always being a *reject*, the slide into resentment, when one is refused a (subsequent) meeting with the other, may be avoided. Already accepting itself to be irreducibly a *reject*, it is not displaced or devastated when the other says *do not approach (again)*. The *reject* in a way always anticipates such an utterance; it is always prepared for it. In the face of it, the *reject* hardly feels any resentment. Resentment in that sense is meaningless to the *reject*: it is indifferent to such a sentiment. In that case, too, there is no (need for any) reactionary restitution or resurrection of the self as a sovereign *subject* certain of itself, no (need for any) reactionary will to defend its constitution by deflecting the other's rejection with his or her own rejection of being in touch with others. In all, the *reject* does not seek to withdraw into a "self-affection" as Irigaray's female *subject* is wont to do. Rather, the *reject* sidesteps all moments of "self-affection," avoiding any (re)foundation of itself as a *subject*.

TOWARD "A PEOPLE TO COME": FROM *LE PRÉTENDANT* TO THE NOMADIC WAR MACHINE IN DELEUZE AND GUATTARI

In my critique of Derrida's philosophy of friendship, I have pointed out that Derrida does not follow through the force of rejection against friendship, particularly against naming "friendship" the event of a future encounter or *nouvelle aimance* that "will never be reduced to the desire or the potentiality of friendship," or "which goes beyond [the] proximity of the congeneric double." In what follows, I would like to demonstrate that Deleuze's philosophy, by contrast, puts forth a stronger or more affirmative force of rejection and therefore also projects a more active figure of the *reject*, which lets (the names of) friendship and community fall by the side. In this section, I will be focusing more on explicating the figure of the *reject* from within Deleuze's philosophy. I will no longer make references to the specific cultural context of teletechnological communication and the hyper-gregarious condition that it produces and disseminates, since I believe the preceding pages have been sufficient in underscoring the stakes or critical urgency of thinking and articulating the *reject* in the face of contemporary network-centric friendship or community. One would just have to keep in mind that any articulation and exposition of the *reject* from now on will always bear a critique of all existing *doxā* of friendship and community. Staying within Deleuze's philosophy will not mean that his figures of the *reject*—the lone philosopher, *le prétendant, homo tantum*, the lover or the beloved—are detached from the real world, though. Deleuze's figures of the *reject* have the function of revealing the real, harsh truths of impossible friendship and syncopic love in relations that we form with other beings in our everyday life. This is even despite the fact that Deleuze himself is never really interested, at least in writing or thought, in friends or friendship that we are so familiar with in lived experienced. As he says in the television interview with Claire Parnet, he is not interested in "an actual friend,"[128] but the figure of the friend that has not simply been appropriated by philosophy as its figure of thought, but manifests itself in heterogeneous forms in the history of philosophy.

Deleuze's engagement with the question of friendship is obvious in his coauthored text with Guattari, *Qu'est-ce que la philosophie?*, especially in the introduction. But Deleuze's own writings—his very early and seldom discussed essay "Statements and Profiles," his *Marcel Proust et les signes*, and his final essay "L'Immanence: une vie"—also revolve around the topic of friendship in equally significant ways, and I will try to cover these texts in the following pages. But to go back to *Qu'est-ce que la philosophie?* a little: it is there where one can say at the outset that friendship in Deleuze and Guattari will be invoked only to have its terrain radically undone. For Deleuze and Guattari, there will be friendship only if it is (already) secant. It will be something of *postfriendship* or *after friendship*, not without a sense of violence, and not without a postapocalyptic inflection. In that regard, one might even speak of the despairing condition where one and the other are all *rejects* in and before friendship and love. Yet, any tearing or rejection of friendship in Deleuze and Guattari, like the force of rejection in Derrida's philosophy of friendship, is not nihilistic, but in fact looks toward another form of relation between beings or a new understanding of relations. In other words, Deleuze and Guattari's endeavor is to reveal existing notions such as "friends" or "friendship" to be but anachronistic misnomers; unlike the case of Derrida, there will be no reversion to these terms or names in Deleuze and Guattari.

I have already noted that Deleuze is not really interested in the real, actual friend, but the friend as a figure or image of thought in philosophy. As he writes with Guattari in *Qu'est-ce que la philosophie?*, the interesting question of friendship would be, "What does *friend* mean when it becomes a conceptual persona, or a condition for the exercise of thought?"[129] One should not expect that the friend as a figure of thought will take on an amicable contour here. Contrary to what philosophy of the Greek heritage has always seemed to suggest, Deleuze and Guattari argue that the friend or friendship does not actually lead to philosophy. That Grecian idea that philosophy is always linked to friendship is mere fiction, according to Deleuze and Guattari. Or, as Deleuze says in his *Marcel Proust et les signes*, the friend as a figure of thought is *never* that which "leads us towards *conversation*, where we exchange and communicate ideas" so that it "invites us to philosophy."[130] Deleuze and Guattari will go further to argue that Greek philosophical "friendship," at the end of it all, is in fact not just devoid of harmonious accord or intellectual conversation but also of "social relation."[131] The philosopher, in truth, cannot bear friendship very much: what he desires is solitude, the silence of which allows a lucidity in thinking. In other words, the philosopher essentially rejects the company, community, and friendship of fellow philosophers. This perhaps explains why Plato's

Symposium ends with an image of a philosopher who stands alone—the image of a solitary Socrates, alone in thinking and without lack of companionship.[132] That is the striking image of Socrates that remains, of which Alcibiades, enamored with Socrates, finds unbearable and injurious.

Deleuze and Guattari surely keep that image in mind in their reading of Socrates as essentially disinterested in dialogues, noting that while Socrates is undoubtedly engaged by, or drawn into, forms of dialogues or dialectical debates, the dialogues mark at the same time Socrates's gradual rejection of those forms:

> Did Socrates not make philosophy a free discussion among friends? Is it not the summit of Greek sociability, as a conversation of free men? In fact, Socrates did not cease to render all discussion impossible, both in the short form of a sparring [*agôn*] of questions and answers and in the long form of a rivalry between discourses. He made the friend the friend of the single concept, and the concept into the pitiless monologue that eliminate turn by turn the rivals.[133]

Philosophy, therefore, is in fact very much averse to discussions, dialogues, or conversations, especially those that take place among friends. As Deleuze and Guattari point out: "Sometimes philosophy is made to be the idea of a perpetual discussion, as 'communicational rationality,' or as 'universal democratic conversation.' Nothing is less exact [...]."[134] Instead, "philosophy has a horror of discussion."[135] Or, "the taste for discussion barely appeals to the philosopher. Every philosopher flees when he hears the phrase 'let's discuss a little.'"[136] Discussion among friends does not mark the activity of philosophy or the trait of a philosopher; it only detracts philosophy or the philosopher from what Deleuze and Guattari see as his or her proper task of concept-creation.

If the philosopher has no time for discussion with the friend, it is because the philosopher has been struck by a force of thought, or one could say that he or she has been called to the task of concept-creation. To focus on the latter, one must learn to walk away from amicable discussions, as Deleuze and Guattari seem to suggest when they say, "We do not lack communication. On the contrary, we have too much of it. We lack creation."[137] In philosophy, one should turn away (from) the friend and follow the solitary line of flight toward the work of concept-creation. This is how philosophy reveals itself to be not really interested in the friend—that real, other corporeal being that one relates to amicably in lived experience. If there is the figure of the friend in philosophy, it is otherwise of the latter. According to Deleuze and Guattari, it has to be recognized that "the friend such as he or she appears in philosophy no longer designates an extrinsic character [*personnage*], an example or empirical circumstance."[138] They go on to add, "With philosophy, the Greeks violently submits the friend no longer to a relation with an other but with an Entity, an Objectness [*Objectité*], an Essence."[139] In other words, philosophy, since the Greeks, has in fact been working out a rejection of the actual friend or actual friendship. Doing nothing for philosophy, the Greeks have been smashing the notion of amicable discussion, if not friendship tout court, from within: "The idea of a Western democratic conversation between friends has never produced a single concept. The idea comes perhaps from the Greeks, but they distrusted it so much, and subjected it to such harsh treatment, that the concept was more like the ironic soliloquy bird that hovered over [*survolait*] the battlefield of destroyed rival opinions."[140]

Deleuze himself had also put forth a forceful rejection of the actual friend or friendship in *Marcel Proust et les signes*. According to Deleuze, "Thought is nothing without something that forces to think, and that does violence to thought. More important than thought is what 'leads to thinking [*donne à penser*].'"[141] Friendship is lacking precisely in that violence or force that will lead one to think or create new concepts. Following Proust, Deleuze argues that "friends are like well-disposed minds that explicitly agree on the significations of things, words, and ideas,"[142] such that these "communications of garrulous friendship" [*l'amitié bavarde*] are essentially "ignorant of the dark zones where effective forces are elaborated and act on thought, forces that are the determinations that *forces* us to think."[143] In other words, one will not find in friendship those dangerous regions of darkness (regions not distant from the abyssal region of syncope according to Clément, as seen earlier in the section on Derrida) from which a force that leads to thought arrives. If philosophy seeks the truth, then "a friend is not enough for us to approach the truth."[144]

LE PRÉTENDANT

While *Marcel Proust et les signes* radically renders the friend an inadequate figure of thought, and while the philosophical task of concept-creation in *Qu'est-ce que la philosophie?* sees the philosopher walking away from all friendly conversations or discussions, one has to be precise to say that Deleuze and Guattari do not negate the relation between friendship and philosophy in an absolute manner: a certain amicable relation remains to be deployed in and by philosophy. Deleuze and Guattari might have shown that philosophy turns away (from) the (actual) friend, but that does not mean that philosophy, at its nascent stage and at its completion, does not need the friend. In fact, Deleuze and Guattari will not fail to explicate that the task of philosophizing always involves a certain apprenticeship in relations at the stage where concepts are created *and* at that where concepts can be perpetuated into the future. I will work backward and consider the question of the future of concepts first. A concept might end up looking like a "pitiless monologue,"[145] according to Deleuze and Guattari's analysis, but it is always highly attentive in terms of a geographical sensitivity to its milieu. In other words, it takes constant survey of its milieu, not at all with an eye to a policing form of surveillance, but to be always alert to components that either continue to make themselves available to the concept, or that have been left out previously. The concept seeks these components out so that it can attach itself to any of these at any moment for its development. As Deleuze and Guattari say, "The concept is in a state of *survey* in relation to its components," or, "the 'survey' is the state of the concept or its specific infinity."[146]

A concept might seem to stand alone at its completion, but it can never deny the existence of other concepts. In fact, it cannot do without other concepts, or without the problematic that other concepts encounter, all of which motivate its own construction. In Deleuze and Guattari's words, "A concept is devoid of meaning as long as it is not connected to other concepts and is not linked to a problem that it resolves or helps to resolve."[147] To reiterate, a concept might at some moment stand above other concepts, but that does not mean that the latter are from then on completely vanquished or redundant. A certain relation with other concepts is always maintained: it is even always at work, either folding one concept into another or unfolding one from the other.[148] That is to say too that a concept might need another to renew itself: "A concept also has a *becoming* that each time concerns its relation with [other] concepts situated on the same plane. Here, concepts link up with one another, support one another, coordinate their contours, articulate their respective problems [. . .]. In fact, every concept, having a finite number of components, will bifurcate toward other concepts composed differently but [...] respond to related problems [*problèmes connectables*], and participate in co-creation."[149]

In that regard, a certain amicable relation is still somewhat mobilized in philosophy for the future of concepts. Concept-creation passes through a certain pedagogy of relations, an apprenticeship in learning how to coexist with another concept even though it is standing above the other at some moment, in view of laying claim to components that it deems critical for its further construction. In other words, for philosophy, or for the future of philosophy, Deleuze and Guattari still need friendship, therefore. They will look for a friend, and they will not fail to acknowledge that friendship might still engender philosophy, that it might even make possible the ultimate question of philosophy, which is the question of what philosophy is, a question that "had to be possible to pose [...] 'between friends.'"[150] Lest one thinks that there is a returning to the figure of the friend or friendship here as one knows it, one should be precise to say that when Deleuze and Guattari seemingly reinvoke the friend or friendship, especially after unveiling the truth of the philosopher's aversion to amicable conversations, and after the irreducible image of the lone philosopher standing at a distance from everyone else, what they are trying to bring to critical awareness in fact is that something has happened to friendship or the friend in the course of philosophy since the Greeks. In creating concepts (and not amicable discussions), philosophy since the Greeks has needed friendship, but it has at the same time transformed the friend or friendship into something else. Given what we have seen of the "amicable" relation that goes on in concept-creation, which involves first walking away from (real) friendship, then standing aloof in solitariness, and then reforming friendships (with other concepts) for the sake of the future of the concept, one is not dealing with what we deem true friendship in this case. A question of sincerity in forming and sustaining friendship is certainly in question here, as it seems that friendship is always posited only to be betrayed, particularly when the concept, at the moment of its triumphal construction, hovers as "a pitiless monologue" over all the other concepts it has surpassed. What Deleuze and Guattari do then, it can be said, is to reveal this true color of friendship in philosophy: they bring to surface the figure of betrayal at the very heart of the mythic image of the friend in philosophy.

To see that in greater detail, I return to the creation stage of the concept. As said, conversations or intellectual discussions between friends do nothing for the philosophical task of concept-creation. Neither does concept-creation arrive by way of a reception of a gift, such as that exchanged between friends, for example. Philosophers "must no longer accept concepts as a gift," or wait to be presented with it like a gift: "Concepts are not waiting for us ready-made, like celestial bodies. There is no heaven for concepts."[151] Concepts must be created out of the singularity of the one who thinks it and be marked with his or her signature.[152] This creative step is not an arbitrary or random act. A very specific act of creation is involved here. The thinker is first absorbed into a field of the problematic, where a problem interests the thinker. That interest is augmented when the thinker is struck by the possibility of him or her addressing or resolving the problem, which then leads to the construction of a concept, a concept that will bear the thinker's signature because of the attention and/or solution he or she brings to the problem. It is in this sense that some sort of friendship comes (back) into play in philosophy (after it has rejected the actual friend), for the thinker must think of himself as "the friend of the concept, [that] he is capable of the concept [*il est en puissance de concept*]."[153] The thinker turns away (from) the friends of conversation or discussion, but he or she nonetheless must turn amicably toward the imminent concept.

Meanwhile, one must never assume that there is only one philosopher seeking the same concept, or that he or she alone is worthy of that concept. The field or plane of the problem is always open to anyone, or, the problematic can interest anyone. For the (lone) philosopher, then, there is always the possibility of competition over the concept. Combat, rivalry, and strife are lurking in the vicinity, posed not only by rival philosophers, but also by the thinker's friend or friends. The philosopher cannot remain the calm or passive friend of the concept, or even of his or her fellow philosopher(s), therefore. He or she has to be more than that: he or she has to be a little more forceful, if not aggressive, with regard to the concept, almost adopting a combative stance in relation to other rival philosophers and philosopher-friends. For Deleuze and Guattari, he or she must *at most* be a claimant or *at least* a lover. He or she must strive toward the concept, always vigilant of the possible competitions or rivalries that abound in the neighborhood. According to Deleuze and Guattari, the philosopher in this case becomes *le prétendant*, the figure that names suitor, claimant, and pretender altogether at the same time. As *le prétendant*, the philosopher can only pretend to be friendlike, while already slowly shedding away the pretensions of friendship or all the niceties that accompany the figure of the friend, since the philosopher cannot allow any friend to reach the concept before he or she does. Not only mistrust cuts across friendship here, but the philosopher must also in effect reject his or her friend(s). He or she must jealously watch over the imminent concept and reach toward it like a lover or claimant to the object of desire, which implies making all other philosophers his or her rivals, leaving them behind in his or her trail of concept-creation. With regard to this philosopher/ *le prétendant*, Deleuze and Guattari will write: "Is [he or she] not rather the lover? [. . .] Or else, is it not a matter of someone other than the friend or lover? For if the philosopher is the friend or lover of wisdom, is it not because he claims it, striving for it potentially [*en puissance*] rather than actually possessing it? Would the friend also be the claimant [*le prétendant*] then, and that which is said to be the friend would be the Thing on which the claim would be made, but not the third [*le tiers*], who would become on the contrary a rival? Friendship would bear an emulating distrust [*méfiance émulante*] with regard to the rival as much as a loving tension towards the object of desire."[154]

One cannot lay claim to any sincere friendship, therefore, in this secant community of philosophers who have gathered around the field or plane of the problematic, from which a concept will emerge in the name of that philosopher who eventually hovers over that plane, that is, the one who emerges victorious in the rivalry to put his or her signature on the concept to come. Here, friendship is very quickly undone, as it betrays an irreducible combative mistrust between friends in philosophy. The philosopher is "but a friend who no longer has a relation with his friend except through a loved thing bearing rivalry [*une chose aimée porteuse de rivalité*]."[155] Once again, at the end of this combat over the concept, the image that remains is the image of a lone philosopher, he or she who has laid claim on the concept and now stands over his or her vanquished rivals, surveying the field of combat as *le survol*. In this image, "there would not be two great philosophers."[156] This image is not shared between friends, in other words, for there are no friends (left). In the eyes of the lone, victorious philosopher, all other fellow philosophers are but *rejects*, since they have failed to lay claim to the concept. In return, the solitary philosopher left standing, in the eyes of the other philosophers, is surely also a *reject*, someone they shun, since that philosopher, in his or her quest to appropriate the concept, has betrayed their friendships by turning them into rivals.

Le prétendant in philosophy, according to Deleuze and Guattari, is the a priori traitorous figure, therefore, always already undoing friendship at the beginning of philosophy, even before philosophy traverses the pedagogy of relations in its work of concept-creation. I read *le prétendant* as a figure of the *reject*—the one who not only rejects but also betrays friendship, and the one who will no doubt in turn be rejected by his or her other philosopher "friends." Any apprenticeship in relations that follows from philosophical concept-creation would then be already tainted, betrayed, or even undone by the mistrust and rivalry of *le prétendant*. *Le prétendant*, or the suitor, claimant, pretender, and *reject*: this is what has become of the friend in philosophy, what happens to friends as a "condition of thought" in the philosophical quest to lay claim to the concept to come. In other words, the aim of the "deconstruction" of friendship in Deleuze and Guattari, which involves the rejection of (real) friendship while maintaining some sort of apprenticeship in relations in the domain of concept-creation, is to undo all the harmonious niceties attached to the notion of friendship and to reveal that the friend is always already the irrepressible traitorous *prétendant* (or *reject*). One must from then on not hesitate to re-cognize friendship as always already secant, and that is why Deleuze and Guattari will always trust the ultimate question of what philosophy is to arrive more from a situation where friendship is rent with distrust and mutual combat, that is, when the question is posed " before the enemy like a challenge, and at the same time reaching that crepuscular hour [*cette heure, entre chien et loup*] when one even distrusts the friend."[157] To put it bluntly, philosophy reproduces the image of the friend only to make use of friendship so as to lay claim to a concept. Otherwise, one can say that the image of the friend is appropriated as the philosopher's foil to soften the force of the claim to the concept, making it easier to sign the imminent concept to oneself. In short, philosophy still needs the friend at times; it even befriends, but only on the condition of making use of the friend for concept-creation. Philosophy in this case serves as a preview to the revelation of a bleak world where friendships or relations are likewise essentially secant, betrayed, or made use of. Or, as Deleuze says in his early "Statements and Profiles" essay, philosophy is "an introduction to an unpleasant world."[158]

If the world that Deleuze unfolds in "Statements and Profiles" is indeed "unpleasant," it is because one finds in that essay the unfolding of an essentially solitary world, where friendship is refused, and where friendship is once again something to be made used of to the benefit of the narcissistic self. According to Deleuze in that Sartrean essay, an "I" creates a subjective point of view of the world and projects this consciousness of the world into the world *as* the world. However, the pure and simple fact of existence of another being—for example, a male counterpart, in his simple anonymity, not yet particularized as a specific identity and therefore a "male-Other," which is "the a priori Other" as Deleuze calls it—complicates and destabilizes that seemingly solitary world.[159] The "I" may conceive that world as a world of fatigue, as in Deleuze's example, but the a priori Other, in his slightest gesture of gaiety contests that representation. In other words, he reveals the fact that the fatigue world "does not have an objective consistency."[160] "I" then comes to see the a priori Other, positing an opposing worldview, to be potentially aggressive: "I" see the Other as an imminent negation, or even denigration, of the subjective certainty of the fatigue world. Things can get worse: the consciousness of the fatigue world begins to overwhelm and flood the "I" with an unbearable insularity, causing him to implode, leaving his "collapsed body [to] [stand] alone."[161] In Deleuze's analysis, this implosive solitariness constitutes the "fundamental mediocrity" of existence or *being*,[162] and a "mediocre-I" is that "I" who has the revelation that the world-as-I-see-it is precisely just that—a particular viewpoint, which is always exposed to the supplement, if not contest, of another viewpoint, either from the body next to "I" or from whoever comes before "I." In that sense, the "mediocre-I" is also nothing less than a despairing or even abject (auto-)*reject*. However, "fundamental mediocrity" can also be where the rent in friendship has its germination. That is because it marks the fundamental contest in viewpoints before all friendships, before any amicable communication or relation with the other. In other words, the first reflex of any encounter with the other, or what quickly gives way in the encounter, is rivalry, a scene of enmity where one "knows itself in solitude, and knows the male-Other in hatred, without breaking with its solitude."[163] One is always already concerned about horizons of viewpoints, concerned whether they touch amicably or threaten to cross (out) one another. One quickly guards one's horizon against that of the other, and this is how the world in which the "I" is always in the presence of others becomes, or proves to be, unpleasant.

Despite this primacy of a secant encounter, Deleuze would argue in this "Statements and Profiles" essay that friendship remains possible. As he says, "The possible world that the male-Other reveals can also be called the offer of a friendship."[164] That is to say, if one could see past the edgy horizons of different worldviews, and negotiate those differences without one negating the other, one could proceed toward a mode of living where living in the world with others is living as what Deleuze calls a "team," which is even close to "a sports team or a social team."[165] According to Deleuze, living as a team could bring relief to "fundamental mediocrity": "The Team is the only way to escape from mediocrity."[166] Unfortunately, the real world is not so amicable, whereby this "Team" can be easily consolidated among people: there remain "those who cannot or do not want to go beyond mediocrity towards the Team."[167] This is where one sees once again how friendship is rather impossible in the Aristotelian-Derridean sense, or how friendship can be formed only to be made use of in order "to go beyond mediocrity." In Deleuze's analysis, two ways present themselves for those who are unable or unwilling to join the "Team." First, there is the absolute anticommunity gesture, the enclosure of oneself within oneself, shutting the world off completely. This is where one would "internalize mediocrity," keeping to oneself, "touches only itself," and not let oneself be touched.[168] In this case, one refuses the violent supplement of the possible worlds of the Other; one refuses to take into account the latter and slips in between them instead: "She parts herself and let herself pass."

Then there is the endeavor "to acquire at least the inner life they lack."[169] Now, the "a prior Other" creates anxiety for the "I" not only because of the possible world he or she expresses, but also because of "an enormous inner life" that he or she holds in reserve,[170] an inner world that is hardly disclosed in the world, and which the "I" can never know for sure if "I" am included or not in that world. According to Deleuze, that reserve is the secret of *being*, that which constitutes the singularity of every *being* in all its plurality and heterogeneity. If there is to be a "team," it then has to be sustained by the acknowledgment of the "inner life" of the other *and* the maintenance of the respective secrets of respective inner lives of all who have come to form this "team." The one who refuses the "team" is he or she who cannot bear the "inner life" of the other. For this "mediocre-I," the "inner life" that is never shared gradually comes to be seen as a lack within him- or herself, and the "mediocre-I" copes with this apparent lack through "the acquisition [. . .] of an inner life [. . .] of the secret."[171] According to Deleuze in this essay, it takes the form of "pederasty," which the translator of Deleuze's essay notes as "either homosexuality among men or the love of young boys by men."[172] It is not difficult to elicit something Greek about this "pederasty," given that Deleuze's example of "pederasty" is set in the context of a lycée, a place of learning, not to mention that in Deleuze's analysis, there is also "something intellectual" in "pederasty."[173] An echo of Greek, philosophical homosexuality, as is often read in Plato's *Symposium*, where Alcibiades desperately seeks to elicit the secret or some sort of "inner life" from within Socrates, surely resonates here.

In "pedastry," the mediocre-being makes the other invest an "inner life" in him. But he has to first create a hint of an "inner life." Thinking he lacks one, he turns "fundamental mediocrity" into "the secret," turning, in other words, the solitariness of "fundamental mediocrity" into "the sign of an abject and painful independence."[174] He "shares [this] with the child," charming the child with such a secret, obsessing the child to create for him a further "enormous inner life," which is only in the end "what *seemed* [. . .] to be an inner life."[175] The desperate need for an "inner life" comes to be disseminated to the "mediocre adolescent,"[176] therefore, and the "mediocre adolescent" in turn desires an "inner life," which he understands he can derive from the one he loves or who loves him. It is here that friendship becomes instrumental, where it is useful only to fulfill the apparent lack of an "inner life" in oneself. Put another way, friendship here is needed only to set up a scene of love where one can witness the beloved investing an "inner life" in oneself. It is here that one begins to look for the friend, so as to overcome one's "fundamental mediocrity," while at the same time refusing the friendship offered by the "Team." Let me quote Deleuze's explication at length:

> The statement of the mediocre adolescent: I have never conceived of the confession of love except in the form of insults. And when I dream a little, [. . .], it is always the same thing. I am hidden in a cupboard at a friend's house. A young girl comes in, and cries: "Pierre (or Paul, or Jacques, and finally my name) is a dirty bastard, a revolting, stinking

pederast [...]." So I come out of the cupboard, and say "It's me." What follows is of little importance, since I know how to make her confess her love, by untying her injury like a complicated knot. But there it is: it is of absolutely no importance that the girl exists; it is much more important that a cupboard is really, effectively, in the room of one of my friends [...] and without a cupboard I could never have given my dream any priority over fixed objectivity. Will I find one? I am looking for a friend.[177]

The instance of "I am looking for a friend" here certainly brings to mind Derrida's critique in *Politiques de l'amitié* of the deployment of friendship in the history of philosophy for a generally narcissistic purpose. In the case of Deleuze's critique here, friendship is the relation through which one makes use of one another to create an "inner life" for oneself, so that there will be someone to embellish one's "fundamental mediocrity" with the contours of an "inner life." One might be tempted here to speak of the "mediocre-I" as some sort of *auto-reject* in the sense of a self that disdains him- or herself because of a perceived lack of an "inner life." However, I insist that there is a difference with the *auto-reject* that I am elucidating in this present work. As I have discussed in the previous section on Derrida, the *auto-reject* that I am theorizing here rejects itself not because of any lack, but because it does not want to be striated by any single thought. Such an *auto-reject* is affirmative and needs to be affirmed, while the "mediocre-I" as *auto-reject* is evidently self-negating or self-denigrating. Furthermore, I have also stated that the *auto-reject* in friendship is one who recognizes him- or herself as a *reject* in friendship, which implies that he or she would affirm the irreducible rent in friendship, rather than seek to create a supplemental suture over it, or to look for a friend and make use of him or her, as is the case of the "mediocre-I."

LOVE (AGAIN)

In the section on Derrida, I pointed out that for Derrida, love, if not *l'aimance*, can play the critical role of "deconstructing" all present friendships, opening them up to another form of relation (without relation) that will bear "the just name of friendship." What role can love play for Deleuze's "Team"? Does love give a hopeful horizon to Deleuze's bleak world as well?

Love, for Deleuze in his "Statements and Profiles" essay, in fact sidesteps the construction of a "Team," if not lures one to reject it. According to Deleuze, not only is the "Team" undone because of rivalry or because "many have only been able to choose rancor," but also because of love, which "expels [lovers] from the Team."[178] Love might take one (and the beloved) out of the "Team," but does love then bring one to another amorous or amicable structure (as in Derrida's *nouvelle aimance* or Bataille's "community of lovers"), otherwise than the plural or more-than-two "Team," such that love here provides a salvation or form of escape from worldly solitariness? Does love not always promise some sort of union with another, promising, as Bennington suggests, to "tend towards a fusion of the parties to it"?[179] Love in Deleuze, however, will not be an amorous or amicable respite from the world of secant friendships. Love takes one away from the "Team," but it does not lift one from the depths of solitariness; love, instead, will plunge one further into that abyss. Reminiscent of Clément's syncopic love, love in Deleuze will be the passage toward the revelation of a world where relations are always already secant, and where solitariness or solitude is indeed "irremediable." That is the lesson of Deleuze's *Marcel Proust et les signes*. There, Deleuze follows Proust in giving preference to love over friendship, even if it is the slightest or shortest of all loves: "A superior mind or even a great friend are not worthy of a brief love."[180] The lesson that love offers with regard to always already secant relations in the world is in fact harsher than friendship. One can always refuse friendship, refuse the "Team"; one can always be mistrusting of an offering of friendship, and even sully that offering with a hue of perceived competition, thereby surpassing friendship with rivalry or hatred. That is to say, one can always choose to withdraw into solitariness in the face of friendship. However, in love, one is lured by the promise of a union with another; one chooses to enter into a union with another, to affirm a relation with the other, to enter into a world where the two bodies in love are always present to each other. It is not a solitary world that one looks for, or even expects, in love. That will only be the disappointment of love, and love will not hesitate to disappoint precisely in that way.

Love begins by an allure of the Other, the beloved, whose secret of her entire "inner life" draws the lover to her. The beloved emits a sign of this allure, which incites in the lover a desire to unlock or unveil that inner world, to elucidate that world completely, so as to know or share it as a common property between the lovers, such that there will be no more secrets between them: "To love is to seek to *explicate*, to *develop* these unknown worlds that remain enveloped within the beloved."[181] But the moment explication proceeds, the lover gradually comes to realize that the beloved's inner world of "unknown worlds" is impassable. Instead of an elucidation of the inner life of the beloved, the lover is met with worlds "reflected from a point of view so mysterious that they are [. . .] like unknown, inaccessible countries."[182] The promise of a world shared between two fades as love progresses. In that sense, love repeats the despairing image of a solitary self under the sign of "fundamental mediocrity," where one realizes that others have existed before oneself, or that a multiplicity of heterogeneous worldviews are always already out there, and that one's worldview is never for certain shared or taken into consideration by the other. As Deleuze writes, "We cannot interpret the signs of a loved person without entering [*déboucher*] into worlds that did not wait for us to form, but were formed with other people, and in which we are at first only an object among others."[183] The goal to reconstruct a world shared between two is essentially denied, and one can perhaps speak of the lover as a *reject* in this aspect. In love, no less than in friendship, a fundamental exclusion or fundamental secant relation is revealed, despite the lover's demands for the reparation of such suture:

> The lover wishes that his beloved bestow upon him her preferences, her gestures, her caresses. But the beloved's gestures, at the moment when they are addressed and dedicated to us, still express *the unknown world that excludes us* [my emphasis]. The beloved gives us signs of preference; but because these signs are the ones that express worlds in which we play no part, each preference by which we profit draws the image of the *possible world* where others would be or are preferred.[184]

Further, the mistrust that haunts friendship (as in the case of *le prétendant*) is present in love too. Mistrust here will be reminiscent of the betrayal function of *le prétendant*/ "friend," a mistrust derived from the beloved concealing the fact that she withholds a world that excludes the lover, a mistrust derived from the beloved's lie that all is shared between the lovers and that no secret remains. It must be said, however, that betrayal here is without conscious or deliberate intent, "not by virtue of any particular ill will of the beloved."[185] Nevertheless, the lover, in his or her fundamental exclusion or rejection from the beloved's "unknown world," is left only with a solitary condition, a "fate […] expressed in the motto: To love without being loved."[186] In that regard, love, as it is spelled out in *Marcel Proust et les signes*, unveils without reserve the condition of living in the world as solitary being, revealing to us, if not exposing us to, a bleaker world.[187]

AFTER FRIENDSHIP: FROM JEAN AMÉRY'S *HOMME DU RESSENTIMENT* TO DELEUZE'S *HOMO TANTUM*

The above has shown that the question of friendship for Deleuze and Guattari is not so much that which unfolds in lived experience, but how philosophy has folded *the image* of the living friend into itself as "a condition for the exercise of thought." That does not mean, however, that they consider friendship in philosophy as distinct from friendship as experienced in real life. That there is ultimately a nondistinction, if not a continuum, between philosophy and life for Deleuze (and Guattari) can be elicited from Deleuze's following of Spinoza, where he would seek a point where "there is no longer any difference between concept and life."[188] In other words, Deleuze and Guattari's critique of philosophical friendship is not, and will not be, without regard for the conditions of friendship as they are lived in the real world. Or else, it is not without consideration of how actual friendship may be transformed or challenged, or how the limits of present actual friendship may be overcome. With regard to examples of friendship in the real world, ordinary friendship seems inadequate to Deleuze and Guattari for their argument of always secant friendship. Instead, they would defer to an extreme case, to say the least, or what Blanchot calls a "limit-experience":[189] friendship in and after Auschwitz. This extreme case is drawn largely from their reading of Dionys Mascolo's reflections on his friendship with Robert Antelme, a survivor of Nazi concentration camps, in *Autour d'un effort de mémoire* particularly, and from Blanchot's thoughts on friendship in light of Antelme's *L'Espèce humaine*.[190]

Auschwitz, for Deleuze and Guattari, is the abyss opened up between humans, which gives them occasion to speak of a friendship that is always rent with distrust or rivalry. According to Deleuze and Guattari, Auschwitz stands for "a too overwhelming ordeal, an unspeakable catastrophe" [*une trop forte épreuve, une catastrophe indicible*],[191] and one might add that it was an ordeal and catastrophe because it testified to a human potentiality for a nihilistic anticommunity and/or antifriendship will and power, which humans have shown to execute with systematic, indifferent precision. In the wake of such anticommunity and/or antifriendship human violence, friendship, and not just poetry according to Adorno, seems almost impossible after Auschwitz.[192] In a move that echoes Antelme's *L'Espèce humaine*, where Antelme makes the unbearable admission that there is in fact very little difference between the SS officer and the rest of mankind, or that the affront against a particular group of humans is also the work of humans as a species, Deleuze and Guattari will say that after Auschwitz, "It is not only our States but each of us, each democrat, who finds ourselves not responsible for Nazism but sullied by it. There is indeed catastrophe, but the catastrophe consists in the society of brothers or friends having undergone such an ordeal that they can no longer look at one another, or each at himself, without a 'fatigue,' perhaps a mistrust [. . .]."[193] The notions of fatigue and mistrust (and distress, as will be seen) are instances where Deleuze and Guattari borrow from Blanchot's and Mascolo's rhetoric,[194] in order to reinforce the idea that actual friendship after Auschwitz, if not postapocalyptic friendship, is such that one cannot avoid distrusting another, including the friend, to advocate or pursue the cause and course of another fascistic nihilism. One cannot trust oneself either (not to do likewise). This is why one looks at the friend or potential friend with a certain fatigue or mistrust, as one and the other bear in their own ways that historical trace of nihilistic anticommunity violence: after Auschwitz, there will be a "turning away, a certain fatigue, a certain distress between friends."[195]

One can certainly be critical of Deleuze and Guattari on friendship here on at least two counts. Firstly, the turning away in friendship because of "a certain distress" can be said to be a reading that Deleuze somewhat forces onto Mascolo's writings. Mascolo, in recalling the experience of helping Antelme evacuate from a Nazi concentration camp, and in helping Antelme heal from his trauma of being tortured there, writes indeed of an "unknown distress" shared between him and Antelme, which he also calls "our complicity" while witnessing Antelme's attempt to recover at least some semblance of his old self, starting from what Antelme calls an "original indetermination," which Mascolo sees as a state of "an *ecce homo* without subject, exposing no one, exposing not a man, but Man reduced to its irreducible essence."[196] Mascolo's notion of distress clearly interests

Deleuze, who wonders in his correspondence with Mascolo if there should also be a "distrust against the friend," in order to bring "'distress' into thought in an essential manner."[197] Later in *Qu'est-ce que la philosophie?*, Deleuze (with Guattari) will modulate Mascolo's distress into "a certain distress between friends," which "converts friendship into the thought of the concept as infinite mistrust and patience."[198] This is in spite of Mascolo's response to Deleuze's earlier letter, in which Mascolo says he is "not able to conceive what mistrust, barring non-malefic disagreements, against the friend would be possible, once he has been accepted into friendship."[199] Also, the distress Mascolo of which speaks, that is, the one shared with Antelme, does not involve a turning away of friends per se. The contrary is true in fact: Mascolo stays with Antelme throughout as Antelme recounts his experience and speaks almost endlessly as he seeks to recover his former self; and Mascolo will say that sharing the "unknown distress" with Antelme made "that period of [their] life [. . .] happy."[200]

Secondly, it requires some sort of leap to trust what Deleuze and Guattari say about real friendship after Auschwitz, given that the question of friendship that interests them, as highlighted earlier, is more a question of friendship as concept rather than real friends. However, if one turns to the essay "Resentment" of Jean Améry, who, like Antelme, is a survivor of Nazi concentration camps, one does get the sense of how (real) friendship and community are indeed almost impossible after Auschwitz. Now, Jews under the reign of the Nazis can be said to be *rejects*, especially *rejects* in the sense of passive figures targeted to be denigrated, banished, and even exterminated in this case.[201] For Améry, the sense of rejection (by others) further degenerates into auto-rejection in *and beyond* the camps: "In the jails and camps of the Third Reich all of us scorned rather than pitied ourselves because of our helplessness and all-encompassing weakness. The temptation to *reject ourselves* [*Selbstverwerfung*, my emphases] has survived within us, as the immunity to self-pity."[202] I note in passing here that auto-rejection in Améry's case does not bear the same sense of the *auto-reject* that I am trying to set out in this present work. The *auto-reject* that I am seeking to trace is, I repeat, of creative regeneration, without the nihilistic self-deprecation or self-denigration, or abject self-scorn that Améry speaks of. Furthermore, if there is an *auto-reject* in Améry, it is borne with *ressentiment*, or it passes through *l'homme du ressentiment*, a figure of aversion in the eyes of Nietzsche.

L'homme du ressentiment is a target of rejection for Nietzsche not just because it represents the inability to act or to actively create its own ways to respond to forces around it, but also because it turns its repressive or reactive forces, which discourage all action, into a rejection of others, to berate others or to put others down.[203] As Nietzsche argues in *On the Genealogy of Morality*, *l'homme du ressentiment* says "'no' on principle to everything that is 'outside,' 'other,' 'non-self.'"[204] This is nothing more than a slave morality or slave revolt of *l'homme du ressentiment*, stemming from "temporarily humbling and abasing himself,"[205] while letting a desire for revenge to brew from within, hoping, through the rejection of others, or through its revenge, "to be powerful one day."[206] It is following Nietzsche's critique of *l'homme du ressentiment* that Deleuze will speak of "the frightening feminine power of *ressentiment*," which is the quest to find those "blamable [*des fautifs*], [or] responsible" for one's state of *ressentiment*, or else the quest to impress upon the world that "others are bad [*méchants*] so as to be able to feel that he or she is good."[207] That would be "the triumph of the weak as weak," which only demonstrates the inability, or rather the refusal, to forget the sense of *ressentiment* and trace a creative or affirmative line of flight from or against it.[208] Despite that supposed victory, *l'homme du ressentiment* will find that the world in general tends to be indifferent to his or her *ressentiment*, and, according to Nietzsche, this is when *ressentiment* degenerates into bad conscience. In Nietzsche's words, bad conscience is "a serious illness to which man was forced to succumb by the pressure of the most fundamental of all changes which he experienced—that change whereby he finally found himself imprisoned within the confines of society and peace."[209] Put another way, *l'homme du ressentiment* here turns the rejection of the world around on himself and "impatiently rip[s] himself apart, persecute[s] himself, gnaw[s] at himself, [gives] himself no peace and abuse[s] himself."[210] In this case, *l'homme du ressentiment* with bad conscience is clearly not the *auto-reject* of creative regeneration but of (auto-)nihilism. In Deleuze's analysis, this *homme du ressentiment* goes further in his or her "frightening feminine power," as he or she also demands the contagion of bad conscience in the world, demanding that the rest of the world suffers as well from this nihilistic auto-rejection.[211]

As I read it, Améry's *homme du ressentiment* bears many of the characteristics of *l'homme du ressentiment* that Nietzsche and Deleuze critique.

This might even be what Améry desires, since he explicitly seeks to oppose Nietzsche's suppression or denigration of the figure of *l'homme du ressentiment* by precisely raising it and affirming it. In line with *l'homme du ressentiment*, there is the rejection of the world contemporaneous to Améry's *homme du ressentiment*: he or she "cannot join in the [postwar] unisonous peace chorus all around him, which cheerfully proposes: not backward let us look but forward, to a better, common future!"[212] There is also the desire for revenge, some "barbaric, primitive lust for revenge" against those who subjected *l'homme du ressentiment* to the tortures of Nazi concentration camps, or the desire to "want at least the vile satisfaction of knowing that [his or her] enemy is behind bars."[213] Or, as Améry says later, following Thomas Mann, "The spiritual reduction to pulp by the German people, not only of the books, but of everything that was carried out in those 12 years [of Nazi rule], would be the negation of the negation: a highly positive, a redeeming act. Only through it would our resentment be subjectively pacified and have become objectively unnecessary."[214] (For Antelme and Primo Levi, however, the thought of revenge is something to be abandoned. According to Antelme in *Vengeance?*, all revenge is useless in the sense that it can never be commensurate with what the victims of Nazi concentration camps have experienced. Levi, for his part, renounces revenge in saying that "violence begets violence, and there is no such thing as good violence to counteract bad violence."[215]) Then there is the bad conscience seeking to disseminate auto-rejection in the enemy of *l'homme du ressentiment*: "I demand that the [torturers] negate themselves and in the negation coordinate with me," Améry says, and he continues later to say that "the problem [of his *ressentiment*] could be settled by permitting resentment to remain alive in the one camp and, aroused by it, self-mistrust in the other [camp of the torturers]."[216] If not, what Germany as "a national community" could do, in general, to assuage *l'homme du ressentiment*, is to "reject everything, but absolutely everything, that it accomplished in the days of its own deepest degradation."[217]

Following Nietzsche's and Deleuze's understanding of *l'homme du ressentiment* and his or her bad conscience, one may deduce that *l'homme du ressentiment* presents an obstacle to any form of friendship or community, rendering any friendship or community almost impossible. Yet, after Auschwitz, and more so in light of Améry's writings, one must reevaluate Nietzsche's and Deleuze's critique of *l'homme du ressentiment*, if not put forth "a genuine anti-Nietzschean ethics of resentment" as Améry has done according to Agamben.[218] If there is a trace of anticommunity or antifriendship in *l'homme du ressentiment* after Auschwitz, one must recognize that an irreparable anticommunity (and antifriendship) force has been first imposed upon the Jews. From then, as Howard Caygill has commented through a reading of Edmond Jabès's *Livre du partage* and *Livre des questions*, "The experience of the *Shoah* shatters not only the memory of community—the sense of belonging to a land, a people, to one-self—but also the sense of belonging to a shared world."[219] In other words, after Auschwitz, one cannot demand *l'homme du ressentiment* to forgive and forget, to elevate him- or herself from his or her *ressentiment* and/or bad conscience to rejoin the world, which, as evident in Améry, is almost impossible.[220] The resistance to forgive and forget stems not only from the "experience of the *Shoah*" but also from the discernment of *l'homme du ressentiment* that the sense of community or friendship offered by what Nietzsche calls "society and peace" is essentially superficial. In fact, "the greater community of all the uninjured in this world" continues the rejection of *l'homme du ressentiment* after Auschwitz: "The social body is occupied merely with safeguarding itself and could not care less about a life that has been damaged."[221]

It is perhaps reasonable then, or even *just,* to leave *l'homme du ressentiment* after Auschwitz (who is really more the passive *reject,* rather than the active *reject*) his or her right and freedom to reject or walk away from all appellations to community and friendship. That is perhaps more ethical than forcing a facile or banal suture between *l'homme du ressentiment* and "all the uninjured" or "society and peace," while rejecting any genuine understanding of the posttraumatic state of *l'homme du ressentiment* after Auschwitz. In other words, and this is what Améry argues, *l'homme du ressentiment* after Auschwitz must have the right and freedom to remain as *l'homme du ressentiment*, to be the (auto-)nihilistic (auto-)*reject*. W. G. Sebald, in defense of Améry, will also argue that one must recognize "the *right* to resentment," or that one must not repress "implacable resentment," the energy of which is "not to resolve but to reveal the conflict," or to "continu[e] to protest."[222] Letting *l'homme du ressentiment* be as he or she is, that is, waiting without expecting [*attendre sans s'attendre*] for him or her to work out, or work through, a yet unthought-of future community or friendship with the rest of the world,[223] is perhaps the least, and at the same time perhaps the most, one can do for this *homme du ressentiment* who has survived Auschwitz.[224] Besides, after Auschwitz, there is no doubt a danger in following Nietzsche to the letter in advocating the rise or *aufhebung* of *l'homme du ressentiment* into its active, creative counterpart, that is, "those artists of violence and organizers."[225] According to Nietzsche, the latter may be "some pack of blond beasts of prey, a conqueror and master race, which, organized on a war footing, and with the power to organize, unscrupulously lays its dreadful paws on a populace," who see to the rise of "a structure of domination," and who "do not know what guilt, responsibility, [and] consideration are," but only "ruled by that terrible inner artist's egoism which has a brazen countenance and see itself justified to all eternity by the 'work.'"[226] We now have the hindsight to say retrospectively that Nietzsche never foresaw that the place of these "artists" would be usurped by Nazism or the Nazis. And even if it were not the Nazis, would this artist-organizer not put in place yet another closed, insular community driven and determined by the work of a self-proclaimed sovereign *subject*, precluding therefore other forms of community nascent alongside those constructed by the artist-organizer-*subject*, other forms that might undo [*désœuvrer*] the work of the latter? In fact, there is not much of community to speak of with this artist-organizer-*subject*. As Nietzsche would acknowledge, any sense of community remains secant with so-called artists-organizers, for their "*perverse* inclinations, all those other-worldly aspirations, alien to the senses, the instincts, to nature, to animals" only "[separate] us more profoundly from them."[227]

But let me return to the question if friendship and community are *absolutely* impossible after Auschwitz. That would seem to be the case with Améry's *homme du ressentiment*. In response to Nietzsche's anxiety of *l'homme du ressentiment*, Améry assures that the *ressentiment* and bad conscience of *l'homme du ressentiment* after Auschwitz do not in effect have the disseminating affect or effect that Nietzsche cautions of: "The fears of Nietzsche and Scheler [author of *L'homme du ressentiment*] actually were not warranted. Our slave morality will not triumph. Our resentments [. . .] have little or no chance at all to make the evil work of the overwhelmers bitter for them."[228] What seems to remain for *l'homme du ressentiment* after Auschwitz, according to Améry at least, is only auto-nihilism. "Soon we must and will be finished," Améry says,[229] and there is always the possibility that the (reactive) auto-nihilism here involves the abdication to death.[230] Yet, must it be that it ends absolutely with self-negation, with the absolute impossibility of community and friendship? The cases of Antelme and Mascolo have shown to be otherwise. I have also suggested that if time allows, a time that does not neutralize or efface the sufferings inflicted on the victims of Auschwitz or the guilt of their torturers, a future community and friendship with the rest of the world, initiated, evoked, desired, and worked out from the side of *l'homme du ressentiment*, may be possible. Deleuze and Guattari seem to suggest that too with regard to friendship after Auschwitz: mistrust and fatigue in postapocalyptic friendship "*do not suppress friendship* [my emphases]" after all, "but give it its modern color and replaces the simple 'rivalry' of the Greeks. We are no longer Greeks, and friendship is no longer the same."[231]

Something like friendship, and yet unlike all friendships that we have known, remains then. The critical point, for Deleuze and Guattari, is to take into account "mistrust" and fatigue in friendship *and* go beyond it.[232] Unveiling "mistrust" and fatigue is then the condition for moving toward a new contour of relation by rejecting all present friendships that still hold on to the archaic and perhaps naïve ideals of amicable relations or harmonious conversations, friendships, in other words, "founded on the community of ideas and sentiments."[233] Perhaps the question of friendship in Deleuze and Guattari, then, is ultimately a question of surviving relations that are always already secant: only by living through the shadows or darkness of those relations (apocalyptic or not) in the world can one pave the way toward new relations free(d) from all present forms, conditions, determinations, definitions, and performativities.[234] As Blanchot would also say, even the fatigue in friendship, once accepted and shared between friends, is what makes friends live.[235] In Deleuze's terms, the question of surviving already secant relations is embodied in his *homo tantum*, that is to say, Dickens's Mr. Riderhood according to Deleuze's reading. Known to be a rogue, which is also to say a *reject*, Mr. Riderhood has a secant relation with the rest of society. However, in meeting with a near-death (or even syncopic) drowning incident, some sort of previously unthinkable friendship or community with this rogue or *reject*, "between his life and death," begins to form, as "everybody present lends a hand, and a heart and soul."[236] In Deleuze's reading, there arises "a sort of urgency, respect, and love for the least sign of life in the dying man."[237] Friendship and/or community remain possible, therefore, after relations have been rent, after the catastrophe of secant relations, and that new constellation of relations is what Deleuze and Guattari are seeking to bring to surface precisely through their critique of friendship or through their unveiling of the shame, despair, mistrust, and fatigue of postapocalyptic friends. One must overcome secant friendship or community, in order to philosophically "resist death, servitude, the intolerable, shame, and the present."[238] That is not all: from there, one must also "form a new right of thought"[239] in respect to a future relation, which, in Derrida's terms, "will never be reduced to the desire or the potentiality of friendship," or which "goes beyond [the] proximity of the congeneric double."

"A PEOPLE TO COME":
COMMUNITY IN DELEUZE AND GUATTARI

One may return to *Qu'est-ce que la philosophie?* to see such an exercise of thought at work at the conceptual level. The creation of concepts passes through secant relations with other concepts: concepts have noncommunicating, nonrelating relations, or rent relations that always resist a harmonious totality. They are marked by tendencies or desires to depart from one another, rather than to cohere. They are like friends who do not talk to each other, friends who say *I have enough of you, my friend*. They seek refuge in their respective reserves of silence, or are inclined to a silence that always seems to project the desire to walk away. All this is without reproach, though, for while concepts "*freely enter* [my emphasis] into relations of nondiscursive resonance," nothing really quite holds together: "They all resonate instead of cohering [*se suivre*] or corresponding with one another. There is no reason why concepts should cohere."[240] Concepts are always tending to break off in heterogeneous trajectories: "[Concepts] do form a wall, but it is a dry-stone wall, and if everything is held together, it is only by diverging lines."[241] They even share rough edges with one another,[242] always already on the edge of rivalry or contest so that each may be, to wit, a cutting-edge concept. Yet, at the end of it all, such secant friendship at the level of concepts in philosophy is but philosophy's vitalism, its force of life, or élan, through which concepts renew themselves or through which new concepts are created: "Philosophical thought does not bring its concepts together in a friendship without again being traversed by a fissure that leads them back to hatred or that disperses them in the coexisting chaos where it is necessary to take them up again, to seek them out again, to make a leap."[243] It is from such philosophical élan, that is to say, in brushing up against the edgy relations of concepts, that Deleuze and Guattari will postulate the emergence of a new, future relation between beings: "The creation of concepts in itself calls for a future form, it calls for a new earth and a people that do not yet exist."[244]

This "new earth and people that do not yet exist" perhaps concern those who reconcile with the fact that secant relations always subtend existence, those, in other words, who are no longer exhausted from the fact that relations are potentially tearing all the time. They would perhaps be those who are always seeking to think and experience unreservedly what new relations would come after present ones, at the same time without deciding on what arrives. They would be at ease, without fatigue, without the need for discussions or reciprocities, and without the anxiety to decide. They would always be at "that threshold of proximity at which everything undoes itself [se défait] and again becomes nebulous."[245] Perhaps they would be those partaking in what may be called a *philosophy of a life*, where *a life*, according to Deleuze in his "Immanence: une vie" essay, would simply be "pure immanence, neutral, beyond good and evil," or "the immanent singular life of a man who no longer has a name, but which does not at all leave him being confused with another,"[246] that is, *a life* that opens itself to all around it. I note that Deleuze's text here once again hinges on Dickens's *reject*, Mr. Riderhood, which then suggests that it is with the *reject* wherein one may find the potentiality for *a life*. In any case, in *a life*, because it is "neutral, beyond good and evil," one goes beyond the "mistrust" and fatigue that haunt present postapocalyptic friendship. That is to say, there will be *a life* after postapocalyptic friendship: one does not self-destruct, or negate life or any encounter, in the despair and mistrust of postapocalyptic friendship. Instead, one leaps over that anguish so as to create everything anew, letting emerge an "incommunicable novelty" or an event that is "neither foreseen nor preconceived,"[247] such as new relations that have no need for, or rather are free from, the existing conditions, determinations, or definitions of community or friendship. For Deleuze and Guattari, "a new earth and people that do not yet exist," or a "shadow of 'the people to come,'"[248] is precisely what lurks *after friendship*.

In the "shadow of 'the people to come,'" one is surely also in the shadow of the question of community in Deleuze and Guattari. Interestingly, like the silence of a shadow, the question of community forms some sort of silent problematic in their philosophy, making it almost incongruous to think that the thought of community lies at their philosophical horizon. This is not just because community is not a theme that is particularly in the foreground of their philosophy, but also because in *L'Anti-Œdipe* and *Mille plateaux*, community hinges on something negative, something that thought must not regress to, if not something that is antithought. For example, in *Mille plateaux*, where Deleuze and Guattari argue for unrestricted or nonregulated movement, "community" is the site wherein lies "the risk of reproducing [. . .] the rigid [*la dure*]."[249] In that respect, it is not surprising if there is a force of rejection against community in Deleuze and Guattari's *Mille plateaux*. However, what remains a critical concept in and for that text is nomadology, which is undeniably something of community, since nomads, from which nomadology takes its image, are irreducibly tribal or of the pack. In other words, the trace of community in nomadology is almost indubitable, despite Deleuze and Guattari's apparent reservation to acknowledge that. How does one then reconcile that irreducible trace in Deleuze and Guattari's philosophy and their apparent rejection, at the same time, of such a concept as community?

Before inquiring into the apparently anticommunity force in Deleuze and Guattari, I would first like to consider if the term *anticommunity* could, or perhaps even should, apply to real-world engagements with the concept of community. Why posit a term that suggests violence against something that has at least put in place in this world some form of harmonious living between humans? Perhaps one could begin less radically by saying *anti-"community"* first, and from there begin to discern why an anticommunity trajectory would seem philosophically desirable today. In *anti-"community,"* the quotation marks around the word community would signal linguistic markers, indexing community as a mark of verbal speech. To be more precise, they would mark community as an *excess* of speech, fallen from any act of thought, rendering community and/or "community" a meretricious speech act. As Zygmunt Bauman has observed, the word "community" as how we have been treating it has been "so loud and vociferous" that we have invoked "community" only to uncritically sing its praises, "telling the others to admire them or shut up," so much so that "community is no more (or not yet, as the case may be)."[250] In other words, within each community, or for anyone who seeks membership to those communities, there is to be no disagreement to the practices, codes, and norms that are already in place. Communities and their practices have become impervious to critique, including suggestions on their futures via altogether different strategies. Such a philosophical letdown with regard to thinking about community becomes evident simply by a quick turn to contemporary affairs of the world. In contemporary geopolitical discourse, there can be no doubt that there has always been much talk about community, particularly about an "international community." However, one is often left thinking what or where such a community is, if not its veracity. Furthermore, the term "international community" has been invoked oftentimes only as an alibi to justify the violent decimation of a state-entity by another of greater global politico-economic-military leverage, when the former resists or deviates from the political and economic interests of the latter. Otherwise, when the "international community" has been invoked or appealed to so that a cosmopolitan collectivity of sovereign states may come together to put in place an effective force to end humanitarian violence, poverty, tyranny, and so on, in some place in the world (and here, one remembers, since the beginning of the twenty-first century, the names Darfur, Sudan, Haiti, and so on), the response unfortunately has been less than desirable, which henceforth only severely weakens the idea of the existence of any such "international community."

Despite the shortcomings of existing communities and the "international community," anti-"community" is *not* about rejecting communities absolutely. The "anti" in anti-"community," to reiterate, operates not so much as the negation of community as an idea or thought as the negation of the linguistic articulation of that idea. In other words, anti-"community" argues for the critical refrain from proclamations of "community," keeping in mid that, according to Bauman, it is really the verbal invocations of "community"—articulated endlessly without submitting it to critical thought, or enunciated as if it could ever adequately give us that thing called "community"—that has so far perverted any future possibility of thinking about community. The force of rejection in anti-"community" acts only against all declaration and proclamation of the myths and false idealisms of community, therefore. It is deployed only to return community to an active process of thought. Put another way, if there is any need or call for a philosophical anticommunity, it is not about anticommunity per se, not anticommunity in the sense whereby one has in view a nihilistic horizon for community. Instead, anticommunity will be called for only to create a clearing for a free space of thought for another thinking of community. That is to say, one projects an anticommunity force not so that we will stop thinking about community but to return community to a thinking without horizon, a thinking that is always open to its futures, open to the newcomer in his or her difference *and* also, without reproach, to the one who departs. That is also what I argue to be the sense of community in Deleuze and Guattari's apparently anticommunity nomadology.

THE NOMADOLOGICAL WAR MACHINE:
AGAINST THE STATE OF COMMUNITY

Deleuze and Guattari's concept of nomadology or the nomadological war machine certainly reads very much as something individual or singular rather than of belonging to some community. After all, as Deleuze and Guattari acknowledge, it "attests to an absolute solitude" (*MP*, 457/ *TP*, 377), not to mention its "social clandestinity" (*MP*, 504/ *TP*, 405) and its rather glaring antisocial "antidialogue" and "noncommunicating" force (*MP*, 468, 472/ *TP*, 378, 380). Furthermore, it seeks to hold on to that space of solitude (only to increase the desert of that space and not to saturate it with accretions of properties or possessions), while it has no similar insistence on holding on to its nomadic tribe, that is, its community. In fact, even within the nomadic tribe, there is the sense that the singular nomadic war machine is already betraying its community by disavowing it or by deviating from it.[251] Yet, one has to be precise to say that the betrayal function of the nomadological war machine goes into operation only when it sees its tribe enclosing both itself and everything else that it receives into, and as, a structural totality. As Deleuze says in an interview with Claire Parnet regarding the betrayal function of the nomadic war machine: "One betrays the fixed powers which try to hold us back, the established powers of the earth."[252] In other words, in the face of any delimiting structuration, nomadology does not hesitate to project its combative force as a war machine in its fullest intensity, so as to dismantle or undo such fixed or established arrangements. Close-knit social arrangements such as communities are not exceptional to this force, and it is under such a condition that the nomadological war machine takes on an explicit anticommunity contour.

To give Deleuze and Guattari a more precise reading, the word "community" is hardly articulated as the primary target of nomadology. Instead, it is the State that the nomadological war machine inclines toward with an angle of attack, and the nomadological war machine conducts war with the State only because the State has delimited ways of movement and thought that are in fact expressions of the nomadological war machine's freedom. In that regard, the State imposes a homogeneity of thought; it discourages, represses, and sometimes suppresses deviations. In that process, the State even captures thought as its rationalizing interiority, through which "thought is [thereby made to be] capable of inventing the fiction of a State that is rightfully [*en droit*] universal, of elevating the State to a status that is universal by right [*de droit*] " (*MP*, 465/ *TP*, 375). In other words, the State appropriates thought so that it can claim to be a force of an enlightened institution, an institution with which none can disagree. To maintain that supreme authority, along with its will to establish spatial integrity, sovereignty, or security, the State also limits the freedom of movement of people within its territory. This can be seen quite clearly in State globalization, where the transnational or transborder movement of information, capital, and goods are almost without restriction, while the movement of people across national or economic communities does not enjoy the same freedom but is still delimited by citizenship criteria. In any case, the State, in Deleuze and Guattari's analysis, is the capture of space, movement, thought, and people into a regulated, policed, and determined zone, or what they call "striated space," and their concept of nomadology is meant primarily to combat against such striation.

If communities become swept up in the combative trajectory of the nomadic war machine, it is because they have become Statelike in their outlook. This is the case when communities become overcoded by their linguistic idioms, customs, economic practices, political inclinations, and so on, and membership into the community is predicated only by the knowledge, acceptance, observance, adherence, and communication of these codes. Here, community becomes nothing less than a political economy signified by a circuitous flow: everything has to circle back on itself, and everything is organized into, or rooted onto, a closed arborescent structure, to follow the rhetoric of *Mille plateaux*. Every face of every body within this community is also reduced to a signifying articulation of the community, each becoming an overconscious investment of community, which also means that the body in such an economy of community gets reduced to a mere denigrating faciality. Faciality, according to Deleuze and Guattari in *Mille plateaux*, is that process by which the face is reduced to a site of signs pointing toward what it invests in, or that which invests in the face, and whence there is no longer any regard for the body in its singularity. It is also with faciality that the operation of quantification begins, that is, when everything counts in this space. Not just bodies count because their faces will add to the progressive façade of the community, but even ethics begins to be quantitatively measured. I cite the example Bauman uses in elucidating some of the myths of community. Within social structures that we mythologize as communities, we take it as natural, or given, that once we have helped someone in the community, "our right, purely and simply, is to expect that the help we need will be forthcoming."[253] In other words, one good turn must be returned with another—no more, no less. Even the friend will be counted. It will be a matter of *my* friend, someone I can count (on) to add quantitative measure to the community (as is the case of contemporary networked-centric friendship that I have critiqued earlier with the aid of Derrida's philosophy of friendship). It will not be that estranging friend, the friend that is the *other*, or the friend that brings to the structure of community a difference or even rivalry (as Deleuze and Guattari's *le prétendant* does) so that community is never a rigid or closed structure. But to return to the point of quantification: Deleuze and Guattari also argue that "the number has always served to gain mastery over matter, to control its variations and movements, in other words, to submit them to the spatiotemporal framework of the State" (*MP*, 484/ *TP*, 389). In other words, when everything counts or begins to count in a community, one is not far from witnessing the community becoming a s/State.

Certainly, a close-knit community where everything is counted or numbered, where every body is subjected to a faciality, or where there may "never [be] strangers,"[254] may offer a nice sheltering architecture. However, because it is not open to any relation that brings it to an exteriority, not open to an invitation to the "friend" or *le prétendant* who brings with him or her the question of rivalry that contests the beliefs of the community, not open, in other words, to any deviation, the architecture of community can become familiarly strange or estranging too. Its architecture will be "like a besieged fortress" as Bauman would say,[255] or to follow Paul Virilio and Deleuze and Guattari, it takes on a bunker architecture: community becomes bunker community. The deathly architecture of a bunker is what one enters into at the limit of that which seeks its own absoluteness or totality, since something is absolute only when nothing else exists beside it, which in turn would only mean the death of the thing itself and/or of those beside it. In other words, with a fortress or bunker architecture of community, the thinking of community—the thinking of its future, or the thinking of its future form otherwise than its present manifestations— no longer has a (horizonless) horizon: there is no longer a free space of thought, or a space of freedom of thought, for community. Community as bunker community, or as Statelike, as State-community, or community-State,[256] is therefore ultimately more anticommunity than communitarian, more anticommunity in the sense of negating all veritable thinking of community than the nomadological war machine.

It is this s/State of community or State-community/ community-State that the nomadological war machine seeks to disarticulate. From within the striated space of State-community, it seeks to reterritorialize a smooth space, a space where tangential trajectories are possible, or where heterogeneous elements are free to come together out of desire and equally free to break away without causing any spatial anxiety. Again, it is a comforting thought, no doubt, that being a member of a community grants one almost automatic hospitality within the community. However, within hospitality, or within a practical ethics of hospitality, there should not only be the right of the host to reject hospitality as Derrida has already observed,[257] but there should also be cases where the receiver of hospitality reserves the freedom to refuse hospitality, the freedom to break away from the enclosures of "hostpitality," that is, the freedom to deviate from, or to not even enter into, that space of hospitality. The smooth space of the nomadological war machine potentially opens up such a freedom, for, having "no homogeneity," it "is precisely the space of the smallest deviation" (*MP*, 459/ *TP*, 371). It is in this sense of opening up a heterogeneous space of deviation—which does not view the absence of organization as a lack and which critiques all homogenizing structures—that the nomadological war machine appears anti-"community" or even anticommunity. But it is precisely in that sense too that it is of community, particularly in the sense that it potentially opens up a space for a community of those who deviate or depart.

In a way, despite Deleuze and Guattari's claim that the nomadic war machine is more a solitary force than a communitarian one, it cannot be denied that the nomadological war machine nevertheless opens a space where beings other than itself come to occupy. Smooth spaces, after all, "are not without people or unpeopled" (*MP*, 631/ *TP*, 506). These people, however, are those who have left behind the striated spaces of State-communities. They do not delimit themselves within a defined territorial organization: "They have a local construction that excludes the possibility of determining in advance a (political, juridical, economic, or artistic) base domain. They have extrinsic and situational properties, or relations irreducible to the intrinsic properties of a structure" (*MP*, 255/ *TP*, 209). Deleuze and Guattari will also call this people "multiplicities" that affirm and exercise the freedom to come together or break away: multiplicities enjoy "a certain flexibility [*souplesse*] following tasks and situations, between the two extreme poles of fusion and scission" (*MP*, 255/ *TP*, 209). According to Deleuze and Guattari, there is also a relation between multiplicities and smooth space: "A heterogeneous smooth space [. . .] is wedded to a very particular multiplicity: non-metric, acentered, rhizomatic multiplicities, which occupy space without 'counting' it and can 'only be explored by legwork'" (*MP*, 460/ *TP*, 371). The bodies of multiplicity may be "non-metric," but, as multiplicity, there is perhaps inevitably the notion of number, or rather the numerous. Yet, there is nothing numerically definitive about it. The number here is no longer that of a quantitative measure: "The number is no longer a means of counting or measuring, but of moving [*déplacer*]" (*MP*, 484/ *TP*, 389). In other words, it constitutes a geography instead, a mapping out of a gathering, whose cartography is constantly changing as the experiment goes along. This number, or "numbering number" as Deleuze and Guattari also call it, participates "in a dynamic relation with geographical directions" (*MP*, 485/ *TP*, 390) and does not function as an index of formal or structural growth, or of historical progress as in State-communities or community-states. The multiplicity of smooth space hence speaks of a mass that is always moving, always breaking away, if not always disappearing, from striated social arrangements—"masses do not cease to leak [*couler*] or flow [*s'écouler*] from classes" (*MP*, 260/ *TP*, 213) — and that mass is strictly not countable either as a singular or combinative crowd.[258] The geographic "numbering number" is more a question of $n-1$ as Deleuze and Guattari would have it, the fragmenting -1 resisting, rejecting, dispersing, or walking away from any form of quantitative and formal totality. It is like the supernumerary in Rancière's terms: that which is not only uncounted (especially by State), but also, more critically, that which refuses to enter into an economy of the counted in homogenizing structures such as conventional communities.

When numbers do not matter, in the sense that they are *not* accumulative supplements to previous quantified constructions, then there is also the possibility of opening up to the outside. According to Deleuze and Guattari, the "numbering number" also makes it necessary "to take into account arithmetic relations that are external" (*MP*, 487/ *TP*, 391). The smooth space of the nomadological war machine hence articulates difference or alterity, and exteriority. As Deleuze and Guattari put it, the nomadological war machine "produces its effect of immensity by its fine articulation, in other words by its distribution of heterogeneity in free space" (*MP*, 486/ *TP*, 391). The rhythmics of the nomadological war machine is therefore also, to wit, "not harmonic" (*MP*, 485/ *TP*, 390), contra the myth of harmonious relations within conventional communities. With the nomadic war machine, there is always the possibility, or the freedom, of a dissonant line rupturing the stability of a melodious line of conventional communities, if not break away with its own *other* trajectory. What matters here, then, is the freedom of trajectory of bodies and thought, the free variation or deviation of the matter of bodies and thought: a question of "materiality instead of imposing a form upon a matter" (*MP*, 508/ *TP*, 408), in other words according to Deleuze and Guattari, a question of the expressive materiality of what gathers *and* deviates, rather than imposing an enclosing form that is often too hastily called "community."

One could say that nomadology concerns *l'in-forme*—that which is without form or even that which de-forms, if not that which forms by deforming. Any striating grasp of community cannot contain the nomadological war machine, therefore, and it is as such that the nomadological war machine appears to be anticommunity: while community tries to hold (on to) everything together in a compact fashion, the nomadological war machine, as "an entire energetic materiality in movement," and which "combine[s] with processes of deformation" (*MP*, 508/ *TP*, 408), gives place to the risk of things breaking down. But that "deformation," along with other "discontinuities" (*MP*, 506/ *TP*, 406) that the nomadological war machine brings about, are in fact critical to nomadology in preventing the smooth space of multiplicity from resembling the circuitous flow of the striated community. To return to the architectural rhetoric used earlier, one may say too that the smooth space of multiplicity created by the nomadic war machine, as it attaches itself to at times threateningly and possibly fragmenting elements of heterogeneity or alterity, is not of a bunker architecture. Instead, it is more a bridge architecture, if not an architecture of moving bridges, or "movable bridges" as Deleuze and Guattari would say in *Qu'est-ce que la philosophie?*, which are always constructing toward a future community. Put another way: if there is any architecture of community that the nomadological war machine projects, it will only be an undefined architecture. It will not be a finished, enclosed architecture, but an architecture that always undoes itself, only to begin again differently: "It is not a question of this or that place on earth [...]. It is a question of a model that is perpetually in construction or collapsing, and of a process that does not cease to prolong itself [*s'allonger*], to break itself apart [*se rompre*], and to start again [*reprendre*]" (*MP*, 31/ *TP*, 20). With the nomadological war machine, the architecture of community is always a question of "relaying" these architectures-to-come or architectures-on-the-way: "only relays, intermezzos, restarts [*relances*]" (*MP*, 468/ *TP*, 377).

It is with such architecture that Deleuze and Guattari's nomadological war machine is always maintaining a thought of community, maintaining the free space of thought of community or the freedom of another thought of community. At the end, it is more *of* community rather than anticommunity in the nihilistic sense. Once again, the nomadic war machine clears a smooth space only for a "movement of people in that space" (*MP*, 526/ *TP*, 422), a people or movement that "is a very special distribution, without division [*sans partage*], in a space without borders or enclosure" (*MP*, 472/ *TP*, 380). Or, to recall the mobile architectural image: it is "an ambulant people of relayers" that the nomadological war machine awaits and for which it clears a path, "rather than a model society [*une cité modèle*]" (*MP*, 468/ *TP*, 377) or a model (of) community. And even if it insists on an "absolute solitude," Deleuze and Guattari will nonetheless qualify that "it is an extremely populous solitude [*une solitude extrêmement peuplée*], like the desert itself, a solitude already interlaced with a people to come, one that invokes and awaits that people, existing only through it, though it is not yet here" (*MP*, 467/ *TP*, 377). In other words, the nomadological war machine smashes present or existing communities from within only to seek another sense of community, or a multiplicity where there is the freedom of coming and leaving, where there is no politics or economies of counting, and where there are always the possibilities of and to the outside. That is to say too that the nomadological war machine conducts war against striated spaces such as the State and overcodified communities only "*on the condition of creating something else at the same time*, which would only be new nonorganic social relations" (*MP*, 527/ *TP*, 423). This *other* social relation is "nonorganic" perhaps because it will be a nonhuman community, nonhuman because it is free(d) from the anxieties of subjectivity, representation, and consciousness of the metaphysical human Being—Being that thinks limitedly and inclusively only in-itself and for-itself, or else only in the image of itself, and Being that only looks toward a One of totality of community. One may also say that it will be "nonorganic" because it will no longer be anthropocentric: everything that exists in this "new nonorganic social relations" can be, or is, shared by nonhuman animals too. In that sense, the nomadological war machine and the "people to come" may even be intensive expressions of what Nancy has called "singular plural" beings.

With Deleuze and Guattari, we are therefore always arriving at, or moving toward, *a* community, *a* community that is as indefinite as its linguistic article, and indefinite not because it is not able to decide itself (as community) or because it is not sure of itself, but because it is always open to something new, always forming itself anew. It is in this way that *a* community guarantees its future, which includes a radical future unrestricted to its present form. It is *a* community that is decisively (an) undecidability, an indecision that is properly in-decision, deciding on its openness to futures and not closures. This trajectory or horizon of (another) community is traced by the apparently paradoxical anticommunity force of the nomadological war machine, a force that goes beyond the sense of *désœuvrement* according to Nancy, veering closer to the radical violence of Bataille's philosophy. In fact, it even seems to go further than Bataille, since it involves not just the silencing of the *subject* or knowledge as is the case with Bataille, but also the disarticulation of community. As mentioned at the very beginning of this discussion on friendship, love, and community, Bataille does not seek the disarticulation of community, but is committed to articulate its presence where its existence, or rather its form of existence, is repressed or threatened. That is why Bataille will remain to speak of a "community of those who have no community." With Deleuze and Guattari, one does not find any articulation of a community of those who have left community, of those who have rejected striated, insular, closed-off, bunker, State-like communities. What is put forth more forcefully instead is anti-"community," if not anticommunity, through the nomadological war machine, which is no doubt a figure of the active *reject* acting against communities that have become overcodified, rigid, closed, and State-like.

To what ends does one articulate anti-"community," or even anticommunity? As this section on Deleuze and Guattari has suggested, community has become an appellation like friendship in contemporary network-centric sociality, that is to say, a term that is excessively invoked without ever submitting its uses to critical reflection, if not excessively invoked only to smother any critical thought on community itself. If the section on Derrida's philosophy of friendship suggests that a sustained rejection of friendship can wrest the concept of friendship back from its abuse, perhaps the anti-"community" or even anticommunity trajectory of Deleuze and Guattari's nomadic war machine can serve a similar purpose: to disarticulate all uncritical enunciations of "community" in order to reopen a space for the rethinking of community. Even though Deleuze and Guattari do not speak of a community of those who reject or depart from striated communities, this does not imply at all any absence of a sense of community. One will always find that sense in "the shadow of 'the people to come'" in them, and this section has tried to demonstrate that the "people to come" is no less of community. I do not think it unreasonable to even call this "people to come" a community of *rejects*, a community of those who are not only refused by totalizing communities but also of those who refuse the latter. Such a community of *rejects* would include those of "nonorganic social relations," which I have suggested above to not exclude human and nonhuman assemblages. It would also include those, such as the nomadological war machine itself, who *auto-reject* themselves in the sense of betraying all new formations of community that they have paved the way for, only to open those forms to newer forms, so as to keep the question of community always open.

3

THE REJECT AND THE "POSTSECULAR," OR WHO'S AFRAID OF RELIGION

Having elicited the figure of the *reject* from the rethinking of friendship, love, and community in Nancy, Bataille, Agamben, and more specifically in Derrida, Clément, and Deleuze, I will now proceed to demonstrate that the *reject* is no less mobilized when contemporary French thinkers take on, or rather problematize, the question of religion. A theory of the *reject* cannot rest content to be just a matter of textual elucidation: it must go beyond conceptual rhetoric and suggest at least potential empirical applications. That was the endeavor of the previous chapter when it situated the question of the *reject* within the contemporary context of network-centric sociality, inquiring how it can potentially resist the present *doxā* concerning the concepts of friendship, love, and community. In doing so, I believe that the theory of the *reject* has the additional force of maintaining, or even pushing further, the radical horizon of those concepts opened by the abovementioned thinkers. The present section follows a similar trajectory. At the textual level, it is particularly interested in contemporary French thinkers who problematize religion almost to the point of abandoning, if not *rejecting* (I will clarify this in a while), religion.[1] Once again, thinkers such as Nancy, Derrida, and Deleuze, are the companions of this chapter, with particular focus here on Derrida and, this time, Hélène Cixous too. It will show how the *reject* is put into circulation when these thinkers question the limits of religion. At the same time, it will situate the *reject* within the context of our so-called secular present and explore how the *reject* can make a critical intervention in our actual negotiations with the contemporary rise of religion.

By saying that Nancy, Derrida, and Cixous put into question the limits of religion, it qualifies any rejecting at work in their texts as never precipitating toward an absolute negation of religion. Perhaps one could borrow the words of John Caputo in his study of the religious contour of Derrida's work and say that these thinkers have religion, except they are without religion's God, especially if the latter is to stand for a symbol of masculine, phallogocentric law or authority.[2] Therefore, it would also be inaccurate to label any of them a pure atheist (if there is any one such), or even "radical atheist," especially if one understands atheism as a condition whereby one's thinking and being in this world is supposedly devoid of any trace of the religious.[3] Even Derrida, who has conceded in allowing himself be considered "radically atheist," especially in the context of thinking the event or the to-come that exceeds all expectations and anticipations, will nonetheless say that he would be, in this case, "an atheist who keeps in mind God, and who likes to keep God in mind,"[4] without any desire to seek or affirm the "essence" or even "hyperessentiality" of God.[5] According to Nancy in his work on rethinking religion in the two volumes of *La Déconstruction du christianisme*, there is in fact no atheism as such.[6] However, if one insists on describing our contemporary condition as atheist, through which one "declares the principle of a negation of the divine principle,"[7] one must then recognize at the same time, Nancy argues, that "the possibility of atheism [. . .] is [already] inscribed at the source of Christianism."[8] To be sure, "the source of Christianism" does not equate to Christianism itself, which only means that there is a source more originary than Christianism that makes "atheism" possible, a source that is not solely attributable to Christianism. That is why Nancy makes clear that "there is indeed a sort of vector of atheism that traverses the great religions" and not just Christianity because "these religions have been witnesses to a complete overhaul [*une refonte intégrale*] of the 'divine,' the profound movement of which goes toward the suppression if not of the 'divine,' at least of 'God.'"[9] Nonetheless, this "profound movement" is more evident, according to Nancy, in Christianism, since it is there where one finds "God who withdraws [*s'efface*], not only God who absents Himself [*s'absente*], as he does for Job, or God who ceaselessly refuses all analogy in this world, as for Mohammed, but also God who makes himself Man [*Dieu qui se fait homme*], forsaking [*délaissant*] his divinity to the point of plunging it into the mortal condition."[10] Atheism, in that case, must be more precisely understood not as a condition that is free from any trace of the religious, but, according to Nancy, as the "auto-deconstruction,"[11] or *auto-rejection* as I would see it, of religion, that is, the simultaneous letting go of its divinity and its *openness* to admit into itself something other than itself, something other than a God-like entity, something like the human or mortal condition.[12] It is through such understanding of the "auto-deconstruction" of religion that Nancy prefers, in place of atheism, to think of the contemporary secular condition in terms of an "absentheism."[13]

Recognizing atheism's religious or even "Christian derivation" [*la provenance chrétienne*] does not, however, mean any "return to the religious" so as "to save religion," or "to revive [*ressusciter*] religion."[14] In fact, one must resist those gestures, especially if they entail regressing to a world in which a particular God, along with a singular religious belief in this One God, determines the guiding principle of being in this world, a principle that evacuates all other forms of reasoning. It is in view of the risk of such a regression that Nancy would even say he "desire[s] to approach the erasure of the name [of Christianity] and of the entire body of references that follow after it."[15] However, "refusing all forms of 'return,' and more than anything else 'the 'return of the religious' [...]" and to think of a "world without God" do not, as Nancy will remind us, place us outside of religion.[16] We remain within the movement of religion's "auto-deconstruction" or *auto-rejection*, which is a movement toward openness, if not an open world.[17] The critical lesson of that movement is that, "without negating Christianity but without returning to it," it allows us to approach that more originary source, more originary than Christianity, which has not only brought us to our so-called atheism, but can also bring us further than that. Or, in Nancy's words, it is through the movement of religion's "auto-deconstruction" that we can

> ask ourselves anew what [...] could lead us towards a point—towards a resource—buried under Christianity, monotheism, and Occidentalism, of which it would be necessary from then on to bring to light: for this point would open, in sum, onto a future of the world that would no longer be Christian nor anti-Christian, neither monotheistic nor atheistic nor polytheistic, but would go forth precisely beyond all these categories (after having rendered all of them possible).[18]

The future, open world, as Nancy elaborates later, "is a world without myths and idols, a world without religion, if this word must be understood as the observation of ways [*conduites*] and representations that respond to a demand of meaning as a demand of assurance, for an end-point [*destination*], and for fulfillment [*accomplissement*]."[19] Clearly, this open world will not be possible if we allow a "return to the religious," such that we reenclose ourselves within religious horizons or principles. Neither will it be possible if we allow the thought of being absolutely outside of religion to be our new principle, making it our new assurance of having a new end in sight, making it our new horizon that we must attain. Put another way, an open world will not be attained if, by claiming to be atheists, we absolutely reject religion and place our belief in our humanism as the origin and end of everything possible in the world. That would only be replacing a principle (of the divine) with another (of the human). Through such atheism, we only return to a world closed off by a certain horizon—previously by a divine horizon, now by an all-too-human one: it "continues [. . .] to close the horizon. Or perhaps it is more precise to say that it continues to form a horizon, precisely where something else should arise."[20] For Nancy, instituting a horizon signals nothing but a "limit, [an] impasse, and [an] end of the world," and therefore an atheism that is bound by anthropocentric and/or anthropomorphic horizons "is nihilism"—a nihilism where nothing remains, or where nothing else can go forth.[21] We therefore need a "thought of alterity opened by and exposed to the outside of sameness [for example, anthropocentrism/ anthropomorphism], which exceeds [sameness] infinitely without being as much its principle [*la pensée de l'altérité ouverte par et exposée hors de la mêmeté, comme ce qui l'excède infiniment sans pour autant lui être en quoi que ce soit principielle*]."[22] Simply put, we need a thought of an "opening [*ouverture*], the Open [*l'Ouvert*] as horizon of sense *and* as the tearing [*déchirure*] of the horizon," a point, in other words, where "the human, all too human, cannot even imagine and to which no philosophical essence of the human can compare."[23] Or else, should thought begin to delimit itself within a humanist or anthropologic and anthropocentric horizon, it must reject itself in ways similar to how religion has "auto-deconstructed" itself.[24] The point here, in short, is to not deny the critical role of religion's "auto-deconstruction" in pointing us toward a way by which thought can be free(d) to move toward infinite possibilities.[25]

In a less philosophical register, that is to say, where the question of the future of thought is not the primary concern, Charles Taylor, in *A Secular*

Age, similarly resists allowing the contemporary world to be understood or determined solely according to humanist terms. Not unlike Nancy, but again, to a less philosophical extent, Taylor acknowledges that the contemporary world is one that is heavily inflected with a post-Nietzschean spirit, that is, a world in which many are convinced that God is dead and that almost everything is humanly possible. It is with this "possibility of exclusive humanism" that one can describe the contemporary world as a world of secularity.[26] However, Taylor is quick to point to the fact that this contemporary world is at the same time punctuated by societies still inclined toward religious or spiritual beliefs. For Taylor, the difference between one society and another, and the difference with regard to spiritual belief or unbelief of one and another, are critical elements that one must consider in order to understand the question of religion in the contemporary world. Such differences are to be respected and affirmed, and not to be dispelled or negated. According to Taylor, there exists "a global context in a society which contains different milieu, within each of which the default option [of spiritual belief or unbelief] may be different from others, although the dwellers within each are very aware of the options favored by others, and cannot just dismiss them as inexplicable exotic error."[27] Or, as he would say more recently, there is in contemporary Western societies "the wide diversity not only of religious views but also of those that involve no religion, not to speak of those that are unclassifiable in this dichotomy."[28] In Taylor's view, the contemporary world of secularity is where spiritual belief and unbelief intersect each other. And in this world, one must have the freedom to practice any religion, as well as the "freedom not to believe"; no particular belief nor unbelief must occupy a "privileged status"; all factions must be heard; and between believers and nonbelievers, one must "as much as possible [. . .] maintain relations of harmony and comity."[29]

Of course, it has to be acknowledged, as Taylor does in his work, that the coming together of spiritual belief and unbelief has not been an easy process. In fact, it has been fraught with violence. To keep in mind this violent history, it is perhaps helpful to deploy the term "postsecular." Scholars such as José Casanova, Hent de Vries, and more recently Jürgen Habermas, have mobilized the term "postsecular" for quite some time now, but it still remains without a fixed, comprehensive, and authoritative definition.[30] If this present work inclines toward this term, unlike Nancy and Taylor who resist it,[31] it is not seeking to arrive at such a definition, or to trace the history or genealogy of the "postsecular." The "postsecular" here would simply be taken to mean what some scholars have discerned as its primary, undeniable characteristic: the "postsecular" gestures toward the militant articulation, in a supposedly secular world, of local religions on the one hand, and the reactionary rearticulation of institutionalized religions on the other. These articulations and rearticulations, however, have brought with them not only symbolic or rhetorical violence, but also real, physical ones. This violence generally manifests itself in the following: violence between local religions, each fighting for its legitimate place in society; violence between local religions and institutionalized religions, as the former contest the latter's position as the dominant religion, or as the latter seek to oppress or repress the former; and of course, the age-old violence between the claim to faith or religion and the claim to knowledge or reason. In any case, what the term "postsecular" in this present work will underscore, just as Taylor's "secularity" does, is that the strangeness of others, more specifically the foreignness of other religions, spirituality, and beliefs, cannot be ignored. To take a now banal example, 9/11 has shown us how the rise of militant, fundamentalist Islamism can have a real, undeniable, and even traumatic impact on almost all of us, regardless if we are of the Christian or Islamic faith, regardless in other words of our religious faith or the putative absence thereof.

The "postsecular" that I am mobilizing here is certainly not that which seeks "to reinstate the divine as a critique of reason," nor that which locates some discursive space "where there would be some place off limits to reason," as Christopher Watkin understands it.[32] That would render the "postsecular" a reactionary movement against secularism, something akin to a return to the religious, and such an understanding of the "postsecular," "as reinforcing Christianity, and as Christianity rediscovering itself," is a misconception according to Manav Ratti.[33] I do agree with Ratti's understanding of the "postsecular," which he takes to be "not anti-secular, nor [...] abandoning secularism or turning to religion"; simply, it "neither proselytizes secularism nor sentimentalizes religion."[34] Or, as Ratti goes on to say, "postsecularism can subsume this deconstruction of the received opposition between the secular and the religious," and it is therefore "an intimately *negotiated* term."[35] In that sense, and with respect to my characterization of the "postsecular" above, it can be said that what is at stake in the "postsecular" is difference. However, one should not rest with just saying that the "postsecular" testifies to a marked rise of religious differences (including differences between inclinations toward the sacred and those toward the secular), which cut across both social groups at the communitarian or nation-state level and civilizations across nation-state lines. In a more critical or even constructive vein, one should also add that the "postsecular" presents us the challenge of affirming those differences and of allowing them to coexist without resorting to physical, symbolic, and rhetorical violence. This is also no doubt what Taylor calls for, and I quote him again:

> In order to place the discussion between belief and unbelief in our day and age, we have to put it in the context of this lived experience [of real, particular differences], and the construals that shape this experience. And this means not only seeing this as more than a matter of different 'theories' to explain the same experiences. It also means understanding the differential position of different construals; [. . .] how one or another can become the default option [of belief and unbelief] for many people or milieu.[36]

Or, as Ratti argues, "the postsecular can be a critique of secularism and religion, but it cannot lead us back to the religious, and certainly not to the violence undertaken in the name of religion or secularism."[37]

No less than Taylor's project, contemporary French thought, especially that of a "poststructuralist" trajectory, can equally make a critical intervention in the "postsecular," given that the overall aim of the "poststructuralist" project has been, to put it very simply here, to elucidate and affirm differences.[38] Nancy's work on the "(auto)deconstruction" of religion is a case in point, through its emphasis on the constant openness toward that which is different from itself and its rejection of any return to sameness. The commitment to others and differences of "poststructuralism" makes it potentially adequate to respond to the contemporary problematic of the "postsecular," that is, the long-standing challenge to affirm and respect both religious and nonreligious differences in ways that would lead toward a more peaceful "postsecular." I will argue that it can indeed do so, especially if one articulates the *reject* that subtends "poststructuralism." In contextualizing the *reject* within the "postsecular," the stakes of theorizing the *reject* are also raised, since a theory of the *reject* now goes beyond the rather intimate and largely personal spheres of friendship, love, and community. Within those latter boundaries, the gestures of the *reject* as discussed in the previous section, such as walking away, or refraining from an initial encounter or making subsequent contact, have relatively little real, physical violent consequences. In the context of the "postsecular," however, which has a global dimension and trajectory, as Hent de Vries reminds us,[39] every gesture has an almost global effect, touching even those who are geographically, culturally, or ideologically distant, if not stranger, to the immediate religious or secular nature of that gesture (as the case, again, of 9/11 has shown). In other words, any gesture of the *reject* in the "postsecular" context is more than a personal act; it goes beyond affecting one's circle of friends, lover(s), and community. The challenge of a theory of the *reject* in the "postsecular," then, is to encourage differences to emerge and affirm themselves, while discouraging such emergence or affirmation from taking place at the price of violence against other differences. That challenge can be met, as I will argue here, through the turn, once again, of the *auto-reject*.

I have mentioned previously that the *reject* in the context of contemporary network-centric sociability is faced with the obstacle of a hyper-gregarious mass. What the *reject* in the context of the "postsecular" must overcome, I would say, is the resurrection of the *subject*, particularly in the guise of the Pauline Subject according to Alain Badiou. Badiou's *Saint Paul—La fondation de l'universalisme* can bear the implicit suggestion that the Pauline Subject can lead us out of the present violent "postsecular" situation. However, that optimistic horizon is really not the case with the Badiou's Pauline Subject. The latter, as I will show, somewhat returns us to the Schmittian sovereign, decisional *subject*, which risks leaving, in the wake of its sovereign decisions, a trail of destruction against others. In that sense, there is instead a danger in staying with the *subject* for the "postsecular." It is precisely Badiou's problematic (Pauline) *subject* that this chapter will deal with in a while. It will then proceed to suggest that, in order to break with the return or resurrection of the *subject*, which at the end of it all only admits the perpetuation of "postsecular" violence, thinking the *reject* might be a better alternative, one that is already implicitly offered, as I will demonstrate, by Derrida's *Foi et savoir*. In the previous section, I argued that Derrida did not go far enough with the *reject*, particularly the *auto-reject*, in his thinking of friendship and love. It would appear that this is once again the case in Derrida's problematization of the question of religion for the "postsecular," especially at the point where I pose the question if there is an *auto-reject* that can open us to a "postsecular" that is not anthropocentric and/or anthropomorphic. Here, I recall Nancy's point that an anthropocentric and/or anthropomorphic mode of thought, be it with regard to a thought of the "postsecular" or of "absentheism," not only pulls thought back within the limited horizons of the human *subject*, but also barely touches on difference: for Nancy, in order that thought avoids that regressive movement, and that it is always open to infinite trajectories, thought must, learning from the "auto-deconstruction" of religion, "welcome [*saluer*] a man other than the son of God or even his double, the son of man, the man of humanism."[40] Thought must be open to "an other, yes, opened in the midst of the same, an other of the same man [*un autre même homme*]," if not "an other otherwise of man" [*un autre que l'homme*].[41] According to Nancy, these others, "these other open bodies" [*les autres corps ouverts*] can be constituted by animals.[42] For a "postsecular" future that is open affirmatively to difference, perhaps the (human) *reject* must also thence learn to auto-reject its anthropocentrism and/or anthropomorphism and thereby welcome the animal-*reject*. This movement from the (human) *auto-reject* to the animal-*reject* would seem to be missing in *Foi et savoir* at first glance. However, as I will demonstrate later in this chapter, a careful reading that brings into relation *Foi et savoir* and the later *L'Animal que donc je suis* will show that an (*auto-*)*reject* or animal-*reject* is not totally absent in *Foi et savoir*. It is already there, without being present. But that also means that the explicit presence and articulation of an animal-*reject* will not be found in Derrida. For that, one must turn to what Verena Conley has rightly prophesized as the "messianic" texts of Cixous, and that is what this chapter will do, following the discussions of Badiou and Derrida.

THE RESURRECTION AND PERSISTENCE OF THE SUBJECT: BADIOU'S SAINT PAUL

In beginning the discussion with Badiou, it must be said that Badiou in fact makes a strange addition to the company of contemporary French thinkers that this work is engaged with. This is because, philosophically, Badiou is always determined to stand apart from the inclinations and trajectories of thinkers such as Deleuze, Derrida, and Nancy. For example, in the early

Théorie du sujet (1982), in opposition to the structuralist wave of anti-Hegelianism of which Deleuze was particularly a strong proponent, Badiou will declare, "neither Hegel nor us are structuralist."[43] More recently, in his *Second manifeste pour la philosophie* (2009), he reiterates that his "target" of philosophical critique in his first *Manifeste pour la philosophie* (1989) had been "the surpassing [*dépassement*] of Metaphysics in the guise of its deconstruction."[44] Or, as he puts it in another way, "the philosophical position that [he] combated twenty years ago was principally the Heideggerian position in its French variants (Derrida, Lacoue-Labarthe, Nancy, but also Lyotard)."[45] In place of the deconstruction of being, the subject, and truth, which is characteristic of post-1968 structuralist French thought, Badiou's self-proclaimed "Platonic gesture" seeks to "reaffirm the possibility of philosophy in its original sense [*sens*], that is to say, the articulation—transformed certainly but still recognizable—of the major categorial trinity [*triplet catégoriel majeur*] of being, the subject, and truth."[46] It is not surprising, then, that in his response to Nancy's project on "who comes after the subject," Badiou—not to mention that Nancy's project (c. 1986) comes just a few years after the publication of Badiou's *Théorie du sujet* (1982)— would insist on the persistence of the *subject*, an endeavor to which he remains faithful today. In other words, and to turn Badiou's rhetoric on himself, Badiou pledges absolutely no fidelity to the break, or even event, of the "deconstruction" of the *subject*, which has ruptured the *subject*'s epistemic foundation or development.[47] He resists, rather reactively, the void in the fabric of the situated or situationized discourse on the *subject* that has henceforth been opened by "structuralist" or "deconstructive" thought, resisting thinking a new figure of thought otherwise of the *subject*, resisting pursuing what Nancy has called "who comes before/ after the subject."

Despite the distance that Badiou takes from "(post)structuralist" thinkers, a diversion to Badiou, especially the Badiou of *Saint Paul: La fondation de l'universalisme*, is necessary for any critical discussion of the "postsecular." To do otherwise is to ignore the surge in interest in the Pauline figure following the publication of Badiou's *Saint Paul*,[48] which includes Agamben's counterreading in *The Time that Remains*. Certainly, Badiou has claimed that "Paul for [him] is neither an apostle nor a saint,"[49] making any endeavor to associate *Saint Paul* with the question of religion or the "postsecular" a potential act of misreading. However, as Badiou himself has acknowledged in limited ways, it is somewhat inevitable, given his "taste" for religious "grand metaphors" such as "Miracle, Grace, Salvation [*Salut*], the Glorious Body, [and] Conversion," that his philosophy may be seen to have religion in its shadows, if not as "a disguised Christianism."[50] The religious trace in Badiou indeed does not escape the eyes of scholars.[51] For my part, I would add to those observations that the religious contour in Badiou's philosophy may be quickly discerned by its emphasis and predication on fidelity, specifically a fidelity to an event, which is the rupturing and now undeniable appearing of what previously did not, or rather could not, exist in the world.[52] Uncannily, faith, as we will see in Derrida and Cixous, also plays a critical role in their "deconstruction" of religion, even though faith in Derrida and Cixous, unlike Badiou's fidelity, is *not* something fixed or monolithic, adamantly or unwaveringly attached to a singular object: faith in Derrida and Cixous is more open-ended, never knowing to what or to whom it is faithful.[53] The uncanny proximity between Badiou and Derrida and Cixous may be further augmented if one begins to consider the Badiouian event, at least in its evangelical trajectory—since it always seeks to announce to the world the element of the new—in messianic terms. The question of the messianic preoccupies the respective writings of Derrida and Cixous, which they will reconfigure in their own ways. According to Adrian Johnston, there is a "weak messianism" to the "revolutionary ruptures" that the Badiouian event brings with it.[54] However, Ed Pluth is right to insist that Badiou is *not* a "messianic thinker,"[55] not in the sense that Derrida might be when Derrida speaks of the event that always arrives in or from the future in its complete surprise. As Pluth points out, "events," for Badiou, "are not things *to come*."[56] The Badiouian event, to reiterate, is the rupturing exposition of things previously denied of their existences, an appearing with such force that the existence of the latter can no longer be denied or ignored.

But to return to the question of Badiou's Saint Paul and the role it can have in contributing to the "postsecular" debate: to be sure, Badiou does not deploy the term "postsecular" in his *Saint Paul* or in any of his works so far (neither, in fact, do the other "(post)structuralist" thinkers in question here). However, in the conclusion of *Saint Paul*, there is a line where Badiou seemingly gestures toward something like a future "postsecular" condition (and I mean "condition" in Badiou's sense—which is to say the empirical and supposedly logical steps put in place, in supplement to the existing "situation" or *dispositif* of people, things, and ideas in the world, following an event, such as a more peaceful "postsecular" world, that ruptures the present *dispositif*), when the Pauline Subject seems to renounce all present secular situations of the contemporary world. There, Badiou writes, "For the subject, [the] subjective logic culminates in an indifference to secular nominations [...]."[57] As I would read it, that "indifference to secular nominations" is nothing less than a dissatisfaction with present secular or even "postsecular" situations. The "subjective logic" that surpasses "secular nominations," then, is a trajectory toward other configurations of the contemporary world, and this is where I think Badiou's Pauline Subject is suggestive of positing itself as a figure of thought for another "postsecular" world.

A qualification is necessary here, however: even if Badiou's Pauline Subject traces a "postsecular" trajectory different from our present "postsecular" situation, it would very much disagree with the future "postsecular" world that I have postulated earlier, particularly the one that affirms the articulation of differences. In *Saint Paul*, the work of the Pauline Subject is defined as nothing less than the declaration of his or her fidelity to the truth of the Christ-event that is the resurrection of Christ, followed by the labor to guarantee the affirmation of that truth in the world. According to Badiou, this is also a project of universalism, since the declaration of the resurrection of Christ is essentially accompanied by the promise of salvation to all, regardless if one is Jewish or not. This project of universalism, at first glance, seems promising for a less violent "postsecular" future, since, as suggested especially by the chapter "Universality and the Traversing of Differences" in *Saint Paul*, it potentially ends all violence between particular differences by demonstrating that Paul's universalism is beyond all particular differences. Badiou even makes sure to say there that particular differences are not to be ignored, disdained, or negated,[58] and that if the "Christian militantism" of Paul "must be a trajectory [*traversée*] indifferent to worldly differences [*différences mondaines*],"[59] this "indifference" must be "an indifference tolerant of differences."[60] However, one cannot help sensing that some form of violence against differences remains with Badiou's Pauline Subject. One can probably sense this from the "militant tonality" of the Pauline Subject, which includes "the appropriation of particularities," the consideration of "the empirical existence of differences" as "essential inexistence," and the too forceful will to "transcend differences."[61] This is not to mention that there is hardly any consideration if particular differences actually welcome the traversing of the Pauline Subject's "universalist militantism" "across them, in them."[62] In that sense, Badiou's Pauline Subject does not really resolve "postsecular" violence. One could even say that in the *subject*'s "indifference" to differences, it is still not that distant from the existing "postsecular" intolerance of differences. In other words, the world that logically entails from Badiou's Pauline Subject is unfortunately not a less violent "postsecular" world. That is because of the (re)turn, precisely, to the figure of the *subject*. Put another way, resurrecting the *subject* tends only to posit another form of "postsecular" violence.

Badiou's Pauline Subject functions more or less in line with his general theory of the *subject*. In other words, St. Paul as a *subject* is not given a priori; the *subject* is not given in the sense that it has always inhered in an existent, waiting only for the latter to discover it and eventually assume for him- or herself the status of a *subject*. To put the point in another way, the *subject* according to Badiou is not constructed out of a conscious decision to found one's individual being as such, and this is where Badiou claims to make a break with the Cartesian *subject*. As he says in *Théorie du sujet*, "the post-Cartesian character of our enterprise" is premised on the claim that "a subject is nowhere given (to or like knowledge)" [*un sujet n'est nulle part donné (à la connaissance)*].[63] "Knowledge" in this case, as we know from Badiou's philosophy, is the state of understanding that claims to have an infallible grasp of an object as if in its epistemic entirety, while effacing aspects of the object that this "encyclopedic" understanding cannot account for. In that case, "knowledge" is admittedly a situation in which gaps or voids regarding certain objects, or even regarding the current state of knowing, transpierce. "Knowledge," however, refuses to acknowledge these gaps or voids and would seek only to repress them. According to Badiou, then, "knowledge" as such is contrary to "truth," which acknowledges those repressed gaps or voids and subsequently works from them or elucidates them through what Badiou calls "truth procedures," in order to articulate what is "generic" or generative of something new in them. In Badiou's perspective, so long as "truth" is out there, unaccounted for or disregarded by "knowledge," the *subject*, which takes itself to be responsible for working out those "truth procedures," and thanks to an event that first grants it to see the "truth" of those gaps or voids, is not only never a given with regard to "knowledge" but also remains a rare occurrence.

Hence, if a *subject* claims to exist under the aegis of "knowledge," then it is barely a veritable *subject*.

It is by keeping in mind the "truth" of the real, that is to say, in acknowledging that there are always gaps or voids in how we see or know the world, which entails understanding that there are always "truth procedures" to work out so as to articulate what has been left out or repressed through these gaps or voids, that motivates Badiou's response to Nancy's question of "who comes after the subject." According to Badiou, that "truth" "allows [him] to deny that it is necessary [. . .] to suppress the category 'subject,'" and he defines the *subject* there as such:

> I call the subject the local or finite status of a truth. A subject is what is *locally born out*.
>
> The 'subject' thus ceases to be the inaugural or conditioning point of legitimate statements. It is no longer [. . .] that *for which* there is truth, nor even the desirous eclipse of its surrection. A truth always precedes it. Not that a truth exists 'before' it, for a truth is forever suspended upon an indiscernible future. The subject is *woven* out of a truth, it is what exists of truth in limited fragments. A subject is that which a truth passes through, or this finite point through which, in its infinite being, truth itself passes.[64]

In this passage, and in fact in this response (c. 1986) in general to Nancy, it is clear that Badiou has yet to mobilize the term "event," which he will soon do in *L'Être et l'événement* (1988), and which he will argue is that which instantiates a *subject*. In place of "event," Badiou here deploys the term "truth." In any case, be it "truth" as is the case of this response to Nancy and also in *Théorie du sujet*, or "event" as will be the case in works subsequent to *L'Être et l'événement*, Badiou makes it clear that if there were to be a *subject*, it would not be decided by any individual being: it is never the *subject* that decides on its subjectivity. To reiterate, the *subject* is inaugurated by "truth," at least in *Théorie du sujet* and in this response to Nancy, and strictly or distinctly by "event," from *L'Être et l'événement* onward.[65] Be it "truth" or "event," it is something that the *subject* has no control of, something that the *subject* does not decide on, and that is why Badiou will also call such a "truth" or event "the undecidable" [*l'indécidable*],[66] which nonetheless brings about the "subjectivation" of the *subject*. It is the "truth"/ event that decides on the *subject*: without the "truth"/ event, there is no *subject*, or, there is no *subject* without a preceding "truth"/ event. As Badiou would say much later in an interview of 2002, when he has decided on the event as that which engenders the *subject*, "the subject is identified by a type of marking, a postevental effect."[67] Preceding the *subject*, the event gives itself, or rather, traces of itself, so that the "subjectivation" of a *subject* can take place. Giving only traces of itself, the event is not from then on encapsulated within the *subject* itself. The event remains free from the *subject*; the *subject* is never the absolute expression of the entirety of the event that engenders it.[68]

In the context of *Saint Paul*, the event, as said, is the Christ-event or the resurrection of Christ, the revelation of which strikes Paul on his way to Damascus. The Pauline Subject is "locally born out" or "woven out" of that event, replacing Paul's former existence as a persecutor of Christians. According to Badiou, it is Paul as *subject* as such, through his "subjectivation" by the Christ-event, that he will begin to learn to live, to experience real living, as opposed to living out an automaton-like, if not dead, existence, which simply follows the dead (Roman) laws of the practical world. However, this new life will be in place only if Paul, following his "subjectivation," enacts the subsequent "subject-process" (according to the rhetoric of *Théorie du sujet*), which is the sustained commitment to declare both the Christ-event and his fidelity to that event. In other words, the *subject* cannot be a pure and simple acceptation of the "truth" or event. There is work to do, or "labor,"[69] in the service of the "truth" of the event. This "labor" is seemingly endless, given that the entirety of the "truth" or event is never given to the *subject*, but only parts of it. The *subject* then, on his or her part, will have to make sense of these parts gradually because, as Badiou explicates in *L'Être et l'événement*, these parts have no material referents as yet in the world. Beyond the linguistic and cognitive matrixes of the present world, they barely exist as concepts that can be formulated or grasped. The *subject*, then, is left with the sole resort of naming, of giving a name to that which has yet to have a referent in the world, and this process or procedure of naming will extend throughout the life of the *subject*, since each naming can only articulate (part of) a part of the "truth" of the event. This is not to mention that Badiou in *L'Être et l'événement* will explicate that the event is essentially "unnamable" or "indiscernible,"[70] which only suggests further that the "labor" of the *subject* is nothing but infinite, "uncompletable."[71]

The Reject and the "Postsecular," or Who's Afraid of Religion   111

In spite of the claims of a new life, one could say, on a negative note, that life after "subjectivation," which is also life under a "subject-process," is rather short of freedom. The *subject* cannot be considered to be a master of his or her own existence. Under the interpellation—and I mean this in the ideological sense following Althusser[72]—of the "truth" or event, after which the *subject* must declare his or her fidelity to the latter and also commit him- or herself to the latter's "truth procedures," one could say that the *subject* enters into an almost (non-Hegelian) master-slave relation with it. Of course, Badiou will deny any such relation between the *subject* and the "truth" or event. So, in *Saint Paul*, he argues that the Christ-event is universal, or equally "offered to all," and any *subject* that is formed by and is subsequently faithful to this event partakes but in an experience of "equality."[73] Equality between *subjects* certainly does not remove the suspicion of a master-slave relation between *subject* and the "truth" or event. Nonetheless, it is via this claim to "equality" that Badiou seeks to dispel any sense of a master in his philosophy of the event. According to Badiou, in declaring fidelity to the Christ-event, "we are all [. . .] co-workers of God," and where there is "conjoined the worker and equality," there will be the "undoing [*défaillir*] [of] the figure of the master."[74] Granted that there will be no God-the-master in Badiou's rhetoric, it remains undeniable (at least to someone without fidelity to the event), however, that the "truth" or event lords over the *subject*. That can be elicited furthermore from the beginning of *Saint Paul*, as one pays particular attention to the rhetoric there concerning the task of the book: "to re-found a theory of the Subject that *subordinates* existence to the aleatory dimension of the event."[75] The subordinated *subject*, or even a subject under subjection (in both senses of "subjectivation" and "subject-process"), can also be elicited in the earlier "On a Finally Objectless Subject," where the *subject* there is considered a "fidelity operator" [*opérateur de fidélité*] of truth.[76] It is not difficult to sense that the term "operator" renders the *subject* something of a mechanical, if not mere, functionary of "truth," something like an automaton, contrary to what Badiou claims the *subject* to be.

Some might argue that servitude (to "truth" or to the event) is a small price to pay for the new that the event promises, or that such sacrifice is worthwhile. But what if sacrifice is not simply the choice of the *subject*, but is in fact a logic inherent to the *subject*-event relation, from which the *subject* cannot escape? To discern this sacrificial logic, one must look deeper into the essential inequality between the *subject* and the event or "truth" that Badiou underscores. In *L'Être et l'événement*, Badiou writes, "Only a truth is infinite, but the subject is not coextensive [with that infinity]."[77] The difference between *subject* and event, predicated on the attribute of infinity, would be articulated in harsher terms in the earlier "On a Finally Objectless Subject": "Being the local moment of the truth, the subject fails to sustain its global adjunction."[78] In light of that statement, and given that Badiou in that same essay calls *subjects* "fragments,"[79] it is not difficult to sense that *subjects*, ultimately, are but mere remains (not, however, in the potentially radical sense of Agamben's remnant) of the "truth" or event.[80] That these remains can even be dispensed with can be elicited from *Logiques des mondes*. According to the latter, the fragment of "truth" or event that a *subject* declares at a particular present can always be taken up by another *subject* at a later time,[81] which implies that each *subject* is really replaceable, an entity that can be sacrificed in other words without much concern. This is perhaps why Badiou will emphasize the notion of "resurrection" in *Logiques des mondes*, which, in order to see to the infinite trajectory of the event or the "truth," allows the "re-embodiment" [*réincorporation*] of the event in another *subject*.[82] With this almost religious faith in the "resurrection" of the event or "truth," it is almost undeniable that it is the master, eternal "truth" or event (or "Master-Signifier," as Žižek calls it) that must be upheld over and above the subservient, transient *subject*. Conversely, as Miller has observed, "the subject is itself [also] never the master of that which is being assembled through it."[83]

Despite the preeminence of "truth" or event over the *subject*, there is an attribute that both event and *subject* somewhat share nonetheless, which is that of exceptionality. In *Logiques des mondes*, Badiou will say that "truths" or events are "exceptions to what there is," and so long as the *subject* declares his or her fidelity to the event, the *subject* is equally endowed with "the exception that truths inflict to what there is by the interpolated clause [as articulated by the *subject*] of 'there is what there is not.'"[84] The exceptional quality of the *subject* can even be elicited from earlier works where Badiou says, "the subject is *rare*."[85] In that case, to go back to *Saint Paul*, the *subject* of the Christ-event is no less rare or exceptional, even though Badiou claims that the Christ-event is "offered to all." Now, in response to the mobilization of a term such as "exception," our contemporary sensibility would no doubt quickly associate it with Schmittian sovereignty.

According to contemporary critique, the Schmittian sovereign *subject* is he or she who possesses the exceptional right, at any time, to make new laws or exceptional decisions, and while he or she singularly embodies the law as its highest authority, the decisive move to institute a new law paradoxically renders him or her outside the law. Badiou certainly may argue that there is really no sovereign decidability or decision on the side of the *subject* in matters of "subjectivation," even though the faithful *subject* cannot escape *deciding on* his or her fidelity to the event and to the commitment to the "truth procedures" in the service of the event.[86] However, Badiou's *subject*, after its "subjectivation" by the event, practices no less the sovereign act of instituting new laws while being outside existing laws, and hence one could say that at least some form of second-order sovereignty is undoubtedly at work in Badiou's *subject*.[87] This is the case when Paul declares the applicability of salvation to all, which effectively makes him "illegal" with regard to the old Jewish discourse that demands access to salvation to be granted only to believers who have undergone traditional Jewish religious rites or practices (such as circumcision).[88] Badiou's reading of Paul goes further to say that Paul is not just outside or beyond the law with regard to traditional Jewish religious discourse, but also with regard to worldly laws. The latter "orders a predicative worldly multiplicity, giving to each part of the whole what is due to it."[89] Paul, however, refuses to accept such distribution of certain peoples to certain stations in life or society as a given or immutable situation in the world. According to Badiou, Paul's declaration of the universality of salvation, which is also the work of love in the rhetoric of *Saint Paul*, breaks with this worldly law. It creates an "interruption" within the latter,[90] exceeding, if not violently supplementing, it: "For the new man [that is, the Pauline Subject or a Christian *subject*], love is the fulfillment of the rupture that he accomplishes [*consomme*] with the law, the law of the rupture with the law, the law of the truth of the law."[91] In all, "the Christ-event is heterogeneous to the law, pure excess over every [legal] prescription."[92] So long as the *subject* is faithful to that event, he or she will share that exceptional condition of being "heterogeneous to the law" or exceeding "every [legal] prescription." Or, as Badiou will say in *Second manifeste pour la philosophie* with regard to the event and the *subject* that is faithful to it: "Every exception to the laws is the result of a law of exception."

Given that the Pauline Subject's second-order sovereignty exposes the fiction, if not "mystical foundation," of every institutionalization of every law,[93] and that it questions and challenges the status quo such that another way of living or managing our lives is possible beyond the determination of State laws, one may be tempted not only to advocate the mobilization of the Badiouian *subject* but also to justify its countersovereign force. However, secondary sovereignty is still sovereignty, and in that sense, it bears consequences similar to those that follow from all other acts or figures of sovereignty.[94] There is, therefore, always cause for caution when the Schmittian sovereign *subject* that decides on the law in an outside-the-law condition rears its head, even if it is in a second-order form, as seems to be the case with the Badiouian *subject*. This is because what typically follows from a Schmittian sovereign figure is an imperialist will to disseminate the new laws he or she desires to put in place, while negating all existing ones, and this dissemination might take on not just a national but a transnational or even universal scope. Badiou seems to have a sense that the universal dimension of the fidelity to declare "truths" or events across cultures, differences, nationalities, and political factions or parties, indeed risks such imperialist contours. This suspicion is articulated in *Logiques des mondes*, when Badiou has a sense that the universality of "truth" or event is "perhaps an imperialist fiction."[95] Of course, Badiou would go on to argue the contrary. However, the fact that Badiou himself has raised the question betrays the sense that an unconscious, but nonetheless very real, imperialist possibility exists with regard to the *subject*'s work of fidelity to an event or "truth." Posing the question, then, only appears to be an attempt to exorcise that unconscious impulse, not to say that it also appears like a defensive, preemptive move to deflect any charge of sovereign imperialism. I would say, however, that this self-reflexive meditation comes a little belatedly. This is because a quasi-imperialist desire has already emerged in the earlier *Saint Paul*. The text seems to betray this desire when it discusses the Pauline Subject's work of love, where a certain imperialist intrusiveness and drive can be drawn from the text's rhetoric. I point to two examples: (1) "The new law [that is, the declared fidelity to the event, and the process or procedure of putting in place conditions for that event] is [. . .] the deployment in the direction of others"; and (2) "It remains that [. . .] fictive beings [that is, beings that are not struck by the event], [. . .] opinions, [. . .] customs, and [. . .] differences are those to which universality addresses, those towards which love is oriented, and finally, through which it must traverse such that universality itself is edified."[96] As I read it, the centrifugal force (but Badiou will say it is a "diagonal"[97] vector) of Pauline love or universality, as it projects itself "in the direction of others" or "traverse[s] through" others, is precisely suggestive of a sovereign, imperialist impulse, since there is no consideration at all if others wish the eradication of their differences, or their being traversed through, in the service of edifying a universality that might be essentially foreign or even undesirable, and hence not universal at all, to them.

One therefore cannot deny that there is a certain sovereign violence in the Pauline Subject's universalist perspective and ambition, which rejects all actual and particular differences as they exist in the present world. Violence, however, is not simply an attribute that one attaches to the Pauline Subject as a point of critique, for violence is not foreign to that *subject*. According to Badiou, the Pauline Subject bears "the polemic against 'what is due,' against the logic of rights [*droit*] and of duty [*devoir*], [which] is at the heart of the Pauline refusal of works [*œuvres*] and the law."[98] Violence, furthermore, is in fact not particular to the Pauline Subject, but rather is consistent with Badiou's theory of the *subject*. Already in the early *Théorie du subject*, there is no lack of violence in Badiou's explication of the *subject*'s entry into the world. The "truth" that inaugurates the *subject* (and I make a reminder here that Badiou has not deployed the term "event" yet in that work), and the trace of the "truth" that the *subject* bears, as highlighted earlier, are always elements of which the present world has not yet seen, known, or heard. The radical newness of the *subject* and the trace of "truth" it bears will therefore not only shock the world but also disrupt it, since, for there to be the *subject* and its declaration of the "truth," the *subject* needs to create a space for itself in the world, which would inevitably involve clearing away certain parts of the previous *dispositif* or order of things. This is why in *Théorie du sujet*, "destruction" is intricately linked to the "establishment [*enracinement*] of the subject" in the world.[99] Badiou also calls this "destruction" *forçage* or forcing there,[100] which describes how the *subject* enacts its "subject-process" in the world, creating conditions that allow elements of the "truth" to come to presence amid the normalized situation of the present world. Bruno Bosteels in his *Badiou and Politics* has argued that this violence of "destruction" dissipates when one arrives at *L'Être et événement* (1988), which suggests that it would be inaccurate to attribute violence to Badiou's Pauline Subject in *Saint Paul* (1997). However, in an interview conducted by Bosteels and Peter Hallward in

2002, that is, just some years before the publication of *Logiques des mondes* (2006), Badiou will suggest that violence is always an underlying motif in his philosophy, and it is only inevitable that it will resurface. Hence, at a point where Badiou speaks of the articulation or appearance of the *subject* in the world, after having undergone the "subjectivation" by an event that previously had no chance to articulate itself, and now appearing as a bearer of the event's "truth," where previously it could not exist as such, Badiou will say, "All of a sudden the question of destruction reappears, ineluctably." He goes on:

> I am obliged here to reintroduce the theme of destruction, whereas in *Being and Event* I thought I could make do with supplementation alone. In order for that which does not appear in a world to suddenly appear within it (and appear, most often, with the maximal value of appearance), there is a price to pay. Something must disappear. In other words, something must die, or at least die to the world in question.[101]

One could say, then, that there are always degrees of violence, at various stages of Badiou's philosophy, that Badiou's *subject* projects or expresses. In any case, "a romance with destruction," as Pluth has commented, "remains a key temptation for any faithful subject."[102] In the later *Logiques des mondes* and *Second manifeste pour la philosophie*, Badiou will bring further nuances to the question of violence in discussing the rare or exceptional appearance of the *subject* in the world. In those texts, Badiou will argue that it is not simply via "destruction" or *forçage* that a *subject* comes into existence in the world, or through which one can recognize a *subject*. According to Badiou now, there are other *subjects—subjects* that are no less cut from the same cloth of the event—that will challenge the *subject* faithful to the event such as the Pauline Subject. There are now, in contestation with the faithful *subject* [*le sujet fidèle*], on the one hand, the reactive *subject* [*le sujet réactif*], who resists radical change as introduced by the event and insists on the old world order; on the other, the obscurant *subject* [*le sujet obscur*],[103] which is similar to the reactive *subject* in opposing the introduction of radical change, but goes further than the reactive *subject* by absolutely negating all bodies or *subjects* that bear that change, conjuring up at the same time a myth of another void in history, the complete embodiment of which, it claims, is only attainable by its subjectivity.[104] In the face of opposition from either the reactive or obscurant *subject*, or both, the faithful *subject* must not abdicate. The latter must not waver in his or her faith in the event and its "truth" or "truth procedures" (and neither must he or she ever question or doubt them), but soldier on with courage to bring justice to the event.[105] This is where the sacrificial logic becomes critical for Badiou's theory of the *subject*. In the struggle against the reactive and obscurant *subjects*, it just might be a fight to the death for the faithful *subject*. And should this faithful *subject* lose in this fight to death, there is always hope that another faithful *subject* will carry on the fight. As Badiou argues, "every faithful subject," which is to say any faithful *subject* that comes after the defeated one, "can also re-embody [*réincorporer*] at the eventual present [*présent événementiel*] the fragment of truth" that was suppressed especially by the obscurant *subject*.[106]

"Re-embodiment" [*réincorporation*] here is also "resurrection" for Badiou, not so much of the particular individual human body that assumes the "subjectivation" of the event, but of the event itself, and the impersonal *subject*-forms that it engenders. In Badiou's words, resurrection here "concerns a supplemental destination of subjective forms."[107] Again, to say that it concerns "subjective *forms* [my emphasis]" ultimately implies a certain indifference to the particular individual human body that bears the "subjectivation" and "subject-process" of the event. Of course, the event and the *subject* that it gives rise to need a corporeal body. It is, after all, the latter that facilitates the *subject*'s work of declaring the "truth" of the event: "borne by a real body, [the *subject*] proceeds according to the inaugural determinations of a truth."[108] But again, the corporeal body is at the end of it all a dispensable functional support. As Badiou writes, what the *subject* seeks is ultimately to be "indifferent to corporeal particularities."[109] That indifference, for Badiou, will even be constitutive of immortality for his *subject*: "being only form, and as form—in the sense of the Platonic idea, the subject is immortal."[110] This quest for immortality, as I see it, is tinged with a certain hubris, a hubris that is rather evident in the final sentences of Badiou's *Second manifeste pour la philosophie*:

> I call "eternity" of truths this indestructible [*inentamable*] availability that renders them being able to be resurrected, reactivated in worlds that are heterogeneous to it where [truths] are created, therefore crossing over unknown oceans and dark millennia. Theory [of the *subject*] must absolutely render possible this migration. [. . .] Descartes spoke

of this "creation of eternal truths." I take up this program once again, but without the help of God . . . ".[111]

What little price to pay then, it seems, in submitting oneself as a "militant subject-of-event"[112] to the sacrificial logic of the event for the chance of immortality, or for the chance to attain eternal truths without God. At the same time, it is not difficult to imagine that such hubris will only intensify the *subject*'s sense of exceptionality,[113] which in turn will only encourage him or her to assert his or her law without concession and to disseminate that law across others, across differences, with greater imperialist indifference. That, in all, is the danger of remaining with Badiou's Pauline Subject, if not any *subject* under his theory, for the "postsecular." As I have tried to suggest above, to go with Badiou's Pauline Subject is not simply going with a passive, benign faithful *subject*. In its tendency for hubris, exceptionality, and an unconscious desire for "imperialist fiction," the faithful *subject* can even reveal itself to be both a reactive and obscurant *subject*. This is because, in the context of the "postsecular," the Pauline Subject, in his unwavering faith in the Christ-event, may just reactively deny another event that is of a non-Christian religion.[114] He risks obscuring the advent of the latter, too, when in denying it he transfers or projects the "destruction" or *forçage* of his "subjectivation" against those who declare the other event, while insisting, in a mythologizing manner, on the supposed universal dimension of the Christ-event. With the Pauline Subject, or with any Badiouian *subject*, one is therefore distant from a "postsecular" future where differences are affirmed and respected. That is to say too that the Pauline Subject and/or Badiouian *subject* offers barely anything new with regard to our existing violent "postsecular" situation.[115]

AFTER DERRIDA'S *FOI ET SAVOIR*: TOWARD THE ANIMAL-REJECT

Given the problems in raising the *subject*, especially Badiou's Pauline Subject, for the "postsecular," I will now turn to Derrida's *Foi et savoir* to elicit the *reject* there and suggest how it is a more adequate figure of thought for a less violent, future "postsecular." Before turning to Derrida, I would like to point out that one may no doubt find several instances of the *reject* in Badiou's philosophy of the *subject*. In fact, one may even say that a theory of the *subject* according to Badiou begins with a question of the *reject*. It is the event that engenders the Badiouian *subject*, but the event, as Badiou tells us, bears elements the existence of which has been previously denied or negated in the world. In other words, the event concerns elements that are essentially *rejects* in the face of the status quo of the present world. Consequently, the arrival of the event, when its advent or appearance becomes undeniable, if not irresistible, followed by the faithful work of the *subject* in declaring the event's "truth" and "truth procedures," marks nothing less than the rise of *rejects*. After their appearances in the world, event and *subject* will in fact remain as *rejects* for some time, a condition that Badiou recognizes through his use in *Théorie du sujet* of the term *horlieu*, or "out-of-place" or "outside place," to describe the *subject* in the world.[116] This is also reflected in his definition of his theory of the *subject*, which he considers as "the emergence of the force where the 'out-of-place' [*horlieu*] includes itself destructively in the space that excludes it."[117] But the *subject* faces another more sustained form of rejection, ironically in the face of the event, because, despite being faithful to the event in declaring its "truth" and despite putting in place its "truth procedures" in the world, the *subject* is always refused the entirety of the event and its "truth."

Furthermore, in bearing the "subjectivation" and the "subject-process" of the event, the corporeal body that the *subject* ineluctably inhabits is disdained, even though a body is nevertheless required for "subjectivation" and "subject-process." The corporeal body is essentially a *reject* in Badiou's theory of the *subject*, and this is exceptionally clear in *Saint Paul*. In speaking of the Christian *subject* formed by being struck by the Christ-event, Badiou argues that this *subject*, struck as such, is also a divided *subject*, as the *subject* maintains on the one hand his or her old corporeal body, while, on the other, on a spiritual, if not formal or "ideational" plane, as Badiou would have it, the *subject* experiences a whole new existence.[118] The latter is of a new, veritable life, unlike the existence that the corporeal body experiences, which is always already conditioned or delimited by the dead, particular laws of the world, and therefore is not really living according to Badiou. That real, bodily aspect of the *subject* is what Badiou would really like to get rid of, as testified by his disdain for it in saying that "the real proves itself [. . .] to be the trash [*déchet*] of every place," and that in the *subject*'s irreducible need for a corporeal support for its material "subjectivation" and "subject-process" by an event, it "must assume therefore the subjectivity of trash [*la subjectivité du déchet*]."[119] It seems that Badiou finds his solution to dispense with the corporeal body through the sacrificial logic in his theory of the *subject*, a logic whereby a *subject* in its corporeal form can always be given up for another since the reembodiment [*ré-incorporation*] of the event can always be taken up or resurrected by another *subject* at another place and time. As I read it, this sacrificial logic only reinforces the sense that the *subject* is irreducibly a *reject*, as the preeminence of the eternity of the event and its "truth" is held above everything else.

To break with the denigrating subordination to the event, Neyrat has suggested thinking the Badiouian *subject* in terms of a *subject to* [*sujet à*], rather than *subject of* [*sujet de*], the event.[120] Neyrat's move here is very close to Nancy's philosophical inclination toward the preposition *à*, for example, when Nancy rethinks *being* or *l'être* specifically in terms of *être-à* or "being-to" in order to signal *being*'s always openness to others, or when Nancy rethinks faith in terms of adoring or *adorer à*, also in order to signal a movement of openness toward the unknown, unanticipated other.[121] It is probably with a similar understanding of the preposition *à* or "to" that Neyrat proposes to think the Badiouian *subject* in terms of a *subject-to*-the-event so as to disentangle the *subject* from a restrictive, retroactive movement with regard to the event. The retroactive trajectory of the Badiouian *subject*, or "the fidelity to the past" as Neyrat calls it, "would be [. . .] a betrayal of the event,"[122] especially of the newness, or even the present condition, of the event, since, as Badiou himself also states, the event is something that hovers over the present and projects itself into the future as well. Reformulating the Badiouian *subject* as a *subject-to*-the-event then, according to Neyrat, would place the *subject* in greater proximity with the event in its present or future trajectory. Changing the preposition from "of" [*de*] to "to" [*à*] may perhaps free the *subject* from a delimiting retroactive orientation in relation to the event. However, I suspect it still will *not* free the *subject* from a closed, monolithic fidelity to a singular event, or moderate its militant or even imperialist force against those who do not share the same faith in that particular event. For that, I would argue that one must drop the *subject* altogether.[123] It would even take more than a *reject*. It would require an *auto-reject*, that third turn of the *reject* that is prepared to question, critique, rethink, and even at times abandon its insistent fidelity to a particular event and the "truth procedures" that it puts in place in an equally insistent manner. It would only be in this manner that the *auto-reject* is also always open to other events, and not fixed by a singular event.

Badiou, however, is not prepared to lose the *subject*, and his persistence in remaining with the *subject*, as I have shown, can be problematic not only for our present "postsecular" situation but also for thinking another future, less violent "postsecular" world. For the latter, I have said that the *reject* can be a more adequate figure of thought. To see how a (nascent or latent) figure of the *reject* can work toward that less violent "postsecular" future, we have to return to (post)structuralist thinkers, thinkers who are invested in the "deconstruction" of *being*, the truth, and the subject, so as to unveil what remains unthought or marginalized in the foundation of that metaphysical trinity. We have to return to thinkers such as Derrida and Cixous, therefore. As said, this section will be on Derrida' *Foi et savoir*, where I will elicit the figure of the *reject* for the "postsecular." In doing so, I am also suggesting that there is a certain force in reintroducing Derrida's text, written in the 1990s, into the discourse on the "postsecular" and to rethink it for a future "postsecular" world. Derrida's *Foi et savoir* remains relevant to our contemporary "postsecular" world because the spirit of the "postsecular" can be said to be an echo, if not an extension, of the context in which *Foi et savoir* situates itself, that is, a world witnessing a "return to religion" or even the "a war of religions."[124]

If we are seeing the extension of "a war of religions" into contemporary "postsecular" violence, this is, according to Habermas, but a consequence of us having felt that there is something missing in our contemporary state of knowledge to account for the undeniable or even irreducible desire for the religious, for "what cries out to heaven,"[125] in a world that has seemingly become-reason.[126] In a way, Derrida's *Foi et savoir* has already provided a response to account for what Habermas has stated to be "missing." For Derrida, it is not so much about adding to existing knowledge to explain or understand the rise or resurrection of religion in the secularized world, but to recognize that despite their differences (which need to be affirmed and respected), religion and reason, or faith and knowledge, proceed via similar ways. In Derrida's terms, religion and reason, faith and knowledge, proceed via a certain paradoxical autoimmune reiterability.[127] In other words, each begins by maintaining a vigilant will to preserve the sanctity or purity of itself, guarding against any contamination from what each believes to be foreign to itself; at the same time, each projects a desire to disseminate itself as widely as possible, so as to assure itself of its vitality or life-force, and in order for not only its practitioners or believers, but also for others, especially other new believers or practitioners, to bear witness and testify to its force and power.[128] It is the latter desire to reiterate itself elsewhere where the paradoxical notion of autoimmunity is located, since, in desiring to spread its word—be it the word of religion or science—to a greater multitude, it would need to go to the outside, opening itself to what it had perceived as antagonistically distinct from itself, risking therefore the desired immunity of its inner sanctity or purity.[129] This auto-dissemination into the outside puts in effect the process of autoimmunity, since it precisely destroys all immunity to the outside. Yet, this paradoxical autoimmune operation does not at all halt the projection of violence against what it had deemed to be markedly alien from itself, a violence that stems from its incessant will to immunity. In autoimmunity, there is also "autoimmune aggression" as Derrida tells us elsewhere, an aggression that "terrorizes most":[130] against the supplemental need to be hospitable to others, there remains the force of rejection against others, a force that has even become structural to religion (and knowledge). It is because of such "autoimmune aggression" in religion that "rejection, as well as an apparent appropriation," according to Derrida in *Foi et savoir*, can take the form of "a structural and invasive [*envahissante*] religiosity" (§45: 86).[131]

In a "postsecular" world where the articulations and rearticulations of religions are met with resistances not only from within religion itself but also from the world of science and reason, not forgetting too that "postsecular" religions are likewise militantly contesting the world of science and reason, what is missing, therefore, is perhaps the recognition of the aggressive autoimmune reiterability, the structure of rejection, in both faith and reason. This structure of rejection needs to be critiqued, if we are to move from a violent "postsecular" that does not know how to accept differences—differences between religions, differences between faith and knowledge, and so forth, to a "postsecular" world where differences are affirmed and respected. We must also be vigilant that the latter is not achieved only in a superficial manner, where we accept differences only if they are passive differences, that is to say, differences that play down their distinctive or rather potentially conflicting edges and integrate or homogenize themselves to us.[132] That would not only be a superficial but even hegemonic "postsecular" world. The future "postsecular" world that we must work toward must be one where differences do not need to smooth out their edges, where differences as such can coexist without destructively negating or denigrating one another. I have tried to demonstrate in the section above on Badiou that a figure of thought such as the *subject* does not really help us move from the structure of rejection to this future, less violent "postsecular" world. I will now try to argue here that it is with the *reject* that we can make that transition, a figure that I find intimated by Derrida in *Foi et savoir*. I will proceed by showing how Derrida's critique of the structure and force of rejection in religion allows the figure of the *reject* to emerge.

RELIGION, OR (AUTO-)REJECTION

If there is a structure of rejection in religion (and I focus here on religion, and not on reason or knowledge, since the question of religion is the concern of *Foi et savoir*, and since what is also at stake in the question of the "postsecular" is more the role, the place, and the force of religion than that of science), it stems from its will to keep its supposed "essence" or inner life sacred and pure, untouched or uncontaminated by what it regards or decides as its outside. In other words, it is religion's militant claim to the sole right and authority to speak about religion in religion's own name that it takes on a force of rejection. As Derrida has noted, non-Christians tend to be precluded from partaking in any discourse on the Christian religion: their responses would not count in any discussion on what the Christian faith means or could mean for the present and the future.[133] Religion has also protected itself with respect to the medium through which its discourse is transmitted and through which it disseminates itself. In that regard, it is only until very recently, as Derrida observes in *Foi et savoir*, that religion has come to no longer resist tele-technologies and their electronic and networked dimension as potential spaces where religion can spread its word and where its discourse can be kept alive. In short, it is in the stubborn insistence, or what Derrida will call *bêtise*,[134] on the supposed authority of its own voice to speak about itself, and on the tradition of how it addresses itself or how it is addressed, that rejection—particularly rejection against others—becomes something structural in religion.

But Derrida will underscore that what eventually plays out in religion is *auto*-rejection, even though religion might not be conscious of this or acknowledge it. Auto-rejection plays out in that very process of spreading its word in order to keep its inner sacred "essence" alive, in the process of transmitting its word to a greater number of people, seeking to convert former nonbelievers into witnesses of its life-force not only for the present time but also for the future. It is in that process that religion takes on the risk of introducing someone or something into its domain that might undermine it from within.[135] In this respect, it risks losing, if not auto-rejects, its claim to indemnity.[136] According to Derrida, such auto-rejection is something of a quasi-suicidal autoimmunity, a gesture that implies taking out its own force of rejection: "all auto-protection of the unscathed [*l'indemne*], the saintly and the uncontaminated [*sain(t)*], the unharmed [*sauf*], the sacred (*heilig*, holy) must protect itself against its own protection, its own policing [*son propre police*], its own power of rejection, its own in short [*son propre tout court*], that is to say its own immunity" (§37: 67). In that sense, and as Derrida has also instructed us in *La Voix et le phénomène* on the question of "auto-affection,"[137] the *auto* in auto-rejection does not concern only the self, but the other too: the other partakes as well, if not more than the self, in the undoing of the supposed sovereignty, or sovereign *ipseity*, of the self. But it is on account of this distribution of the *auto* with the other that religion refuses to abdicate completely its power or force of rejection. Religion might accept auto-rejection in method, in service of its dissemination, but it hardly accepts it in principle, especially, as said, that part of sharing auto-rejection with the other. Realizing that it loses all sovereign claims to the monolithic indemnity of itself in autoimmunity, religion from then on builds for itself a defensive narrative of being under the threat of violation from the outside, which becomes an alibi, justification, and pretext for the (preemptive) resurrection of its initial power of rejection with greater force, if not in more terrifying manifestations. In Derrida's terms, this is the "perversion" of autoimmunity.[138]

Derrida, of course, does not agree with religion's violent rejection and counterrejection emerging from its "autoimmune aggression" against others. In fact, for Derrida, what would have been critical for religion is for religion to stay, if not go further, with auto-rejection, except *without* the reactionary counterrejection against others. One must recognize that there is no religion *in itself* per se, no sacrosanct *essence* of religion,[139] since, in Derrida's analysis, religion's desire to preserve its sacredness, its desire to maintain sole authority to address, respond, or partake in a discourse on religion itself, and its desire to extend itself over time and space in a manner as infinite as possible, are already gestures mobilized by systems of thought otherwise of religion, systems of thought such as science or philosophy. It makes no sense, then, for religion to insist on its own way of thinking about itself, to insist on certain determined ways of speaking about itself, and to insist on the prohibition of interventions from others. These are just phantasms of the institution of religion. For Derrida, these bring nothing new to religion: there is no future for, or of, religion, if religion holds on to the phantasm of its sovereign ipseity. This is where Derrida insists on auto-rejection in religion, an auto-rejection that always opens to the other, an auto-rejection that does not pervert itself into a reactionary violence against others. As Derrida says in *Foi et savoir*, "One would not speak of [religion] if one spoke *in its name*, if one was contented to *reflect* on religion speculatively, religiously" (§27: 38–39). One must "break with [religion]," "to suspend for an instant religious belonging [*l'appartenance religieuse*]"; "it would be necessary in any case to take into account, in an a-religious or even irreligious manner, if possible, of what religion presently may *be*, and of what is *said* or *done*, of what *arrives* at this very moment, in the world, in history, *in its name*. There where religion no longer reflects nor at times assumes or bears its name" (§27: 39). It is also there where a figure of the *reject* may be elicited from Derrida's text.

REJECTS

The *reject* is no stranger to religion, especially Christian religion. One can immediately think of Adam and Eve as *rejects* when they were banished from Eden after eating the fruit of the Tree of Knowledge. In my under-standing of the *reject*, they would constitute the first turn of the *reject*, figures that are abandoned, exiled, or banished. But even before Adam and Eve come to be regarded as *rejects*, one could be audacious to think that God was some kind of *reject* too when Adam and Eve defied his command-ment to not eat the forbidden fruit. One can also turn to chapter 14 of Luke and see the mobilization of the active *reject* when it is said that only those who reject their families and reject even their own lives can be true followers of Christ.[140] These would very much be *rejects* of the second turn, figures that *first* exercise a force of renunciation so overwhelming and over-bearing that they are subsequently rendered *rejects* by others around them.

One may find a combination of the passive *reject* and *auto-reject* in the figure of the *homo tantum* at the heart of the psalms of David, the figure that recognizes that he is rejected by all around him and is left alone existentially, as *only human, just human,* to cry out to God. In short, one could argue that the *reject* figures in the Bible. But the pertinent question here is if the *reject* or any aspect of the *reject* is at work in Derrida's deconstructive understanding of religion in *Foi et savoir.*

Perhaps a quick candidate would be the figure of "radical evil" that Derrida mentions in that text. "Radical evil" is not so much what Kant speaks about in *Religion Within the Limits of Reason Alone,* which is a question of one's inner heart and its fidelity to what Kant calls the universal categorical imperative to act morally. For Kant, "radical evil" manifests itself when the inclination toward that imperative is perverted. In Derrida's text, "radical evil" takes on a more contemporary meaning, naming certain fundamentalist religious groups that deploy extreme violence such as terrorism in order to declare their rejection of other religions. One finds echoes of such "radical evil" in our contemporary post-9/11 world, echoes that are made to resound no less by the Bush administration's appellation, immediately after 9/11, of "the axis of evil" with regard to enemies of the American State. "Radical evil" in that sense quickly became a term to label terrorist groups predicated on militant or jihadist Islamism. But what the State did not and does not readily acknowledge is that the term "radical evil" is also a means to politically define other states or religious groups not aligned to the Christian faith that resist the global hegemony of American political economy, especially that under the Bush administration, which has been held up by a no less hegemonic, fundamentalist Christian faith or ideology.

"Radical evil" as such would seem to be a manifestation of the second turn of the *reject,* that is, the *reject* that either initiates an extreme force of rejection against others or retaliates with a similar force against an oppressive or repressive hegemonic entity. That might be the case, but I bring to mind again the aim or stakes of rereading Derrida's *Foi et savoir* and theorizing the *reject* today, which is to think of a future "postsecular" world of reduced violence. To that end, I would say that one should hold back projecting the active force of the *reject.* I do not mean that one should repress that aspect of the *reject.* That aspect at times remains necessary, especially when a certain religion or mode of thought is targeted to be suppressed or repressed by a dominant force, except it must not be expressed in such violent or terroristic ways that certain fundamentalist religious groups no doubt put into action, ways that bring along with it the fatal cost, collateral or not, of innocent civilian lives. In that case, I would say that the *reject* that is needed for a less violent "postsecular" world is one that hinges more on its passive turn, one that rejects any impulse to (counter)violence. Weak as the force of such a *reject* may be, I would posit that it is more critical, for that future "postsecular" world, to *just* articulate the existence or presence of (passive) *rejects* in the world, *rejects* that are rendered so by sovereign, dominant, hegemonic forces.[141] This would raise awareness of the oppressive actions of the latter and pressure them, *just* by the exposition of *rejects*, to abdicate such actions.[142]

I would argue that passive *rejects* can be found in *Foi et savoir*, and they are the two figures articulated by Derrida before the reference to "radical evil." There are two figures that stand before "radical evil," then, and which are in effect not so different from each other: they are the messianic figure, or more precisely, the messianic figure that is of "messianicity without messianism," and *khôra*. According to Derrida, if religion wants to have a chance at a future, that is to say, for its discourse to continue into the future, or for it to be constantly thought about or thought through anew, it must have an element of the event. The event in Derridean terms, as is well known now, is that which arrives in and of the future in its complete surprise, never programmed, unanticipated, and incalculable.[143] For religion (and, I would add, the "postsecular" world) to have a future, religion (and the "postsecular" world) must be open to such an event. For Derrida, it is the messianic figure without messianism that will lead religion (and the "postsecular" world) toward an opening to the event. It is with this messianic figure without messianism opening itself to the event that one could speak of a passive *reject* here, since its opening to the event in the event's complete incalculable nature would mean that it (auto-)rejects all subjective determination or decision as to what is to come.[144] It neither selects nor denies what or who arrives, but *just* lets be what or who arrives. Underlying this figure hence is a mode of justice that opens to "a universalizable culture of singularities" (§22: 31). In this passivity to the event, the messianic figure without messianism also has to accept the risk that it is something or someone of "radical evil" that arrives, which can consequently precipitate into the complete, denigrating rejection of the messianic figure by that "radical evil."[145] That would be the suffering, if not passion, that the messianic figure without messianism as *(auto-)reject* will have to bear before the event.

What is to be done with this "radical evil" that arrives then? In a sense, there is nothing to be done on the part of the messianic figure without messianism. He or she can only have faith that the trajectory of who or what comes is traced by peace and justice.[146] He or she will just/ *just* have to have faith that the other who comes bears likewise the passive *reject* or even *auto-reject* in himself, herself, or itself, such that it will not project any aggressive force of rejection against its host. In this case, one could question if thinking the *reject* becomes something programmatic, seeking to determine the contour of the encounter between the messianic figure without messianism and the future. In a way, the very thinking of the *reject* admittedly has a programmatic contour, just as Derrida's thought of a "messianicity without messianism" is in certain ways undoubtedly programmatic too (in the sense of rejecting all messianism, for example). But the thinking of the *reject*, like the thought of "messianicity without messianism," does not preclude the possibility that the future or the other that arrives is *not* a *reject* in any way. And even if it is, there is no telling how the encounter will play out between two *rejects* or *auto-rejects*. In other words, with regard to a theory of the *reject*, there will always remain the question, which can be posed in the following manner: What will happen in an encounter or meeting between two *rejects*, when each of them, in their own heterogeneous ways, rejects any move that will decidedly determine the outcome of the encounter? This is where *rejects* exceed all programmatic determination or calculability, for the suspension of decision, if not hesitation, taken differently from both sides of both *rejects* when they encounter each other, will open the thinking of the *reject* to what remains unforeseen or unforeseeable in any present theorization of the *reject*.

In its opening to the event, I have said that the messianic figure without messianism takes on a contour of a passive *reject*. However, a certain active force of rejection in this *reject* must not be ignored, which is its rejection of any appurtenance to any religion, especially to any Abrahamic religion: it is "without prophetic prefiguration" and "does not depend on any messianism, [it] does not follow any determined revelation, it does not properly belong to any Abrahamic religion" (§21: 30; §21: 31).[147] Yet, its rejection of any allegiance, alliance, or affiliation with any religion does not imply any negation or denigration of religion. What this rejection seeks is simply

walking away from the dogmatic or even doctrinal force of religious institutions and their systems of thought. Put another way, what the messianic
figure without messianism as *reject* seeks is its freedom to depart from the
delimiting dimensions of religious thought. In its departure, it seeks, in
turn, another place, another space, free from the delimitations of dogmatic or doctrinal religious thinking, or even evacuated of the latter, so
as to think through religion anew and differently. It is on this question of
seeking another space that the messianic figure without messianicity turns
toward *khôra*.

Khôra, according to Derrida, will be that place where new thoughts or
new ways of thinking (about religion) receive, in their instants of articulation or arrival, what Derrida calls "unconditional hospitality," which is
hospitality that does not discriminate or calculate what or who arrives. In
other words, it is a space that rejects past or existing thoughts or ways of
thinking as obstacles to the new. Again, like the messianic figure without
messianism, rejection here does not involve denigrating or negating past
or existing thoughts and ways of thinking. *Khôra* rejects them only in a
way that it does not allow them to become its defining traits or horizons,
not allowing them to become regulating ideas that would discourage the
arrival of the new in its complete alterity or heterogeneity.[148] It should be
said too that it does not allow what arrives as new to eradicate the old or
the existing, or to allow it to become a new force of resistance against what
comes to disagree with it. To that end, in order to be neutral—rather than
to be immune or to claim to a sacrosanct indemnity—to all that arrives,
Derrida will state that *khôra* can never be defined, determined, or identified as this or that place. *Khôra* rejects localizing itself: it rejects determining a place of or for itself. It is *no place* or a *nonplace*.[149] It is almost
an impossible place, yet always necessary to claim a proximity to it, or an
approximation of it, in order to give voice or place to the new.

This impossible but necessary place, to deploy Derrida's rhetoric, is
played out in the philosophical personage of Socrates in Derrida's reading
of Plato's *Timaeus* in *Khôra*, and it is perhaps in this personage where *khôra*
takes on a clearer contour of a *reject* or even *auto-reject*. According to Derrida, Socrates assumes a semblance of *khôra* when he acknowledges that
he in fact does not occupy, own, or has the right to access, the authorized
space to speak, for example, about politics, or even philosophy. If he speaks
on politics or philosophy, then he does so by pretending to assume such a

space. For Derrida, at play here is an "auto-exclusion."[150] But by doing so, another form of rejection is also in place, since, in Derrida's analysis, Socrates also points to the phantasm of the institutionalized space from which politicians exercise their presumed authority to assume political discourse or to determine the practice of politics. In other words, *khôra* unveils that there is no one place—*plus d'un lieu*—where the supposed "essence" of a subject—be it politics, religion, or philosophy—finds its place, a place where a supposed right way to speak about the subject can take place.[151] For a future thinking of religion, or even for a future of religion, one must therefore reject (without eradicating) any adherence to or grounding on any particular site of religion or religious institution, but move toward the nonplace or *opening* of *khôra*, which is that "spacing" that does not let itself be "dominated by any theological, ontological, or anthropological instant," or which "remains absolutely impassible and heterogeneous to all the processes of historical revelation or anthropo-theological experience" (§24: 34).

But perhaps the most radical figure of the *reject* that can be found in *Foi et savoir* is the figure of Abraham that Derrida invokes there. This Abraham is not the Abraham that Derrida discusses in *Donner la mort*, that is to say, the Abraham that obeys without questioning God's commandment to sacrifice Isaac. The Abraham of *Foi et savoir* says no to God's commandment: "an Abraham who would from then on refuse to sacrifice his son [. . .]" (§37: 65). As such, this Abraham breaks with, if not rejects, in the language of *Donner la mort*, the "absolute alliance" with God.[152] This Abraham refuses to respond responsibly to God's test not only of his obeisance but also of how he maintains the secret link between himself and God as "the absolute singularity."[153] The Abraham who responds and assumes the responsibility to carry out God's commandment, as in the case of the original story, that is, the Abraham who takes up the role of the executioner or even murderer in what could be, or would have been, "the worst sacrifice" [*le pire sacrifice*], is, however, essentially an irresponsibility in the face of a general ethics toward Isaac and the rest of the human(e) world, according to Derrida, following his reading of Kierkegaard's *Fear and Trembling*. Instead of going with this responsible-irresponsible Abraham, the Abraham of *Foi et savoir* puts in suspension any response or responsibility to God's commandment and God's "absolute singularity." I would even say that this Abraham puts in suspension the *différance* between the responsibility to God and the irresponsibility to mortal beings and the mortal world. This time, he refuses the subjectivity given by God through God's secret call, which requires him to respond to the commandment of sacrificing Isaac. This time, he refuses to respond: "Here I am" [*me voici*]. However, this does not mean that this Abraham falls back to the arms of Isaac and the ethical human world: there is no telling if he would do that. There is another secret at work in Abraham this time, therefore, a secret more radical perhaps than the secret he has with God when he accepted the commandment to sacrifice Isaac. This time, it is a secret that is no longer "unilaterally assigned by God,"[154] a secret that perhaps God does not even know. That is not to say, however, that a decision of a sovereign subjective type is at work here, since there is essentially no Kierkegaardian "mad decision" on Abraham's part to go either with God or with the human world.[155] Decision, and therefore subjectivity as well, is effectively put in suspension here. I would hence refrain from saying that a *subject* is at work. Instead, there is something of a *reject* here: a *reject* that rejects any alliance with the "absolute singularity" of God and any allegiance to one's mortal community; and an *auto-reject* that refuses the force of subjectivity to decide to go with one or the other, or one *and* the other, but remains in the undecidability between the two.

At this point, one could perhaps let this Abraham resonate with another figure that also appears to be something of the *reject* (even though I will demonstrate in the next section on politics that this figure is somewhat far from the *reject* as I understand it): Melville's literary figure, Bartleby the scrivener, who states quite simply but enigmatically: "I would prefer not to." This is not an arbitrary invocation, since Derrida does relate this Bartleby to Abraham in *Donner la mort*. In the context of *Foi et savoir*, it would not, however, be Abraham who says "I would prefer not to" *after* having accepted God's commandment, that is, Abraham who retracts his acceptance of the responsibility upon further reflection on the nature and consequences of the commandment. Instead, it will be another Abraham-Bartleby who says to himself "I would prefer not to" when asked to respond, and/or when given the commandment, that is, neither accepting nor refusing the commandment. In this case, one (including God) really "does not know what [this other Abraham] wants or means, one is ignorant of what he does not want to do or what he does not mean or want to say."[156] The "I would prefer not to" of this other Abraham-Bartleby then "evokes the future without prediction or promise; it enunciates nothing that was hypostasized [*arrêté*], determinable, positive or negative."[157] This Abraham is no longer "the unique Abraham in a singular relation with a unique God,"[158] nor Abraham who would choose to restore all ethical or communitarian relation with his fellow human beings at the cost of disobeying God. Here, "we no longer know who Abraham is, and not even he can tell us" [*Nous ne savons pas qui s'appelle Abraham, et il ne peut même pas nous le dire*].[159] What remains then is perhaps an *auto-reject*, and perhaps a silent one too, who no longer has to respond to God, and hence sacrifice all human ethics, nor turn to his fellow human beings, sacrificing in this case the absolute duty to God.[160]

FROM THE AUTO-REJECT TO *DIVINANIMALITÉ*

For a less violent "postsecular" world, that is, a world where differences between religions and difference between faith and reason can be articulated without each difference compromising its alterity or letting its radical edge destructively negate or denigrate other differences, one should *not* put forth vehemently the active *reject*. For that less violent "postsecular" world where differences withhold projecting their defensive or preemptive violence against others, one would need to foreground the *auto-reject* instead. At this point, I would like to go further with the thought of the *auto-reject* whereby the *reject* rejects its own anthropocentric or anthropomorphic aspect. I do this, on the one hand, in keeping with Nancy's argument that an anthropocentric or anthropomorphic horizon presents a closure, instead of an openness, for thought. On the other hand, I do this also because it seems that a nonanthropologic, nonanthropocentric, and nonanthropomorphic figure of thought is also missing in the question of the "postsecular," and I would like to address this gap in "postsecular" thought. Now, for Habermas, if one is to resolve "postsecular" violence, a communicative dialogue between religious sectors and secular sociogovernmental institutions must be in place. The aim of such communicative action is for secular society to witness and accept the fact of how religious discourse can, as effectively as other nonreligious or "more scientific" discourses, explain "postsecular" transformations in society, such as the surge in religious activism. It is also for religious sectors to understand that for the peaceful and respectful coexistence between citizens of different cultures and races in society, there must be put in place certain secular, normative laws to guide society along this process. Rather evidently, this communicative action is anthropologic and anthropocentric. It is based on human language, or what an interlocutor to Habermas in the debate on "postsecular society" calls "the use of an understandable language," a language that in turn works toward "an inclusive community to which all those belong [. . .] are capable of understanding" the difference between faith and knowledge, religion and reason.[161] In other words, it is based on a language and a communitarian teleology that exclude nonhuman animals and their voices and silences.[162] What is therefore also missing in the present "postsecular" discourse, and in the discourse of a future "postsecular," is the consideration of animals. However, if a future "postsecular" world where no difference is discriminated against or rejected is to be desired, then this future "postsecular" world must also include the difference of animals, rather than exclude it. For that future, perhaps one must also think the *auto-reject* in relation to animals, if not shift thought from the *auto-reject* to animal-*rejects*.

In a way, animals are missing in Derrida's *Foi et savoir*, more absent than the visible absence, as Derrida notes, of Muslim and female interlocutors in the debate on religion at Capri (since Derrida did not even mention animals at that point).[163] Put another way, animals are some sort of *rejects* in Derrida's text: Derrida never puts animals in explicit relation to the messianic figure without messianism, to *khôra*, and to the other Abraham.[164] However, I would say that animals there are not *rejects* in the sense of beings that are abandoned or denigrated. Animals are *rejects* in *Foi et savoir* only in the sense that their coming to explicit presence is somewhat veiled. That means to say, too, that the thought of animals is not absolutely detached or rejected from Derrida's "deconstruction" of religion in *Foi et savoir*. In fact, I would argue that the thought of animals is at the heart of the question of religion in *Foi et savoir*. This is because, if, according to Derrida there, the thinking of religion is not so much about what religion "is" but "the question of the question" (§35: 61),[165] it is then also the question of the animal, since, as Derrida puts it in the later *L'Animal que donc je suis*, the question of the animal is also "the question of the question."[166] And "the question of the question," for Derrida, is a question of what is presupposed and entailed in the naturalized understanding of a response. It concerns, therefore, the question of what constitutes or counts as a response; the consequent question of who, or what, can or cannot be considered capable, legitimate, or authorized to respond; and the question of to whom one responds. With regard to religious and/or "postsecular" discourse, what counts almost absolutely as response is human language, as seen in the invocation of "understandable language" in the discussion with Habermas on the "postsecular" as the regulative idea of what constitutes a response. In other words, a response is typically predicated on human language enunciated by a human subject, a subject having mastery over language, a mastery that becomes evident to others by impressing it upon them, who are then made to recognize or acknowledge this subject's subjectivity. Derrida in *L'Animal que donc je suis* will remind us that Lacan goes further to say that the constitution of a response must be supplemented by the ability to erase the trace of one's response and to not only feign a response but to pretend to give a false response or to "feign to feign." Lacan claims that animals are incapable of these supplementary gestures and that they are neither capable of responding in the way described above whereby a relation with another is established, that is, whereby another can recognize animals as "subjects of enunciation" just as humans are. The denial of the animal as a "subject of enunciation" or a subject *tout court*, and therefore the denial of its capacity or even right to respond, can be said to account for their exclusion in much thought about religion (except as sacrificial objects or metaphors, for example, "lamb of God") and/or the "postsecular." Animals lie outside, or are totally other or *tout autre*, of what many have judged to be norms of "proper" respondents and responses in discourses on religion and/or the "postsecular." In the domains of those discourses, animals are, in a word, *rejects*.[167]

However, as the discussion above on Derrida's messianic figure without messianism has underscored, the future of religion needs to let something or someone totally other arrive, something or someone that responds to religion or its discourse in a way yet unthought of, or in its unique or even secret way. This other may even reject responding at all, like the other-Abraham in *Foi et savoir*: an other who says, "I decline all responsibility. I no longer respond, I am no longer responsible for what I say [*je ne réponds plus de ce que je dis*]. I respond that I no longer respond."[168] Religion needs a totally other or a *tout autre* that is beyond the horizon of its past and present thought. For Derrida in *Donner la mort*, one must open oneself to the *tout autre* that is "human or not,"[169] and respect it in its absolute singularity;

or, to continue the rhetoric of *Donner la mort*, one must respect it as much as the "other other" or "other others" [*l'autre autre, les autres autres*].[170] In *L'Animal que donc je suis*, this *tout autre* becomes "an instance of the animal, of the animal-*other*, of the other *as animal*, of the *other*-mortal-life [*l'autre-vivant-mortel*], of the non-similar in any case, of the non-fraternal [*non-frère*] [. . .]."[171] It is at this point where Derrida brings the absolute alterity or the absolute singularity of the divine in proximity with that of the animal, claiming that the instance of the divine and that of the animal are "inseparable" or are linked [*s'allient*] to each other.[172] This is also where Derrida will invoke the word "divinanimality" or *divinanimalité*, in order "to break [*rompre*] with [. . .] the similar, to situate oneself at least in a place of alterity radical enough whereby one must break with all identification with an image of oneself, with all similar living beings, and therefore with all fraternity or all human proximity, with all humanity."[173]

The thought of animality is therefore not absent in Derrida's thinking of religion. The question of animals and the question of religion are interlaced in Derrida, as *L'Animal que donc je suis* demonstrates. However, as said, any explicit articulation of the animal-*other*, or *divinanimalité*, is missing in *Foi et savoir*, which undoubtedly gives the impression that the animal-*other* is some sort of a *reject* there. If it is a real forgetting of animals in *Foi et savoir* (which is not the case, as I have tried to demonstrate), then the text risks repeating the rejection of animals in Christian religion, a rejection that manifests itself not only in terms of treating animals only as sacrificial objects, of discriminating certain animals as impure and therefore prohibited to human contact and consumption as pronounced in chapter 11 of Leviticus, but also of marginalizing them the moment biblical narratives proceed to underscore the imperative to obey divine commandments as Cixous has noted. But Cixous has also reminded us that without animals, religion or religious experience will not have seen itself through: according to her, Abraham's journey up Mount Moriah to obey God's commandment to sacrifice Isaac would have been infernal and impossible without his donkey.[174] And, as Dominick LaCapra would remind me, without the ram, which is so often passed over as a mere "extra" not only in the biblical narrative but also in critical discourses on the narrative,[175] Isaac would have ended up as the sacrificial object; one cannot imagine, if that were indeed the case, what kind of relations would entail between Abraham and the rest of humanity, and between Abraham and God. In other words, religion and/or the "postsecular," if they are to see themselves and their respective futures through, will continue to need the animal. Or, to put it in the rhetoric of this study, the *reject* or *auto-reject*, if it is to lead religion and/or the "postsecular" to their futures, must *follow after* the animal.

I have italicized "follow after" above because these words are in fact of critical significance in Derrida's *L'Animal que donc je suis*, words that may offer us a way to better understand in what particular way the animal-*other* or *divinanimalité* is missing in *Foi et savoir*. According to Derrida in *L'Animal que donc je suis*, the gesture of *following after*, or the move that chases after (another) [*démarche suivie*], is something of the animal: it "will have to resemble that of an animal seeking either to hunt or to escape."[176] Derrida will go on to say that *following after* will also resemble

> an animal trail [*la course d'un animal*], which, orienting itself by scenting [*au flair*] or by hearing, goes over more than once [*repasse plus d'une fois*] the same path to retrace tracks [*relever des traces*], either to scent the trace of another there, or to efface its own by multiplying it there, precisely as that of an other, scenting [*flairant*], as this trail makes evident to it, that the trace is always of an other [*la trace est toujours d'un autre*].[177]

Given this passage from *L'Animal que donc je suis*, one can perhaps say that, if any trace of the animal-*other* or *divinanimalité* is missing or effaced in *Foi et savoir*, it is because Derrida is already *following after* the animal, if not already approximated himself beside an animal that is already erasing its traces, already placing himself without place, that is, without fixed visible localization *à la khôra*, *following after* this disappearing animal. Perhaps the animal-*other* or *divinanimalité* is already escaping the restrictive limits of existing religions and religious discourse and already seeking another space where the discourse on religion can take place in a totally different way involving nonhuman animal participants or interveners. Is this not the same move that Derrida makes with regard to the apparently absent discussion of the sacrificial ram in the Abraham story in *Donner la mort*, only to say later, as recounted by Michael Naas, that that is because he has (already) taken the "side of the sacrificed ram"?[178]

In that sense, can one say that there is already in *Foi et savoir* an auto-rejection of all traces of anthropocentrism and anthropomorphism, or else a figure of the *reject* that also rejects its own presence, as it *follows after* the animal-*other* that is effacing its traces? Has *Foi et savoir* in fact advanced "into the risk of absolute night" (§22: 31), the night where animal eyes may open, as Derrida writes in "De l'économie restreinte à l'économie générale: un hégélianisme sans réserve"? I would think so, and any rereading or rethinking of *Foi et savoir* must *follow after* such a trail too. That would be the sense of the *after* in the title to this entire section on Derrida ("After Derrida's *Foi et savoir*"). Any reinvestment in *Foi et savoir* for the "postsecular," which comes *after* the publication of *Foi et savoir*, must *follow after* the animal. To reiterate then, the *reject* or *auto-reject* for the "postsecular" must *follow after* the animal. It is only then that the *reject* or *auto-reject* can open religion and/or the "postsecular" to a future where differences not only between anthropocentric and anthropomorphic religions and reason, but also those between humans and animals, are affirmed and respected, that is, a future where animals are no longer excluded or rejected from the domain of religious or "postsecular" discourse, no longer judged to be incapable of bringing something critical to that discourse.

To see at work an *auto-reject* that follows after the animal, we need not, in fact, wait for an unforeseeable or unanticipated future. The critical function of such an *auto-reject* for a nonanthropologic, nonanthropocentric, and nonanthropomorphic "postsecular" future is in fact already understood by Cixous, especially in her texts written in the 1990s. In other words, it is from Cixous that one can elicit that *auto-reject* that follows the animal. To be more precise, Cixous shows us how we can move from auto-rejection—and in Cixous's case, this would mean rejecting our human vision, human knowledge, and finally our human selves—to an animal perspective for, or on, the "postsecular." But before doing that, one must begin with the question of religion in Cixous's *œuvre*.

DIVINANIMALITÉ, OR THE ANIMAL-MESSIAH IN CIXOUS

I begin this section by recalling the remark John Caputo made in relation to the question of religion in Derrida: "Jacques Derrida has religion, a certain religion, his religion, and he speaks of God all the time. The point of view of Derrida's work as an author is religious—but without religion and without religion's God."[179] The same could be said of Cixous too: the religious is never absent in Cixous's works. As Hugh Pyper has observed, "The range of

[Cixous's] engagement with the Bible is considerable," and that "scattered throughout her writings are [. . .] often quite sustained engagements with particular biblical texts."[180] Or, as Sal Renshaw puts it, "It would be hard to find a Cixousian text that does not in some way refer to the religious."[181] Yet, as in Derrida, one would not find in Cixous "religion's God." In the words of Charlotte Berkowitz, "For Hélène Cixous, [. . .] God embodies the sacred. But in Cixous's lexicon, God is not the Father."[182] To be "without religion's God," however, especially in Cixous's early works, is not just refusing to acknowledge God as "the Father." Like many Cixous scholars, Berkowitz will point out that Cixous "disdains those parts of the Bible that represent Paternal Law,"[183] and she explicitly challenges "religion's God," or the masculine, prohibitive law that it has come to represent.[184] Claude Cohen-Safir goes further to suggest that Cixous in this way inscribes a "counter-Bible" [contre-Bible], where "the known metaphors: the tree, virile elevation, and the fall, are subtly hijacked of their original meaning into a resolutely humanistic and feminine perspective."[185] For Cohen-Safir also, the consequence of Eve eating from the Tree of Knowledge in Cixous is no longer the apocalyptic "millennial deprivation of knowledge," but something creative, whose "conquering" and "exploratory" spirit ought to be celebrated.[186] The affirmation of such "humanistic and feminine" transgression against "religion's God" has also been noted by Susan Sellers. Reading Cixous's "Sorties" in La jeune née (1973), Sellers notes a "feminine willingness to risk [God's] prohibition."[187] "Eve," Sellers continues, "follows her desire and defies God's incomprehensible prohibition not to eat from the Tree of Knowledge. Eve's refusal, Cixous writes, creates for herself and the world the opportunity for knowledge, innovation and uncensored choice."[188] To put it in terms of this current work, it could also be said that Cixous, especially in her works of the 1960s and 1970s, reverses the judgment of Eve as a reject—a reject from the perspective of God who banishes her (and Adam) from the Garden of Eden, and a reject from the perspective of those who blame her for the Fall of Man. In other words too, Eve in Cixous's earlier works is no longer a passive reject; rather, Eve becomes an active reject, as she explicitly rejects God's authority, while affirming her own desires.

Any explicit project of active rejection tends to bestow upon one the image of a sovereign subject. It is not surprising then that both Sellars and Renshaw see in Cixous's earlier texts the emergence of a feminine subject.[189]

Granted that something like a *subject* might be in the process of (violently) supplementing Cixous's early writings, as she inscribes there a figure of thought that bears the force of active rejection against religion's God, I would like to point out that the more passive *reject* has been accompanying her thought nonetheless. This is evident in one of her later essays, as she reflects particularly on the state of women, animals, and writing: "Each one of us—the whole of mankind, irrespective of sexual difference—must deal with the feeling of things being *taken away* from us. What is interesting is that birds, writings, and many women are considered abominable, threatening, and are *rejected*, because others, the rejectors, feel something is taken away from them."[190] It could be said then that there remains in Cixous a consideration of passive *rejects*, a sense of their potentialities, or even perhaps a hint of an awareness of the critical importance to foreground them, in spite of the early anxiety to articulate the active *reject*, which tends to lead to the nascent formation of the *subject*. Here, I am interested in how animals, women, and writing, precisely as *rejects* that are more passive than active, that is, *rejects* that resist all becoming-*subjects*, are sustained in Cixous's later writings, and how they affect her continued engagement with religion there.

In that regard, the works that appeared in the 1990s become interesting sites of inquiry. I would argue that they, like the early writings, are no doubt "without religion's God." However, they cannot be said unequivocally to be "without religion." In fact, it can even be said—especially if one follows Verena Conley's observation, if not prophecy, that Cixous's works of the 1990s would bear "messianic tones"[191]—that the point of view there takes on a religious turn, a turn from "without religion" to *within* religion. Texts such as *Beethoven à jamais* (1993), *Messie* (1996), "Savoir" (1997/1998), and "Conversation avec l'âne" (1997) will indeed suggest a slight religious shift or conversion in Cixous's writing, as they trace a messianic trajectory rather than religious defiance.[192] To be sure, the conversion is *not* one that acquiesces or abdicates to "religion's God" or to dogmatic religion or religious dogmas. In the words of Cixous, there is "no Christian repentance."[193] Or, there is no nostalgic or regressive "return to the religious," of which Nancy warns us against; there is no "postsecular" turn in Cixous, if "postsecular" is misconstrued, according to Ratti, "as reinforcing Christianity, and as Christianity rediscovering itself."[194] In this particular conversion, Cixous's writing does not abandon the endeavor to undo, or go beyond, the masculine and prohibitive biblical law. That endeavor remains, except, unlike in the early works, there is no outright celebration of religious transgression, no explicit renunciation of religion, no open declaration of being "without religion." In other words, the active force of *rejection* against religion is played down in the works of the 1990s. A subtler strategy is adopted instead, which involves remaining *within* religion. This is because there is the realization—and the personages in Cixous's narratives would come to display this—that it is from within religion that one can more effectively sidestep or surpass the masculine, prohibitive biblical law and its apocalyptic effects. It is a strategy that perhaps recalls Derrida's endeavor to think beyond metaphysics in the 1967 essay, "La Structure, le signe et le jeu," where Derrida argues that "to have done with metaphysics, there is no sense in doing without the concepts of metaphysics," or that "the passage beyond philosophy does not consist in turning the page of philosophy [. . .] but to continue to read philosophers *in a certain manner*,"[195] a particular manner not bound by the need to absolutely negate or reject the thing that one seeks to go beyond. I argue that such a strategy is indeed deployed in Cixous's "messianic" works of the 1990s. They certainly do not seek to do "without religion," or to inscribe a radical "counter-Bible" as Cohen-Safir argues. Instead, they remain within the pages of the Bible, even within the pages where the Paternal Law is at work. In other words, just as Derrida does not turn the pages of metaphysics or philosophy, Cixous's "messianic" works do not turn the pages of religion either, but read them "in a certain manner," such that what can perhaps be called an *other* Bible—Cixous after all speaks of an "other book" [*autre livre*], if not "the Bible that is mine" [*la Bible à moi*][196]—unfolds from within those pages.[197]

Before going on, let me quickly say that I do not presume the term "religion" to be unproblematic in Cixous. I recognize that "religion" is an equivocal, if not difficult, terrain in Cixous's works in general. In fact, she herself will say: "The word *religion* doesn't work, I don't know how it's said."[198] I do not seek to accomplish the monumental task of defining "religion" in Cixous here. My aim here is less ambitious: I only want to highlight in this section the apparent shift from being "without religion and without religion's God" in Cixous's early works to something like being "without religion's God" but now remaining *within* religion in the works of the 1990s. This shift involves playing down the second turn of the active *reject*, that is, the forceful rejection of religion and of religion's God, while foregrounding the third turn of the *auto-reject*, which in turn sees to a following of the animal-*reject*. In other words, it is the move from the *auto-reject* to the animal-*reject* in Cixous's "messianic" works that enables Cixous to be "without religion's God" while remaining *within* religion, or which allows an *other* Bible to unfold. Now, if this *other* Bible is still to be "without religion's God," sidestepping the prohibitions and apocalyptic effects of biblical law, yet not "without religion" per se, it would need to be structured around a particular point of view. It would need a point of view radically different from those that have determined every authoritative (and masculine) reading of the Bible, but which nevertheless remains *within* religion's Genesis. Evidently then, and this is what the "messianic" texts of Cixous will suggest, the unfolding of an *other* Bible cannot be hinged on any anthropocentric or anthropomorphic point of view, not even on the "resolutely humanistic and feminine perspective" of the earlier works as Cohen-Safir has noted. Instead, it must follow an animal point of view.

An animal point of view can be considered to be *within* religion and "without religion's God" at the same time. This is because, on the one hand, it is a point of view that accompanies the human at the moment of his and her transgression of religious law, and one may therefore regard it as treading on the edge of the desire to be "without religion's God." On the other hand, it remains free from the malediction of the knowledge of shame of nakedness, which inflicts the human after his transgression of religious law. One keeps in mind that animals, in the Genesis story, were never given the commandment to not eat from the Tree of Knowledge in the first place; whether the human eats from the Tree of Knowledge or not, the animal is that which never knows the divine damnation of "religion's God," never knowing shame nor knowing how to have shame.[199] In other words, the animal point of view is indifferent to that *death by knowledge* from which Adam and Eve suffer after eating from the Tree of Knowledge. In that case, the animal point of view sidesteps both divine prohibitions and the damning consequences when divine commandments are transgressed, and one could say that the animal point of view is always *within* religion and never outside it.

The animal point of view can be further said to be *within* religion in the sense that even though the animal follows the human in his and her subsequent Fall from Eden, it has never in effect been banished from Paradise.

Perhaps the animal has never known the loss of Paradise then, but remains to keep sight of it. Without this sense of loss, an *other* Bible with an animal point of view may even be said to be free from a certain work of mourning that bears on the human point of view. Having eaten from the Tree of Knowledge, death by knowledge of shame and nakedness is what human vision sees, or what his or her eyes are opened to. In other words, so long as the human sees, every living moment is a work of mourning with regard to that death by knowledge. To exacerbate the problem of human vision, one notes from Genesis 3 that the human, after his or her eyes are opened, does not, however, see everything, despite his or her vision of good and evil, a vision that places the human in a parallel position with the godly. According to the narrative of Genesis 3, there remains a blinding effect to this human vision, which comes from humans' anxiety to conceal themselves from God, as if wanting to blind themselves from the presence of God.[200] In that sense, humans have opened their eyes only to lose sight of divine presence. The animal, by contrast, not only has no cause to mourn for any death by knowledge of shame, but has never needed to blind itself to divine presence either, and hence also no cause to mourn for the lost vision of divine presence. The animal point of view, therefore, with regard to the question of religion or even the "postsecular," is essentially indifferent to the human work of mourning, and an *other* Bible with an animal point of view will be one that is done with mourning the Fall of Man, the loss of sight of God or the divine, the loss of Eden, and the damnation of Eve. In that respect, one may also postulate that in this *other* Bible, there is no longer an Eve who defends and lays claim to her right to desire knowledge. Neither is there an Eve who justifies her eating from the Tree of Knowledge as an ultimately creative act that paves the way for humankind's wondrous discovery of knowledge. There is also no longer the desire to construct another Garden of Eden, as is the case with *Le Vrai jardin* (1971), in explicit opposition to the Garden of Eden in Genesis. In place of Eve the active *reject*, as is the case of Cixous's early works, can we thence speak of Eve the *auto-reject*, Eve who relinquishes her disposition as a rebel against religion, or as an affront to religious doctrines and judgments? Or, can we even be more radical to say that in the "messianic works of the 1990s," which put in effect a shift toward an animal point of view, which is also to say an auto-rejection of all anthropocentrism and anthropomorphism, there is no longer any need for an anthropologic Eve? Supposing there is an auto-rejection in Eve, if not an auto-rejection of Eve, it is important to reiterate that there is no supplication to any return to the original garden here, as if remorseful for one's previous rebellious or transgressive gestures. One keeps in mind that with Cixous, there is "no Christian repentance." But to get back to the animal point of view: free from the preoccupation with the human work of mourning, the animal might even be said to veritably inhabit every instant of living. Every instant for the animal is a moment of intense living, going into the very heart of living or the interiority of life. As such, this *other* Bible might even accomplish Cixous's project of writing without mourning, as articulated in her essay "De la scène de l'Inconscient à la scène de l'Histoire" (1987), where she declares her wish "to arrive at an epoch where one will write not to mourn the past, but to become the prophet of the present."[201]

In any case, an animal point of view would play a critical role in the unfolding or inscription of an *other* Bible that remains within religion but is "without religion's God" and without mourning. Unfortunately, the animal point of view, as Cixous notes, is not something valued but oftentimes ignored or forgotten. In *Messie* and "Conversation avec l'âne," Cixous observes that the animal perspective has hardly been taken into account by the Bible. Instead, it is always abandoned at the margins, as the narratives proceed to make manifest divine law and power and to underscore male obeisance to divine commandment.[202] Animals, in the Bible, are more or less *rejects*. Nevertheless, in order to allow an *other* Bible to unfold, one must follow the animal-*reject*: one must write with, or toward, an animal point of view, rather than to marginalize or denigrate it. That is what Cixous's "messianic" texts do. The question that remains is how Cixous's texts arrive at that animal point of view. Among the "messianic" texts of the 1990s, "Conversation avec l'âne," in my view, provides comprehensive steps toward such a point of view. To elucidate those steps, which are no less steps of auto-rejection, I propose then a close reading of "Conversation."

BLINDNESS, OR THE REJECTION OF HUMAN VISION

> What I love is: the proximity of the invisible.
> —HÉLÈNE CIXOUS[203]

An animal point of view is not an immediate given. As "Conversation" demonstrates, the passage toward an animal point of view, which is also the passage toward an *other* Bible, first requires the rejection of human vision, and that is precisely what "Conversation" puts to work before it moves into, or attains, an animal point of view.[204] I have suggested above that human vision after the Fall can be read as an unending work of mourning, and so, it is perhaps not surprising that one finds in a text such as "Conversation" a move to reject human vision in order to interrupt such a work, if not to have done with it, and hence arrive at a writing free of any burden of mourning. However, the rejection of sight, at first glance, seems to contradict the beginning of "Conversation," which opens with an apparent jubilation of recovering from a myopic malediction. The experience of gaining uninterrupted vision in fact parallels the narrative of Cixous's "Savoir," which is precisely about being able to see with the naked eye following a laser surgery to rectify a myopic condition, and the jubilant proclamation to see in "Conversation" is even executed in a rhetoric of unveiling similar to that deployed in "Savoir": "I lift the visor from my eyes, I turn my naked eyes towards the world. And I see. I am seeing! With the naked eye, and this is exaltation itself. I pass from non-seeing to seeing-the-world" (82). As in "Savoir," too, the sensation of seeing the world with the naked eye in "Conversation" is likened to receiving a miraculous gift.[205] Yet, this gift seems to be ultimately refused. This is because, even though one has gained the ability to see with the naked eye, the myopic condition remains to be articulated in the present, as if the ability to see with the naked eye is at the end of it all renounced, or even disdained: shortly after the beginning of "Conversation," the narrator writes, "By misfortune or secret chance I *am* [my emphasis] born very myopic," and that "before being a woman I *am* [my emphasis] myopic" (81). In other words, if "Conversation" is written, as is the case of "Savoir," after the surgical operation to correct the myopic condition, given the passage of exalted seeing that echoes "Savoir," myopia seems to be affirmed and reinstated instead, at the end of it all. This is reinforced indeed toward the conclusion of "Conversation," where the narrator calls for the removal of any shame in inscribing bespectacled or myopic literary heroes, no matter how ridiculous that image may seem. In other words, by the end of "Conversation," the text's opening passage of exalted seeing is undoubtedly problematized, as the text inclines toward nonseeing, if not blindness, rather than vision.

The rejection of human vision goes further than simply sidestepping or merely renouncing the work of mourning that post-Fall human vision bears. It in fact plays a critical role in the commencement of *writing* an *other* Bible, and in order to "see" that, it is necessary to return to the passage of exalted seeing. That passage ends with the narrator stating that vision is a gift given to her by the world. What follows is a space, or gap, in the text. As I read it, this spacing is deliberate, or strategically placed, as if to suggest that there is nothing more to be said or written with the return of sight, as if the narrator has no desire to say or write anything else after possessing vision. If this spacing seems to suggest an implicit disdain for seeing, this hypothesis can be confirmed by the passage that follows the spacing, which begins, "Now I write" (83). It is important to note that in this writing, vision is not at work, for an earlier passage in "Conversation" will have already stated that when the narrator writes, writing takes place *not* in the realm of sight or vision, but in darkness or in the blindness of night. According to the narrator, "I write the night. I write: the Night" [*J'écris la nuit. J'écris: la Nuit*] (80). There is barely any visibility in this night, given the distinction the narrator draws between this night and the light of day. She turns to night because, according to her, the immediacy of the world brought about by seeing in the light of day—a light that swarms vision with a hurtling "appearance-ing" [*l'apparitionnement*] or "abrupt appearance" [*brusque apparition*][206] according to "Savoir"—only interrupts and obstructs writing. Under the capture [*captation*] of such immediacy in the world of sight, writing becomes impossible. As it is said at the beginning of "Conversation," daylight vision blinds instead, and there is no knowledge to be gained from such an illuminated world, and hence there is nothing to write about under such optical condition:

> What we call day prevents me from seeing. The solar day [*le jour solaire*] blinds me to the visionary day. The glaring day prevents me from hearing [*entendre*].[207] From seeing-hearing [*voirentendre*]. From hearing myself [*m'entendre*]. With me. With you. With the mysteries.
>
> For me to go towards writing, I must escape from the broad daylight that catches (me by) my eyes [*j'échappe au gros jour qui me prend (par) les yeux*] and fills it with crude grand visions. I do not want to see what is shown. I want to see what is secret. What is hidden among the visible. I want to see the skin of light. (79)

Once again, whatever joy in seeing the world in "Conversation" is more or less renounced here. Instead, what is affirmed is to disappear from the light of day that enables vision, or to seek the unseen or "what is hidden among the visible." This seeking to see "what is hidden among the visible" can be compared to the notion of *l'invu* or the unseen in "Savoir." *L'Invu*, as the narrator in "Savoir" will slowly come to recognize, is the miracle given to the myopic, which is his or her creative privilege of seeing "the not yet" [*le pas encore*]: "There had never been the unseen. It was an invention."[208] She will also realize that she herself was an "unseen" in her previous myopic state, since her inability to see properly everything around her also entails an inability to see herself being seen by others. And she will understand that being an *invue* herself has in fact been a blissful condition: "Not seeing, she did not see herself being seen, this was her lightness of blindness that was given to her, the great freedom of the effacement of the self."[209] This is a clear contrast to the chaotic "war of faces" she confronts in the world when she sees with the naked eye after the laser surgery.[210] This yearning for *l'invu* or "the nostalgia of the secret nonseeing," which is also to say, the "unexpected mourning" for "her 'my-opia'" [*sa 'ma-myopie'*], suggests that in both "Savoir" and "Conversation," myopia, if not blindness, is the condition that one must affirm, especially with respect to writing, and not the attainment of vision.[211]

But to go back to the question of night in "Conversation": to write, one must not only "slip away from the world and from diurnal sociality" (79), but one must also slip into the night. One slips into this night by shutting one's eyes, and hence one can do this too in spite of the glaring day: "I close my eyes" (79), and "behind my eyelids I am elsewhere" (80). That is how writing begins, not with vision but with blindness: "I write without seeing that I am writing and what I write" (99). The desire for blindness will be further affirmed when the narrator even regrets that myopia is not adequate to the blindness of the night of writing: "myopia is not sufficient to make night" (81). Thus, when the narrator begins again to say that writing resumes after the passage of exalted seeing, it will not be writing with vision but "writing blind" [*écrire aveugle*], to follow the subtitle of "Conversation." "Now she writes," the narrator says, and "in my *dark* [my emphasis] interior softness, the rapid steps of a book that arrives imprint themselves" (83).

WRITING THE PASSAGE OF INSTANTS, OR WRITING BEYOND MOURNING

But what takes place in the process of writing that proceeds in the night or in the blindness of night, such that an *other* Bible, "without religion's God"

The Reject and the "Postsecular," or Who's Afraid of Religion   147

and beyond mourning, begins to imprint itself? According to the narrator, writing in this case passes into the very interior of the body of words,[212] tracing the birth of words at the very moment of their genesis as they are engendered by other words of an existing phrase. This will be a writing that inscribes the temporal "before" or *l'avant* before things manifest themselves. As the narrator says in "Conversation," "I want to write, *before*, at a time still in fusion before the frozen time of the narrative" [*je veux écrire, avant, au temps encore en fusion d'avant le temps refroidi du récit*] (84). In this case, "I write the genesis that befalls [*survient*] before [*avant*] the author" (86). To ensure that this *avant* is not a nostalgic investment in the past, for example, a seeking to return to the moment before the Fall, the text will quickly state that a certain instantaneity or now-ness instead is at stake in this *avant*. This becomes clear when "Conversation" states that writing the "before" is also a question of living, as it "takes place like life arriving to us" (86), whereby one needs "to grasp [*prendre*] the living instant with the closest and most delicate words" (93). The sense of urgency in needing to take hold of the living instant in the "before" or *l'avant* of "Conversation" resonates no doubt with the myopic experience of the "not yet" or the "pas encore" in "Savoir." The latter is a mode of seeing where "everything is perhaps," but it is precisely because of that "perhaps" that living becomes more intense or urgent: with regard to living as a myopic, the narrator in "Savoir" would say that "to live was in a state of alert."[213] That "state of alert" is surely no less called for in writing the *avant* in "Conversation." Writing in this manner would after all also mean to write with a certain speed—"I write to touch the body of the instant with the ends of words" (94),[214] and it is "all now" (85), with no time for knowledge acquisition: "This is an attempt [*essai*] to write down what goes quicker than my consciousness and my hand. But—the passage, by chance, leaves traces. One must act quickly. And no time to learn" (88). There is no time to master the knowledge transpiring at any passing instant—"I do not order, I do not conceptualize, I pursue what has overtaken me" (88).

Inscribing such instants, however, is a delicate, if not paradoxical, negotiation. That is because these instants cannot be inscribed with an immediacy that recalls the violent immediacy that characterizes vision or seeing-with-the-naked-eye. Rather, it is a question of inscribing a passage, the passage of one instant unfolding onto another. Specifically, it is the inscription of the passage "between night and day" (82) at the moment when one writes in the darkness or blindness of night. In the context of the beginning of "Conversation," this passage is experienced precisely in a state of myopia, and myopia, as one understands from "Savoir," is no less an experience of a passage, akin to "swimming across the channel between the blind continent and the seeing continent."[215] Vision, or seeing with the naked eye, by contrast, lacks this sense of passage. Vision, as noted earlier from "Savoir," implies instead an "abrupt appearance," and so seeing in "Conversation" is never associated with the word passage. The closest it gets—and this is speaking strictly in orthographic terms only—is *paysage* (83), which is landscape, and does not suggest any sense of passage.[216] For the narrator of "Conversation," however, "What is important to me is not appearance, it is the passage. I like the word Passage. All the words of passage or passing [*passe*], all the passing and traversing words [*les mots passants et passeurs*]" (81). Devoid of any sense of passage, seeing serves little to grasp the unfolding of one instant into another: it does not help writing move toward an animal point of view, not helping writing therefore to pass into an *other* Bible.

According to "Conversation," a mode of writing that inscribes a passage, particularly the passage of unfolding instants, following the renunciation of human vision and knowledge, is critical in bringing one closer to a writing that is done with mourning (and hence closer to an *other* Bible). In "Conversation," to be done with mourning is after all to accept the fact that everything is passage, or that everything passes (on)—or, as I would put it, everything is *auto-rejection*, and that there is no future, no new instant without the passing of a previous one: "What just arrived will perish. Strange and exalting meeting of the living [*le vif*] and its end. One advances in leaving behind oneself. Human destiny: to be of the flesh of forgetfulness [*être de la chair à oubli*]" (93). Once that fact is accepted, the "combat with mourning" (93) can begin, and one can begin anew without the past (for example, the Fall, the damnation of Eve, the loss of Eden, and so on) haunting or violently supplementing the present. That rebeginning is a question of letting go,[217] if not a question of forgetting: "One must forget in order to re-present oneself as virginal [*se re-présenter vierge*], to offer oneself as virginal [*s'offrir vierge*] to the new year" (93). Writing the passage, or writing without mourning, is then a question of writing that rejects holding on to things obsessively: "I do not write to keep" (93).[218] As hinted in "Conversation," this will require something other than human spirit: writing beyond the work of mourning must be taken up outside of "human destiny."

ANIMOTS

True to going outside of "human destiny," "Conversation" looks to the animal condition to facilitate writing the passage, and that is why "Conversation" in general can be said to be preoccupied with sliding into an animal perspective. The turn to the animal is irrefutable at the moment prior to, or "before," the text's insistence on approaching the passage by not tarrying with a word, by not seeking "to learn" or "conceptualize" it, that is, where the narrator speaks of Abraham's donkey. In conventional wisdom, the donkey is hardly an intelligent animal. However, in "Conversation," both the donkey and its apparent ignorance are not to be slighted. Placing the image of a donkey before the passage on the insistence to not tarry with words in fact suggests that the animal, without the human desire to conceptually master or comprehend every word that arrives, *hears* [*entendre*] and *receives every* word. In other words, it is the animal condition of being apparently ignorant, of being without human learning and intelligence, that will precisely facilitate a writing that registers every word of every instant, facilitating writing's approach toward the passage. Such understanding of the animal is no doubt grasped by the narrator when she compares herself to a donkey, as she undertakes the writing of the passage: "I am only an ideal donkey, I bear and I hear, I admit it [*je l'avoue*], mine is a work of acceptation [*mon travail est d'acceptation*]" (85). To reiterate, in order to write the passage of the instant without stopping to learn or conceptualize, one must abandon the human condition and follow the animal, or pass into an animal point of view or condition. As the text says, "With the donkey, one goes immediately to the essential" (88). The critical proximity, if not nondistinction, between writing and the animal or animal condition can be further established in the following phrase, where the narrator writes, "I write on the donkey" [*J'écris sur l'âne*] (88). One recalls that the narrator, some moments before, had written with a similar syntactic structure: "I write on writing" [*J'écris sur écrire*] (86).

Writing the passage, which is also a writing from which an *other* Bible potentially unfolds, is also, to use a term from "Conversation,"[219] a matter of *animots*, which Eric Prenowitz translates as "animal-words." It is a matter of following or chasing after the animal, of assuming an animal perspective. Or else, to use a word akin to the word "passage," it is a matter of *smuggling* oneself into an animal point of view or condition, and I note here that the word *passeur*, one of the "passage" words or *les mots passants et passeurs* that the narrator likes, can also have the sense of a smuggler or smuggling.[220] The book that entails from such a *passeur* or smuggling, according to "Conversation," is furthermore not only "an anarchic thing" but also "an untamed animal" (100). It is also in view of that smuggling or *passeur* that the narrator, in response to her own question as to "how does a book arrive," will say, "like a cat" (103). At this point, the rejection of human sight in the writing of an *other* Bible is not at all forgotten, for these *animots* are inscribed under the cloak of nocturnal or myopic blindness. As the narrator says, "When I am in pursuit of a thought that runs away before me like a wonderful game [*gibier*], my eyes no longer see" (80). Vice versa, the experience of writing in blindness or darkness is no less an animal condition: it is an experience, according to the narrator, that takes place "barely at the break of dawn [. . .] still on all fours" (82).

With *animots*, that is to say, with the rejection of human sight and human *savoir*, and with the passage toward the passing moments where words are engendered, one can perhaps finally speak more affirmatively of a mode of writing from which an *other* Bible that is beyond or done with mourning unfolds. I stress again that this *other* Bible remains within the pages of the religious Bible; elements of the latter, like the Fall, are neither repressed nor denied here. With regard to the Fall, the narrator in "Conversation" does not fail to write that she has been "driven out of paradise" (104). In other words, we are still dealing with some form of a *reject* here, very likely one that bears traces of that Eve who was banished from the Garden of Eden. Yet, the Fall is accepted almost indifferently, without bitterness, guilt, or remorse. Instead, with respect to the Fall, it will be met with joy or even *jouissance* (85). But I argue that there can be such indifference or *jouissance* only because one has smuggled oneself from the human subject to the animal point of view, which does not see what humans see, does not know what humans know, and therefore does not mourn that *death by human knowledge*. Simply put, one must *auto-reject* one's anthropocentrism and/or anthropomorphism, so that one can first approach the animal and then attain that indifference and *jouissance*. This point is no doubt well-grasped by the narrator, which perhaps explains the smuggling into an animal condition right at the beginning of "Conversation." I bring to mind again that writing there is a question of writing in the realm of night, of writing with eyes shut, with myopia, or which in short rejects human vision. I now add the observation of something like a Fall that accompanies this rejection of human sight there, although it is not a Fall that seeks to play out the biblical Fall, which could serve to expiate the latter, but one that is a passage toward the animal condition: "When I close my eyes, the passage is opened, the dark gorge, I descend. Or rather it [the passage] descends: I trust myself to the primitive space, I do not resist the forces that overwhelms me. *There is no more gender* [my emphasis] [*Il n'y a plus de genre*]. I become a thing with raised ears" (80). Having already mentioned the donkey in "Conversation," it is not without reason to say that the "thing with raised ears" that one becomes in this Fall is in the image of that animal.[221] But to explicate how the animal condition opens the way toward an *other* Bible where the Fall is received and accepted with indifference or *jouissance*, it is necessary to explicate the phrase *il n'y a plus de genre.*

I have translated *il n'y a plus de genre* as *there is no more gender.* Certainly, *genre* can be translated as "genus," or "genre" in the sense associated with types of writing such as the essay genre or the genre of the novel. The French *genre* can also mean *gender* though, and I tend to see it as the case here. I would argue that *gender* here also refers to *human gender* or sexual difference, or if one prefers, the *genre* of gender difference that befalls and afflicts humans in Genesis after eating from the Tree of Knowledge. I am certainly not saying that the notion of gender does not exist for animals, but gender for animals surely does not bear the accompanying human vision and knowledge of shame when one animal sees another animal naked, or when one is seen naked by another animal. In short, gender in animals is not supplemented by the human knowledge of shame in the face of gender difference. In "Conversation," *il n'y a plus de genre* can be translated as no more (human) gender because a shift toward animal gender can be said to be occurring there, more specifically a shift that wants to renounce human gender difference. I proceed slowly to demonstrate this. I first note that the question of writing in "Conversation" is also a question of "receiving the message," the message that is of "paradisiacal nudity" and "without censure" (82). The narrator further elaborates that to receive that message, "one can only receive it nude [*nue*]. No, not undressed. The nudity of before all clothing [*La nudité d'avant tout vêtement*]" (82). Such that "Conversation" does not regress to a work of mourning sustained by a post-Fall human sense of shame, "paradisiacal nudity" cannot be nostalgic of human nakedness before the Fall. Cixous ensures this by saying that "paradisiacal nudity" is to be with "neither pride nor shame" (104). A "paradisiacal nudity" that is with "neither pride nor shame," that is to say, without the human pride of defying divine commandment to eat from the Tree of Knowledge, and without the sense of human shame that comes after that defiance,[222] is more an animal point of view rather than a human condition. "Paradisiacal nudity" therefore cannot be human nakedness here. Instead, it inclines toward animal nakedness where a human perspective of gender does not come into play. It is only as animal nakedness, or via an animal perspective, that "paradisiacal nudity" can participate freely—"knowing neither limit nor hesitation" (82)—in the *jouissance* guided by a "law of life," which enables an "erotic and fertile genius" to see to the "couplings," "hybridizations," or "crossings" of words (96). In this *jouissance*, there is no more human shame of nakedness, no more mourning for the Fall through the human knowledge of shame and nakedness. To be sure that this *other* garden of "paradisiacal nudity" is strictly of animal nakedness and perspective,[223] the Adamic or human act of naming will not be at work here.[224] In this *other* garden or *other* Bible, only words are received, in the way animals, such as the animals that accompany humans in the Bible, receive every word that is said, muttered, and even unsaid. Here, there will only be the witnessing of the birth of words, witnessing every living instant of the birth of every word.

Jouissance in "Conversation," which is without the denial or bitterness of the biblical Fall of Man, and which immerses itself in the instants of living by not seeking to conceptualize or retain what passes, might seem to echo what Cixous has called "second innocence" in one of her seminars given in the 1980s.[225] According to Cixous there, "second innocence" has nothing to do with that "pregiven [and] paradisiacal" Edenic innocence.[226] In other words, it does not yearn to regain or return to the latter. It keeps the biblical Fall well in mind, but, at the same time, it also understands that if the guilt inherited from that Fall is pursued to its extreme limit, that is to say, by developing a discourse that incessantly plays out this guilt, by projecting it ad infinitum, there will reach a point where this guilt becomes almost meaningless and is transformed into innocence. As Cixous puts it,

"At the end of infinite guilt, one can become innocent."[227] One must therefore work toward this "second innocence": it is "to be earned" and "should
be our goal, our ambition."[228] This work, however, is nothing but a question
of living, a living that is "a very delicate movement of detachment" where
"we know something but we do not hold on to it."[229] In other words, it is a
question of living that does not hold on to any particular knowledge, especially that knowledge of shame or guilt. Such living is also called "grace"
in Cixous's terms, and it is through such grace that one achieves "second
innocence," since, according to Cixous, "second innocence is precisely the
grace one gives to oneself."[230]

As will be seen later, there is also something of grace in *jouissance* in
"Conversation," which further gives the impression of its close proximity to
"second innocence." However, I am inclined to think that that *jouissance* is
more, if not less, than the "second innocence" that Cixous speaks of in her
seminar. As I have been arguing, Cixous's "messianic" works of the 1990s
such as "Conversation" move away from outright religious defiance and
make a turn toward being within religion. *Jouissance* in "Conversation"
involves such a turn. "Second innocence," however, is consistent with the
trajectories of Cixous's works before the 1990s in relation to the question of
religion, which means that it retains a tinge of religious contestation. The
resistance to Man's condemnation through the biblical Fall is almost evident when Cixous writes, "We are not free falling because we do not *want*
to fall."[231] Also, the quest for "second innocence," which deploys no doubt a
rhetoric that advocates "feminine curiosity,"[232] since it is predicated on Clarice Lispector's notion of "wanting" or "thirst,"[233] seems to be another rebellious celebration of Eve as the creative seeker of knowledge. In that case, the
perspective of "second innocence" still belongs very much to the "humanistic and feminine" perspective adopted or projected in Cixous's earlier works.
That undoubtedly anthropocentric "humanistic and feminine" perspective
is further enforced as Cixous also makes a distinction between humans and
animals in this "second innocence." Through a reading of Heinrich von
Kleist's "Marionette Theater," particularly with reference to the figure of the
bear there, Cixous makes a marked separation between humans and animals, stating that animals continue to possess a "status of purity" while post-
Fall humans have lost theirs.[234] *Jouissance* in "Conversation," however, does
not, as discussed, make that demarcation between humans and animals. In
fact, for there to be a veritable indifference to the biblical Fall, and for there to

be *jouissance* in "Conversation," there is, as shown, a smuggling of oneself to the animal point of view. With this passage to the animal condition, it would also seem that one leaves the terrain of an anthropocentric and/or anthropomorphic "second innocence" and enters perhaps what may be called instead a "third innocence," an innocence not only not foreign to the animal but also does not delineate animals from humans.

FROM *JOUISSANCE* TO *MESSIANICITÉ SANS MESSIANISME*

The *jouissance* of experiencing the passage where every engendered word is received, that is, the *jouissance* of writing in "paradisiacal nudity" without shame and therefore beyond mourning that *death by human savoir*, may be articulated as the passion of the animal.[235] Passion, according to Derrida in *Demeure*, is not only "the experience of love," but also "witnessing" or "testimony" [*témoignage*].[236] Derrida's understanding of "passion" can be applied to the animal condition in "Conversation," since love and complete receiving or acceptation (of the engendering of words)—and therefore testimony too—are at play with regard to the animal there. One example of the passion of the animal in terms of bearing witness in "Conversation," mentioned before in the section on Derrida, is perhaps the untold dialogue Cixous believes to take place between Abraham and his donkey on their way up to Mount Moriah. It would be the dialogue in which, one might assume, Abraham confides in his donkey of his despair at obeying God's commandment to put Isaac up for sacrifice, the dialogue without which, Cixous believes, the journey would be unbearably "infernal" (87). In terms of the loving passion of the animal in "Conversation," there is no less the loving touch between the narrator and her cat. This touch does more than establish a physical connection between them, for the touch or passion of the cat is in fact instrumental in giving the narrator access to "touch the body of the instant" in her writing of the passage. The latter is after all preceded by a passage on the touch of an animal: "I touch the soft and wild touch of my cat, my female cat [*ma chatte*], my female cat that I follow and am [*la chatte dont je suis la chatte*], and nothing of appropriation between us except moments of grace, without guarantee, without security, without a glance [*sans regard*] thrown to the following moment" (84–85).[237]

With regard to the word *passion*, I do not ignore the fact that it has borne overtly religious senses in the history of its usage. With that in mind, and having stated that "Conversation" is traced by a passion of the animal, perhaps the discussion can return to the question of whether "Conversation" is "without religion and without religion's God." At first glance, "religion's God" still seems to figure in "Conversation," especially when the narrator says, "I have never written without God" (101). Yet, it has to be noted that when the narrator speaks about God, she is not speaking about God per se but "the word *God*" [*le mot* Dieu] (100). From this marked distinction between word and concept or thing, perhaps it is not difficult to discern a distancing from "religion's God," a distancing that manifests itself further when the narrator lets reverberate the word(s) *d'yeux* ["of eyes"], which is homophonic to *Dieu* ["God"], in the proximity of the latter: "Le mot *Dieu*: le mot d'yeux"—"The word *God*: the word of eyes" (100). Things regarding eyes that see are generally renounced in "Conversation," and so if God is the word of eyes, it will not be surprising that "religion's God" is similarly set up only to be undone.[238] The renunciation of "religion's God" in "Conversation" in fact takes place quickly when the narrator proclaims that "God is not that of religions" (100). Instead, God is but a word or another word in the process or passage of writing, a word that articulates and temporarily provides hospitality to all the future words that will arrive: "God is the name of everything that has not yet been said," and "the word God [functions] to give lodging to the infinite multiplicity of everything that would be said" (101). Further, not only will God in "Conversation" be "not the Father" (as Charlotte Berkowitz has noted), but even the monotheistic dimension of "religion's [Christian] God" will be done away with, as the narrator goes on to say that the unfolding of an *other* Bible will reveal that there are *gods* rather than a single god: "This page writes itself [*s'écrit*] all by itself, this is the proof of the existence of *gods* [my emphasis]" (100).

That "Conversation" is "without religion's God" can be established then. But is it absolutely "without religion"? I bring to mind that I have suggested that an *other* Bible is not inscribed outside of religion's Bible, but within it. The endeavor to create an outside does not lead one beyond the work of mourning. Instead, with the outside, there is in fact *no* "forgetting" or no letting-go of the trauma suffered on the other side of the boundaries of the outside: the outside itself will always mark the work of mourning with regard to that trauma. (I also bring to mind again Derrida's point that to get beyond metaphysics is not to do without metaphysics but to remain within it and (re)read it "in a certain manner.")

In my reading of "Conversation" above, I have tried to demonstrate that to get round the problem of the outside is to smuggle or slide into an animal point of view or condition. Now, the animal may be considered to be "without religion," since, receiving no injunction against eating from the Tree of Knowledge, it was never subject to divine law and commandment, and hence it is beyond religion in this sense. However, in another sense, the animal is not absolutely outside of religion, for it has never been in fact banished from Eden, and therefore remains within religion. The animal, then, occupies an equivocal region where all the turns of being without religion *and* being within religion are at play. It occupies the limit, the frontier, the passage between within-religion and without-religion, or better, the point where one is beyond (and not outside) religion but remains within religion. Perhaps Derrida's notion of "messianicity without messianism" may be useful to better express this animal perspective or condition of being beyond/within religion. I have discussed "messiancity without messianism" in the section on Derrida, and I reiterate here that "messiancity without messianism," according to Derrida in *Spectres de Marx*, is a question of allowing the future to arrive in its full surprise as a true event, in other words, a condition that does not exclude opening oneself to the complete risk of what arrives from the future.[239] In a way, this "emancipatory [*émancipatoire*] affirmation"[240] can also be said to be an intense living-in-the-instant, akin to Cixous's notion of a passage, because it does not cast any headlong vision in order to anticipate what is to come. Derrida will argue that such a "structure of experience" is a secular one, "a certain experience of the promise that one can attempt to liberate from all dogmatic and even metaphysical-religious determination, from all *messianism*."[241] For that reason, Derrida chooses to underscore the adjective "*messianic*, [. . .] rather than *messianism*, in order to designate a structure of experience rather than a religion."[242] However, Derrida makes clear that this "messianicity without messianism," despite being without, or beyond, religion, does not absolutely exclude the religious. As Derrida argues, the religious, along with the messianic, will form the "injunction" for us to affirm and respond to the emancipatory "messianic spirit."[243] The critical point is to not let "messianicity without messianism" be guided or (pre)determined by any religious figure or commandment. It is only in that sense that "messiancity without messianism" is "without religion," or as Derrida says in *Foi et savoir*, that "in itself, [messianicity without messianism] does not belong to any Abrahamic religion," or that it is "older than every religion."[244]

Such "messianicity without messianism" presents itself in "Conversation." There is after all no lack of a messianic force in inscribing the passage that welcomes the "infinite multiplicity" of instants to-come. Accompanying the narrator is "the *always unforeseen Messiah*," which she avows to be "the force that makes me write" (101). Like Derrida's "messianicity without messianism," which detaches itself from all appurtenances to any religion, the messianic force in "Conversation" cannot be identified with a religious messiah or religious messianism. The narrator in "Conversation" refers to "the always unforeseen Messiah" as "you" (101), a "you" that comes and goes freely and that leaves the narrator no certitude as to whether it will return or not, but nonetheless gives the narrator an unwavering belief that it will. This "you," unlike all religious messiahs or messianism, is not a human messiah, though. Instead, this "you" points to an animal, if not a cat, to be specific. This postulation of a messianic cat in "Conversation" can be derived via a reference to Cixous's *Messie* (1996). The messianic figure in *Messie* is none other than a cat, which the narrator there will say not only accompanies the trajectory of the text but also the characters in the text. This cat nonetheless remains free to come and go as it wishes, but always returns miraculously. Such characterization of the messianic cat in *Messie* surely foreshadows the description of the messianic "you" in "Conversation," and therefore brings the two messianic figures into an uncanny proximity, not to mention that the narrator in *Messie* also addresses the cat as "you." The messianic "you" in "Conversation" is no less a cat than the messianic cat in *Messie* then. And if the messianic cat in *Messie* is always that which leads one to the future, the cat in "Conversation" plays a similar critical role: it is with the "female cat" that "moments of grace, without guarantee, without security, without a glance thrown to the following moment" arise. Such rhetoric, which resonates rather clearly with the Derridean rhetoric of the "to-come" or the "eventness" of the future, surely places the "female cat" in "Conversation" (and *Messie*) within Derrida's "messianicity without messianism" in terms of its "structure of experience," which, being absolutely invested in the instant, allows the future to arrive in its "absolute surprise."[245] In this case, it would even seem that "Conversation" (and *Messie*), more than the works of Derrida perhaps, demonstrate how one succeeds, by recognizing the messianic force in the passion of the animal or in an animal condition or perspective, in approaching that "messianicity without messianism" where there "would be the opening to the to-come [*l'avenir*] [. . .] without prophetic prefiguration."[246]

The "messianicity without messianism" in "Conversation," borne by the passion of the animal, or by the animal point of view or condition, then consolidates the unfolding of an *other* Bible that is "without religion's God," without mourning, and without appurtenance to any religion, while not needing to be outside of religion. I would now like to conclude the discussion on Cixous by returning to the question of the "postsecular." To reiterate, "postsecular" thought, while still lacking definition, can be described as the attempt to recognize the trace of the religious in our contemporary world, despite our belief that we have been living through secular times. I have also suggested that there can be a future "postsecular" thought too that acknowledges the rise of local religions without laying claim to any existing dominant or primary religion (for example, Christianity) to which those religions must defer. This future "postsecular" thought can be said to have similar horizons to those of Cixous's "messianic" *other* Bible. I have also said that "postsecular" thought at present remains largely anthropocentric and anthropomorphic, which risks privileging, or inclining toward, the perspective of a certain group of people or human community. Actual "postsecular" violence, such as the militant assertion of a local religion in opposition to its being appropriated or homogenized by a dominant religion, has already shown us the precarious outcome of such anthropocentric or anthropomorphic "postsecularism." If "postsecular" thought is to be sincere in welcoming the articulations of a multiplicity of religions where no one religion dominates another, it should take a page from Cixous's "messianic" texts. In other words, it would be in need of an *other* Bible similar to that which unfolds in Cixous's "messianic" works: it is in need of an *other* Bible that opens a space of thought not predicated on any religion, on any religious law or dogma, or on any prohibitive law of any "religion's God." Such an *other* Bible for "postsecular" thought can be attainable not by a limited "humanistic and feminine" perspective. It needs a turn—a turn that is no less the auto-rejection of anthropocentric or anthropomorphic vision, knowledge, and selfhood—toward the animal-*reject* (to keep in mind that animals are still largely marginalized or disregarded in religious and "postsecular" discourse), toward its point of view.

The Reject and the "Postsecular," or Who's Afraid of Religion 159

THE ANIMAL-(AUTO)-REJECT: BALAAM'S DONKEY

To conclude this entire section on the question of religion in contemporary French thought, I would like to turn, just as Cixous has done in "Conversation," to a donkey. I would like to *follow after*, to keep in mind Derrida's rhetoric, a donkey in the Bible. This donkey is not Abraham's donkey though, but Balaam's donkey in chapter 22 of Numbers in the Old Testament. Numbers 22 begins with Balak, king of Moab, finding his territory surrounded by the Israelites. Fearing that the latter will swarm his land, Balak summons Balaam, known to be successful in his blessings and curses, to curse the Israelites in order to keep them out of his land. Balaam did not agree immediately to the invitation to Moab, but said he would seek counsel with God first. God tells Balaam that the Israelites are blessed and that Balaam shall not curse them or go with Balak's messengers. Balaam heeds God's counsel and refuses the invitation. But the insistent Balak sends more messengers with more promises of greater honor to convince Balaam to take up the invitation. Balaam again seeks counsel with God, and this time, not without irony surely, God says go with the messengers if they call to him, but also "do only what [God] tell[s] [him] to do." God's irony being completely lost to Balaam, Balaam follows Balak's messengers and sets out on the journey to Moab on his donkey. Furious, God puts a sword-wielding angel before the path of Balaam and his donkey. Balaam does not see this angel, but his donkey does, which then swerves off the intended but now fatal path. Balaam strikes his donkey to get back onto the correct route, but this time the angel stands before them in a vineyard path with a wall on each side. The donkey crashes into one of the walls in order to escape the imminent wrath of the angel and in the process crushes Balaam's foot against the wall, consequently suffering Balaam's second wrath. The angel then appears where there is no longer any way to turn, so the donkey falls to the ground, landing on Balaam this time round. For the third time, then, Balaam strikes his donkey and cries out that if he had a sword he would kill it. God opens Balaam's eyes and now Balaam sees the deathly angel and knows he is wrong.

Many things can be said about this passage, for example the quasi-(auto)-sacrificial gesture of the donkey and perhaps especially the part where God gives voice to the donkey (which I omit above). However, what I would like to highlight here is that the donkey does *respond* in its way. It responds to the deathly angel standing before it and Balaam, responding in a way that Balaam is too stubborn, stupid, or *bête* to understand. In any case, Balaam's donkey responds in a way that preserves the respective lives of its own and Balaam's. (Contrary to what Heidegger would claim, Balaam's donkey knows what is to die.) In order to save itself and Balaam, in other words, to save differences—the difference of humans and the difference of animals, or to preserve the respective life-force of these differences—Balaam's donkey is willing to *auto-reject* itself, in the sense of willingly suffer Balaam's strikes, and is accepting of Balaam's treatment of it as a *reject* when Balaam claims to kill it were he in possession of a sword. For a future, less violent "postsecular" world where not only differences are affirmed and respected, but where life-forces of these differences are also maintained, perhaps it is this animal-(auto)-*reject* that will lead us there. As I have been trying to suggest throughout this section, perhaps it is the figure of the *reject*, particularly the *auto-reject* that renounces all anthropocentrism and anthropomorphism, that will help us follow after, in turn, that animal-(auto)-*reject*.

4

PROLEGOMENON TO REJECT POLITICS

From Voyous *to Becoming-Animal*

PLUS D'UNE DÉMOCRATIE

What deserves to be reiterated, with regard to unveiling and mobilizing the *reject* in contemporary French thought's rethinking of friendship, love, community, and religion, is that the affirmation of differences is at stake. One may go further to say that this affirmation is an affirmation of radical differences, if not a radical affirmation of radical differences, without this affirmation ever having the intention to assimilate any of those differences within its discursive space. Indeed, its objective cannot be the neutralizing or the taming of *rejects*. Put another way, a theory of the *reject* critiques or disagrees with *rejects* that express or project their differences at the cost of others. Affirmation here must leave *rejects* free to remain as *rejects* or *auto-rejects*, such as the "friend" who walks away and who might never return to any existing friendship, the lover who puts in suspension or syncope all existing love, or the other-Abraham or animal-messiah that prefers not to respond to any particular religious injunction. This is only how any affirmation is constantly a "dis-closing" [*déclosion*], constantly undoing all attempts to close the other—regardless if this other is a *reject* or not—in or within a homogenizing space or thought.

In the course of eliciting and affirming *rejects* or *auto-rejects* in contemporary French thought, the preceding chapters have also raised several notions that have political import, if not, are already political in themselves. An example is Deleuze and Guattari's nomadic war machine, which was discussed in the chapter on friendship, love, and community. The primary target of the nomadic war machine is typically not so much community, but the State, which has come to embody that which is absolutely organized, and from which hardly anyone can deviate or escape. Community comes under attack by the nomadic war machine only when it takes on such State-like striating structure. In that same chapter, love was subjected to a rethinking as well. Love can also have political potential, if we are to follow Hardt and Negri's argument in *Commonwealth*, where, according to them, love can be a force that ruptures the appropriating network of global capital. The love that Hardt and Negri speak of is not so much romantic love. Rather, it concerns "solidarity, care for others, creating community, and cooperating in common project," particularly within the multitude that is deprived of the riches of those who control, manage, and perpetuate the global capital Empire.[1] It is through these acts that spring forth a Spinozean joy, that is to say, an "increase of [their] power to act and think," which potentially "marks a rupture with what exists" and which sees to "the creation of the new."[2]

In speaking of "messiancity without messianism" in the chapter on the "postsecular," one is also no doubt in the proximity of political thought, especially when one refers not only to Derrida's *Foi et savoir* but also to his *Spectres de Marx*. As Derrida argues in *Spectres de Marx*, "messianicity without messianism" has everything to do with the thought of *démocratie à venir* or "democracy to come." One needs to be precise, however, to note that what is critical in the phrase *démocratie à venir*, as Derrida underscores in an earlier interview with Michael Sprinker, is not so much *démocratie* but the *à venir*.[3] The *à venir*, which is undeniably something of the future, is markedly different, however, from *the future* [*le futur*] according to Derrida. *The future* [*le futur*] for Derrida is something programmed, the arrival of which is most oftentimes already expected or anticipated and is always something of the order of the possible. In the eyes of Derrida, there is nothing of the event of *the future*, therefore. The promise of the event lies instead with the *à venir*, since it arrives in complete surprise, or rather in its complete surprise, as Nancy would say with greater precision, since he argues that the event is the surprise itself and vice versa.[4] Derrida will go on to explicate that what is at stake in the *à venir* is the arrival of the other: the other of which we have no, and will not have, knowledge, that is, the other that we were neither expecting nor anticipating. Derrida will also regard this other as *anyone*. That is to say, it does not matter *who* he or she is, or *what* it is: *anyone* is the one "before [its] metaphysical determination [. . .] in the subject, the human person, and consciousness, before all juridical determination in the similar [*le semblable*], the compatriot, fellow creature [*congénère*], brother, neighbor, fellow-believer [*coreligionnaire*] or citizen," or, more simply, the "anonymous 'anyone,'" "whoever," the "undetermined 'each one.'"[5] In a *démocratie à venir*, this other or *anyone* arrives without the need to identify himself, herself, or itself: there would be no such demand in exchange for hospitality within this space. As Derrida would have it, that would be the unconditional hospitality of *démocratie à venir*. That is to say too that in the space of *démocratie à venir*, the other or *anyone* has the *right to reject* disclosing himself, herself, or itself, and the right to reject all belonging, appurtenance, and subscription to any—if there are indeed any—community, ideology, and political inclination there. In that regard, there is always the chance that this other or *anyone* is nothing less than a *reject* to any existing communitarian construct or political configuration. Nonetheless, it is the ethical task of *démocratie à venir*, or it is within the ethical contour of its unconditional hospitality, to receive without question and prejudice this other-*anyone-reject*. One can say that *démocratie à venir*, in short, concerns more the *reject* than the *subject*.[6]

To be precise, *démocratie à venir* does not only receive the other-*anyone-reject* coming from the future; in a retroactive manner, it is also committed to open itself to the other-*anyone-reject* that has come before, but has been repressed, oppressed, silenced, eradicated, or made to be erased from memory by a previous or existing political regime or ideology. *Démocratie à venir* recalls these others who have been violently rejected; it allows their voices or traces to resurface, resound, and disseminate anew and into the future. According to Derrida in *Spectres de Marx*, this is the "hauntology" [*hantologie*] that underlies the "messiancity without messianism" of a *démocratie à venir*. To remain with one of the motivations behind the writing of *Spectres de Marx*, the "hauntology" of "messianicity without messianism" would also mean the chance for a different take on Marxism, not only one that has been marginalized or even discounted from the dominant and conventional mode of reading Marx, but also one that deviates from orthodox Marxism, if not practices a certain infidelity to Marx's writings. A "hauntology" must allow the exposition of this different take, and the different political trajectory that can be drawn from it.[7] This is why Derrida stresses that it is the *à venir* that is more important than *démocratie* in the phrase *démocratie à venir*. This is also why, for Derrida, democracy, in place of other modes of political practice, is written in simply because it is the better one at the moment: Derrida is prepared to abandon it when something better than democracy comes along.[8] In that respect, I would like to say that there is also a mechanism of *auto-rejection* in *démocratie à venir*: *démocratie à venir* does not hypostasize itself on any particular political thought, not even democracy, despite "democracy" being inscribed in the phrase itself. There is *no one* mode of thinking and practicing democracy on which *démocratie à venir* predicates itself. Rather, it is open to *more than one* mode of thinking and practice that *démocratie à venir* can assume. Given that there is *no one* form of democracy to which it adheres, but is open to *more than one* form, one can deploy the Derridean rhetoric to say that in *démocratie à venir* there is *plus d'une démocratie*. There is *plus d'une démocratie* because, according to Derrida, democracy is structured around autoimmunity,[9] which lets in something foreign and even potentially fatal within its internal organization, only in view of perpetuating itself beyond its own spatio-temporal context. In other words, autoimmunity, before being a calculated move undertaken by so-called democratic states, and perhaps even before it is properly of the biological sciences, is ethical in the sense that it concerns the affirmation of the other, since it involves a body opening itself up to what it would normally reject, at the same time putting in place, in a highly risky or even suicidal fashion, an *auto-rejection* within itself.

Affirmation, however, as Nancy tells us, is not political. It is philosophical, rather, and does not belong to the order of politics. Affirmation and politics are distinct, therefore, and are not to be confused with each other. This does not prevent politics from having any link to affirmation, though. According to Nancy, politics, which has to do with space or spatiality, can task itself to create a place [*lieu*] to maintain or guarantee the affirmation of the "dis-closing" of others or differences.[10] In Nancy's view, there can be a politics that foregrounds or gives place to the fact of every being existing and living alongside another (a politics that surely is not so distant from Derrida's "unconditional hospitality"). In that case, the place of politics must foremost be a place of openness, not a place of exclusion. It must be open to those who have been excluded by previous or existing political practices and ideologies. Having done this, the place of politics must not entail any holding on of all these beings within a particular space: it must not seek any fusion of all these beings into a communitarian unity, of which politics will manage or govern in a totalizing manner. In other words, politics here must acknowledge that relations between beings are always undergoing transformation, which includes involving some beings walking away from existing relations. Politics must accept such dynamics of dispersion and not force any rapprochement or reconciliation. It must maintain every being's liberty to free itself from any present relation and to form new ones beyond the determination of politics. Incidentally, that would also entail ensuring each being's liberty to free itself from the very place of politics.

Politics, in other words, must not violently supplement every space or delimit every being or thing within its determination and contours. Otherwise, as Nancy notes, one ends up with the fascist notion of "everything is politics/political."[11] When every space is captured by politics, or when politics begins to determine every space, demanding every being there to adhere to a certain political ideology, it is necessary, according to Blanchot, following Foucault's caution in *Surveiller et punir* (1975) that visibility is a trap, to think "the right to disappear" [*le droit de disparaître*].[12] Or, as Nancy has suggested, for a place of politics that is always open to the other or to radical differences, that is, a fluid place of politics that adjusts itself to transformations in relations between beings and that never founds, hypostasizes, or disseminates itself in an imperialistic manner as *the* place of affirmation, one must put in place a thought of politics without the *subject*. The place of politics that assures or affirms the "dis-closing" of radical differences must be wary of the *subject*—not so much the *subject* that develops a conscious certainty as to how he or she singularly determines his or her thought, action, and existence, but the *subject* that extends that certainty with a sovereign ambition, that is, the *subject* that decidedly positions his or her existence as the foundation of an exceptional worldview, to which all must accede and not resist.[13] The place of politics, Nancy argues, need not be occupied by such a Schmittian sovereign *subject*.[14] The renunciation of a sovereign *subject* does not equate to a renunciation of sovereignty, however. A minimum sovereignty remains, or must even remain, with politics. This is because a certain force, a certain power even, is required to effectively put in place a space of affirmation; with force or power, or even with the moment of affirmation, there is irreducibly sovereignty at work.[15] The question, then, for Nancy, is to articulate another sovereignty that sidesteps a Schmittian imperialist sovereignty: one can be "sovereign otherwise" [*autrement souverain*].[16] And since Schmittian sovereignty is largely predicated on a thinking of the *subject*, or, because the *subject* more often than not assumes some form of Schmittian sovereignty, perhaps the question of being "sovereign otherwise" must depart from any thinking of the *subject*. As I would argue, for this *other* sovereignty, if not for a place of politics that maintains the affirmation of "dis-closing" radical differences, the thinking of politics must be accompanied by the thought of the *reject*.

Before eliciting the *reject* from the political writings of contemporary French thought, particularly from those of Derrida and Deleuze, perhaps it can be said at the outset that politics in fact begins with the *reject* for most contemporary French thinkers (even though, I reiterate, they do not articulate it in that manner). This is even the case for Badiou who takes distance from Derrida, Deleuze, and Nancy and from the "poststructuralist" project concerning the "deconstruction" of the *subject*. The political event arrives, for Badiou, when the presence or force of those who have always been disregarded or denigrated by the existing ruling political regime as "inexistent"—or *rejects*, as I would put it—is no longer deniable. However, Badiou would disdain to allow the "inexistents" to remain as *rejects*. According to Badiou, once the force and presence of "inexistents" is undeniable or irresistible, which is to say, following the uprising that is the political event, the "inexistents" must also raise themselves from mere *rejects* to the status of *subjects* of that political event. As we have also seen in Badiou's theory of the *subject*, it is the *subject* that must remain faithful to that political event and do whatever it takes in order that the event and the "inexistents" can no longer be repressed or suppressed by the ruling political regime. In that regard, violence is oftentimes inevitable, if not critical, for Badiou's militant political *subject*. For Badiou, the uprisings of the masses in the Arab Spring of 2011 is a manifestation of such critical violence, a violence that he, in *Le Réveil de l'histoire* (2011), considers to be constitutive of "historical riots," in contrast to riots that do not change the course of things in the world but are only of frivolous violence. Badiou has also called for these movements to not lose momentum, or abdicate to the democratic practice of elections, which only risks neutralizing the force of the movement.[17] Sustained violence is sometimes necessary, therefore, according to Badiou, such that one does not compromise the existence of the political event, or that there is no compromise with the current political regime. The *subject* must take courage to carry on with this violence, and this is why the soldier will be the exemplary figure for Badiou's political *subject*.[18] However, Badiou's *subject* risks taking on a sovereign, imperialistic contour, especially when it develops a deep conviction of the universal dimension of the event to which it is faithful and begins to disseminate it across all differences, indifferent to other political trajectories that do not coincide with the supposed universality of the *subject*'s event. The rise of the *subject* in the place of politics then betrays any affirmation of "dis-closing" with regard to others and/or differences. This is evident in Badiou's political thought when he categorically rejects democratic thought, including the thought of *démocratie à venir*, as a possible form of emancipatory politics [*politique d'émancipation*], but insists that the latter is possible only by being strictly faithful to the "communist hypothesis," if not by following through the "Idea of communism."[19]

Apart from Badiou, other contemporary French thinkers whose political thought can be said to begin with the *reject* include Jacques Rancière and Étienne Balibar. As explicated in key texts such as *La Mésentente* and *Le Partage du sensible*, politics, for Rancière, begins with what he calls "the part that has no part" or *le sans part*, that is to say, those who are discounted by State politics from being considered as those whose voice, works, and even existence count.[20] In the eyes of the State, these *sans parts* do not add up to what it counts as its political subjects. Consequently, the State further deems them incapable of, or rather prohibits them from, political participation and intervention. Their political exclusion has consequences for their existential condition, since, being *sans part*, they are supernumerary to the calculation made by the State in its distribution of space to accommodate its subjects and its distribution of economic resources to those same subjects. In other words, they will not be accorded any hospitality with respect to those spaces, or the benefits that the State's (recognized) political subjects receive. The State will furthermore ensure that such unjust and unequal distribution remains in place, which is to say too that the State will do whatever it can to render the *sans part* silent and invisible, insensible to the rest of the community. This art of State politics, which determines what is sensible or not, is, according to Rancière, not true politics; instead, it constitutes politics as a form of policing [*la police*], vigilantly guarding the frontiers between the sensible and the insensible, making sure that one domain does not cross over to the other.

The *sans part*, like the "inexistent" in Badiou, is surely not distant from the *reject*. However, just as the "inexistent" in Badiou's political thought must not remain in its state of rejection after the political event but must become a *subject* of the latter, the imperative in Rancière's political thought is to not allow the *sans part* to passively remain insensible to the rest of the world. True politics therefore must first address the *sans part*, the "wrong" [*le tort*] constituted by the State's policing practices. It must recognize and expose this "wrong," or give exposition to the *sans part*, articulating or inscribing it as an exposé amidst current political discourse, so as to rupture any political rhetoric or practice that perpetuates that "wrong." Such exposition/ exposure/ exposé marks the beginning of "disagreement" [*mésentente*] or "dissensus" in politics, which, according to Rancière, constitutes the veracity of politics. It is in "dissensus" that the *sans part* is no longer simply *sans part*. As Rancière explicates in a piece on Derrida's *démocratie à venir*, which is clearly in disagreement with the latter's renunciation of the *subject*, it is in "dissensus" that the *sans part* inscribes itself as a political *subject*:

> A dissensus consist in putting two worlds, two heterogeneous logics on the same stage, in the same world. It is a form of commensurability of the incommensurables. This also means that the political *subject* acts in the mode of the *as if*. It acts as if it were the demos, that is, the whole made by those who are not countable as qualified parts of the community. This is what I see as the 'aesthetic dimension' of politics: the staging of a dissensus—of a conflict of sensory worlds—by *subjects* who act as if they were the people made up of the uncountable count of the anyone.[21]

This is not the space to discuss Rancière's work in detail, given the commitment of the present section to highlight works that engage the *reject* in a more sustained, albeit subterranean or implicit, manner. Let me say, however, that in calling for the becoming-*subject* of the *sans part*, it seems that one risks the neutralization, if not end, of politics in its veritable sense according to Rancière. This is because—supposing that the *sans part* as political *subject* is able to make the existing ruling political regime acknowledge its presence and accord it its rightful place and status in society, and to present itself on the political stage and make itself count as a legitimate political *subject*, supposing further too that from then on it can coexist with the State—it seems that one works teleologically toward the end of "wrong" or "dissensus" in politics. Even if there are numerous "wrongs" or "dissensus," the sense is that, given time, the dissipation of all these "wrongs" and "dissensus" is perfectible. In that case, I wonder if the neutralization of "wrong" and "dissensus" also teleologically neutralizes the singularity or radical difference of the *sans part*. When the State and the *sans part* claim to be able to coexist, or to resolve the "dissensus" between them and therefore reconcile their differences, is this, at the end of it all, an assimilation of the *sans part* to the State, that is, an appropriation by the State of the *sans part*, in the guise of acceptation, which only sees to the reduction of the political force of the *sans part*? In the "commensurability of incommensurables," is there not the risk of regressing toward "consensual" politics, against which Rancière's notion of "dissensus" was primarily raised? Furthermore, I am not sure if any State has ever transferred any responsibility of its governing body (or even part of it) to former *sans parts*, or if any governing body of the State has adopted the political vision of the *sans parts*. I doubt it. If Rancière's political thought here degenerates into a situation whereby the radical difference of the *sans part* is compromised in relation to the existing political organization, Badiou would argue that this is because of the democratic trace that is inscribed in the negotiation between the *sans part* and the State. I might disagree with Rancière's raising of the *subject*, but unlike Badiou, I do not believe that there is no trace of hope in democratic thought for an emancipatory politics; neither do I hypostasize my thoughts on politics on any particular or singular Idea, be it on the Idea of communism that Badiou insists, or the Idea of democracy (though, in that sense, I do align myself more with Derrida's *démocratie à venir*.) For my part, then, I would say that Rancière's political thought risks blunting the political edge of the *sans part* when it articulates the *sans part* in terms of the *subject*.

To be sure, I am not suggesting that the *sans part* must always remain as *sans part* in the sense of always being deprived of its political voice, its juridico-legal rights, and its share of economic resources and wealth. What I am resisting is the becoming-*subject* of the *sans part*. The *sans part* must fight for and (re)gain his or her voice, rights, and shares. However, in order to maintain its political edge, such that it does not compromise any aspect of itself with the status quo, the *sans part* must also learn how to walk away from all measures to assimilate it into some sort of "commensurability" with a dominant group. It is in that sense that I am more sympathetic to the Rancière of *La Nuit des prolétaires* (1981), where he celebrates workers in the nineteenth century who, instead of organizing themselves for the next proletarian movement at the end of their day's work, not only dream of being poets and artists, but also, precisely because of such dreams in the previous evening, fail to turn up for the political march the next day.

PLUS D'UNE ÉGALIBERTÉ

While the *reject* as *sans part* has been rather consistent in Rancière's *œuvre*, the more explicit surfacing of the *reject* in Balibar's political thought comes only recently. It has become more evident in his recent explication of "anthropological differences."[22] Close to the "poststructuralist" project to affirm differences, Balibar's "anthropological differences" have the objectives of acknowledging the differences that traverse each human being in him- or herself and the other and not allowing these differences to become psychological, physiological, ideological, and legal frontiers between one human being and another. These differences include gender and transgender differences, legalistic differences that label criminals in decimating ways, and, picking up from Foucault, pathological differences that demarcate supposedly mad, abnormal beings [*les anormaux*] from the supposedly normal. What Balibar wants us to recognize is that the differences that we relegate to or even condemn in others, through which we render these different others *rejects*, may be found within ourselves too. According to Balibar, we, in all our differences (including unavowable ones), and in our misdemeanors too, no matter how great or small, are all irreducibly *malêtre* or "mis-beings" in one way or another. We might want to repress our *malêtre*, but it always remains something undeniable and inevitable that we not only bear but also share in our being-with or existence with others. In other words, we, and the world, are traced and traversed by the *malêtre* of ourselves and others, and this is why Balibar will also say that *malêtre* is the "subject of relation" [*le sujet du rapport*].[23] Reconstituting, or rather acknowledging, *being* [*être*] as *mis-being* [*malêtre*], as I see it, is also saying that we are all undeniably *rejects* in some ways. Tracing a Foucauldian trajectory of thought in rethinking *malêtres*, Balibar has also called for the rethinking of Foucault's heterotopia in order to acknowledge and affirm these *malêtres* and their "anthropological differences." In contrast to utopias, which tend to be ideal places set or imagined in another world and time, heterotopias are places existing *here and now*, except they have been marginalized or tucked away in the design of city-spaces because they accommodate beings (living or not) bearing differences markedly distinct from so-called normal human beings, such that the latter are only anxious to exclude from their everyday lives.[24] For heterotopias to aid in articulating positively today the "anthropological differences" of us all *malêtres*, they must no longer be marginalized but disseminate themselves into the consciousness or sensibilities of public spaces. In that sense, heterotopia according to Balibar is close to Nancy's thought of politics as place, as heterotopias become critical spaces that allow the affirmation of *malêtres*. However, contra Nancy, and more like Rancière in his thinking of the *sans part*, the thought of the *subject* is not distant from Balibar's *malêtre*. Like Badiou too, Balibar has never aspired to depart from any thought of the *subject*, despite the "deconstruction" of the *subject* by "poststructuralist" thought.

In his response to Nancy's invitation to think "who comes after the subject," Balibar has stated that one must not be so quick to relinquish the category of the *subject*. As Balibar cautions, when it comes to thinking or even critiquing the *subject*, there are in fact two aspects of the *subject* that one must keep in mind. The first concerns the *subject* as *subjectum*, which allows the *subject* to define itself through its consciousness of its ability to singularly think, affirm, and found its existence or self, apparently without the intervention of another. There is not much disagreement from Balibar with regard to the critique of the *subject* as *subjectum*. There is, however, the second aspect, which concerns the *subject* as *subjectus*, and it is this aspect that Balibar seeks to preserve against all critique of the *subject*. Balibar reminds us that the experience of the *subject* as *subjectus* has a longer history than the *subject* as *subjectum*: the *subject* as *subjectus* recalls its relation, or rather subjection [*sujétion/assujetissement*], to a sovereign master, be it human or divine, before the *subject* attains its subjectivation as a self-determining *subjectum*. Balibar argues that one must never forget "the long history" of the *subject* as *subjectus*,[25] because it is from the memory of oneself as *subjectus* that one begins to think about one's liberty, to seek to be free from being subjected to another (sovereign) entity. As Balibar suggests in his response to Nancy, "Liberty in effect can only be thought as that of the *subject*, of subjected being [*l'être assujetti*]."[26] For the freedom of one and all, then, one must not, according to Balibar, abandon the thought of the *subject*, particularly the *subject* as *subjectus*.

Recalling the *subject* as *subjectus* is not sufficient, however. Going back to Rousseau's thought on the collective sovereignty of citizenship, Balibar insists, as is consistently the case throughout his political philosophy, that the figure of the citizen must accompany the thought of the *subject-subjectus* on its way to freedom or liberty. According to Balibar, the figure of the citizen and its constitution

> put into operation a *reduction of verticality* that brought the instruments of power and law *to the level of the community* (ideally at least, but this ideality [*idéalité*] can "grip the masses," as Marx would say, and therefore engender material effects). More precisely, they transform [power and the law] into instruments immanent to "co-citizenship" [*concitoyenneté*] (and into offensive or defensive arms, when the need arises): because, conflicting as this community of citizens is [. . .], it is always by an essentially horizontal fashion, through the effect of a reciprocal procedure, that individuals and the collective of which it is composed mutually "confer" upon themselves an equal freedom [*une égale liberté*].[27]

In other words, for Balibar, it is in the figure of the citizen wherein lies the political potentiality to break with any sovereignty monopolized or appropriated by a singular person; with the figure of the citizen, one sees to a sharing or redistribution of sovereignty with other citizens, ensuring at the same time that one and the other are equally free or freely equal (a condition that Balibar elsewhere calls *égaliberté* or "equaliberty,"[28] where equality and liberty must be thought simultaneously and not one without the other, not even one less than the other, which, in either case, only results in neither equality nor liberty). Taking the 1789 Declaration of the Rights of Man and of the Citizen as his point of reference, Balibar argues that what is at stake there is "the constitution of citizenship—in a radically new sense," and "what is new is the sovereignty of the citizen," which challenges "the idea of sovereignty [as] always been inseparable from a hierarchy, an eminence."[29] What citizenship posits is an "egalitarian sovereignty" [*souveraineté égalitaire*] predicated on "the equality in human nature," which is nothing but the fact of "equality 'by birth,'" that is to say, based on the fact that all "humans 'are born' not as 'subjects' [in the sense of *subjectus*] but 'free and equal in rights.'"[30] According to Balibar then, it is with citizenship that "the concepts of sovereignty and equality need not contradict each other."[31]

The political potentiality of the figure of the citizen to let emerge such "egalitarian sovereignty" is what motivates Balibar to respond to Nancy's question in the following manner: "*The citizen comes after the subject.* The citizen (defined by his rights and duties [*devoirs*]) is the *non subject* that comes after the subject, and his constitution and recognition puts an end (in principle) the subjugation [*l'assujetissement*] of the subject."[32] However, there is no dropping the *subject* in Balibar's thinking of the figure of the citizen: "After the passage from the subject (*subjectus*) to the citizen," there remains "the passage from the citizen to the subject (*subjectum*),"[33] that is to say, to the *subject* that is conscious not only of his or her self-representation as a being existing freely and equally as the next being, but also of the "equaliberty" of others to exist likewise too. This *subject* is conscious of maintaining a thought of an "infinite liberty" [*liberté illimitée*], a liberty that is equally extended to all, which is also a "self-regulated" [*autolimitée*] liberty, in the sense that it has "no other limits except that which it assigns itself to be able to respect the rule of equality."[34] This is "the becoming-subject of the citizen," and the *subject* here "will be the new 'subject,' the citizen subject."[35] At this point, I wonder if the *reject*, or even *auto-reject*, more than the *subject* or *citizen subject*, is a more adequate figure for Balibar's thinking of "egalitarian sovereignty" and *égaliberté*, or that "egalitarian sovereignty" and *égaliberté* are traced more by the *(auto-)reject* than the *(citizen) subject*. Firstly, if the thought of liberty begins with the *subjectus*, the *subjectus* is no less a (passive) *reject*, deprived of the liberty to be equal with his or her sovereign master, deprived of the power that allows the sovereign being to lord over him or her, and deprived of the freedom to free him- or herself from that subordination. And when it does take up enough courage to challenge sovereign authority, does it not also involve its expression as an *active reject* counteracting against all external forces that are oppressing it? The aspect of an *active reject* does not end there, though. In fact, it continues to express itself even when the former *subjectus* has assumed the figure of the citizen. According to Balibar, this can be found in the citizen-figure's civic disobedience, which he argues is exigent from time to time, since it is through which the citizen-figure reaffirms or recreates the notion of citizenship each time.[36] A passive citizen, who does not fight for the institutional recognition of the changes or expansion in citizenship, or who does not reject the institutional delimitation and determination of citizenship, only abdicates "egalitarian sovereignty" to the State. Acts of civic disobedience, as Balibar makes clear, are not nihilistic with regard to laws, however. Instead, "they recreate the conditions of a legislation or of the 'general will.' They do not attack the concept of law, they defend it."[37]

Aspects of the *active reject* and the *auto-reject* become clearer in Balibar's notion of the "becoming subject of the citizen." In the latter's putting in place of *égaliberté* for all, it seems that there is nonetheless some form of *auto-rejection* at stake, as Balibar underscores the meticulous care needed to articulate "infinite liberty" [*liberté illimité*] more precisely as liberty that is self-checked [*autolimitée*], so that one's liberty does not violently supplement another's: what is at stake therefore is an *auto-rejection* that keeps in check one's liberty so that it is not excessive to the point of compromising another's. Furthermore, Balibar has also said that in relation to equality, especially equality that admits differences without allowing certain differences to be privileged over others or to dominate others, there is a certain "nondetermination" to the figure of the citizen.[38] This is no doubt in contrast to the *subject*, since the *subject* never fails to determine itself through certain predicates, or by some auto-foundation. The "nondetermination" of the figure of the citizen, as Balibar explicates, involves its being "*neither* the individual *nor* the collective,"[39] which only means that no particular person or group stands for the model of the figure of the citizen, according to which others must identify themselves with in order to partake in an "egalitarian sovereignty." Neither individual nor group, any being in all his or her "anthropological differences" or even *maltêre* (which I have suggested can be articulated in terms of a *reject* as well) can therefore, theoretically, become a citizen. In this "nondetermination," it seems that, more than the *subject* as *subjectum* (a *subject* conscious of his or her possibility of self-representation), it is the *auto-reject* that underlies the figure of the citizen. Still with regard to the notion of "nondetermination," Balibar will say further that "the nondetermination of the citizen [. . .] manifests itself also as the opening [*ouverture*] of a *possibility*: the possibility for all *given* realization of the citizen to be put in question and to be destroyed by a struggle for equality."[40] In other words, the figure of the citizen, or the thought of citizenship, must *auto-reject itself* the moment it inclines toward any naturalized figure, or when it hypostasizes on the latter. It must *auto-reject itself* the moment when a different figure of the citizen is at risk of not having an equal affirmation. Balibar will put this another way, and here we see the return of the *active reject* at work: the figure of the citizen is "the author of a *permanent* revolution,"[41] especially in its dialectical relation with institutions to which the thought of citizenship, according to Balibar, always remains tied, as it negotiates with them on the one hand for its "institutional definitions" or affirmation and legitimation,[42] and contests them on the other, in its "insurrectional moment,"[43] when institutions do not accommodate the transformation, evolution, or expansion of citizenship with regard to other "anthropological differences." In all, the *(auto-) reject*, instead of the *subject*, seems to better capture the sense and force of the movement from subjugation (as *subjectus*) to *égaliberté* or the sharing of "egalitarian sovereignty" (as citizen), up to maintaining the opening of the latter to both existing noncitizens or *malêtres* and to *malêtres* to come. This is not to mention a moment in Balibar's writing when he is also seen willing to do away with the *subject*: "I prefer," he says, "the terminology of the political actor (hybrid, collective, transitory [*transitoire*]) to that of the *subject of politics* [. . .]."[44]

My critique of Balibar's "citizen subject" does not touch only on the term "subject." The notion of "citizen" or "citizenship," for me at least, is equally problematic. Of course, Balibar endeavors to open up the thinking of "citizenship" beyond all past and existing understanding of the term. He therefore seeks an "extended citizenship,"[45] one that extends beyond national frontiers, "beyond the sacrosanct equation: citizenship=nationality,"[46] or else a "trans-national or post-national citizenship."[47] Or, as he puts it another way, "extended citizenship" must be an open and in-complete [*inachevable*] citizenship.[48] Nonetheless, one cannot deny that "citizenship" is very much an Occidental concept, which goes back to the Greeks.[49] The Occidental trace of "citizenship" is not unmarked in Balibar either. However, instead of going back to the Greeks, Balibar aligns his notion of "citizenship" or the figure of the citizen to the Declaration of the Rights of Man and of the Citizen of 1789, which is undeniably grounded in French history. So, on the citizen that "comes after the subject," Balibar will say that that "is already given and we have it all in our memory. We can even date it: 1789."[50] One has to ask, however, who is this "we" that Balibar speaks of? Is the non-French, who does not share the French history of 1789, and therefore cannot properly claim to have 1789 in his or her memory, included in this "we"? Given this Occidental or French trace of "citizenship," one also has to question what happens when one extends this concept to those living in countries without any real history of such a term, in the sense that the concept of citizenship was only imposed upon them as a consequence of some form of colonization. Does this trace, undeniably determined by a particular history and nation, risk being a violent supplement to the thinking of the liberty of all beings, including the equal liberty or *égaliberté*—without reducing this notion to the French trinity of *égalité, liberté et fraternité*—of the difference of each being? Does it paradoxically become a singular, regulatory "political 'idea'"[51]—in spite of Balibar's attempts to radicalize it as open, in-complete, transnational, and postnational—upon which *égaliberté* is possible, as if *égaliberté* is ineluctable from a French-inflected thought of citizenship, and hence as if there is only one form of *égaliberté*, deriving itself from the thought of citizenship? If *égaliberté* is open to all differences, or if it does not practice within itself "differential inclusion" that essentially excludes certain differences,[52] it seems to me that *égaliberté* cannot be one, but rather, there must be *plus d'une égaliberté*. As I would argue, then, for *plus d'une égaliberté*, one must free *égaliberté* from being singularly predicated on the "political 'idea'" of citizenship or on the figure of the citizen.

Balibar, of course, does not fail to recognize that citizenship is a problematic term. As he notes of the French working-class society, citizenship more often than not perpetuates the marking of differences in a derogatory and negating way. It is not uncommon, according to Balibar, that citizenship quickly becomes "a second segregation" or "a supplemental segregation" [*sur-ségrégation*].[53] This is when the working-class immigrants, previously segregated from "native" citizens when they first arrived, but now living out their existential conditions as "citizen workers" after being granted citizenship (which still does not immunize them from certain continued segregation by "native" citizens), segregate the next wave of noncitizen immigrants, that is, illegal immigrants or the *sans papiers*, even though these later immigrants, through their labor, equally constitute the "working mass" [*ouvrier-masse*] of which the "citizen workers" are undeniably a part, and contribute to the country's economy.[54] Along with the "native" citizens, albeit lacking any true solidarity with them, the "citizen workers" make the new working but noncitizen workers the scapegoat of social insecurity.[55] In this case, citizenship becomes an attribute (or even property) for a group of beings with which they *reject* others that are devoid of that attribute. No doubt at work here too is the raising of the *subject* in the citizen, in his or her self-representation as a citizen; the citizen does this in a sovereign way too, in his or her auto-position as the more privileged being who is entitled to denigrate, negate, and *reject* the noncitizen other. The latter now becomes the *subjectus* subjected to the segregating practices of both "native" citizens and "citizen workers." Within this political space, then, there are "not only 'citizens' but also 'subjects,'" subjects-*subjectus* that are "*less foreign than foreigners* [*moins étrangers que des étrangers*] and yet more different *or more 'foreign'* [*étranger*] than them," subjects-*subjectus* that are prohibited to cross frontiers more than foreigners, subjects-*subjectus* therefore that are worse than citizens or "citizen workers."[56] According to Balibar, this is the situation where the "citizen-subject" has been appropriated as some form of norm that segregates those who have no claim to that category, if not as some form of "national normality" that is "*interiorized* by the individuals" such as the "citizen workers," making that norm "a condition, an essential reference of their collective or communitarian sentiment, and therefore, their renewed identity (or of the order, the hierarchy that they put in place in their multiple identities)."[57]

To sidestep such appropriation or interiorization, which only degenerates into a negation of *égaliberté*, I would suggest, again, that it will be more helpful to articulate the *(auto-)reject* instead of the *subject* or even the citizen. One must *auto-reject* all claims to the status (or privilege) of a citizen or a subject that potentially place oneself above the noncitizen immigrant-worker. One must remind oneself, especially if one is a former-immigrant-turned-citizen-worker, that one has been, or even remains to be, a *reject* in relation to the "native" citizens. This will help serve to recall the suffering that one has endured as a *reject*, which in turn will present a better chance of one refraining from extending that injustice to the new immigrants, short-circuiting any reincarnation of that injustice that one might perpetuate when one thinks oneself a sovereign "citizen subject." Recalling one's experience as a *reject* (which might, as noted, still continue in some other ways), and rethinking oneself as an *auto-reject* in the sense of refusing any preeminence, privilege, or superiority in one's recently acquired label of "citizen subject," one might even be motivated to make a political intervention, alongside the new noncitizen immigrant *rejects*, as past and current fellow *rejects*, to end all existing injustices against them. I reiterate that one must be cautious here in such political intervention to not resurrect the *subject* (in oneself) once again. The danger is that with the *subject*, one may assume a position from which one speaks *in place* of the non-*subject*/noncitizen other, as if the latter is incapable of articulating his or her existential condition that is severely short of *égaliberté*. Furthermore, when this political *subject* decides to represent itself as a collective body, there is also the risk that each singularity, or else each *reject* in his or her own different degrees of being rejected and of auto-rejection, gets reduced to a homogenized body. Any sublimation toward a *subject* must therefore be interrupted. *Rejects*, in their multiplicity, must manifest themselves in their respective ways, in other words, as plural and heterogeneous *rejects*.

To take up Rancière's rhetoric, it is through these *rejects* who are no less an exposition, exposure, and exposé of the "wrong" [*le tort*], or the *sans part* that currently exists in society in its denigrating distinction not only from "native" citizens but also from immigrant "citizen workers," that politics can begin again. It is not my intent to be so severe in my critique of the figure of the citizen as much as of the *subject*, since I am well aware that, unfortunately, there are many in various countries who still need citizenship before they are granted basic rights such as the right to live, the right to abode, the right to work, and even the right to medical assistance. Nonetheless, I would call for the practice whereby the appeal to rights, not even the "right to have rights" as Arendt would say, but *just* the right to exist—that is to say, to exist without being subjected to rejection or to a denigrating segregation, so long as one is an honest worker contributing to the economy and does not exert any real violence against others—need not be conditioned by citizenship. If *égaliberté* is a constant struggle, as Balibar reminds us, and if it concerns as well the constant fight for the very basic right to existence, I would say that this fight or *égaliberté* comes before and after citizenship. Balibar has said that we are not born *subjects*,[58] but I would add that we are neither born originarily, or rather ontologically, as citizens. *Égaliberté* lies in our fact of existence, in our fact of being born tout court, and not in our historically and nationally determined condition of being citizens, which really comes after our fact of being born. Besides, given that we are still far from being "postnational" or even "transnational," Balibar's dream of an "extended citizenship" still remains a distant future.[59] In that case, such a dream can risk deferring to the future all endeavors to ensure *égaliberté* to all, as one becomes content to wait for an "extended citizenship" to be institutionalized before one acts to address existing injustices or "the wrong" in politics. In this indefinite wait for the institutionalization of "extended citizenship," existing *rejects* can only despair at the fact that such citizenship remains absent in the *here and now*, and that its chances to exist in *égaliberté* are in fact really slim. In place of predicating political thought on the "citizen subject" and/or "extended citizenship," I would argue that a politics that begins with the *reject*—which is both a concept that really knows no boundaries whatsoever, indifferent therefore to all national frontiers and identity, *and* an existential condition that many of "the wrong," the *sans part*, or the *malêtre* experience in real terms while the notion of the "citizen" largely remains an ideal to them—can address the question of *égaliberté* in a more urgent manner *here and now*, and no longer defer it to the future. In other words, a political intervention that seeks to be a veritable rupture in politics must recognize the fact that Man is not just born free but also not born as citizens, and hence not take recourse to, but free itself, from the historically determined and institutionally given term such as "citizen." Certainly, one must not refuse intervention to help existing *rejects* such as illegal immigrants, refugees, stateless people, and *sans papiers* attain citizenship, especially in cases where they need it urgently, but one can also begin with their condition as *rejects* and, instead of waiting for institutions to grant them citizenship or legitimize them as citizens, work precisely from their *reject* condition and modulate or supplement without delay existing laws such that they will prevent their further denigration, negation, and the denial of basic rights to them, including the right, or rather freedom, to exist. The latter course, I would argue, is how one lets the other who comes in or from the future in a *démocratie à venir* be free as *anyone*, rather then compelling the other to identify with either "native" citizens, "citizen workers," or whatsoever citizen.

FROM *VOYOUS* TO AN UNCOMMON BARTLEBY

Predicating the thought of *égaliberté* on the "citizen subject" or even citizenship is problematic. Derrida also has his suspicions of the limits of both the figure of the citizen and citizenship, and that is why, in his thinking of *démocratie à venir*, cosmopolitism, unconditional hospitality, and the impossible but necessary sharing of sovereignty (instead of allowing its appropriation or monopoly by a singular entity), Derrida would say that they are "beyond citizenship."[60] Indeed, one will find in Derrida a figure of thought otherwise than the "citizen subject," if not a figure that is neither "citizen" nor "subject." As I will now try to show, it is the *reject* that subtends those thoughts instead, a figure that no doubt problematizes at the same time the category of the citizen and/or the "citizen subject." The figure of the *reject* in Derrida's political thought can be said to be surfacing since *Spectres de Marx* (1991). There, the *reject* takes on either a spectral dimension, coming (back) from the past, or a messianic one, where it comes from (or as) the future. Be it the revenant or the messianic figure, Derrida's *reject* there is dissimilar, or else does not (cor)respond, to any existing political configuration or ideology, and we see this becoming clearer with *Politiques de l'amitié*. It is Derrida's *reject* in the later *Voyous* (2003), though, that I want to highlight here, which takes on a more actual, more present, or more corporeal contour. This is because this *reject* has a certain resonance with a political movement that has recently touched our contemporary world, and its articulation can perhaps have implications for that movement's future. This *reject* is none other than the one named in the title of Derrida's text: *voyou*, or "rogue" as it has been translated.[61]

The term *voyou* or "rogue," especially in the wake of the Bush administration that witnessed the 9/11 terrorist attacks in the United States, and which retaliated with the global and indefinite "war on terror," has come to signify, on the global stage of international politics, states that are either against the "war on terror," or pose a potential threat to international peace and security. However, as Derrida reminds us, *voyou*, before its political appropriation by the Bush (and Clinton) administration, can also be a nonstate actor, or can have a more local, quotidian meaning. "The *voyou*," Derrida tells us, "is idle [*inoccupé*], sometimes unemployed, and at the same time actively occupied to occupy [*occupé à occuper*] the street, either to do nothing there but to 'roam the streets' [*courir les rues*], to lay about [*traîner*], or to do what one must not do normally in the streets according to the norms, the law, and the police [. . .]."[62] It is because of such idleness that the *voyou* is regarded, or rather disdained, by others as some sort of *reject*: "They are labeled [*désigné*], denounced, judged, condemned, pointed out, as actual or virtual delinquents, by the State, or by civil or good society [*bonne société*], by the police, sometimes by international law and by armed police that watches over the law and morals, over politics and civility [*politesse*], over all traffic routes—pedestrian zones, vehicular, maritime, and aerial zones, computer network [*l'informatique*], the e-mail, and the Web."[63] Consequently, they are commonly categorized as "those apart, the excluded or the strays [*égarés*], the marginalized [*excentrés*] who roam the streets, especially those of the suburbs [*banlieues*]," even though they "are sometimes brothers [*frères*], citizens and fellows [*semblables*]."[64] Here, one can no doubt hear echoes of Balibar's *malêtre* or Rancière's *sans part*.

In general, the "rogue-being" [*être-voyou*] is one that is preoccupied with occupying space,[65] especially public spaces, to the extent that it violates the hospitality such spaces grant to anyone. In a way, we have recently witnessed the gathering and uprising, largely on a massive scale, of such *voyous*, starting with the *indignados* in Spain in 2011, which then mutated into the Occupy movement, with Occupy Wall Street as the pivotal event before spreading to other cities in the United States and then to other major cities in the world. Declaring themselves as the 99%, that is to say, the (global) majority that are denied the wealth or financial resources of the rich 1%, declaring themselves no less as *rejects* therefore, they refuse to passively or silently further accept this economic inequality. They refuse the banking policies that favor the rich, or the irresponsible banking practices that have resulted not only in that unequal wealth distribution but also in financial crises that have degenerated into housing foreclosures, unemployment, and poverty for many of this 99%, while banking CEOs continue to receive extravagant bonuses. Such active rejection on their part manifested itself in their occupying of public spaces, especially those in proximity with key financial districts such as Zuccotti Park in New York City or La Défense in Paris. In doing so, one can say that they took on the form of a multitude of *voyous*. The term "multitude" will no doubt recall the recent works of Hardt and Negri. From *Empire* and *Multitude* to the more recent *Commonwealth*, the endeavor of Hardt and Negri has been to articulate a "multitude of the poor," whose poverty is not merely limited to "misery or deprivation" but is also constituted by a resistance to "the individualism and the exclusive, unified, social body of property."[66] In fact, Hardt and Negri do not hesitate to associate the Occupy movement with their concept of "multitude," as they write in the wake of the movement in the journal *Foreign Affairs* that the movement has precisely "developed according to what [they] call a 'multitude form.'"[67] Incidentally, the force of active rejection is not missing in Hardt and Negri's "multitude." As they argue in *Empire*, the "multitude" bears the force of refusal. According to them, this refusal can be found in Bartleby, Melville's literary figure that I have mentioned a little in relation to Derrida's thought in the previous chapter on the "postsecular." Calling Bartleby the "figure of absolute refusal," Hardt and Negri read in Bartleby's enunciation of *I would prefer not to*, in response to his employer's demand to copy legal documents, to carry out other odd jobs, and later in the narrative to leave the premises, "the refusal of work and authority, or really the refusal of voluntary servitude."[68] That refusal, for Hardt and Negri, is also "the beginning of liberatory politics."[69] They will underscore, however, that Bartleby's enunciation "is only a beginning,"[70] and it cannot remain as such, resonating only within the persona of Bartleby. If so, it will remain only an inadequate voice, "empty" in the eyes of Hardt and Negri, because it is too solitary, and which "leads only to a kind of social suicide."[71] According to Hardt and Negri, the enunciation of refusal must disseminate itself and be embodied by a larger collective, a "common" as they would say. In other words, something more is needed following the enunciation of refusal: "What we need is to create a new social body, which is a project that goes well beyond refusal. [. . .] [We] need also to construct a new mode of life and above all a new community."[72] (I have, with references to Nancy, Derrida, and Deleuze, provided a critique of such construction of community in an earlier chapter of this work, so I will not comment on the question of community in Hardt and Negri's quote here.) There must be, then, for Hardt and Negri, and to adopt their rhetoric in *Commonwealth*, a *becoming-common* of the figure of Bartleby: or, Bartleby and his force of rejection must be embodied by a multitude.

The multitude of the Occupy movement would seem constitutive of that "new social body" that Hardt and Negri find lacking in Bartleby, since it claims to represent "the 99%." Even though Hardt and Negri in their *Foreign Affairs* contribution do not mention Bartleby in their discussion of the Occupy movement, one could nonetheless argue that there are certain resonances between the movement and Bartleby, not to mention that Bartleby was in fact mobilized as a figure of thought for the Occupy Toronto movement.[73] For example, while we find in the movement the preference to occupy key public spaces or financial centers rather than mobilizing potentially violent general strikes against the present financial management of society, we find in Bartleby a similar insistence, according to the narrator, "to keep *occupying* my chambers, and denying my authority; [...] scandalizing my professional reputation; [...] and in the end perhaps outlive me, and claim possession of my office by right of *his perpetual occupancy.*"[74] Like the Occupy movement then, Bartleby, in his "immobile [...] pure passivity,"[75] displaces all sense of sovereign property and propriety of authority.[76] And yet, I would like to question if Bartleby is really the literary figure of thought, or "conceptual persona" as Deleuze and Guattari prefer to say, of, or for, the Occupy movement. Or, to pose the query in another way, is the "multitude" of the Occupy movement the "people to come," to use another of Deleuze and Guattari's formula, that Bartleby prefigures?

I do not deny that there are resonances between Bartleby and the Occupy movement, but I would say that these resonances are really limited. I would even say that what is shared by them is only the gesture of occupying spaces that are not actually, or rightfully, theirs, a gesture therefore of occupying spaces in ways that violate the notion of hospitality. Otherwise, there is nothing much in *common* between them. If, for Hardt and Negri, something common is shared within the multitude, there is actually nothing common about Bartleby; or, there is nothing about him, or in him, that is desirable to be shared by others. When Bartleby refuses to verify his copy, the narrator notes that Bartleby refuses "a request made according to *common* usage and *common* sense" of the norms or normativity of the copyist vocation.[77] When Bartleby refuses the collective verification with other colleagues of the multiple copies he has made, and the other odd jobs that the narrator asks of him, the narrator will remark that Bartleby's refusals are "strange peculiarities, privileges, and unheard of exemption."[78] Furthermore, there is hardly any solidarity between Bartleby and his colleagues. Upon hearing Bartleby's refusal to verify his own copies, Nippers, one of Bartleby's colleagues, wanted "to kick him out of the office."[79] Given such relation with colleagues, the figure of Bartleby, contrary to Hardt and Negri's aspiration for him, will always remain estranged from any common, collective spirit. Bartleby can never count as part of the common workforce: he is *not* of the common; he is "the unaccountable."[80] In other words, Bartleby is the uncommon.[81] The common is what Bartleby cannot bear in fact; it is against which Bartleby projects his enunciation of *I would prefer not to.* And it is perhaps because he ends up in the "*common* jail,"[82] after being removed by the police for refusing to evacuate the premises, that Bartleby finally meets his end there. But even in that "common jail," one notes that he nonetheless has the rights to haunt a section of the prison that is "not accessible to the common prisoners," a section where it is said too that he sleeps not among other prisoners but among "kings and counselors."[83]

If there is "a refusal of work" in Bartleby, as Hardt and Negri see it, it must also be noted that it is not a refusal of work tout court. In fact, Bartleby has no resistance to work initially. Upon his arrival, contrary to his half-competent and near redundant colleagues, he did an immense amount of copying. He "ran a day and night line," "wrote on silently, palely, mechanically," with "incessant industry," to the point where the narrator acknowledged Bartleby to be a "valuable acquisition" and that he "felt [his] most precious papers perfectly safe in [Bartleby's] hands."[84] In short, Bartleby *works*, not to mention he works in an exceptionally industrious way with respect to the rest of his colleagues. Bartleby's "refusal to work" comes into effect only when something common inflects his working condition. To be specific, it is when the word "prefer" becomes a common office lingo, when "it involuntarily rolled from [Nippers's] tongue,"[85] and that is when Bartleby prefers to stop copying altogether.[86] Bartleby has an anathema for that becoming-common of the word "prefer" probably because—even though Nippers "did not in the least roguishly accent the word prefer"[87]—Nippers's reiteration manifests itself as a travesty of the force of refusal in Bartleby's enunciation. There is no refusal in Nippers's usage at all. What resounds in Nippers's reiteration of that word is but an unconditional ascension or subservience to the request of his employer: "Oh certainly, sir, if you prefer that I should."[88]

The uncritical acceptance of the employer's sovereignty is what Bartleby resists. That is to say, Bartleby will work, efficiently even, serving the purposes of the company, but he will work only if working does not entail sacrificing the integrity of the manner by which he carries out his task. In other words, he will not allow his subjectivity as an individual, unique copyist to be violently supplemented or suppressed by the sovereignty of his employer; he will not allow himself to be reduced to yet another invisible, anonymous cog in the production machine. This is perhaps why Bartleby refuses any task that falls outside his job-scope as a copyist, preferring "never on account to be dispatched on the most trivial errand of any sort" such as going to the post office to collect his employer's mail.[89] More critically, this is also perhaps why Bartleby refuses the work that was handed to him by his employer via "a high green folding screen, which might entirely isolate Bartleby from [his employer's] sight, though not remove him from [his employer's] voice,"[90] a screen that might recall that which Pythagoras, the sovereign master-teacher, put between himself and his disciples during his acousmatic lessons. Bartleby simply would not submit to a condition whereby those in a sovereign position render others invisible or to be without presence.

In Bartleby's refusal to work, or to become-common, there is certainly no lack of an affirmative subjectivity in him that serves as a counterpoint to his employer's sovereign subjectivity. There is no doubt that that subjectivity manifests itself most forcefully in Bartleby's "persisting in occupying" his employer's premises.[91] As a *subject* that knows, or is conscious of, what he prefers (not to), that is to say, as a *subject* that holds his ground and not leave, it can even be said that there is also something sovereign in Bartleby's will to remain or occupy, not forgetting that the term "occupy" does take on an imperialistic connotation in the context of war, carried out by a sovereign state of greater military power in relation to another weaker state. The imperial force of Bartleby's subjectivity is undeniable, as it makes the narrator-employer gradually abdicate his sovereignty. That sovereignty was already threatened when the narrator-employer first discovered Bartleby occupying the premises on a Sunday. Being told by Bartleby that he was "occupied" and to come back later, the narrator-employer "incontinently [. . .] slunk away from [his] own door, and did as desired."[92] Upon further reflection that it was a subordinate who dictated to him what to do, and who sent him away from his own premises, all the narrator-employer could summon up in himself were only "sundry twinges of impotent rebellion," which only further deepened his sense of being "unmanned."[93] Eventually, it will be the narrator-employer who first gives in, or who first gives up his sovereign position: "Since he will not quit me, I must quit him. I will change my offices; I will move elsewhere; and give him fair notice, that if I find him on my new premises I will then proceed against him as a common trespasser."[94]

In "persisting to occupy," which is really nothing less than a violation of an ethics of hospitality on the side of the guest, Bartleby renders himself what Agamben has called "the ungrateful guest."[95] He is some sort of *voyou* no less, since, as already noted from Derrida, a "rogue-being" [*être-voyou*] is preoccupied with occupying spaces in ways that violate the hospitality conferred by those spaces. Certainly, Bartleby is not occupied with occupying the streets (a preoccupation more accurately that of the participants of the Occupy movement). However, if one follows Derrida's "deconstructive" analysis of the term *voyou*, it is not so unreasonable to call Bartleby a "rogue-being." According to Derrida, "To speak of a rogue [*voyou*], one makes a call to order [*on rappelle à l'ordre*], one has begun to denounce [someone else as] a suspect, one makes an interpellation, even an arrest, a summoning [*convocation*], a writ [*assignation*], an investigation: the rogue must appear [*comparaître*] before the law."[96] Indeed, not too long after the narrator-employer has quit his premises, one finds Bartleby, in refusing to leave those same premises, being arrested by the police and sent to the "common jail." "When one speaks of rogues, the police is never far,"[97] as Derrida reminds us. This is also what the participants of the Occupy movement eventually realize or experience. Bartleby and the Occupy movement, then, even though they diverge on the question of the *common*, nonetheless share certain aspects of a "rogue-being."

As evident in Bartleby's displacement of his employer, and in the Occupy Wall Street movement's disruption of the normal functioning of Wall Street, there is a certain countersovereign force of the *voyou*. Or, there is a politics of "rogue-being." Derrida will even suggest that politics begins with the "rogue-being": "The question of a democratic politics of the city must always begin by the serious question" of "what is a *voyou*," if not "under what conditions is a *voyoucratie* possible."[98] In other words, Derrida suggests that the *voyou* can be the figure following which one may begin to rethink existing democratic thought and practices; or, more precisely, the question of hospitality that surrounds a "rogue-being" can have implications for the question of democracy. According to Derrida, democratic practices so far, while seeking "to offer hospitality to all the excluded," have paradoxically excluded, within their spaces, "in particular bad citizens—rogues, noncitizens, and all sorts of dissimilar and unrecognizable others."[99] Welcoming the *voyou*, which is a gesture akin to "unconditional hospitality," may pave the way toward a *démocratie à venir*, where sovereignty will not only be something of the State's monopoly and hegemony,[100] but shared by *anyone*.[101] In this case, a dissociation between sovereignty and "unconditionality" may even become possible,[102] that is to say, a situation in which whoever or whatever that is welcomed is not subjected or indebted to the gesture of the host, a gesture that typically marks not simply the hospitality of the host, but also the latter's sovereignty as displayed by his or her power or authority to either offer or deny hospitality.

In that regard, Derrida has also argued for the consideration of rogues or *voyous* and their countersovereign gestures, such as the simple act of occupying public spaces, as potentially playing a critical role in questioning the State's supposed right to "retain and assure of itself the monopoly of violence."[103] As witnessed in the police actions in Oakland and in the University of California campuses in Berkeley and Davis against the Occupy movement's peaceful encampment, and in the New York Police Department's eviction of the occupiers at Zuccotti Park, it is evident that the State today still has no intention to relinquish that monopoly. However, the questioning or critique of that monopoly can nevertheless begin with the "rogue-being." The latter possesses a certain "counterpower" or a "criminal and transgressive countersovereignty" that "defies" the sovereignty of the State; therefore, it is an element that the State must inevitably reckon with.[104] This is especially so when there is more than one rogue (*plus d'un voyou*) or when there is a multitude of rogues, such as the participants of the Occupy movement seem to be. These participants in their sheer mass, in their gathering as an assemblage or *demos*, and even though they were "not destroying anything"[105] in occupying the streets or public parks or squares but were committed to the legal act of civil disobedience through "nonviolent protest,"[106] can take on a semblance of an entity or even a *cratie*, a "*voyoucratie*" as Derrida would say (following Flaubert).[107] It is this potentiality of a *voyoucratie* that the State finds *voyous* threatening to its sovereignty, since *voyoucratie*, as Derrida has also noted, can "give itself the power to render less viable or weaker" the police,[108] the laws, and norms. Derrida will go on to say, "*voyoucratie* is also a corrupted and corrupting power of the street, an illegal power that is outside the law regrouping in a *voyoucratic* regime, and therefore in a more or less clandestine organized formation, in a virtual State, all those that represent a principle of disorder—not of anarchical chaos but of structured disorder, [...] of plot [*complot*], of conspiracy [*conjuration*], of offense or premeditated offensive against public order."[109] Such a description of *voyoucratie* is certainly not far from the profile, the mode of organization, and the trajectory that characterize the Occupy movement, and this can explain the reactionary and oftentimes violent actions taken by the State and its police force against the participants of the movement.

But to return to the problematic link between sovereignty and hospitality: certainly, there is a critical need to call for an unconditional hospitality on the side of the (sovereign) host—and this is in the order of Derrida's ethical philosophy—not only to the *voyou* but also to *anyone*, in order to attempt to dissociate sovereignty and hospitality. One can in fact argue that this was practiced in some sense by Bartleby's employer, since he accepted Bartleby even though the latter "had declined telling who he was, or whence he came,"[110] allowing Bartleby to even violently supplement his sovereign right to the office space.[111] However, the guest, surely, must also have some respect for the host and not usurp or appropriate the latter's place and even drive the latter away. Otherwise, what follows is nothing but a return to a conditional hospitality, in other words, a hospitality predicated on the sovereignty of the new host and his or her new laws, where not everyone or anyone feels welcome or at ease. That is no doubt the sense that Bartleby gives to the people who work in the office or even in the building, to the people too who are just passing by the offices there. There is, therefore, for the *voyou*, a part to play too, such that his or her "countersovereignty" or "counterpower" does not violently supplement that of the host to the point where what changes is but the sovereign figure, as the new sovereign subject continues to act in ways that are indifferent to the perspectives of others. I note that the latter does not happen only when the *voyou* takes on the ("legitimate") sovereign position. It can also occur prior to that, when the *voyou* assumes a *subject* position, that is, when it insistently decides to claim or appropriate public places to the extent that it becomes difficult or even impossible for others to access these places, that is to say, when these places are no longer *public* spaces but become territories of the *voyou*. Such occupation surely infringes upon the peace and safety of neighboring locales, and one must question or critique this practice of the *voyou*, its politics of the streets,[112] which sees to the dissolution of all sense of hospitality. One underscores, therefore, that such occupation can disturb and annoy neighbors, which the Occupy movements certainly did, which consequently did not assist them in garnering greater public or collective support for their causes.[113] And if these *voyous* lost a certain sense of a commons with the rest of the world when they started to become a nuisance to those around them, the sense of a commons within the sphere of the *voyous* also began weakening. This happened when some of the *voyous* assumed the position of sovereign subjects, as many of the

Occupy participants did in the course of the movement, which allows a polemical divide to arise between them and the other *voyous*, especially between them and the *voyous* of the homeless and the poor. They charged the latter of causing disorder within the encampment sites, proceeding to even reject the "original" homeless and poor *voyous*, even though the Occupy movements in part were to speak for them.[114] From then on, any sense of a multitude of commons and any possibility of a shared sovereignty sure began to dissipate, remaining but a distant goal.

I acknowledge that I am oversimplifying things with regard to the Occupy movement here and have not taken into further considerations that some of these homeless and the poor were encouraged by the police to infiltrate encampment sites to create difficulties or to break down the growing solidarity amongst the participants. Let me just say that I do not claim to offer any sophisticated or in-depth analysis of the movement or of the intricate developments that have taken place within it.[115] My doubts and reservations raised here in relation to the movement are made based on my sense and observation that the movement was taking on a contour of a collective (counter)sovereign body or *subject*, as it grew in number and voice, and as it auto-positioned itself in strategic places (claiming even to own them too) with its mode of ordering itself through "frequent assemblies and participatory decision-making structures" as Hardt and Negri have noted in their intervention in *Foreign Affairs*.[116] My aim in making reference to the Occupy movement here is simply to warn against the raising of a *subject* in politics, including revolutionary politics. To be sure, I am not at all in disagreement with the cause or aim of the movement. In fact, I am all for it, except I would like to be a little critical of its strategies or trajectories, especially when they take place at the price of the well-being of others, or even at the risk of the lives of the participants. It is with this critical slant that I suggest one must ask to what ends such a politics of the streets or politics of occupation move toward. As the cases of Bartleby and the Occupy movements show, it tends unfortunately toward a nihilistic politics: Bartleby as a sovereign *subject* of occupation eventually gets reduced to a *subject* that is subordinated to the interpellation of the police and ends up in prison, a fate that most of the participants of the Occupy movements have also met with.

I would argue that what the *voyou* must do instead is to know when to walk away, and not to occupy a space to the extent where it begins to exercise another monopoly or hegemony over that space. That is to say too that the *voyou* must stop short from grounding itself as a sovereign *subject*. It is not just that when Bartleby insists on standing his ground, he is reduced from a *subject* of occupation to a *subject* submitted to the interpellation of the police. It is also the case that from then on, there is no longer anything uncommon or "original" about Bartleby. The only thing left with Bartleby is that he remains a constant *subject* of occupation and is almost *common* as such a *subject*, doing nothing but haunting the premises. In that case, he no longer makes any other moves that will shock the order. He becomes just another figure of a "politics of 'resistance' or 'protestation,' which *parasitizes* upon what it negates."[117] In other words, in occupying the former sovereign's premises, Bartleby has also subsequently renounced his freedom to move along on another trajectory. Furthermore, in becoming easy to predict, as Bartleby grounds himself in the position of a *subject* of occupation, and therefore easy to manage too, one just awaits his arrest by law enforcement officers for being a "common trespasser." In a way, this has also been the trajectory of the participants of the Occupy movement. Everything falls into ruin then, the moment Bartleby and the participants of the Occupy movements, or the *voyous* in short, decide to ground their sovereign subjectivity by insisting on occupying their chosen premises and not walking away.[118]

How does one put in place a thought whereby the *voyou*—be it Bartleby or the participant of the Occupy movement—is encouraged to be perhaps more radical than it already is, and walk away, and therefore prevent founding itself as a sovereign *subject*? I would argue that articulating the figure of the *reject*, in place of a "political subject of the poor" as Hardt and Negri would want it, can mobilize such a thought. I have already mentioned that the Occupy movement, consisting of the 99% that are refused adequate economic resources or economic equality because of unequal wealth distribution, implicitly claims itself to be a multitude of *rejects*. Bartleby is no less a *reject* either: as noted, he is largely sidelined by his fellow copyist.[119] At first sight, then, both Bartleby and the multitude that makes up the Occupy movement are already *rejects* in the passive sense. But there is no doubt that they bear the second turn of the *active reject* too, when Bartleby projects his force of rejection through his enunciation of *I would prefer not to*, and when the 99% decide to occupy public places to manifest their discontent of being denied the wealth the 1% enjoy. At this point, I note once again that it is usually the overprojection of the active force of rejection, first against the oppressive forces, then against whoever or whatever is in the vicinity (just as Bartleby became a nuisance to the new proprietors of the premises), that one witnesses the claims to the foundation of a sovereign subject. This is why it is important to put in place the third turn of *auto-rejection* in order to prevent any (re)articulation of the *subject*. In other words, in the case of Bartleby especially, after the first enunciation of *I would prefer not to* in the face of the demand to quit the premises, the *reject* must know how to auto-reject by not allowing his or her gesture of occupation to become a singular, monolithic, fixed strategy. He or she must know how to walk away from that strategy, and that is perhaps how the *(auto-)reject* will always be a shock to the system or to the political order, and also prevent its interpellation by the police. (I have also suggested that this walking away may be important or critical when the *reject*'s strategy becomes harmful or life-threatening not only for itself but also for other [fellow] *rejects*, and also when it begins to come at the cost of affirming and respecting the well-being of others.) It is via such a movement that the *reject* can continue to carry out political rejection in ways unanticipated or incalculable.[120] That means to say that the fight is *not* over for the *reject* when it walks away: instead, it seeks out other, better, effective, and life-affirming means. At times, the ends might change or even appear to disappear, but that is only because the *reject* has managed to find for itself another horizon that can neutralize, if not surpass, that which has formerly limited or oppressed it.

In any case, it is by walking away that Bartleby can perhaps be what Žižek deems "a kind of *arche*," whereby his force of rejection is never delimited to "the refusal of a determinate content as, rather, the formal gesture of refusal as such."[121] In Agamben's reading of Bartleby, he has written that "the hardest thing [. . .] is not the Nothing or its darkness, in which many nevertheless remain imprisoned; the hardest thing is being capable of annihilating this Nothing and letting something from Nothing be."[122] I would like to think, however, that harder is the endeavor to return to the Nothing, in order, as Agamben would have it, "to save what was not."[123] The latter is what the *auto-reject* is potentially capable of, as it rejects all present predispositions in order to start everything anew again, constantly articulating an "each time" where "everything re-begins at zero,"[124] reaching (back) to the "what was not" that gets left out in all present actualizations.

When Bartleby becomes a *subject* of occupation, he clearly is not able to return to the Nothing to begin again, since, each moment from then on is *filled* with him, in a "motionless" manner,[125] filling out the office space around him. In that regard, he loses "the mode of Being of potentiality that is purified of all reason."[126]

It is to be able to reject everything that one has built, to reject one's subjectivity in other words too, only in order to constantly rebegin at zero, that I suggest one must begin to mobilize the figure of the *reject*, especially the *auto-reject*, alongside the *voyou*. At this point, I would like to highlight that Bartleby and the Occupy movement, as *voyou* and/or the *reject*, may seem to recall Marcuse's "Great Refusal." When Marcuse called for the "Great Refusal" in 1964 in *One-Dimensional Man*, there were at least two phenomena against which the "Great Refusal" had to project itself. The first was the production by the State of a sense of imminent war, a war that only had as its horizon an absolute nuclear fallout between the United States and the Soviet Union. The production of such an apocalyptic vision only served to "justify" the accelerated research and development of the US State war machine, which also had implications for the future militarization of society, such as the translation of military technics (for example, the Internet) into society. The second phenomenon was the technological advancement of society, which was increasingly capable of satisfying consumer material desires on a larger scale, which in turn produced the illusion that there was little that society could be dissatisfied with, hence discouraging any sort of resistance to, or "dissensus" with as Rancière would say, the status quo. According to Marcuse, it is when society loses its capacity, or even its will, to resist both the domination of militarized thinking in society and the management of society via technological gratification, that society is flattened out, reduced to something that is "one-dimensional." It is then that one must resurrect the "Great Refusal," which is nothing less than a "protest against that which is,"[127] and which Marcuse found its manifestations in nineteenth-century workers' movements and Marxism. According to Marcuse, to project that "Great Refusal," one must also seek a "new historical subject,"[128] which Marcuse saw in characters or "conceptual personae" of literary works especially of the Romantic tradition.

It is perhaps because of Marcuse's inclination toward the Romantic tradition that he does not make reference to Bartleby in relation to the "Great Refusal." That does not, however, prevent one from discerning the proximity between Bartleby and the "Great Refusal." One can argue that Bartleby's *I would prefer not to* is a form of Marcusean refusal of "that which is." Or, Bartleby's "refusal to work" can be said to find its echo in Marcuse when the latter argues, following Valéry's poetics that celebrates the poetic articulation of absent things, that the "Great Refusal" also concerns "that which is not seen, not touched, not heard,"[129] which means that in articulating the unseen, the untouched, and the unheard, the "Great Refusal" is willing to go so far as being "non-operational"[130] (if not "inoperative," to follow Blanchot's or Nancy's rhetoric). The proximity between Bartleby and the "Great Refusal" is clearly not missed by Hardt and Negri. When they speak of the "absolute refusal" of Bartleby, they do not fail to make reference to Marcuse's *One-Dimensional Man*. But Hardt and Negri would no doubt depart from Marcuse, for Marcuse ultimately does not renounce solitariness, but celebrates it. As seen earlier, Hardt and Negri consider Bartleby's solitariness "social suicide" and argue that "absolute refusal" must be embodied by a "social body." Marcuse, in contrast, takes solitariness as the mark of a "Great Refusal": "Solitude [is] the very condition which sustained the individual against and beyond his society [...]."[131] Such solitude or solitariness is something Bartleby never surrenders throughout the narrative. To put it in Marcusean rhetoric, Bartleby resists the "desublimation"[132] of both solitude or solitariness and his "refusal to work" into some aspect of the *common*. In that regard, Bartleby is truer to Marcuse's "Great Refusal" than to Hardt and Negri's "absolute refusal."

The Occupy movement, for its part, seemed to have had actualized a particular form of the "Great Refusal," one that Marcuse envisioned one year after the publication of *One-Dimensional Man*. As he prophesized, there will be an "opening of the one-dimensional society," and "this prospect of a rupture with the continuum of domination exploitation has its material basis, its emerging basis in the aggravating economic stress of the global system of corporate capitalism, such as: inflation, international monetary crisis, intensified competition among the imperialist powers, escalation of waste [...]."[133] The motivations for the Occupy movement are certainly not much different from the "material basis" that Marcuse has spoken about for a future "Great Refusal": the Occupy movement in general has essentially been a refusal to accept that "global system of corporate capitalism." The proximity between the Occupy movements and Marcuse's

"Great Refusal" can also be further elicited from Žižek's remarks on the movement. When he says that the movement in general has been nothing but "a stopping point [*point d'arrêt*] in the quotidian course of life, to sabotage the normal functioning of the system,"[134] he echoes Marcuse no less, who had foretold that there will come a time "when man calls a halt to the rat race that has been his existence, [...] and decides that instead of going with the rat race, instead of producing ever more and even bigger for those who can and must buy it, to subvert the very mode and direction of production, and thereby of their entire life."[135]

I certainly do not disagree with the necessity of a force of rejection against that which suppresses or represses "instinctual revolt."[136] I would like to think no less that there remains a critical pertinence to Marcuse's "Great Refusal." However, I question if the figure of the *subject*, as invoked by Marcuse when he calls for "a new historical subject" for the "Great Refusal," is an adequate figure of thought for an effective "dissensus" against "that which is." Given the apparent failures of Bartleby and the Occupy movement as *subjects* of occupation, it seems rather futile to found a (counter)sovereign *subject* that insists on an explicit but dangerously (auto)nihilistic "Great Refusal." I would argue that a subtler and certainly more life-affirming strategy is needed today. For that, it is no longer the *subject* projecting a (counter)sovereign force that one must look to, but a figure with a "weak force" perhaps, as Derrida would say,[137] a figure that does not insist on, or is not preoccupied with, its sovereign subjectivity or subjective sovereignty. I have suggested above that the *auto-reject* who walks away may be that figure.[138] With the *auto-reject*, perhaps it is also no longer adequate to speak of a "great" refusal. Instead, I would follow the organizers of the 2011 Marcuse conference at the University of Pennsylvania to call this subtler and life-affirming strategy "critical refusals." With "critical refusals," I would take it to mean that refusal takes on plural forms, rather than a fixed, singular program, and that "critical" would imply some sort of constant movement and self-critique, if not auto-rejection, where any enunciation of refusal does not become hypostasized, banal, or even common. More importantly, "critical" would also mean a nonnihilistic refusal, but a life-affirming one.[139] For that, one not only needs a politics of the *(auto-)reject*; at times, it even calls for a strategy that *rejects politics* altogether, as hinted by the notion of *walking away*.

For the rest of the chapter, I would like to go further in considering how the *auto-reject* in walking away from its "insurrectional moment" (Balibar) against State politics can ensure the nonreturn to the *sovereign subject*, that is to say, the *subject* that does not share sovereignty with others but monopolizes it and its hegemony of force, or else the *subject* that negates the affirmation of the opening toward *anyone* or the other in its complete difference. For that, I would argue that one must turn to a figure of the *reject* that seems impossible in the domain of political thought. The impossible, however, as Derrida would say, is necessary, and this also applies to *démocratie à venir*. As he says in the interview with Michael Sprinker, "Democracy, for me, if I can wager an aphorism, is the political experience of the impossible, the political experience of the opening to the other as possibility of the impossible."[140] This impossible figure would be the animal, since the animal has always been rejected as a possible figure of thought in politics or political philosophy, and so, following the preceding chapter on the "postsecular," I will follow after the animal a little further. Derrida, of course, does not rule out thinking the *voyou-reject* in relation to animals. He notes of Charles Nisard's suggestion that *voyou* can be derived from "*loup-garou*," which translates into English as "werewolf."[141] However, Derrida has his suspicion of this link and prefers to put his trust in the English *rogue* as having greater resonance with animals. As is common in English, *rogue*, beyond (and before) its appropriation by politics for political significations, also describes animals "whose behavior appears deviant or perverse," such as "rogue elephants" or "rogue horses," when they conduct themselves in a "lawless" [*hors-la-loi*] or "devastating" [*ravageurs*] manner, contrary to what is expected of them, for example, to be a "disciplined racing or hunting horse."[142] In *L'Animal que donc je suis*, Derrida will also suggest that the animal has the political potentiality to leave all forms of politics predicated on fraternity and alliance or friendship (which he "deconstructs" in *Politiques de l'amitié*) suspended, undecided, or undecidable, which then allows all existing forms of politics to be questioned or historicized, opening the thinking of politics to elements that political thought has always rejected, marginalized, or forgotten (again something Derrida does in *Politiques de l'amitié* and *Spectres de Marx*). Derrida intimates as much when he says that the animal is "like the every other that is every (bit) other in such intolerable proximity that I do not as yet feel I am justified or qualified to call it my fellow, even less my brother. For we shall have to ask ourselves, inevitably, what happens to the fraternity of brothers when an animal appears on the scene."[143]

Derrida will also mobilize the figure of the animal in his *La Bête et le souverain* seminars in order to destabilize, displace, and perhaps discredit the concept of sovereignty, especially that which has been appropriated and monopolized either by a human individual or by an institution constituted by like-minded human subjects, that is, a sovereignty that presupposes and entails others as incapable of responding to the call to decisively assume a point of authority. I do not follow after Derrida's animal-*voyou* here, however. Instead, I propose in the following to track Deleuze and Guattari's concept of becoming-animal, which I will show to prove itself to be more *voyou* than Derrida's animal-*voyou*, particularly in the context of our contemporary post-9/11 politics. In the shadow of the latter, radical politics, especially that which resists State politics, can be an impossible task, and I explicate this later. Becoming-animal, by contrast, as I will argue, can posit a political trajectory that, to deploy Deleuze and Guattari's rhetoric, smashes State politics from within. What follows is a sustained engagement with Deleuze and Guattari's becoming-animal. It will not tire readers with a detailed explication of the turns of the passive, active, and auto-, *reject* in becoming-animal, but hopes those turns unfold themselves in an evident manner in the process of the discussion. The greater interest here instead will be to inquire into the implications of becoming-animal's turns or forces of (auto-)rejection for political thought, not so much in relation to a theoretical *démocratie à venir* or *égaliberté* this time round, but, as said, to contemporary politics.

From the outset, it can be said that becoming-animal constitutes some form of a *reject* with regard to political thought. This is even the case with some Deleuze and Guattari scholars, given a general hesitation in them in considering becoming-animal's political potentiality. There are certainly those who explicate the concept of becoming-animal, and while they do not hesitate to extend its application to literary works, they do not discuss its political possibilities.[144] Then there are those who are keen to define the ambiguous political terrain of Deleuze and Guattari's philosophy, yet stop short at including becoming-animal within that political cartography.[145] In other words, when it comes to elucidating the politics of Deleuze and

Guattari's philosophy, becoming-animal is very much a missing concept, if not a *reject*, in Deleuze and Guattari scholarship.[146] The refusal to take into account becoming-animal may be said to be a humanist or anthropocentric reflex, even though Deleuze's philosophy of becoming, if not Deleuze's philosophy tout court, is explicitly mobilized against such a reflex. That reflex becomes evident when such scholarship makes appeals, for example, to "actualized or actualizable elements of democratic political normativity," or to "limits of what is possible under present [political] conditions."[147] Such appeals are undeniably anthropologic and/or anthropocentric, since "what is possible under present [political] conditions" tends to exclude things animals or the animal condition of life.[148] Only the (rational) voice of the human reverberates within the limits of "present political normativity."[149] Even when the issue of animal welfare turns up as an element in the latter, it can always be reduced to a gesture made in the name of human's ethical progress; or when it concerns the protection of animal lives in relation to ecological sustainability, it is but in the name of perpetuating human habitation and alimentation in the world. In short, it is only in the image of the rational human, if not "the average adult-white-heterosexual-European-male-speaking a standard language,"[150] that development in political thought is recognized and put into practice. Any figure less than, or in excess of, this rational human being will not count in the space of such a thought, and so animal life barely forms any part of "present political normativity," especially becoming-animal, which, as Deleuze and Guattari say, makes the rational human figure reel. This perhaps explains the rejection of the question of becoming-animal in the political thought of Deleuzo-Guattarian scholars, so long as they predicate their thought on "present political normativity," for an inclination to such a normativity cannot, or is unable to, conceptually and empirically account for such a question as becoming-animal.

The anthropologic and anthropocentric limits that haunt Deleuzo-Guattarian political thought, however, must not prevent thinking becoming-animal as integral to the political force of Deleuze and Guattari's philosophy. As they suggest in their book on Kafka, *there is a politics* of becoming-animal: "To the inhumanness of the 'diabolical powers' responds the sub-human [*le sub-humain*] of a becoming-animal: become-beetle, become-dog, become-ape, 'head over heels and away,' rather than lower one's head and remain a bureaucrat, inspector, judge, or be judged."[151] In other words, becoming-animal, as Kafka's stories have shown, can constitute a politics that serve as a counterpoint to the striating bureaucracy or oppressiveness of institutional politics. In *Mille plateaux*, Deleuze and Guattari will go beyond a Kafkaesque context and say in more general terms, "*There is an entire politics of becomings-animal,* [. . .] which is elaborated in assemblages that are neither those of the family nor of religion nor of the State. Instead, they express minoritarian groups, or groups that are oppressed, prohibited, in revolt, or always on the fringe of recognized institutions, groups all the more secret for being extrinsic, in other words, anomic" (*MP*, 302/ *TP*, 247, my emphasis). I will return to a discussion of this quote later. For the moment, the point that I would like to make here is that the political potentiality of becoming-animal must no longer be marginalized or ignored. Instead, there is a certain urgency, if not necessity, to recognize, or even put into effect, the political force of becoming-animal in our contemporary world. This is because there exists, on the one hand, a certain trap in constructing political philosophies that remain within "present [democratic] political normativity," and on the other, a certain impasse in contemporary radical politics that seeks to counter such normativity.

A few notes on the trap in remaining within "present [democratic] political normativity" are in order: it is by now undeniable that the horizons of democratic thinking and practice in our early twenty-first century, that is, the post-9/11 world, have been under siege. Exploiting the global anxiety for an international democratic peace and security, those horizons have been captured by the sovereign State war machine, namely the American one, such that international democratic politics is thinkable only in terms of a total submission to a global "war on terror." Every state in the world, and every democratic citizen of the world, must accede to support the "war on terror" and not resist it, no matter what form that war has taken, and no matter if its proceedings were adequately justified or not. Such politics has also demanded that every entity in the world presents itself as a singular, *identifiable* body, meaning that none must resist its exposure to the State's globally prevalent technics of surveillance or identification (CCTVs, Unmanned Aerial Vehicles [UAVs], body scanners, biometric passports, and so forth) that seek to contain that body within that politics. Nothing less than a politics of *identifiability* is at work here, and preemptive strikes will be "justified" not only against a territory but also against an individual body that has appeared to deviate from this politics. This condition, which echoes Deleuze's fear of a "world State [...] of absolute peace still more terrifying than that of total war,"[152] has more or less institutionalized itself as the sole normative dimension of so-called democratic geopolitics today. Agamben has certainly put all these in more apocalyptic terms, arguing that all democratic principles in the world are "entirely lost," and that all that remains is the "state of exception" everywhere.[153] Here, I would like to state that I do not follow Agamben so far as to think that the "state of exception" or a "politics of identifiability" will be an absolute condition or horizon without redemption for political thought in a post-9/11 world. However, if it seems that I allow the image of an almost absolutely delimiting State politics to inflect my rhetoric here, I do so only to underscore that such State politics undeniably remains a very real condition today, of which radical politics or even a politics of the *reject*, in the guise of becoming-animal, cannot and must not ignore. It is the challenge or obstacle from which radical politics and/or politics of the *reject* must not back down. In staging a confrontation with State politics formulated in almost absolute terms, I also do think that this can be a valuable or critical lesson for future radical politics, particularly in the case where future political apparatuses project a similar extreme or totalizing horizon.

One could certainly oppose any pessimistic view of contemporary politics by pointing to the fact that the Obama administration replaced the Bush administration in 2009 and has ended post-9/11 American military operations in Iraq. However, we still do not have a world completely free from the "war on terror." In fact, some still describe our contemporary situation as a time of war, and not without justification, since reports of UAVs taking out terror suspects in Pakistan or Afghanistan continue beyond the Bush administration, not to mention that in early 2010, the United States and Britain still considered extending the "war on terror" to Yemen. Furthermore, one has not witnessed a reduced intervention by the State's global military and surveillance technics in public spaces under the Obama administration.[154] The increasing affirmation, if not celebration, of security imaging as a highly competitive and therefore profitable enterprise only signals that neither the United States nor other democratic countries are moving toward dismantling the politics of identifiability and its militarized surveillance structures. Instead, such politics and technics, to reiterate, are becoming naturalized as a norm in democratic states the world over, regardless if one is still in the "war on terror." It is as such that there is a certain trap in deploying the rhetoric of "democratic political normativity": either it risks limiting oneself to the horizon of the State's politics of identifiability, or worse, risks implication in such State politics. In any case, it is evident that political thought, especially one that seeks to inscribe a veritable democracy, cannot go far by deferring to "the limits of what is possible under present condition," especially when those limits are essentially captured or determined by a questionable State "democratic" geopolitics.

In place of a political thought that defers to "democratic political normativity," radical politics, unfortunately, does not present a real alternative. Under the militarized architecture of "democratic" geopolitics, radical politics, or in fact any politics that seeks to counter the ideology and technics of a State-determined "democracy," appears more to be at an impasse, if not impossible. State surveillance apparatuses and preemptive strike machines will guard against any minimal political deviation. (This is also why, if one desires to rethink Marcuse's "Great Refusal" today, if not "the refusal to behave" according to norms or normativity dictated by the State (or even society),[155] any contemporary refusal cannot in effect express itself with such explicit force as manifested by the Black Panther movement, the Vietnam War protests, and the revolutions of 1968, all of which Marcuse witnessed just slightly after the publication of *One-Dimensional Man*. One needs a subtler form or strategy otherwise than an explicit and forceful rejection.) This is not to say that one has stopped conceptualizing radical political thought in the post-9/11 world. Contemporary theorists such as Hardt and Negri, Virno, Galloway and Thacker, and Casarino have taken up the task of constructing radical politics in and for the twenty-first century. Their point of attack, however, is not the highly militarized horizon of the post-9/11 world. The imperative, for them, is to critique and undo the capitalist network empire (structurally not unrelated to the militarized world of surveillance technics), which has captured and controlled communicative discourses of people everywhere. In opposition to that empire, they have called for either a "multitude" or a "common," with its idiosyncratic form of communication that both eludes the appropriation of the network empire and undoes the empire's demand to convert all discourses into economically productive information.[156] More radical is the strategy suggested by Galloway and Thacker, who call for "tactics of nonexistence,"[157] which seek to smash that empire network from within by disappearing into that very network to create a counternetwork. Such network-based radical politics face certain dangers, however, if not a certain nihilism, if the State's advanced military and surveillance technics is not taken into consideration. For instance, one can sense how "tactics of nonexistence" easily risk falling short, just by the reminder of the existence of the 8th Air Force, a combat-ready squadron created and tasked by the American State war machine in 2006 to locate and destroy such counternetworks in cyberspace.

Present radical political thought is therefore quite inadequate or ineffective to sidestep the force of the State war machine. However, that does not mean that one should then give up resisting the ideology of existing State-determined "democratic" geopolitics, no matter how impossible such resistance may seem today. Resistance remains necessary, a necessity that Deleuze and Guattari insist on via their lament that "*we lack resistance to the present.*"[158] Becoming-animal, I would argue, is that trajectory of resistance, if not force of rejection, that we need today. In other words, becoming-animal can resist or sidestep the force of the State war machine and hence lead us out of the impasse of contemporary radical political thought. One has to recognize the political potentiality of becoming-animal today, therefore. But before eliciting the political promise of becoming-animal, I note here that becoming-animal is *not* an exception to the preemptive violence of the State's military and surveillance apparatuses, which would seek to obliterate it with force and acceleration the moment becoming-animal presents itself as an explicit affront to the State. Resistance needs a subtler strategy today; it must not give itself an explicitly defined political program or contour, or even project an explicit force of rejection or disagreement against State politics. Becoming-animal, as I understand it, does proceed with such a subtle strategy: it is a strategy that *auto-rejects* all hypostases on a particular political trajectory and all determinations that would give it a political profile. That is becoming-animal's critical political force in the face of our early twenty-first-century "democratic" geopolitics, which helps avoid many of the risks borne by existing radical political thought defined by explicit programs, targets, and strategies in the face of the latter.[159]

To take on board becoming-animal, one must be prepared to push existing political thought beyond its anthropologic and/or anthropocentric limits. One must in fact be prepared to even *depart* from existing models of political thought, rather than to assimilate or even tame becoming-animal within their norms or normativity. It is this very departure that constitutes becoming-animal's first steps in sidestepping the striation of State-determined "democratic" politics.[160] According to Deleuze and Guattari, becoming-animal is a matter of spatiality—a zone of proximity with the animal—and the temporal immersion into that spatiality.[161] It is an experience of being-at-the-edge, a border experience, or "a phenomenon of bordering" (MP, 299/ TP, 245) opened up between the human and the animal. And this border experience of becoming-animal is about *sensing* the animal, or the actualization of the force or *affect* of the animal within us, which, according to Deleuze and Guattari, is "the effectuation of a power of the pack that throws the self into upheaval and makes it reel. Who has not known the violence of these animal sequences, which uproot one from humanity, if only for an instant, making one scrape at one's bread like a rodent or giving one the yellow eyes of a feline? A fearsome involution calling us toward unheard of becomings" (MP, 294/ TP, 240). We must respond to those calls (and I will explicate this question of response in the following discussion on *aisthēsis*), and it is in responding to those animal affects, which is also to say, in *rejecting* one's anthropologic or anthropomorphic forms and limits, which include the supposed propriety of behavior such as not scraping at one's bread, that one can begin that traversing or "crossing" [*passage*][162] toward an animal space.

In taking that step toward an animal space via becoming-animal, one in fact initiates the process of counteracting the militarized surveillance architectures of State politics. Now, "present political normativity," or conventional anthropocentric politics, which also includes contemporary State "democratic" geopolitics, has hardly concerned itself with animals: it largely *leaves them to be*. In other words, so long as State politics *reject* taking into account animals within their sphere of control or influence, animals, as political *rejects*, are never subjected to the same political determinations, delimitations, and obligations that humans experience as "political animals."[163] Put another way, animal spaces largely escape the gaze and capture of politics. This also means that it is by recovering the very space of exclusion, which the animal occupies after it has been left aside by the frames of normative politics, that critical thought has a space to slide into and sidestep State politics.[164] One must nonetheless be meticulous to ensure that this animal space is *not* outside of the militarized s/

State of contemporary global politics, or that it explicitly marks a space that tears away from the State—I make another precautionary reminder here that seeking such an outside is nothing short of a death wish today.[165] Becoming-animal must be vigilant to *auto-reject* any such desire or even death-drive for an outside. Rather, it will be an *adjacent* space, which escapes the gaze and capture of State military and surveillance apparatuses, where becoming-animal can posit a political resistance that counters and goes beyond the terror and limits of early twenty-first-century "democratic" normativity.[166]

But perhaps one must be even further meticulous to say that this *adjacent* space would allow becoming-animal not only to slip toward a space that is the blind-spot of the gaze of State politics, but also to remain before all technics of identifiability, hence preserving itself from all State preemptive violence. As I would put it, this *adjacent* space is where becoming-animal can let play its doubling effect of *I remain, I become*. This subtle strategy, especially critical in the face of militarized surveillance architectures, and which is no less an artifice or ruse and not without humor,[167] is suggested by Deleuze and Guattari themselves when they say, "becoming is always double" [*que le devenir aille toujours par deux*] (*MP*, 374/ *TP*, 305). As they explicate, what that means is that in becoming-animal, the original entity, the human for example, remains as he or she is. This part of his or her entity can still present itself as a singular, identifiable body before any technics of identifiability, so as to preserve his or her life from the State's deadly preemptive measures. However, something happens at the same time at the edge of his or her body: imperceptible molecular movements are taking place there, deterritorializing themselves from the human body and traversing toward an animal affect. In effect, becoming-animal here involves an *almost* literal disappearance, as it puts forth "an objective zone of indetermination or uncertainty" (*MP*, 355/ *TP*, 273), or tends toward the in-visible or "the imperceptible" (*MP*, 305/ *TP*, 249). In a way, the disappearing, if not dis-appearing, condition of becoming-animal disrupts the real, or it dislocates the perception of the real (*MP*, 292/ *TP*, 239). It makes itself difficult, almost impossible, to be located in the real, but it is nevertheless real and not the stuff of dreams or fantasies (*MP*, 335/ *TP*, 273). It is a problematic real, therefore, a real that is nondeitic, nondefinable, unidentifiable. In other words, one cannot capture in visual terms that aspect of human life that is becoming animal, that aspect that is in-visibly occurring at the edges of the human form: becoming-animal proceeds by being "something more secret, more subterranean" (*MP*, 291/ *TP*, 237) than what the real would like it to display to visibility.

If traversing toward an animal space constitutes becoming-animal's initial sidestepping of State politics, the dis-appearing part of becoming-animal is its challenge or resistance to the State's technics of surveillance, while letting the visible human body remain before those same technics.[168] In other words, it is the *I become* of becoming-animal that one may speak of a political trajectory that counters or rejects State politics, for its dis-appearing aspect always poses a difficulty for any identifying technics of the State to trace or chart at present or in advance. It always slips into an *adjacent* space that is the blind-spot of the gaze of State politics, where the body is not limited to a singular form but can fully and freely engage (with) its own multiplicity. In the face of a politics of identifiability, becoming-animal surreptitiously contests the demand for a totalizing coming to presence and presents at best a haziness before all gazes of the State apparatus. In that sense, and in keeping in mind that the dis-appearance of *I become* is a matter of molecular investment in an animal affect, one may also speak of a "molecular politics" (*MP*, 339/ *TP*, 277) or even "a revolutionary micropolitical action" [*une action révolutionnaire micropolitique*][169] of becoming-animal. As Deleuze and Guattari will tell us, "molecular politics" or "micropolitics" resists any apparatus that attempts to striate or delimit a body to a singular entity according to codes determined by that apparatus, and "molecular politics" or "micropolitics" will counter such striating operation by setting free the "intensive multiplicities" or "diverse modalities" that a body desires to express—multiplicities and modalities that not just reject but also exceed and escape all codifications by the apparatus.[170]

But before one can put into effect "molecular politics" or "micropolitics," there is always the question of how one becomes-animal, a question that readers of Deleuze and Guattari's philosophy will constantly pose, since Deleuze and Guattari give us only a vague sense of the process. As Deleuzian scholars have never failed to underscore, becoming-animal is nothing like a mimetic repetition of the animal form, which means that to become-animal, one cannot rely on an image of a particular animal that the human form will gradually take on or resemble. And if there are no visual signposts to point one toward becoming-animal, Deleuze and Guattari will add to the difficulty of becoming-animal by insisting that there is no prescriptive methodology, "no preformed logical order" (*MP*, 307/ *TP*, 251), to it. In other words, one cannot refer to any foundation of reason, *logos*, norms, or normativity to become-animal. In becoming-animal, "being expresses [the human and the animal] both in a single meaning in *a language that is no longer that of words*, in a matter that is no longer that of forms, in an affectability that is no longer that of subjects" (*MP*, 315/ *TP*, 258, my emphasis). To put it briefly, becoming-animal cannot be pinned down by rational human discourse. Common sense and intelligible sense serve no purpose here; they are powerless before becoming-animal. In a sense, becoming-animal just becomes; it rejects the linguistic and rationalizing performatives of *logos*. According to Deleuze and Guattari, it can even be "done with enough feeling" [*si on le fait avec assez de cœur*] (*MP*, 337/ *TP*, 275), although they will be quick to underscore that this feeling is nothing subjective—"the affect is not a personal feeling" (*MP*, 294/ *TP*, 240). Instead, this particular affect or feeling opens one to a plural alterity or heterogeneity within *and* without. Becoming-animal, as said before, is then a question of being worthy of such affects, of opening oneself to the *sensation* of animal affects and responding to them affirmatively, (auto-) rejecting any anthropocentrism or anthropomorphism that blocks those responses.

This particular "feeling" or sensation of animal affects may perhaps be found in the originary and communicative *aisthēsis* that humans and animals share. *Aisthēsis*, as Aristotle himself has observed, is the irreducible feeling of "pleasure and pain" that both humans and animals sense and which enables both humans and animals to immediately "communicate" a wrong done to them.[171] To cross to the adjacent space of the animal, it is perhaps a question of recovering that originary *aisthēsis*, that is, of recovering a sensation of the milieu[172] of *aisthēsis* that humans and animals originarily share.[173] Originary *aisthēsis* has to be recovered because we have somehow lost it when Aristotle supplemented it with an anthropocentric *logos* in his political philosophy. It could be argued that originary *aisthēsis*, in its immediate sensing and communication of pain or wrong done to a human or animal, is of political potentiality, that is, *aisthēsis* in itself is already adequate to demand, without delay, an addressing of the wrong committed against a human or animal. Aristotle, however, refuses to recognize the political potentiality of *aisthēsis* as such. For *aisthēsis* to become politics "proper," Aristotle insists on the supplement of rational speech (or *logos* as rational speech), which will transform *aisthēsis* into an all too human "perception of good and evil," or "a sense of justice" that "decides what is just" in an institutional or legalistic manner.[174] From here, it could be said then that to recover *aisthēsis*—before it is supplemented by a form of *logos* that has been appropriated by, and reduced to, the human—is not only a way toward the adjacent space of becoming-animal, but also an unveiling of becoming-animal's potentiality for a future political project of justice. Participating in an affect "that is no longer of words," becoming-animal becomes invested in an immanent response, "here and now" in Deleuze and Guattari's words,[175] to the injustices enacted against any singularity with or without *logos*, without the delay entailing legal processes that translate injustices and corresponding legal actions into the linguistic performativities of institutional jurisprudence.[176] Such a project of justice certainly departs from, if not displaces, the economy of illocutionary exchanges that sustains the spirit of democratic parliamentary discussion. Yet, as suggested, its immanent responsiveness might even be more effective than all existing political normativity based on some communicative action that is in turn conditioned by some preexisting common knowledge or linguistic idioms shared between speech actors.[177]

The shift to originary *aisthēsis*, or the refusal to predicate itself on any logocentric system, gives becoming-animal a further radical political edge as well. Being an experience that is hardly rationalized or rationalizable (since it is an experience without method and without program, as noted above) and therefore barely known or knowable, becoming-animal can be said to disrupt, in a word, biopolitics, that is, the political condition that regulates life in a hegemonic manner and which thinkers such as Agamben have considered the contemporary world to be in.[178] Biopolitics, as Foucault has already analyzed it, is perfectible only if it has knowledge of its subjects, or if its subjects are always knowable; biopolitics cannot consolidate its management of its subjects if there exists a life, such as becoming-animal, which (auto-)rejects conceptualization.[179] With becoming-animal's refusal to be conceptualized, we are once again in the domain of "something more secret, more subterranean" of becoming-animal's politics, which we have seen in its molecular trajectories: there is no doubt a posture of secrecy in becoming-animal's escape from any methodology that seeks to pin it under a rationalizing gaze. In fact, as Derrida has noted, there has always been a secret to the animal, the secret that inheres in what it thinks and whether it even thinks at all: in that respect, the animal can therefore never be the complete epistemic object of total knowledge, and its secret will always remain to be a madness for any economy of rational thought, which hence always troubles philosophers.[180] Yet its secret is also precisely that radical condition that allows it to be free from any conceptual capture that Man is subjected to, such as his or her striating categorization as political-being or "political animal." Becoming-animal, which reiterates the unconceptualizable secret of the animal, challenges any (State) politics that seeks to totalize and homogenize every human life as its knowable, singular, political *subject*.

Speaking of the unconceptualizable contour of becoming-animal, one may perhaps transpose the *aisthēsis* of becoming-animal to an aesthetic modality, or more specifically, to the Kantian experience of aesthetic sensation, which is derived not only from art objects but also from things of nature.[181] The proximity between the Kantian aesthetic sensation and the *aisthēsis* of becoming-animal is almost undeniable, since they share many similar traits. For one, if the originary *aisthēsis* that concerns becoming-animal is of an (immediate) communicable feeling of pleasure or pain, one finds a corresponding "universal communicability" in the Kantian aesthetic sensation.[182] And if aesthetic sensation, for Kant, escapes the grasp of human cognition,[183] or is essentially and ultimately unknowable and contributes nothing to knowledge (*The Critique of Judgment* §1 [42], §15 [71]), or is without concept (§15 [70]), all these traits are certainly encapsulated by the unconceptualizable contour of becoming-animal. The *aisthēsis* of becoming-animal can even be said to be close to the Kantian *sublime* aesthetic sensation, considering that Kant has argued that we sense such sensation through things in nature that exceed what our existing knowledge of nature has prepared us for, or that exist beyond the limits of recognizable or humanly perceptible forms[184]—and becoming-animal, as discussed above, is of such a thing. Kant has also said that things of the sublime are of an immense magnitude beyond measure (§26 [99]). However, becoming-animal, as seen, proceeds at the molecular dimension, and hence, if there is a magnitude to becoming animal, it would be at a level of what Deleuze and Guattari would call an n-1 degree of magnitude. Despite this difference, what remains critical, for the attainment of either the Kantian sublime or the *aisthēsis* of the Deleuzo-Guattarian becoming-animal, is an affirmative receptivity via an immanent response,[185] an enthusiasm,[186] or the free play and movement of thought and imagination (§9 [58]).[187]

Deleuze and Guattari themselves do not fail to articulate the aesthetic dimension of the *aisthēsis* of becoming-animal.[188] As they say in an instance in *Mille plateaux*, "it is through writing," in the sense of literature such as Kafka's writings or Melville's *Moby Dick*, "that you become animal" (*MP*, 229/ *TP*, 187). There is no doubt that art is the site that Deleuze and Guattari frequently turn to in order to locate the nascence or emergence of becoming-animal. And if sensation is the critical mode of responding to animal affects in becoming-animal, they reiterate the importance of the role of art in relation to this aspect of becoming-animal when they say that "the aim of art" is "to extract a bloc of sensations, a pure being of sensations."[189] But the question that I would like to pose here is if it necessary to turn to art in order to elicit and elucidate becoming-animal and its political potential as a counterpoint to State politics. No doubt, art, for example the cinematic arts as Deleuze argues in *L'Image-temps*, has the political potentiality to articulate a "people to come" or a yet unthought-of assemblage such as the "intensive multiplicities" of becoming-animal, in opposition to the State's proclamation that no other assemblages exist except those it had constructed and organized. However, Deleuze also warns us that such art risks being eventually appropriated by the State, which would then transform it into State apparatuses serving only to disseminate State politics.[190] Furthermore, art is always in a way untimely: it comes too early in expressing or projecting sensations such as becoming-animal before they are recognizable or acceptable by the world, which entails that any turn to art in order to finally pursue that trajectory of becoming-animal is at the same time always too late a gesture. In that sense, perhaps one must look elsewhere to be able to respond immanently to the sensation of becoming-animal, and hence put in effect an immanent political response to State politics.

According to Deleuze and Guattari, this elsewhere is none other than life itself, or rather the experience of the space of everyday life where perceptible and imperceptible matter or elements traverse one another. In that sense, one may perhaps regard the sensation of becoming-animal as an "ambient awareness" of the "intensive multiplicities" or "diverse modalities" around oneself.[191] For Deleuze and Guattari, this would be the sensation of "life lines" or "real becomings that are *not* [my emphasis] produced only *in* art, [...] that do not consist in fleeing *into* art, taking refuge in art, [...] [and] that never reterritorialize on art" (*MP*, 230/ *TP*, 187). Life itself, if not *only* life itself as Deleuze and Guattari will claim, contains enough creative force to engender those multiplicities or modalities.[192] (As I will explicate later, I am not saying at all that life *is* political. I agree with Deleuze and Guattari that the contrary is true instead. What is suggested here is that certain elements of life itself can potentially have political force, without them having to serve solely political ends.) There is always already an aesthetic trajectory in life itself, therefore, which is also to say that the sensation of these molecular multiplicities or modalities can *already* be found in life itself, prior to any fabrication of artworks seeking to express such a sensation.[193] That is why Deleuze and Guattari will say that "art is never an end in itself" (*MP*, 230/ *TP*, 187) for becoming-animal or becoming tout court. It is more critical that one immerses oneself "in life, in real life" (*MP*, 229/ *TP*, 187), and be affirmatively receptive and responsive to the encounter with all the molecular animal affects there.

As Deleuze would also suggest, there is always a political potentiality in participating in such molecular dimensions of life, a certain power or subversive contour in the molecular "art of encounter outside knowledge," or in short, in "aesthetic existence."[194] I would argue here that such encounters break with what may be called the politics of (dis-)friendship that underlies post-9/11 State geopolitics. In claiming to defend international democratic peace and security, State politics has demanded that one not offer friendship, support, or hospitality to forms of life that disagree with, or resist, the technics of identifiability. Otherwise, one would, like those who resisted the "war on terror," be given the name of "rogue," a name that would only announce a "justified" preemptive military force against the thus-named. Such State politics has the effect of discouraging one from building any affinity with anyone, even though the latter might be an advocate of the politics of "war on terror." But even without the dictum to alienate deviant forms of life, even without the threat of labeling anyone who befriends the latter a "rogue," the global military and civilian surveillance apparatus itself already has the force to discourage relations between one and another. After Foucault, one knows that the logical end of institutionalized surveillance would only be the translation of surveillance practices into the individual itself. In other words, it conditions the individual to adopt not only a consciousness of surveillance but also a *surveillance-consciousness*, whereby the individual begins to conduct surveillance on him- or herself *and* on other individuals, watching the next person beside him or her. Such individualization of surveillance surely hinders the construction of any friendship or trust, and such has been the politics of friendship of the early twenty-first century, where the State has been advising one—implicitly or not—to be wary of the next person, whom the State would conjure in the image of a possible terror-suspect, terror-perpetrator, terror-advocate, terror-mastermind, or rogue-terrorist.

Becoming-animal, in its molecular encounters with "intensive multiplicities" and "diverse modalities," breaks with such State-conjured paranoid narratives of human interaction, or the State's biopolitical will to manage its subjects by the relations they form. In contrast to the State's determination to control and delimit relations between beings, becoming-animal's "transversal communications between heterogeneous populations" (*MP*, 292/ *TP*, 239) open a body to an unlimited relation with any (number of) living entities. In other words, becoming-animal invites unrestricted participations; it constructs its own milieu of friends, its own politics of friendship or assemblages: "There is an entire politics of becomings-animal, [...] which is elaborated in assemblages that are neither those of the family nor of religion nor of the State. Instead, they express minoritarian groups, or groups that are oppressed, prohibited, in revolt, or always on the fringe of recognized institutions, groups all the more secret for being extrinsic, in other words, anomic" (*MP*, 302/ *TP*, 247). The alliance with the "anomic" is indeed how becoming-animal sharply challenges the State's politics of (dis-)friendship. The "anomic" is an "exceptional individual," with whom "an alliance must be made in order to become-animal" (*MP*, 297/ *TP*, 243). This "anomic" individual, however, is not exceptional in the sense that it is outside the law, or "has no rules or goes against [*contredit*] the rules" (*MP*, 298/ *TP*, 244), in the manner in which one tends to think of the exception. The "anomic," and the becoming-animal that follows it, are more subtle or discreet than to announce themselves as being outside the law or directly antithetical to the State. The "anomic" and becoming-animal perfectly understand that doing so will only invite their destruction by preemptive militarized politics. The "anomic" therefore remains within the boundaries of what is politically determined as normal, except it is always at the thresholds of those boundaries. It is like a shadow there, and one can never be sure if the shadow has already inclined toward the outside or adjacent spaces. One can never be sure which way the "anomic" is going to turn: back inside, outside, or beside? Like the animal and its secret, the "anomic" is the figure of uncertainty, "the unequal, the rough [*le rugueux*], the rugged [*l'aspérité*]" (*MP*, 198/ *TP*, 244), the figure without conceptualization. It does not violate the law, but it disturbs the stability or equilibrium of the law precisely because of its undefined or ambiguous political alignment.

Yet, one should note that an alliance is not a necessary condition for becoming-animal. This is particularly helpful in the case when the "anomic" treads too close to being outside the law, which would then attract the attention of the State's surveillance apparatuses and hence put becoming-animal at risk of a preemptive strike by the State. This nondependence on an alliance for becoming-animal can be elicited in Deleuze and Guattari when they state that the sensation of animal affects within us does not require an actual, physical proximity with animals. In other words, the empirical presence of an animal is not a necessary condition for becoming-animal. The desire to exceed our singular anthropocentric and anthropomorphic selves can already be sufficient. Deleuze and Guattari suggest this when they question the necessity of an outside: "A fascination for the outside? Or is the multiplicity that fascinates us already related to a multiplicity dwelling *within us* [my emphasis]?" (*MP*, 298/ *TP*, 240). In *Qu'est-ce que la philosophie?*, they would add that the affect of becoming-animal "concerns *ourselves here and now* [my emphasis]; but what is animal, vegetable, mineral, or human in us is no longer distinct [. . .]."[195] All these imply that an adjacent space, which is at stake in a politics of becoming-animal, need not be one literally beside our bodily forms: it can also exist within us. In responding affirmatively to becoming-animal, that is, to the sensation of animal affects within, an adjacent space can be created *involutionarily* within us: "Becoming is involutive [*involutif*], involution is creative" (*MP*, 292/ *TP*, 238). In this case, the "involutionary" creation of a free space from within one's bodily form once again avoids the hasty determination to articulate an *outside*, or to form an alliance with a rogue "anomic" in explicit opposition to State, evading thus the fatal intervention by the State's preemptive military and surveillance apparatuses.

To be sure, elucidating the political trajectories of becoming-animal today, which no doubt resist or challenge State politics, will not be about disseminating the ideologies or advocating the conductivity of terror as it is understood and executed in contemporaneous times. If becoming-animal assumes a combative anti-State posture, it is because it puts into question the supposed "democratic" normativity the State has claimed necessary for the defense of a global democratic peace and security. It is also because the State would have *first* delimited the freedom of becoming-animal in that process: it is when the State seeks to determine becoming-animal's possibilities of relations with other beings, and when it demands a totalizing singular presence from becoming-animal, that becoming-animal will adopt a disposition in opposition to "organizations such as the institution of [. . .] the State apparatus" and "continually work them from within and trouble them from without, with other forms of content, other forms of expression" (*MP*, 296/ *TP*, 242). In short, it is only when its freedom is at risk that becoming-animal "is accompanied, at its origins as in its undertaking, by a rupture with the central institutions that have established themselves or seek to become established" (*MP*, 302/ *TP*, 247). Yet, as it may already be evident throughout the discussion of the politics of becoming-animal, becoming-animal in fact does not launch an explicit combat with the State. The political force of becoming-animal is always more a matter of "uncertain combat,"[196] if not "war without battle lines, with neither confrontation nor retreat, without battles even: pure strategy" (*MP*, 436/ *TP*, 353). That also means that, unlike the radical politics mentioned earlier, there is never a clear political directive, program, or contour with becoming-animal, and that is how it will always escape the capture and destruction by twenty-first-century State militarized "democratic" geopolitics. That is to say too that when becoming-animal does eventually put in place a political critique against the State, the State will only at best have a little (or hazy) suspicion as to where that critique comes from, little knowledge as to how it is done.

At this point, I would also like to point out that becoming-animal does not reject democracy tout court. Like Patton in his essay "Becoming-Democratic," I do believe that a spirit of democracy remains a backdrop to Deleuze and Guattari's philosophy, only if democracy is meant to be the constant project of recognizing the freedom of life, or the right to life, of anyone or anything in its heterogeneous terms or voice. I have suggested that becoming-animal can further open the terrain of democratic thought when it goes beyond the boundaries of a rationalizing *logos*, which only serve to reduce existing democratic normativity to an anthropocentricism and/or anthropomorphism. Becoming-animal, in departing not only from all anthropologic and anthropocentric political normativity but also from anthropologic and anthropocentric thinking in general, allows a nonlogocentric terrain to emerge, which negotiates the freedom and justice due to each living entity—human or animal—via the fact of the entity's singularity. In other words, this negotiation will not make acceding to *logos* (or "rhetoric" in Bennington's reading) a condition for justice, a condition that only creates a delay, if not an obstacle, to the due address of a violation done against a singularity.

One could perhaps say that above everything else, the question of a life free(d) from any form of striation is the ultimate concern of becoming-animal. It is the pursuit of such a life that becoming-animal will trace a "line of flight" toward an adjacent space that sidesteps a space of capture. The horizon that one must keep in sight, if there is one, when thinking about Deleuze and Guattari's politics is therefore life, or, to be precise, the freedom of life; any gesture that entails from such a politics would always be engaged in undoing apparatuses that delimit life.[197] Todd May is only accurate to say that the premise of Deleuze and Guattari's political philosophy of life, or "what is most 'vital' about life is its capacity for disorganizing what is organizing and repressive."[198] However, I am a little uncomfortable when May puts the question of politics and life in Deleuze as such: "Life is what politics is about and, concomitantly, politics suffuses life."[199] I would like to think that life and politics do *not* necessarily turn around each other endlessly; that life is not always striated or reterritorialized by politics. One may recall Nancy here: things might pass through politics, but not everything is politics or political. I would therefore like to think instead that there is life beyond the frames of politics.

Politics must not be the unsurpassable limit for life. To think life as only political through and through, not only because it is captured by State biopolitics, but also because it is absolutely committed to some political movement for the good of itself and others, would only risk letting life be striated by the domain of politics. In this case, one must then "tempt [life] into an uncertain combat" as Deleuze and Guattari say,[200] and wrest it away from the confines of politics. I am not saying that the "question of freeing life" from political capture or from politics in general need not involve any political moves. On the contrary, I do recognize that certain political steps must be taken in order to "free life wherever it is imprisoned,"[201] hence my endeavor so far to trace becoming-animal's political potentiality to critique and resist contemporary State "democratic" geopolitics, and to open up a terrain of political thought beyond the limits of anthropocentrism and anthropomorphism. If I am arguing at this point for a life beyond the frames of politics, or that a life free(d) from politics is the ultimate aim of becoming-animal, I am saying, without denying the political potentialities of becoming-animal's trajectory, that a political contour must not define the *ends* of becoming-animal.[202] Or, put another way, becoming-animal must *auto-reject*, as it does, political horizons not only set by others or the State, but also those that might emerge in the course of its political trajectory. To be sure, I also do not mean any return to human or anthropocentric life here. Instead, I follow Deleuze's definition of "a life" here, according to which, "the life of the individual has given way to an impersonal yet singular life, which unleashes [*dégage*] a pure event liberated from the accidents of interior and exterior life, that is to say, from the subjectivity and objectivity of that which arrives."[203] In other words, "a life," in Deleuze's terms, is also indifferent to the categories of the *subject* and *object*.

One could indeed raise a disagreement here and cite a line in *Mille plateaux* where Deleuze and Guattari say that "before being, there is politics" (*MP*, 249/ *TP*, 203). That phrase in itself could suggest that politics does seem to be the first and last concern of Deleuze and Guattari's philosophy. But a careful reading of its context would indicate otherwise. That phrase follows from Deleuze and Guattari's reading of how schizoanalysis perceives the "lines of flight" traversing a living body (lines that can also pertain to the trajectory of becoming-animal, since there are also "animal lines of flight" (*MP*, 248/ *TP*, 202)). The fact that these "lines of flight" are *read by* schizoanalysis as political, however, could also mean that "lines of flight" *in themselves* are *not* necessarily political. They become so only under the interpretative lens of schizoanalysis. In other words, their political disposition is only a supplemental aspect given by schizoanalysis. Following Fernand Deligny, Deleuze and Guattari will in fact state beforehand that "these lines mean nothing" (*MP*, 248/ *TP*, 203). They will also elaborate that these lines are essentially "without a model," "have nothing to do with language," "have nothing to do with a signifier, the determination of a subject by the signifier," "nothing to do with a structure," and without "imaginary figures [or] symbolic functions" (*MP*, 248–49/ *TP*, 202–3). In that case, they inherently do not articulate a "politics" that one can associate with any existing political thought, be it democratic or revolutionary. Or else, "lines of flight" do not essentially belong in any *a priori* way to politics. Like becoming-animal, they exceed politics or any endeavor to confine them within political frames. They are ultimately just "life lines," which, however, can in fact be unbearable to any form of normative anthropologic and anthropocentric political thought because of their disavowal of all political norms (*MP*, 248–51/ *TP*, 203–5). It is as such that normative political thought, finding these "life lines" an affront to existing political normativity, renders them political or rather counterpolitical, which hence gives place to the false judgment that politics is at the beginning and end of these "life lines."

The sense that becoming-animal is not ultimately delimited by politics can also be affirmed when one brings to mind again the ends of becoming-animal. I have noted that for Deleuze and Guattari, the end of becoming-animal is becoming-imperceptible (*MP*, 304/ *TP*, 248). The rejection of coming to presence surely has little use for politics as we know it, especially when it pertains to prescribing a political program.[204] But it should be noted that this becoming-imperceptible is not a reductive, nihilistic gesture. On the contrary, it is something generative. In becoming-imperceptible, a body's form loses its organized totality; it loses molecules at the edge of its form, but from then on, they come into contact with, or are exposed to, other molecules riding on a cosmic force that moves the world and that flows through the world. Becoming-animal, in becoming-imperceptible, "brings into play the cosmos with its molecular components" (*MP*, 343/ *TP*, 280). It is this active and affirmative interplay with the world's molecules that the becoming-imperceptible of becoming-animal regenerates a thought of the world. In contrast to the apocalyptic teleology of twenty-first century State politics, the becoming-imperceptible of becoming-animal "is to world, to make a world of worlds," leading us "to be present at the dawn of the world" (*MP*, 343/ *TP*, 280), the dawn of life.[205]

To reiterate, there is a life to live beyond the frames or domains of politics. So far, human life in this early twenty-first century has been captured almost absolutely as political subjects of a global State politics driven by the perfectibility of an international democratic peace and security. To retrieve the freedom of life from the appropriation of the State, human life cannot do it on its own today, but must approach the animal. In becoming-animal, one is also presented the possibility to create an adjacent space where life is free(d) from the capture of striating State politics. Such a process no doubt implicates becoming-animal in a certain political trajectory, as elucidated by this section, but the point, once again, is not to place politics as the horizon of such a life or its life-liberating strategies. One can put it simply by saying that politics must only be a means of liberating life but not an end in itself. If there is a politics to becoming-animal, as Deleuze and Guattari do not fail to acknowledge, this politics must be understood as something transitional or transversal, a political affect where affect here would mean "purely transitive, and not indicative or representative," as Deleuze defines elsewhere.[206] "Transversal" also implies perpetual, and even uncertain, movement. I would say that everything bears on the "transversal," and this is the case for becoming-animal, when it moves from taking on a political trajectory in order to resist State politics to freeing itself subsequently from politics in order to live life. Becoming-animal, in other words, as it charts a politics against the State, if not traverses the State with its politics, also *transverses* such politics, leaping on a line of flight toward a life beyond the frames or striation of politics. The "transversal" element, that is to say, that which prevents all hypostasis or localization, is what enables becoming-animal to sidestep the capture of politics or the political.[207] From not resisting the State's prohibition to create an *outside* that can oppose State politics, to a becoming that dis-appears into an adjacent space to overturn State measures, and to the eventual abandonment of all political ambitions for a life free(d) of politics, that is, to the point where it exercises the freedom to *reject politics* altogether, the "transversal" trajectory of becoming-animal, in this sense, can also be said to bear all the turns of the passive, active, and auto-*reject*.

5

CLINAMEN, OR THE AUTO-REJECT FOR "POSTHUMAN" FUTURES

In following the animal in the last two chapters—first the animal-mes-siah in Cixous, and then becoming-animal in Deleuze and Guattari—one could say that the question of the *reject* has progressively taken on a "posthuman" contour, especially if one follows Cary Wolfe's "posthu-manism," or Rosi Braidotti's "posthuman critical theory" (even though, as I will explicate in a while, one should heed Braidotti's "posthumanism" only in limited ways). According to Wolfe in *What is Posthumanism?*, the animal question—particularly that which Derrida in *L'Animal que donc je suis* takes as its point of departure—is what "posthuman" discourse, if it is to free itself from the limits of anthropological and anthropocen-tric humanism, must let itself be inflected with, complemented at the same time by considerations of Niklas Luhmann's second-order systems theory and Disability Studies. In that regard, Wolfe's "posthumanism" can also be said to be a question of the *reject*, since—as one has to unfortunately acknowledge—disabled beings, systems theory, and animals remain in many ways excluded from any complete appurtenance to "normal" human communities, or to discourses that hinge on the "normal" human being as their primary concern. In fact, even before Wolfe's "posthumanism," *rejects* have already been no strangers to "posthuman" discourse. This is surely the case of Donna Haraway's "posthumanism" of the 1980s, through which one has witnessed the emergence of figures of the *reject* typical of that epoch: figures such as cyborgs and genomic replicants. Undoubt-edly, almost thirty years after Haraway's cyborg manifesto, the notion of cyborgs has been progressively naturalized in contemporary ways of living and contemporary understandings of bodily operativity and interactions. That is due to advances in the medical sciences, which have made common today the introduction of technical and robotic prostheses to the human body so as to enhance or supplement failing human parts. Furthermore, robots are also gradually being accepted as companions for the aged and people with physical disadvantages. Genomic replicants, especially of the human type, however, remain some sort of *rejects* today, since the replication of human selves through genomic experimentation is still very much forbidden territory.[1] In any case, it can be said that "posthumanism" so far has been motivated and mobilized largely by *rejects*, that is, figures excluded, marginalized, and even banned by existing sociocultural norms and dominant intellectual discourses that determine what constitutes a human and what belongs to human communities. It can be said further that *rejects* in "posthuman" discourses have been raised in large part not only to counter that rejection but also to contest the certitude or foundation of the human male *subject*, especially his insistence on his unitary, organic holism and what he believes he can do with that supposed holism. The critique of the human *subject* can even be found in Luhmann's systems theory, which constitutes a basis for Wolfe's "posthumanism." It is true that machinic categories tend to proliferate in Luhmann's systems theory, and one does not expect any organic entity such as the human *subject* to show up. Yet, in the preface to the English edition of *Social Systems*, the question of the human *subject* is raised, as Luhmann questions why people cannot "let [the category of the *subject*] go," or why it has been "overlooked [. . .] for so long" that each *subject*, "as an observer of his observing," tends to denigrate others.[2] That denigration, as Luhmann puts it, arises "because every subject conceives of itself as the condition for the constitution of all others, those others could be subjects, but not real, so to speak, *subjective* subjects. From the perspective of each subject, each other one possesses merely a derivative, constituted, constructed existence."[3]

Braidotti's brand of "posthumanism" in *The Posthuman* launches a similar critique of the human male *subject* (not to mention that her vested interests in the "postsecular" and becoming-animal resonate with the present work). As she puts it unequivocally, her "posthumanism" involves a direct, critical response to "the unitary subject of Humanism, including its socialist variables," that is, the *subject* that is essentially human, occidental, and male and who exploits his environment and denigrates others that are different from him, so that he can establish some sort of central, authoritative position in the world.[4] Even though she does not use the term, she highlights the fact that "the unitary subject of Humanism" produces *rejects*:

> All other modes of embodiment are cast out of the subject position and they include anthropomorphic others: non-white, non-masculine, non-normal, non-young, non-healthy, disabled, malformed or enhanced peoples. They also cover more ontological categorical divides between Man and zoo-morphic, organic or earth others. All these "others" are rendered as pejoration, pathologized and cast out of normality, on the side of anomaly, deviance, monstrosity and bestiality.[5]

Like Haraway in her empathy with cyborgs, Braidotti situates herself amid those *rejects*: she recognizes that "[her] feminist self, partly because of [her] sex, historically speaking," in relation to Humanism, "never quite made it into full humanity [. . .]," and so "[her] sex fell on the side of 'Otherness,' understood as pejorative difference, or as being-worth-less-than."[6] It is from the recognition of being such a *reject* in the wake of Humanism's construction of "the unitary subject" that Braidotti launches her "posthumanism," which, not unlike Haraway's or Wolfe's, is therefore born of *rejects* no less. However, contrary to what Wolfe and I consider to be a possible future trajectory of "posthumanism," Braidotti resists any departure from the notion of the *subject*. She seeks, instead, "to replace [the unitary subject of Humanism] with a more complex and relational subject," a "critical posthuman subject" that is in more specific terms "a relational subject constituted in and by multiplicity, that is to say, a subject that works across differences and is also internally differentiated, but still grounded and accountable."[7] In place of the *subject* of Humanism, Braidotti posits a "non-unitary subject" bearing "an enlarged sense of inter-connection between self and others, including the non-human or 'earth' others."[8]

I certainly do not disagree with the more general ethical and political dimensions of Braidotti's "posthumanism," such as her call for greater respect and empathy for others, in reaction to Humanism's uncritical celebration of a human male *subject* that rejects others and their differences, and her resistance to the biopolitical determination and control of life and its "multiple practices of dying," which include programming death by unmanned combat vehicles—which Braidotti calls "tele-thanatological machines"—that stealthily proliferate the world over.[9] However, given the objective and outlook of this present work, I find Braidotti's tarrying with the *subject* specifically problematic, for reasons that I have been spelling out throughout this work, and for others that I will try to highlight in the course of this chapter. For the moment, let me give further consideration to a "posthumanism" that not only is committed to a critique of (male) human organic holism but also suggests a departure from the *subject*. One could say that in such a "posthumanism," there is a trace of French "poststructuralism," especially the trace of the "poststructuralist" endeavor to critique or "deconstruct" the *subject*. One could even go further to say that a "posthumanism" that continues the unfinished project of critiquing or "deconstructing" the *subject* may appear to posit itself as an heir apparent to "poststructuralism." That does seem to be how Wolfe positions his "posthumanism," of which he does acknowledge its other debt to "poststructuralism" beside the one to Luhmann's systems theory, and for which he would suggest the critical task of providing a response to Nancy's question of "who comes after the subject."[10] Ivan Callus and Stefan Herbrechter, in their work on "posthuman" theory, also articulate the trace of "poststructuralism" and likewise take up Nancy's question in their "critical posthumanism."[11] However, Callus and Herbrechter, like Braidotti,[12] are hesitant to radically depart from the *subject*, and continue to postulate "posthuman subjectivities."[13]

While I share Callus and Herbrechter's concern for a more critical explication of the link between "posthumanism" and "poststructuralism" in general, such that the specific difference of each term is never effaced,[14] I would like, in this chapter, to build on the thread that ties "posthumanism" to the "poststructuralist" project to posit a figure of thought otherwise than the *subject*. In other words, what I think is more pertinent for this present work is the question that remains from the "poststructuralism"-"posthumanism" connection, which is whether the *rejects* of "posthumanism"—its cyborgs, genomic replicants, machinic systems, animals, and disabled beings—are adequate responses to Nancy's question, or if they further the critique of the human *subject*. Or else, is it the case that more still needs to be done, in a way whereby the debt of "posthumanism" to "poststructuralism" goes even farther? What I am suggesting here is that the *reject*, or more specifically the *auto-reject*, which I have elicited and developed so far from contemporary French thought, not only can make a critical intervention in present "posthumanism" but also can pave the way toward a future "posthuman" discourse that really goes beyond anthropocentric and anthropological limits. In that regard, merely deploying or identifying *rejects* in "posthumanism" is inadequate, especially if "posthumanism" is to provide a response to Nancy's question in a way that leads to an "undoing far more comprehensive [...] [than any] deconstructive engagement" of the human *subject*.[15] I would even say that "posthuman" discourse risks being some sort of philosophical letdown when it in-corporates or assimilates aspects of these *rejects* for the human. This is because "posthumanism" in that case only exposes itself, in a regressive fashion, to return to the human *subject*, or to be nothing but the work of the all-too-human *subject*, keen only to accumulate for itself predicates previously left out in its foundation. One could even borrow Braidotti's words to say that such "posthumanism" is not really "free [...] from the provincialism of the mind, the sectarianism of ideologies, the dishonesty of grandiose posturing and the grip of fear."[16] Worse, *rejects* are no longer "free" in their abandonment to be as they are, but are now striated within the gaze and reach of the "posthuman" *subject*. In this case, "posthuman" discourse runs the ethical risk of circumscribing, taming, regulating, and acculturating the differences or heterogeneity of *rejects*.

The above ethical danger has been noted by Wolfe himself, and by Keith Ansell Pearson much earlier in the late 1990s, when Pearson expressed his suspicion of "posthumanism" as an (unconscious) "vicious return of outmoded grand narratives" of the human *subject*, especially when "posthuman" discourse begins to rein in elements previously regarded as alien to human life, only to further the futures of and *for* that human *subject*.[17] I fear that Braidotti's "posthuman subject" unfortunately bears the potential to fulfill Pearson's prophecy. That is because, while she claims that her "posthuman subject" "exceeds the boundaries of [...] anthropocentrism," taking into account—and I state again that it is a respectful account—of all human and nonhuman others rejected by humanism, there remains in her "posthuman subject" the all-too-human ambition of "*encompassing* the human, our genetic neighbors the animals and the earth as a whole."[18] The use of the possessive pronoun "our," which disregards Deleuze's caution on the rhetorical and philosophical danger of such possessive determiners, is already problematic in itself, as it betrays an appropriative gesture or desire.[19] But I highlight here the anxiety to archive or reinscribe (which is another way of circumscription) every *reject*—both historical and contemporary—within the cognitive consciousness and epistemological boundary of Braidotti's "posthuman subject," so that that *subject* can "make sense of contemporary global culture and its posthuman overtones."[20] Braidotti also says that all this be done in "an understandable language."[21] One suspects that this language is not communicable to those who do not share human language, since one does not forget that "the human subject" remains the foundation and horizon in Braidotti's "posthuman subject."[22] In other words, despite her good intentions to go beyond anthropocentrism and give due consideration to nonhuman others, Braidotti's "posthuman subject" only reiterates a grand narrative that serves in large part the interest of the human. Consequently, a certain hierarchy that privileges the human is also put in place: as she declares without reservation, she aspires for her "posthuman subject" to embody "posthuman recompositions of a pan-*human* cosmopolitan bond."[23] The unconscious remainder of all this is that Braidotti's "posthumanism" reiterates the production of *rejects*, albeit lesser *rejects* in the sense of no longer being marginalized or banished, in nonhuman others.

To avoid any regression to the human or "posthuman" *subject* that still renders some others *rejects*, "posthumanism" must therefore go beyond recognizing and mobilizing *rejects* in a way whereby *rejects* remain somewhat passive to "posthuman" theorizations. In other words, one must also recognize the active force of rejection that the other might be expressing, in resistance to any "posthuman" theoretical endeavor to bring it within proximity, if not appropriate, frame, or delimit it as its rhetorical tool or arsenal against that which it critiques. Perhaps one must also go so far as to allow such active rejection from the side of the other, in and through which is expressed with full force the other's difference. What follow is not only a veritable supplement to the human *subject* but also a more adequate affirmation of the irreducibility of the other and its difference. This is where I would argue for the importance of foregrounding the aspect of *auto-rejection* or the *auto-reject* in "posthumanism," which will indeed allow the full expression of active rejection on the part of the other. This is a move that remains for "posthumanism" to accomplish because, while "posthumanism" has recognized and sought to affirm the *reject* in others, it has not yet adequately recognized the *reject* in itself. That does not mean that all one has to do is to recognize the cyborg, the machinic system, or the animal in oneself: that would still risk appropriating the other and/or its predicates for oneself, or identifying oneself with the other, all of which amount to reducing the other to oneself. That does not mean either to recognize oneself as a *reject*, such as the female/feminist other of Humanism's male *subject* in Braidotti's case, and then proceed to identify and recruit other *rejects* in order to found a new subjectivity that will discredit and overthrow the incumbent *subject*. Instead, one must, perhaps before everything else, take into account that one may always be regarded as a *reject* by others—others that even include the *rejects* mentioned so far: animals, cyborgs, and systems themselves. In other words, one has to recognize that in one's approach toward the other, even if it is to recognize and affirm the latter's existence and differences, the other may not desire at all that encounter or proximity. A distance, instead, may be desired by the other, and one has to respect that distance. That distance can be maintained through *auto-rejection*, whereby one refrains from reducing the distance between oneself and the other by keeping in mind that the other might reject any thought of proximity with oneself. In this case, one refrains from making the first move to approach: the *auto-reject* lets the other arrive only if the latter desires to do so. *Auto-rejection* here also guarantees that the *reject*, which refuses to assume any sovereign power over others, never demands the total disclosure of the other and its predicates or qualities, as if it possesses a certain right or prerogative to make that demand.[24] As the *reject* would recognize, that right or prerogative is essentially a false presumption, which only leads one to appropriate the other and/or its attributes. The *auto-reject* here, contrary to the *subject*, ensures that there is no circumscribing of the other within its determinations. Put another way, the other here, before the *auto-reject*, is always free to depart, always free even to *not* arrive before the *auto-reject*.

In such *auto-rejection*, "posthumanism" must be willing to take the risk of allowing any assemblage or new forms of relations it seeks with the *reject*-other to fall into a state of inoperativity [*désœuvrement*]. Here, one may posit, after Nancy's "inoperative community" [*communauté désœuvrée*], an unworked [*désœuvré*] "posthumanism," that is to say, a "posthumanism" that refrains from totalizing all the *rejects* within its discourse, or a "posthumanism" that refuses to be productive in the sense of constructing a domain where *rejects* can be unified or be in fusion. Or, to borrow

Callus and Herbrechter's term, which they would like to let resound in the word "whither" in the title "Whither Posthumanism?" of their panel at the 2011 MLA conference, one must take the chance of letting "posthumanism" *wither* away.[25] *Auto-rejection*, by which the other is always free in its movement to arrive *and* leave, or even to not appear, and by which "posthumanism" risks withering into some sort of "inoperative community," is a move clearly absent in Braidotti's "posthumanism." I have already noted that her "posthumanism" is driven to encompass every possible *reject*. Implied in this drive is also the resistance to entertain the thought of other *rejects* moving away from her "posthuman subject." Hence, despite Braidotti's declared fidelity to Deleuze's philosophy, not only to his philosophy of becoming but also of movement, the rhetoric of her "posthuman" theory once again problematizes, if not betrays, that fidelity, as she seeks "a position that transposes hybridity, nomadism, diasporas and creolization processes into means of *re-grounding* claims to subjectivity [...]."[26] In other words, there will be no absolute line of flight for other *rejects* in Braidotti's "posthumanism"; instead, the movement of others will always be a limited one, always reterritorialized within the perceptual and cognitive frame of the "posthuman subject." The delimitation of movement of others further threatens to compromise Braidotti's call to contest biopolitics, which seeks to master the knowledge of the location and movement of every human life through forms of technology that include global-positioning systems. This is because we see in her "posthumanism" the raising of a similar ambition, when she says, "a primary task for posthuman critical theory [...] is to draw accurate and precise cartographies for [...] different subject positions as spring-boards towards posthuman recompositions of a pan-human cosmopolitan bond."[27] Granted that Braidotti lays claim to a proximity with Deleuze's philosophy rather than with Nancy's, which means that one should not expect her "posthuman" theory to align with the thought of an "inoperative community," her thought of community, nevertheless, runs counter to Deleuze's. I have shown in the chapter on community that Deleuze also resists any thought of community as something of a bond or fusion, or as an assemblage where there is no exit: in the face of such a thought of community, Deleuze (and Guattari) will mobilize the nomadic war machine to smash it from within. Yet, we find in Braidotti's "posthumanism," through her "posthuman subject," the project of "community bonding and social belonging," or the endeavor "to re-assemble a discursive community out of different, fragmented contemporary strands of posthumanism."[28]

On the point of letting "posthumanism" wither away, or letting it fall into inoperability, I adopt a rather critical stance also with regard to Luhmann's second-order systems theory. It is not in the interest of this current work to explicate Luhmann's complex theory of systems, but let it be said simply (and admittedly in an unjustified manner) that if a "posthuman" world or condition arises, as Wolfe sees it, from Luhmann's world of interacting systems, then this "posthuman" world is a world of increasing complexity. According to Luhmann's systems theory, a system (be it a human entity, a nonhuman organism, a physical object, or even a machinic program) is always situated in a complex world where systems are already interacting with other systems in complex ways. To partake in this world of complexity, the system generates a more complex process, not only to intercalate itself into the existing complexity but also to overcome or surpass it, if not to *reject* the complexity of another system.[29] This process allows Luhmann to arrive at his axiomatic (and paradoxical) phrase: "Only complexity can reduce complexity."[30] To be sure, the more complex process that a system generates is not born of a solipsistic closure of the system itself. Instead, it is fed by the difference that exists between itself and its environment: it is the "difference [that] holds what is differentiated together."[31] As I would read it, there is, in that case, some sort of use-value, in the eyes of a system, of differences disseminating in the environment. For a system, something productive can result from interacting with these differences, which is to keep or hold all differences together. To put it in Bataillean-Derridean language, there is a restricted economy here between system and its environment. The question that I would pose is: Why not let flow a general economy instead, a pure expenditure into differences without taking into account any possible return for one's complexity, that is, an unproductive immersion in complexities, and see what new assemblages or networks (which can be complexities in themselves that negotiate with existing complexities in unforeseen ways) evolve, or rather devolve?[32] To remain within the restricted economy of "complexity to end complexity,"[33] I would argue, only runs the risk of resurrecting the *subject*, if not raising a more complex operative *metasubject* (not unlike Braidotti's "posthuman subject") hovering over other systems and environments. Certainly, Luhmann has insisted that this process is a "subjectless event."[34] However, I would say that the (unconscious) return of the *subject* is already at work in Luhmann, as betrayed by his reference to the concept of the self when he speaks of the higher complexity as "*self*-description, *self*-observation, and *self*-simplification within systems."[35]

As I see it, it is the absence of *auto-rejection* in complexity, in other words, the refusal to let itself wither away or run into inoperativity, that allows the *subject* to haunt Luhmann's "posthuman" second-order systems theory. It is also the absence of *auto-rejection* in Braidotti that allows the *subject* to problematize and compromise her "posthumanism." This is why I am stressing the *auto-reject* for "posthuman" discourse, if it is not only seriously committed to the "poststructuralist" project of critiquing the *subject* or of seeking a response to "who comes after the subject," but also committed to the respectful affirmation of others, including other-*rejects*. The *auto-reject* would put in place a radical *auto-rejection* that will prevent any return to a human (and humanist) *subject* in "posthumanism": it would involve a rejection of any claimed structure that presumably founds any supposed constitution of a self or subjectivity. Such *auto-rejection* may bring to mind once again the notion of autoimmunity, which we have seen in the earlier chapter on the "postsecular." Just to briefly recall then, autoimmunity, as Derrida tells us, is a mechanism within a body that acts against "its own protection, its own policing, its very power of rejection [*son propre pouvoir de rejet*], its properness in short [*son propre tout court*]."[36] The undoing of one's own power to reject through autoimmunity might appear appealing to the discourse of "posthumanism" or any discourse that seeks to let arrive and affirm the other.[37] However, Derrida has also warned us that autoimmunity, especially when enacted or mediatized spectacularly by a State possessing politico-economic-military power such as the US State war machine, may conceal or dissimulate a will to reconsolidate a more terrifying monolithic self. In other words, the proper [*le propre*] may still lie behind deceptive or simulacral forms of autoimmunity. In this case, any image of a limitless opening-up of one's own borders to anyone or anything, which in turn gives rise to an image of a defenseless self, becomes mere expediency. The (extreme) difference of others, and especially the rejection by others of all assimilatory processes that the proper or the self demands in its (conditional) hospitality, become exploited or manipulated by the self and get woven into the latter's paranoid narrative of clear and present danger. With that narrative in place, it only allows the proper or the self to "justify" all claims to immunity or indemnity from laws limiting extreme and preemptive counterdefensive measures to eradicate others. It essentially allows the proper or the self to put in place a calculated preclusion of the other, "justifying" at the same time its new clinical indifference to the other's desire to approach.

Autoimmunity, as described above, which Derrida calls "autoimmunitary aggression" that "terrorizes most,"[38] or the terrifying and terroristic "pervertibility" of autoimmunity,[39] and which implicates the violent rejection of others, is *not* the *auto-rejection* that "posthumanism" must put in effect. Besides, one must also not forget that before autoimmunity inscribes for itself the paranoid narrative to reject the other, it has in fact already programmed its inner destruction: for that eventual expedience of rejecting the other, "autoimmunitary aggression" would have had, Derrida tells us, "in its own *interest* [. . .] to expose its vulnerability, to give the greatest possible coverage to the aggressions against which it wishes to protect itself."[40] Such nihilistic or "quasi-*suicidal*"[41] operation that eventually feeds the conjuration and "justification" of an "autoimmunitary aggression" is *not* the trajectory, *not* the horizon of the *auto-reject*. As I have tried to underscore throughout this present work, if the *auto-reject* rejects itself, it is certainly not in the abysmal spirit of nihilism, but creative regeneration. The question is how to sidestep the terror of "autoimmunitary aggression" in *auto-rejection*.

Recent developments in the world of microbiology seem to provide a response, particularly from research in bacterial life, that is to say, research concerning an element conventionally considered to be some form of *reject* in the domain of human life, especially in the eyes of those who are anxious to maintain the latter's supposed sanctity. Bacterial life no doubt has been regarded as something of a *reject* in human eyes (save for the bacteria lining our stomachs or those used for making cheese), since, as Myra Hird has observed, not only have "bacteria [. . .] always occupied abject status," but also, in general, a "pathogen matrix overwhelmingly defines" our human perspective of bacteria, seeing any interaction with bacteria as "military encounters—invasion and defense—between my (nonbacterial) individual self and disease (bacterial)."[42] But back to the research to which I was signaling: I am thinking here of the controversial work published in *Sciencexpress* in 2010 by the biochemist Felisa Wolfe-Simon on the bacterium GFAJ-1.[43] This bacterium was placed in an extreme condition of high arsenic presence. Other living beings in a similar environment would find themselves at the brink of death, since phosphorous, which has so far been considered to be one of the necessary building blocks of life, will react with arsenic to produce fatally poisonous results. The GFAJ-1 strand of bacterium, however, supposedly proved itself to be adaptable to such toxic environments. It does that through what can be considered an "auto-deconstruction" of the supposed necessity of phosphorous for life. In other words, instead of relying on phosphorous as an irreducible or exigent necessity for life, it does away with such reliance and develops a taste for poison, "a taste for arsenic,"[44] and lives on. Here, the supposed constitutive structure of life, of what is proper to life, to the self, to the *subject*, is *auto-rejected* or undone, and one witnesses an uncalculated symbiosis (or even complexity, to use Luhmann's term) between bacterium and arsenic.

Certainly, life, or even *sur-vivre* (that is to say, to survive more than mere survival), remains at stake for the GFAJ-1 bacterium in this *auto-rejection*, or in what may be considered a true autoimmunity (where the rejection of oneself is the greater concern than rejecting the other). After all, the GFAJ-1 bacterium is like any other being—living or nonliving, human or nonhuman—exposed to the world. As such, it is traced by what Derrida considers to be an irreducible logic of the *pharmakos*, which means that it will risk empoisoning itself by immersing itself in the outside, in the hope that this empoisoning will in turn transform into a remedy that will free it from its present specific spatial and temporal delimitation. However, life here, in dispensing with the dependence on phosphorous as the supposed necessary condition of life, is now made "to live in a different way,"[45] cleared of all references to any underlying structure that seemingly promises to (re)constitute the self or what is proper to the self. Perhaps it would even be better in this case to speak of what Deleuze calls "a life," where, as seen in the chapter on politics, "a life" is the immanent affirmation of all singularities of existence, without any determination of a *subject* or *object*, without any notion of self and the other, without privileging one life over another. It is precisely because there is no reiteration of the previous state of life or of the (insular) *subject* in a hidden form as in the case of "autoimmunitary aggression" (which would see the GFAJ-1 surviving by rejecting, for example, the arsenic elements in its environment) that one might claim for the *auto-rejection* in the GFAJ-1 bacterium a true autoimmunity. It is such *auto-rejection* that a "posthumanism" seeking to truly depart from the human *subject* or subjectivity must put in place.

It seems then that "posthumanism" can learn something from the GFAJ-1bacterium if it is to put in place something of a true *auto-rejection* or autoimmunity. Should "posthumanism" then turn to bacterial life, after having turned to the cyborg, genomic replicants, systems theory, and animals? Perhaps it should, just to keep itself mindful of *auto-rejection*, so that it will not reduce the *reject*-others that it is invested in to its terms. However, I would add that should the discourse of "posthumanism" engage itself with bacterial life, it must be meticulous to not cultivate or acculturate the latter such that any recognition or consideration of bacterial life serves only to supplement and perpetuate the survival (*sur-vie*) of the human *subject*. This is where I depart from Hird's "microontology." "Microontology," as Hird defines it, is "an ethics that engages seriously with the microcosmos" of bacterial life.[46] That is to say, instead of adopting a naturalized, pathogenic view of bacteria, which not only entails the refusal to give bacterial life any proper thought, but also drives us to eradicate them completely, "microontology" teaches us that not *all* bacteria are pathogenic, but some are even instrumental to our well-being, such as the bacteria that line our intestines. The latter example also demonstrates that we are always living with bacteria, not just with those without in the external environment or in the air, but also with those within. Or, as Deleuze and Guattari put it more radically, *all* things in the world, including nonhuman entities, engage in a "peopling [*peuplement*] by contagion" that is disseminated by bacteria.[47] I certainly have no disagreement with the above aspect of "microontology." I take precaution with "microontology" only when, through its serious undertaking of studying "bacterial self-organization, communication, complexity, division of labor, and communities," it claims to be able to teach us how to live with others, since "microontology" highlights that "bacteria are not only social in and of themselves, but also—through symbioses—weave all organisms into cultural and social co-constructions and co-evolutions."[48] On the one hand, in gleaning from bacterial life what can be productive for human communities and human sur-vival,[49] "microontology" runs the risk of being a calculated move on the part of the human *subject* to totalize bacterial life within a new grand narrative of human "ethics." On the other hand, in a too rapid embracing of the productive symbioses or interactions that can take place between humans and bacterial life, it also risks blurring, and hence not respecting, the distinction or difference between one and the other, as betrayed by Hird even, when at one point, she proclaims that "'I' am bacteria, [and] that bacteria are us."[50] Here, we are in danger of appropriating the bacterial-other such that we can assume its identity, while the bacterial-other is reduced to a human "us."

At this point, I would like to pose the question if it is always necessary to mobilize the other in order to think about *auto-rejection* for, and in, "posthumanism": Must one always look to the other-*reject* to remind oneself of *auto-rejection*? Can we never see the *reject* in us, or rather see ourselves as *rejects* (in order to not confuse "the *reject* in us" with our intestinal bacteria), and therefore deploy the *auto-reject* without the turn to the other? The ethical risk of looking to others may become evident if we retrace some of our tracks and critically review our taking up of the animal question in the previous two chapters, especially with respect to Cixous's animal-messiah and Deleuze and Guattari's becoming-animal. No doubt, an *animal turn* can be useful in critiquing or challenging biopolitics. As Wolfe in a more recent book has argued, taking into account how humans have always negatively framed animals—in terms of not possessing language or rational thought and therefore lie outside the anthropocentric frame of enjoying having rights—can make us reflect on the similar condition humans are undergoing today in the face of biopolitics.[51] Biopolitics, to reiterate, does frame our lives in terms of letting us live if we are obedient political *subjects*. The moment we make a radical political deviation, the mechanisms of biopolitics is always ready to exclude us from the frames of what is politically acceptable. That is to say, when biopolitics decides to view that deviation as dangerous, it can systematically terminate our existences, just like how some animals are set apart for industrial farming and then systematically slaughtered. Seen in this light, that is to say, seeing that "we are always already (potential) 'animals' before the law [of biopolitics]—not just nonhuman animals according to zoological classification, but any group of living beings that is so framed [by biopolitics],"[52] we can, Wolfe suggests, begin not only to resist biopolitics and to rupture its frames in order to liberate human lives but also to critique the cruelty involved in industrial farming.

However, according to Nicole Shukin, such a theoretical move can be guilty of turning animals into what she calls "animal capital" by "freeing animal life into a multiplicity of potential exchange values,"[53] such as when one foregrounds the plight of animals in order to invoke sentiments of resistance against a political condition. Another instance whereby discourse might be capitalizing on animals is when it deploys them as "powerful substitutions or 'political objects' filling in for a lost object of desire or originary wholeness that never did or can exist, save phantasmatically."[54] (We no doubt risk this move if we can only turn to *rejects* other than ourselves to think of *auto-rejection*.) To avoid such trappings of the animal turn, Kari Weil suggests a "coming of age" of animal studies, by which we must recognize that "animals are and should be of concern not only as instruments of theory, not only because they affect us, but because our lives also affect them."[55] She goes on to say that we have to "recognize and extend care to others while acknowledging that we may not know what the best form of care is for an other whom we cannot presume to know. It is a concern with and for alterity, especially insofar as alterity brings us to the limits of our own self-certainty and certainty about the world."[56] In what seems to me a bizarre rhetorical turn, she calls this "coming of age" of animal studies "critical anthropomorphism," whereby "we open ourselves to touch and to be touched by others as *fellow subjects* [my emphasis] and may imagine their pain, pleasure, and need in anthropomorphic terms, but stop short of believing that we can know their experience."[57] The reliance on the terms "anthropomorphism" and "subject," in my view, risks making some steps back to a mode of thinking that centers on the human. As I read it, that is betrayed by the "we" in Weil's rhetoric, a "we" that is undeniably human. Sure, recognizing the alterity of animals might make us "unthink" animals in ways "without claiming an essentialized otherness," but this is in exchange for a revelation of what our previous way of thinking has "deterred *us* from thinking, what it has made *us* leave behind or whip into submission" and hence "enlarge or change the possibilities for what *we* can think and what *we* can do in the world."[58]

To break with the process of capitalizing on animals and others, should we not stop looking to them for our theoretical rhetoric and purposes? Returning to the question of *auto-rejection*, we can break that process by recognizing ourselves as *rejects*. Once again, contemporary French thought can be shown to have already put in place this possibility of looking to ourselves (without, to be sure, reconstituting or refounding a holistic, monolithic self or *subject*) to see how we are already in the midst of *auto-rejection*.

That possibility is offered to us through contemporary French thought's inclination toward the thought of *clinamen*, which is clearly evident in the works of Michel Serres, Deleuze (and Guattari), and Nancy.[59] The thought of *clinamen*, in short, is predicated on some sort of subtractive thinking, since *clinamen* names the process by which atoms detach from a living body or matter without the latter controlling that detachment. This is evidently contrary to the accumulative impulse that drives the thought of the human *subject* or subjectivity, an impulse that seeks to gather as many predicates as possible to augment and consolidate the foundation of that *subject* or subjectivity. In other words, the thought of *clinamen* takes into account that one is always already in the process of *auto-rejecting* some part of oneself, even though this takes place at a molecular or atomic scale.

The question of *rejection* and/or *auto-rejection* is also present in Serres's explication of *clinamen* in *La Naissance de la physique*. According to Serres, "There are only two objects, constitutive of all things: atoms, the void [*le vide*]."[60] Things come about, or rather the *event* of things arises, when a minimal declination occurs in this void, allowing the fall or *clinamen* of atoms. Now, even before we speak of rejection in *clinamen*, Serres would have already signaled the notion of rejection with regard to this void. As Serres notes, "The void, *inane*, has for its root [a] Greek verb [. . .] which signifies 'to purge,' 'to expel,' or, in the passive, 'to be driven out [*chassé*]' by a purge.'"[61] And if the *reject*, or rather *auto-reject*, underscores the need to respect the distance between one and the other, Serres would also highlight the critical need for distance in *clinamen*. It is only with distance that a minimum angle of difference can take place, and hence for there to be *clinamen*. "Things," as Serres would conclude, "are born [therefore] from distance [*l'écart*]."[62] But to underscore the thought of *clinamen* as a clear departure from the human *subject*, Élisabeth de Fontenay has noted that *clinamen* is a phenomenon not restricted to human entities and therefore not the sole property or predicate of human *subjects*, but is also shared by animals.[63] Or, according to the early atomist philosophers Lucretius and Epicurus, it can also be found in nonorganic elements such as rain or fire.

In the event of *clinamen*, where these deterritorialized atoms end up escapes the determination or control of the bodies to which they originally belong; these bodies cannot control or even have knowledge of which deterritorialized atoms they are coming into contact with. Each body, through *clinamen*, is then equally exposed to any number and type of atoms; or, according to Deleuze, each body is immanently exposed to a plurality of heterogeneous singularities.[64] I have mentioned earlier that "peopling," in the sense of the encounter between plural and heterogeneous beings, which include nonhuman beings such as plants, animals, and even atmospheric elements, occurs, for Deleuze and Guattari, via contagion by bacteria. Nancy also speaks of "peopling," but not as much as "the people" [*le peuple*]. "The people," according to Nancy, is not something restricted to human beings, but includes, like Deleuze and Guattari's "peopling," nonhuman entities such as animals, vegetation, minerals, and even divine beings (and such understanding of "peopling" or "the people" surely recalls all the questions of community, the "postsecular," and (animal) politics that have been crucial in this work). As Nancy would argue, these nonhuman entities get brought along, consciously or not, when one goes about evoking a "people," in which "are traversed, without joining up, the whole and the part, the high and the low, the excluded and the included, the right and the left, subjectivity and subjection, the one and the multiple, order and disorder, identity and indistinction."[65] Nancy attributes such a "people" or "peopling" to *clinamen*, rather than to bacterial activity.[66] *Clinamen*, for Nancy, is also contact, which, in his philosophy, involves touch *and* the withdrawal of that touch: "gestures, encounters [*rencontres*], approaches, distances [*les écarts*]."[67] It is also via *clinamen* that a "people" keeps (d)evolving, allowing certain elements free to depart and remaining ones to welcome other new elements, allowing therefore "the invention of an other people, an other contact freed from identifications and adherences deposited in the word 'people.'"[68] The re-cognition of *clinamen* in those terms can give "posthumanism" what Keith Ansell Pearson has called a "viroid life," that is to say, a "viroid life" that does not need to cultivate viruses or bacteria. Instead, one is already immersed in, and one already is, the "viroid life" of deterritorialized atoms.

The fact of *clinamen*, in other words, will always unhinge any subjective desire or fantasy to ascertain one's constitution as a whole, unified *subject*, or to sovereignly determine the development of one's corporeal entity, supposedly held intact by the *subject*.[69] Put yet another way, the *auto-rejection* of *clinamen* gives place to the auto-deconstruction of the *subject*. For a "posthumanism" that continues the "poststructuralist" deconstruction of the *subject*, or which responds to Nancy's question of "who comes after the subject" by articulating the *reject*, especially the *reject* that is not borrowed, if not, worse, appropriated, from other-*rejects*, but draws from itself as an *auto-reject*, *clinamen* may be its point of departure. Furthermore, thinking *clinamen* can have political stakes for the posthuman *auto-reject*. In the interview "Il faut bien manger: ou le calcul du sujet" for Nancy's question of "who comes after the subject," Derrida has intimated that so long as one stands before laws—and the contemporary or "posthuman" world undeniably remains to be governed by laws—one is always somewhat a *subject*. However, with the deterritorialized atoms of *clinamen*, it would seem that "posthumanism" may begin to free itself from any attachment to the *subject*, since these atoms, like viruses or with their *élan viral* or *élan bactériel*, are always free to move anywhere, never governed by laws that restrict their movements across frontiers.[70] To be sure, this thought of *clinamen*, which is also the thought of the *auto-reject* that is free(d) from the category of the *subject*, is not to be put in place just to transgress laws for the sake of transgressing laws, or even to provoke some form of frontier-smashing anarchy. Instead, it is to generate the possibility of thinking how our *being* and our movements need not be always, if not solely, reduced to legal determinations or regulations.

I should add that the "posthuman" *auto-reject* in *clinamen* certainly does not align itself with the dystopic "posthumanism" of disembodiment that N. Katherine Hayles critiques, that is, a "posthumanism" that is too quick to forget or lose the corporeal body, only to reify it as downloadable data in the "distributed system" of teletechnological networks to which almost every "posthuman" body is connected.[71] Thinking *clinamen*, or thinking *auto-rejection* via the deterritorialization of one's corporeal molecular elements, is not a call for the body to precipitate into a doing or wasting away of itself. It is not a negation of the body. If anything, it is a reaffirmation of the body, paying attention to how a body is *always already*, to use the Derridean phrase, interacting with another, *without* the control or determination of a human *subject*. This puts a "posthumanism" of *auto-rejection* close to Hayles's countermove against a "posthumanism" of disembodiment. Yet it is not Hayles's "posthumanism" of embodiment either. The distance between a "posthumanism" of *auto-rejection* and a "posthumanism" of embodiment rests once again on the question of the *subject*. Now, Hayles has clearly stated that she is "not trying to recuperate the liberal subject."[72] Well aware of all the problems that have been associated with the *subject*, she "[does] not mourn the passing of a concept so deeply entwined with projects of domination and repression."[73] Despite being in agreement with the "poststructuralist" deconstruction of the *subject*, Hayles is not prepared to lose the *subject*. In other words, the question of "who comes after the subject" is not one to which she feels the imperative to respond. She does not seek another figure of thought other than the *subject*. The category of the *subject* still has some currency, except that is has to be redefined in terms of a "posthuman subject," which, according to her, is "an amalgam, a collection of heterogeneous components, a material-informational entity whose boundaries undergo continuous construction and reconstruction."[74] One must therefore be precise to note that Hayles's *subject* is *not* the self-proclaimed unitary, masculine, human(ist) *subject*, but a *subject* that experiences a "splice"[75] between him- or herself as behind-the-screen user of teletechnology (what Hayles calls "enacted body"), and him- or herself as represented on screen (what Hayles calls "represented body"). It is the celebration of the latter at the expense of negating the former, or the rush to push to the extreme the virtual possibilities of the human in certain "posthuman" discourse, that Hayle's "posthuman subject" resists. In the face of a "materiality/information separation" of the body,[76] the "deconstruction of the liberal humanist subject" presents to Hayles "an opportunity to put back into the picture the flesh that continues to be erased in contemporary discussions about cybernetics subjects."[77]

One can borrow the Derridean term and say that Hayle's "posthuman subject" puts in effect a *différance* between the corporeal "enacted body" and the virtual "represented body" of oneself in the contemporary network-centric world. That is to say, the "posthuman subject" is always negotiating how one body differs *and* defers from the other, never grounding on one body and alienating the other. The "posthuman subject" does this not only in relation to itself but also in relation to other "posthuman subjects" and their respective "enacted body"-"represented body" continuum. To capture all these senses of *différance* of the "posthuman subject," Hayles will also call the latter a "flickering signifier." The term gestures toward an absence of a stable, reducible, singular body. The flickering highlights, when it *flickers on*, the presence of the virtual "represented body," but it also signals, when it *flickers off*, to the corporeal "enacted body" behind that "flickering signifier," which is not (fully) present on the screen. As a "flickering signifier," which calls for the attention of another, it is an acknowledgment that there is no recognition of itself without the other. Or else, it is flickering because it is responding to another "flickering signifier." In any case, the "flickering signifier" is always in relation to the other. Yet, I would ask: What happens with a "flickering signifier" that is more insistent in its flickering than others, whose flickering can become like a demand, if not command, for others to give it recognition, for others to give its corporeal boundary due "construction and reconstruction"? As I see it, the "flickering signifier" can become a signal of the return or haunting of the *subject* that holds itself in higher eminence than others, and hence risks being a suture of that problematic *subject* that "poststructuralism" has put into deconstruction.[78]

It is in light of that anxiety to create certain sutures, which are again too operative rather than "inoperative," and which risk resurrecting the *subject*, that a "posthumanism" of *auto-rejection* takes its distance from a "posthumanism" of embodiment. As I have tried to suggest so far, for a "posthumanism" that not only opens to those who have been excluded or rejected from all consideration of what founds and establishes the human, but also a "posthumanism" that does not tame or circumscribe these others or *rejects* within a strictly defined discourse, we would need a "posthumanism" *without subject*. This "posthumanism" would not be so keen to be so productive, or to produce a totalizing discourse or operation by which it ascertains itself. Instead, it would be open to the chance of breaking down, to the chance of being rejected by others. Such a "posthumanism" is what I have been trying to outline as a "posthumanism" of *auto-rejection*. Or else, in order not to forget or deny the technological aspect of "posthumanism," one could follow Timothy Murray in his *Digital Baroque* and think about the Deleuzian fold in a digital register, which would enable one "to remain open to the multiple becomings and machinic eventfulness of the fold rather than to seek refuge in preconceived universals grounded in self-presence."[79] Thinking the fold, as Deleuze suggests in his discussion of perception in *Le Pli*, indeed sidesteps all thoughts of the *subject*, especially that which seeks to impose upon others its particular point of view of the world. In any conventional understanding of perception, a perceiving body or *subject* is commonly presupposed, after which entails a spatiality that extends from the perceiving body to the perceived point. The bodily *subject* of perception in this case comes first: it is the center or centripetal locus of perception. However, in Baroque philosophy according to Deleuze, the order is reversed.[80] The perceiving body, or the point of view, is not a priori of perception. Rather, one begins with perception, which is also the fold, since Deleuze also says the fold consists of "a thousand minute perceptions." Perception in the order of the fold is a priori of the perceiving body; it precedes independently of a perceiving *subject*. It is with perception that the body subsequently comes into being in the sense of formalizing itself as a *subject*. In other words, the *subject* is always secondary in the Baroque conceptualization of perception or the fold.[81] Or, as Murray puts it, "folds expand infinitely in all directions rather than definitively in the shape of a cone, line, or sight that culminates in a single, utopian point of subjectivity."[82] There is no desire for sutures with the fold either. Rather, things are punctured. According to Deleuze, matter that constitutes Baroque architecture is always cavernous, and the ceiling is always prepared to be smashed through, only to allow folds (from the past and the future) to pass through it and continue into infinity.

But perhaps more than the fold, it is more critical, as Murray underscores, to pick up on the Deleuze-Leibnizian notion of the incompossible, even for "posthumanism." The incompossible concerns entities that were previously rendered to have no possibility in this world. In that regard, the incompossible with respect to certain "posthuman" discourses, such as those of Braidotti for example, would be the *auto-reject* and/or the body in and amid *clinamen*, or else, a "posthumanism" *without subject*, without that which needs to know or be in control of the movement of oneself and others. To go beyond the present limits of "posthuman" discourse, or for a "posthumanism" that can respond to Nancy's question of "who comes after the subject," and for a "posthumanism," as Wolfe would have it, that not only concerns "the decentering of the human by its imbrication in technical, medical, informatics, and economic networks" but also "[engages] directly the problem of anthropocentrism and speciesism and how practices of thinking and reading must change in light of their critique,"[83] it is not a "posthuman" *subject* to which we should (re)turn. Instead, we should try to follow the folds or *clinamen* of an incompossible "posthuman" *auto-reject*.

6

CONCLUSION

*Incompossibility, Being-in-Common,
Abandonment, and the Auto-Reject*

The previous chapter concluded with a consideration of Deleuze's reading of Leibniz's incompossibility. Perhaps it is only apt to close this present work on that same note of incompossibility. After all, this work has called for the affirmation of "inoperative community" (especially in terms of a community of those who depart), the friend who leaves town, secant or even postapocalyptic friendship rent with fatigue or distress, syncopic love, the roguish *homo tantum*, the traitorous nomadic war machine, the "postsecular" coexistence of faith and knowledge, the animal-messiah, a democracy-to-come open to the transversal politics of becoming-animal, if not becoming-animal itself, and "posthuman" bacterial life or *clinamen*. And all these need to be affirmed because they are still very much incompossibles in our present world, incompossible to our present conceptualization of the world, that is, to what we think is the best world for us, or what we think is best for this world. By extension, the figure that lies behind or subtends all the above, that is to say, the *reject*, as I have tried to demonstrate throughout this work, is also incompossible. The discussions on Badiou, Balibar, and Rancière have shown that the mode of *being* still considered best in and for the world, or the figure supposedly bearing the promise to create the best world, is the *subject*. All conceptualization, figuration, or embodiment, of the *reject*—even though it is upon which Badiou's *subject* of the event, Balibar's *citizen-subject*, and Rancière's *sans part* are based—will have to be abandoned, left aside, or *rejected*. Abandonment or rejection indeed constitutes the construction of a world predicated on compossibility, as that world brackets out elements that deviate or diverge from the rest that are converging and adhering together into some sort of harmony, which is really nothing less than a totalizing unity. That is to say too that nothing short of a sacrificial structure—the sacrifice of incompossibles or *rejects*—belies the construction of a world that is considered best.

Consistent with Deleuze's combat for the affirmation of life wherever it is threatened (and it does not matter if this life is incompossible or not), Deleuze argues for a rethinking of incompossibility. In other words, instead of negating deviant or diverging elements, Deleuze calls for their affirmation. Another mode of abandonment would have to be in place: an abandonment of what we think or decide as the best world, and an abandonment of our supposed responsibility to bring about or create that best world. In short, there needs to be an abandonment of all suppositions of the *subject*—the *subject* that would represent to him- or herself what the best world would look like, the *subject* that would consciously decide as his or her position, authority, and responsibility to organize that world according to his or her principles. With that abandonment, a "new harmony" would be in the air: no longer one where elements have to compromise certain aspects of themselves so as to "fit" nicely within an existing or presupposed order, but one where elements are free in their dissonant trajectories, free to be radically different, without them needing to add up, or be reduced, to some homogenizing totality. In other words, this "new harmony" does not mark out dissonances as against the rule and hence must be neutralized according to some preexisting principle governing harmonic cadences. Instead, it resounds in ways by which "dissonances are no longer to be 'resolved,'" and "divergences can be affirmed."[1] According to Deleuze, this "new harmony" is the world of incompossibles, and this is what we need to let unfold.

One could say that what is at stake in a world of incompossibles is Nancy's notion of "being-in-common." As I have noted in the earlier chapter on friendship, love, and community, "being-in-common" is *not* a phrase from which, or toward which, we put to work a project of commonality or homogeneity. I recall here that the "in" in "being-in-common" does not signal a trajectory that delineates some form of fusion among all *beings*. Instead, it is first and foremost an abandonment (and therefore not an abandonment *after the fact* of deciding what a best world is), where *beings* are "abandoned" to be "first [. . .] received, perceived, felt, touched, managed, desired, *rejected* [my emphasis], called, named, communicated." In other words, "in" concerns both the coming together of *beings* that desire that gathering, *and* the diverging trajectory of others seeking other relations or other forms of harmony. One could also say that in "being-in-common," each *being* is as *uncommon* as the next, if not incompossible to the next. I would indeed argue that Nancy's "being-in-common" is not distant from the Baroque conceptualization of incompossibility, given that when Nancy speaks of the world in which "being-in-common" takes place, or more precisely, of the worlds of "being-in-common," he at times takes recourse to a rhetoric close to the Baroque articulation of the world of incompossibility, that is, the world as a multiplicity in which worlds fold into and unfold from one another. So, according to Nancy, "The unity of a world is nothing other than its diversity, and the latter, in its turn, is a diversity of worlds"; or, "The unity of a world is not one: it consists of a diversity that includes disparity and opposition."[2] Nancy would say further that in this world, "each [*being*] opens onto and closes on a multiplicity of worlds [*plus de mondes*], in itself as well as outside itself, burrowing [*creusant*] the outside with the interior, and vice-versa"[3]—a rhetoric that no doubt recalls the Baroque conceptualization of existence in monadic terms.

For the "new harmony" of incompossibles then, it is the *uncommon* that we need to underscore, perhaps more so than any theory of the commons or the multitude as proposed by Hardt and Negri, Virno, Casarino, and Thacker and Galloway.[4] I have suggested in several endnotes in this work that the commons or multitude as argued for by these theorists tend to exclude not only nonhuman animals and/or aspects of animality such as the nonparticipation in, or nonappurtenance to, human language, but also those who wish to stand apart from any commons or multitude. In that regard, I suspect these theorists remain quite estranged from any "new harmony," if not grounded in some ideology of a world of compossibles, so long as they bracket out elements or aspects that do not cohere with their theoretical conceptualizations or models. To be sure, I certainly do not disagree with them on account of their resistance to the dominance and hegemony of global capital in the world, a dominance and hegemony that is globalized further today by its manifestation in the form of a digital network empire. One does not forget that this network empire unapologetically renders other worlds incompossible, especially worlds that seek to construct ways of life extricated from the total dependence on capital. Driven by "economies of abandonment," it also makes many, as Judith Butler and Athena Athanasiou have observed, subjects of dispossession.[5] Subjects of dispossession are, on the one hand, beings dispossessed of their modes of living and of their properties, as they are compelled to abdicate to labor patterns dictated by global capital, and as they find themselves helplessly stripped of their possessions when financial markets, investments in which global capital also make it almost necessary, crash. On the other hand, they are also disposable beings, whose dispensability is once again conditioned by global capital, which determines the necessity of their labor, and hence their livelihood, depending on the real and/or speculated burgeoning or dwindling of certain markets. As Athanasiou has stated, "In the context of neoliberal forms of capital—combined with tightened migration policies and the abjection of stateless peoples, *sans papiers*, 'illegal' immigrants—bodies (that is, human capital) are becoming increasingly disposable, dispossessed by capital and its exploitative excess, uncountable and unaccounted for."[6]

The Occupy movement of 2011 has underscored how many of us in the world are such subjects of dispossession, and how much we reject both that interpellation and the condition of dispossession. What the Occupy movement has also shown is that another mode of living and working, not necessarily incompossible with the world of capital, is or has been latent in the world, and it should not rest incompossible any further if we want to address the injustice of the condition of abandonment or dispossession without delay. According to Butler, the Occupy movement is "the expression of justifiable rage" that not only says *we*—the dispossessed, disposed, and disposable—*are here*, but also "'We are *still* here,' meaning: 'We have not yet been disposed of. We have not slipped quietly into the shadows of public life: we have not become the glaring absence that structures your public life.'"[7] However, just as theories of the commons or multitude run the risk of rendering incompossible elements that diverge or stand apart from their project, the Occupy movement likewise risks closing off a world of incompossibility. This occurs when, as noted in the chapter on politics, it begins to insist on its world as the best and drops all respect for others with which it deems incompatible, others that it considers noncritical to its cause. All this has only led to the movement losing its (street) credibility. To reiterate, the challenge for a world of incompossibility is to refrain from positing a particular world as better than another, if not the best, such that one becomes indifferent to the existence or even extermination of other worlds. In the world of incompossibility, there is no hierarchical order. According to Deleuze, what unfolds in this world is "a pure emission of singularities," and since there is no hierarchy according to which these singularities unfold, no particular singularity has preeminence over others. Hence, everything in the world of incompossibility is effectively "ordinary": "Everything is regular! Everything is singular!"[8] This is also how a "new harmony" reverberates throughout the world of incompossibility. There is neither preference for elements that harmonize perfectly nor for those that are dissonant. Every element is free to resound equally there. Or, each voice "sing[s] its own part without knowing nor hearing [*entendre*] that of the other, and yet 'harmonize [*s'accordent*] perfectly.'"[9]

What the world of incompossibility implies then would be the letting-be of the world predicated on global capital, letting it develop according to its trajectories. However, to be precise, that does not mean any abandonment of resistance to that world when it threatens to denigrate or negate other worlds. Resistance is necessary in that case, but it has to be negotiated such that it does not, in turn, negate the world it resists. Negotiated resistance here has to pave the way by which disparate worlds can coexist, so that we will never lose sight of a world of incompossibility. This negotiated resistance will always be necessary, for there will be occasions when the edges of disparate worlds come into contact again, and they might still disagree with one another, but they will no longer seek the decimation of the other world. What transpires between disparate worlds in the world of incompossibility then is "vice-diction," by which the relation between those worlds is paradoxically constituted by divergent trajectories, and not by "contradiction," which typically entails the anxiety for its resolution, if not the eradication of what is perceived to be the contradicting entity.[10] In Deleuze's terms (which anticipate the strategies of the nomadic war machine), negotiated resistance in a world of incompossibility is also "a Non-battle"; rather, it is "closer to guerilla tactics than the war of extermination, closer to Go than the game of chess: one does not seize the adversary to render it absent, one delineates its presence to neutralize it, to render it incompossible, to make it recognize divergence."[11] In other words, negotiated resistance, with "vice-diction" or the "non-battle" as its approach, keeps in mind that the world of incompossibility is a world *not* of common values.

The question remains: How to let unfold the world of incompossibility where divergent worlds have the freedom to exist in their singular, if not radical, difference, and yet without that difference menacing or threatening the existence of other worlds? According to Nancy, this world, even though without any imposed totality that keeps things in order or harmony by evacuating dissonant elements, still needs a law. This law, however, is not that typical or ordinary law that needs to be founded, inaugurated, and imposed. It has neither origin nor horizon or limit, upon which or following which the world might attain some sort of perfectibility: there is no *arche*, no *telos*, to this law.[12] This is also not the law *before the law* in the Kafkaesque or Derridean sense, which awaits a *subject* to assume it, to make it a law, and to enforce it. In other words, it is not the law before which "the structure of every subject" is constituted,[13] which in turn gives the law its "mystical foundation of authority."[14] In Nancy's terms, it is not the law before which one stands or appears [*comparaître*] "under such and such head of law."[15] It is more originary than the law before the law. Nancy calls it "law of the law," and according to him, is "more ancient than any legislation, and more archaic than any legislating subject."[16] At the same time, it also exceeds all existing forms or representations of the law as the "beyond" of all those representations and the "beyond of subjectivity in general" that takes itself as responsible for those representations.[17] It will not be in the service of the conclusion of this work to belabor it with a critical, extended discussion of the "law of the law" according to Nancy.[18] What I hope suffices here is to highlight that this law affirms the freedom of each being to exist; or, put inversely, the fact of existence of each being is the expression of that law and the freedom that accompanies it. That is to say, there is already this law, in the fact of existence of each being in its singularity or difference from other beings. Or, more precisely, *there is* [*il y a*] always this law, at each time [*à chaque fois*] as Nancy would say, as each being exists in its difference with itself and with others. In short, this law is never the "auto-production" of any subjective will.[19] Neither is it conjured from any fictional or "mystical foundation of authority," but accompanies the "factuality" of *each and every* being's existence in their existing, free from any hypostasis on a Being "signified in terms of principle, substance, and subject."[20]

In recognizing that every element, in accord or in dissonance with the rest, has a place in the world, the "law of the law" is no less the recognition of a world of incompossibility, given also that Nancy articulates that law in terms of *nomos*, which is "the distribution, the sharing out [*répartition*], the attribution of parts," according to "the exceptional singularity" of each element.[21] Such that no element will be incompossible, this *nomos* is never a "completed distribution," but always sees to the "universe in expansion" in terms of the "non-delimitation of individuals," which is to say, an "infinite tension" that always moves or brings the world forward, always giving place to "each existent *and* to the infinite, or indefinitely open, circulating, and transforming community (or communication, or contagion, or touch) of all the existences of existents."[22] As I have pointed out in earlier chapters, "communication" here has to be understood in the Bataillean sense, that is, the coming together and departing of existents before they constitute themselves either as *subject* or *object*, and "contagion" here is also a matter of *clinamen*, that is, the detachment of corporeal molecules and their subsequent free attachment with other molecules without any corporeal entity determining or essentializing any of these dissociations or encounters. "Touch" here also needs to be thought in similar terms. As Nancy has frequently stated in texts such as *Corpus*, *Noli me tangere*, and *Le Sens du monde*, touch must never be an unrelenting grip but always a matter of contact that proceeds with tact. In other words, touch must be that which knows how to withdraw, and that is how touch can open up a world of "being-in-common." Incidentally, *nomos* is also an important term for Deleuze and Guattari's nomadic war machine. For Deleuze and Guattari, *nomos* concerns the recognition of forces other than those already recognized, or rather institutionalized, as instrumental in keeping the world in order or in giving the world some form of ordered rationality. These other forces do not contradict those that have been institutionalized, but they "do not proceed from them either, do not depend on them, but testify to always supplemental events," as they conduct themselves with speeds driven by "*clinamen* or minimum divergence [*écart*]."[23] According to Deleuze and Guattari, this aspect of *nomos* gives us a "heterogeneous smooth space," which "supports [*épouse*] very peculiar types of multiplicities: nonmetric, acentered, and rhizomatic multiplicities, which occupy space without 'counting' it, space that can be 'explored only by advancing [*en cheminant*] through such multiplicities.'"[24]

Nancy and Deleuze and Guattari all acknowledge that *nomos* is always (violently) supplemented by other laws that do not recognize, or worse, banish, divergent elements that do not add up to the existing harmonic order. That is why Deleuze and Guattari mobilize the nomadic war machine in order to set free all the forces of *nomos*.[25] Nancy has a less forceful or violent approach. In addition to what we have seen above, that is, recognizing *nomos* or "law of the law" as the very fact of existence of every existent in and as his or her freedom, Nancy will also underscore that *nomos* or "law of the law" is not enacted or enforced as how other ordinary laws proceed by bearing a certain right [*droit*] or "force of law."[26] *Nomos* or "law of the law" must be regarded in terms of the *categorical imperative*, though not in the order of the Kantian categorical imperative that demands its institutionalization based on a subjective consciousness of an *as if*, by which he or she acts according to some fictive universal law. (Once again, the insistence on the *fact* of existence in the "law of the law," if not its inherence in that factuality, marks precisely its distance from the Kantian categorical imperative.) Because this non-Kantian categorical imperative is precisely not derived from any *subject*—it "does not belong to the nature of the subject,"[27] evacuated therefore of the *subject* or any subjectivity, this categorical imperative does not proceed by any willed enforcement: it "does not force," or "it does not have the nature that we recognize under the name of 'command.'"[28] Or, "it does not threaten [*menace*], it does not force its execution," as it is devoid of "all executive power" [*toute puissance exécutoire*],[29] or all "power of coercion."[30] In a way, this categorical imperative is already enacted, or it is always in action (specifically as an "unconditioned action"[31]), by the very act or fact of existing of each existent at each time. Corresponding to that act or fact of existing at each time, this categorical imperative is also always "a beginning, an initiative, or an initiation without end [*initialité sans fin*],"[32] which in turn testifies to the "beginning, inauguration, or initiative of a world as an in-finite series of phenomena of freedom itself."[33] If one insists on speaking of force in this "law of the law" or categorical imperative, perhaps it is but the "free force" inhering in the very "existence of a body," a force that is "neither of the 'mind' [*l'esprit*] nor of the 'body'" but "is existence itself, which is not to be confused with a subjectivity [. . .] or an objectivity."[34]

Without any command or order for its enforceability, all that the categorical imperative asks for [*exige*] is respect: the respect for every of its beginnings, inaugurations, and initiations. Again, this respect is not a demand, coming as if from some higher, superior place, for servile obedience. It is not respect dictated by "an obligation," which is a "rather sterile behavior [*comportement*] in general."[35] Rather, respect here concerns a certain regard, a regard that does not involve subjective perception or vision. As Nancy argues, this respect/regard "does not lift the eyes and perhaps does not even open them,"[36] as if there is a fixed, visible object or maxim to which respect must be paid. In fact, effectively, "there is nothing to see," or it does not concern vision [*il n'est pas à voir*].[37] It is but a "consideration,"[38] a consideration of one's coexistence with others, which is always already there, and which takes place through constant gathering or dissociation, that is, through a "with" [*avec*] that is always "proximity and its spacing [*espacement*]."[39] And, perhaps it cannot be reiterated enough, it is also a consideration that precedes and exceeds all subjective contemplation. More recently, Nancy will articulate respect or consideration in terms of *esteem*, which can be said to be an immediate sense, at each instant, of all the singularities surrounding one's existence, before any subjective estimation or calculation of how one wants to treat them. Put another way, *esteem* would be the opening of the body to the existence of other bodies around it, an opening of which the body has no control because what *esteem* is attuned to is the ephemeral nature and nuances of the multiplicity of existences at each time, which essentially escape all efforts of the *subject* to absorb or capture within its time of contemplation or attention span.[40]

According to Nancy, what takes place in *esteem*, or consideration, or respect, is *abandonment*, which is *not* abandonment as mentioned earlier, that is, abandonment conditioned and determined by global capital or by any conceptualization of the world predicated on compossibility. It is also certainly not abandonment as put to work by the *subject*, which either involves the abandonment of others and their perspectives in its endeavor to establish a certitude of itself or its point of view of the world, or the conscious abandonment of certain aspects of itself in its interaction with other *subjects* in order to be acknowledged as a fellow *subject*.[41] The abandonment to which Nancy refers is something more ontological, an ontological phenomenon given by the fact that an existent can articulate its manner of existing in a multiplicity of ways, or that it is available or open to "a profusion of possibilities" of articulating itself.[42] By that fact, an ontology of abandonment would recognize that *being* is originarily "abandoned of all categories and transcendentals."[43] And if, indeed, ontological abandonment gathers and collects all the predicates that a *being* gives to itself only to the point of exhausting [*épuisant*] them or in bringing them to "the extreme poverty of abandonment,"[44] that poverty must not be thought of with a nihilistic horizon in view, or as an abject condition (even though Nancy calls it a "miserable condition,"[45] and Agamben "the irreparable"[46]). Instead, impoverishment must be thought of as that which allows *being* to give itself other attributes. That is because, if abandonment sees to "the cessation or suspension of discourses, of categorizations, of interpellations and of invocations," it is precisely because of the profusion [*foisonnement*] of such abandonment that allows *being* to articulate itself in other ways, which thereby "constitutes," ontologically, "the being of being."[47] It is in that regard that abandonment is in fact closer to the thought of "abundance,"[48] if not an abundance-to-come.

Abandonment that sees to an abundance-to-come takes place only if being is "neither the author nor the subject of abandonment."[49] That abandonment will also not be one that takes place only once, as if abandonment is abandonment once and for all. There is no end to abandonment: it is "infinite," or "there is no permanence of abandoned being [*l'être abandonné*]."[50] That is how abandonment opens every existent to unlimited ways of existing with regard to both itself and others: it opens every existent not only to "its infinite difference of finite exposition in the absence of essence,"[51] leaving it to a mode of existing that is "a scattering without recourse" or "a dissemination of ontological fragments [*miettes ontologiques*]," but also, "without caution [*garde*] and without calculation,"[52] to every entity around it, even to those that it might consider incommensurable or incompossible to itself in its subjective disposition.[53] That is also how, according to Nancy, abandonment is always an abandonment to "the law of the law,"[54] which, as discussed above, sees to the freedom of existence of *each and every* being, or the freedom of how *each and every* being exist at each time. Given also that existing in abandonment does not order itself into any unity,[55] one could say that abandonment always and already abandons every existent to a "new harmony," that is, a world of incompossibility.

(Ontological) abandonment, according to Nancy, is not something for us to inscribe in our being or existing: we are always already "abandoned being." However, given that we are still far from any "new harmony," or that we still delimit ourselves within a world of compossibility, to which the global network empire of capital stands as its bulwark with its forced abandonment of certain peoples and worlds in terms of dispossession, it is more likely that we have forgotten our existence as "abandoned being."[56] To help remind ourselves that we are as much abandoned as the other, abandoned to this world driven by a *nomos* that sees to the freedom of existence of every being as an undeniable fact in this world, that is to say, to remind us not to make unjustified decisions as to who is to be abandoned in this world, we might just need to reiterate or reinscribe our sense of "abandoned being."

Following what I have been suggesting throughout this work, perhaps articulating the *reject* can serve as that reminder and turn us (back) to a world of incompossibility. The first turn of the *reject*, that is, the passive *reject*, would remind ourselves of our originary "miserable condition" of being devoid of any category that could definitively define our mode of existing, hence leaving us always free to a process of differentiation in relation to ourselves and to other beings around us (which also differentiate themselves at each time). That would also remind us that all the discourses we mobilize in order to gather all the predicates or attributes that we think could build toward a transcendental category for our being (for example, the *subject*) are but fictions, to which the fact of our existing always remains indifferent, therefore proving them to be superfluous and always inadequate. Of course, not all of us will be willing to accept our originary status of "abandoned being" or *reject* and would still seek some form of sublimation toward that supposed or fictional "elevated" status of the *subject*. The *subject* becomes dangerous when it proceeds to militantly negate differences that are not commensurable with itself or its point of view of the world, or to traverse differences in order to end all differences in a dialectical move to reduce everything to a supposed unity, harmony, or totality as determined by his or her principle. This is where the second turn of the *reject*, which concerns its active force, is ready at hand to counter or resist the force of the *subject*, or any force that seeks to neutralize, negate, or eradicate it, such as the mechanism of dispossession put into operation by the global network empire of capital.

As I have underscored throughout this work, the second turn of the *reject* must always proceed with caution. Its resistance must not be carried out to the point of annihilating that which it resists, in which case, the *reject* only repeats the gesture of that which it counteracts. This is why the third turn of the *reject*, or the *auto-reject*, is always the critical turn in the theory of the *reject*. Turning the force of rejection on itself, the *auto-reject* checks its active force of rejection, keeping in mind that every other being has the right and/or freedom to exist. In other words, the *auto-reject* has in mind the "law of the law," or is always in respect of *nomos*, through which it considers or esteems others, especially radically different others, not in terms of a contradiction that needs to be resolved or made to disappear but in terms of "vice-diction," where each is free to pursue its own divergent trajectory. Those trajectories can indeed be incommensurable to one another, so long as one does not endanger the other. In that regard, the *auto-reject* effectively holds on to no principle that would tempt it to decide what is best for itself or for the world, no principle as to what a world of incompossibility would or should be like, and no principle as to what the "new harmony" should sound like. As an *auto-reject*, it keeps in mind that others can always reject its point of view or world; therefore, there would be no forcing of one world onto another. There can only be the acknowledgment that there is already a world of incompossibility in which there is "the free dissemination of existence."[57] Finally, the *auto-reject* would also always refuse any auto-positionality, renouncing any move to occupy space in any permanent manner. Here, the *auto-reject* keeps in mind that in our mode of existing, we are always abandoned, constantly abandoned to a spacing [*écart*] of space,[58] from which the *auto-reject* would also elicit the fact that the world is always in formation, whereby *each and every* being have the right and freedom to exist.[59] The world as always in formation would mean that there will always, if not equally, be another spacing of space elsewhere to allow the coming to presence of another being, not to mention that the space left by the *auto-reject*, as it is abandoned or abandons itself to another spacing, can be filled by another.

The *reject*, in all, can be said to respect the "law of the law," which, as seen, concerns the categorical imperative to be attuned to the multiplicity of existence in the world, which is also to hold in *esteem* the fact and therefore freedom of every existence in the world. Or, each time the *reject* is mobilized, it is done in respect of the "law of the law." It is in that regard that the *reject*, in line with the "law of the law," or *nomos*, or the world of incompossibility, understands or respects the very fact of existing as "unsacrificable" [*insacrifiable*],[60] in contrast to the world of compossibles. It is also in respecting the "law of the law" that the *reject* is in respect of abandonment.[61] As this work has been suggesting throughout, the *reject* indeed concerns abandoned community,[62] abandoned friendship, abandoned love, abandoned belief, abandoned politics, and abandoned humanism and/or anthropocentrism, all of which manifest themselves in the names of "inoperative community," community of those who depart, secant or postapocalyptic friendship, syncopic love or *aimance*, the "post-secular" animal-messiah, becoming-animal, and "posthuman" bacterial life of *clinamen*. Once again, there is nothing nihilistic about these abandonments. They do not signal the end, destruction, or ruin of community, friendship, love, faith, politics, or even the human. Instead, abandonment here concerns the opening up of thought and existence to other forms of relations, faith, politics, and human life that go beyond, if not are incompossible to, their present appellations or conceptualizations.

It is perhaps with the *reject* that we could indeed witness the inauguration, or more precisely the un-closure or dis-closure [*déclosion*] (since it is already *there*), of the world of incompossibility. Put another way, as long as "inoperative community," the community of those who depart, the friend who walks away, postapocalyptic secant friendship, syncopic love or *aimance*, the roguish *homo tantum*, uncommon Bartleby, the *sans papiers* or *sans-part*, becoming-animal, the animal-messiah, and the "posthuman" *clinamen* are more or less regarded as incompossibles, we need a theory of the *reject* to reaffirm both their existences and the world of incompossibility. And yet, and yet . . . In keeping in mind the nonpermanence of abandonment of "abandoned being," which is also in keeping with the spirit of the *auto-reject*, one must always allow for the possibility of witnessing the abandonment of the term *reject* in an unforeseeable, uncalculated future. A theory of the *reject* must be open to that abandonment at any time, so that "abandoned being," in another register, or by another name, whose senses and meanings are still incompossible to the language to which it belongs, can emerge or articulate itself in the world of incompossibility.

NOTES

1. INTRODUCTION: LET'S DROP THE SUBJECT

1. Letter of February 1986, reproduced in Nancy's "Introduction" to Cadava, Connor, and Nancy, eds., *Who Comes After the Subject?*, 5. The book is an extended version of the special issue (bearing the same title) of *Topoi* 7(2) (1988). The French original appeared slightly later in *Cahiers confrontation* 20 (winter 1989), with the title *Après le sujet qui vient*. Nancy's letter is also reprinted in the French journal in the "Présentation." I have chosen to use the translated version in *Who Comes After the Subject?* since it is more readily available. I do likewise for Gilles Deleuze's and Alain Badiou's interventions for the same reason.

2. Derrida, "'Il faut bien manger,'" in *Points de suspension*, 279. This interview with Nancy also appears in *Who Comes After the Subject?* Readily available, I have chosen to refer to the original French text. Translations of this text are mine.

3. See Nancy's "Introduction," in Cadava, Connor, and Nancy, eds., *Who Comes After the Subject?*, 5.

4. Ibid., 4.

5. Here, I follow Brian Massumi's translation of Gilles Deleuze and Félix Guattari's *A Thousand Plateaus*, 105. The French original says "Homme-blanc-mâle-adulte-habitant des villes-parlant une langue standard-européen-hétérosexuel quelconque" (*Mille plateaux*, 133).

6. Just as the birth of the modern *subject* can be found in Descartes, as many scholars, including Nancy, have argued, the sovereign-like negation of others can also be located in Descartes. In the second meditation of his *Meditations on First Philosophy*, Descartes seeks to establish the certitude of his thinking. It proceeds via the unrestrained touching of the honey wax before him, but one finds Descartes more than ready to make nothing of that experience of touching the object, or worse, to dispel the existence of that object by claiming it to be possibly a mere object of his imagination or dream.

7. To be sure, the picture of contemporary French thought in relation to the question of the *subject* is not so clear and straightforward: the critiquing or "liquidating" the *subject* does not follow a simple, linear progression. The rejection

of the *subject* is no doubt evident in early, pre-1968 French structuralism—in the works of Claude Lévi-Strauss, Jacques Lacan, Roland Barthes, and also Michel Foucault, for example. Things get a little complicated from 1967 onward. Via a different and more dynamic mode of structuralism, or what is fashionably called "poststructuralism," Jacques Derrida and Gilles Deleuze would continue the rejection of the *subject*, a project they never abandoned in their respective philosophies. Foucault, meanwhile, would return to the *subject* in the 1970s but rethink it in more corporeal and plural terms, not just away from the Lacanian *subject* reduced to a linguistic structure, but also away from the classical *subject* that assumes itself to be a unitary male human in a singular or exceptional position of power. For the complex intellectual history of the *subject* in relation to contemporary French thought from structuralism to "poststructuralism," see especially François Dosse's two-volume *Histoire du structuralisme*. Étienne Balibar and John Rajchman in their *French Philosophy Since 1945* also do not neglect this rejection and rethinking of the *subject* in contemporary French thought. Whether it is rejection or rethinking, they argue that it is something not quite the *subject* that contemporary French thought seeks, but "something in our lives, or in our ways of being and being-together, that can't simply be self-reflected or constituted by continuities of memory, that is im-personal or irreducible to persons of speech or discourse, that can't be individualized any more than collectivized, that can't be centered or made present in a consciousness or a 'proper body,' with its voice and its gaze" (*French Philosophy Since 1945*, 193–94).

8. Deleuze, "Philosophical Concept," in Cadava, Connor, and Nancy, eds., *Who Comes After the Subject?*, 94, trans. modified. A version of Deleuze's French text, "Réponse à une question sur le sujet," can be found in *Deux regimes de fous*. The quote is on page 326. The original, "Un concept philosophique," appears in *Cahiers confrontation* 20 (winter 1989): 89–90.

9. Derrida, "'Il faut bien manger,'" in *Points de suspension*, 274.

10. On the "lost" or "fading" *subject* in Lacan, see his "Of Structure as an Inmixing of an Otherness Prerequisite to Any Subject Whatever," in *Structuralist Controversy*, 189, 194.

11. Derrida, "'Il faut bien manger,'" in *Points de suspension*, 272.

12. Ibid., 271.

13. Ibid.

14. Ibid., 275, 277.

15. Ibid., 277.

16. Deleuze, "Philosophical Concept," in Cadava, Connor, and Nancy, eds., *Who Comes After the Subject?*, 95. See also Deleuze, "Réponse à une question sur le sujet," in *Deux regimes de fous*, 328.

17. Derrida, "Il faut bien manger," in *Points de suspension*, 286.

18. Ibid., 286–87.

19. Ibid., 282.

20. Ibid., 282. Deleuze would also say that "a concept [such as the *subject*] does not die simply as and when one wants it to [. . .]" ("Philosophical Concept," 94, trans. modified).

21. As noted earlier, the responses were first published in English in *Topoi* 7 (2), 1988; then in the original French in *Cahiers confrontation* 20 (winter 1989); and finally in English again as *Who Comes After the Subject?*

22. Beyond, or even without, Nancy's question, Balibar and Rajchman, in their introduction to *French Philosophy Since 1945*, would say that despite the negative criticism and reception of "French Theory," it has to be recognized that "translated into many languages, ["French Theory"] remains a key philosophical inheritance and resource for the twenty-first [century]. It was [in the twentieth century] not only a matter of the academic discipline of philosophy. It was the sort of philosophy that would exert an often transformative influence in many fields, sometimes assuming an ongoing role within them; no area would remain unaffected. It is hard to imagine, for example, what the current study of humanities or social sciences in English-speaking countries would be without it" (*French Philosophy Since 1945*, xvii).

23. This is rather evident from one of his chapter titles—"Learning from Temple Grandin: Animal Studies, Disability Studies, and Who Comes after the Subject" (Wolfe, *What Is Posthumanism?*).

24. For the analysis and critique of Descartes's *ego sum* as "self-supposing" and "self-positioning," see especially Nancy's *Ego sum* and "Un sujet? " (in *Homme et sujet*, 47–114).

25. See, for example, Critchley and Dews, *Deconstructive Subjectivities*, or more recently, Rothenberg, *Excessive Subject;* and Howells, *Mortal Subjects.* I do not forget that psychoanalysis, since Lacan, is heavily invested in problematizing the *subject*: see, for example, Smith, *Discerning the Subject;* Žižek, *Ticklish Subject;* Cavell, *Becoming a Subject;* and Chiesa, *Subjectivity and Otherness.* Nancy's response to the question of the *subject* in psychoanalysis appears as *Le Titre de la lettre.* In this present work, I heed Nancy's advice in "Un sujet?," where he warns of the confusion that can arise in conflating the question of the *subject* in philosophy with that in psychoanalysis or even psychology. Given the philosophical contour of this present work, I will not be bringing psychoanalysis into the discussion.

26. From Nancy's letter, dated February 1986, in Cadava, Connor, and Nancy, eds., *Who Comes After the Subject?*, 5. On a related note, Derrida has likewise observed and foresaw that there are "those who would want to reconstruct today a discourse on the subject that is not pre-deconstructive, on a subject that no longer assumes the figure of the mastery of the self, the figure adequate to the self, the center and origin of the word, etc., but would define the subject rather as the finite experience of the non-identity to the self, of the underivable interpellation

[*l'interpellation indérivable*] that comes from the other, from the trace of the other, with the paradoxes and aporias of being-before-the-law, etc." (Derrida, "'Il faut bien manger,'" in *Points de suspension,* 280).

27. Just to name a few here: see, for example, Butler, *Subjects of Desire,* though Butler recognizes the problem of inscribing the *subject* more explicitly in *Dispossession;* Braidotti, *Nomadic Subjects,* which, while adopting Deleuze's nomadic thought, seems to me not to take into account Deleuze's rejection of the category of the *subject;* Mahmood, *Politics of Piety;* Varma, *Postcolonial City and Its Subjects;* Liu, *Stateless Subjects;* and Jabri, *Postcolonial Subject.*

28. In the following chapter, I will show how Clément does that through her notion of syncope. Here, I will just note how the *subject* is so distant, if not absent, in Cixous's conceptualization of "feminine writing" or *écriture féminine* in "Sorties" (in *La Jeune née*). We do find the *subject* in the earlier *Neutre,* but Cixous mentions it only to critique it as that which forces a suture over the openness of a text. According to Cixous there, a text is always traversed by the neutral, which is "without-subject" [*Sans-Sujet*] (37), before and after a *subject* intervenes in both the reading and writing of the text. And if there is such a thing as a smooth text, in other words, without suture perhaps, it will be one wherein there is the "effacement of the faces of the subject" (32).

29. Derrida, "'Il faut bien manger,'" in *Points de suspension,* 282, 282–83.

30. Ibid., 283.

31. "Introduction" to Cadava, Connor, and Nancy, eds., *Who Comes After the Subject?,* 4.

32. Ibid., 6.

33. Nancy, "Un sujet?," 51.

34. As Nancy notes, "*Hypostasis* is only another word for *hypokēimenon* (placed below, supposed [*supposé*], a very important word in Aristotle), which in Latin is translated as *subjectum.* There is an entire family—'substance,' 'subject,' 'hypostasis,' 'hypokēimenon,' of which one could say that it is all the family of the *suppositum*" ("Un sujet?," 67).

35. This is perhaps close to the *sense* of Nancy's "who" or "some one" [*quelqu'un*] in place of the *subject.* According to Nancy, this "who" or "some one" "makes sense by itself, without this 'self' being a substance itself; makes sense by itself without being a subject, or makes sense without supposing itself sensed [*sensé*]" ("Un sujet?," 113). This *sense* is neither intelligible nor logical sense. It is "sense [*sens*] that has no relation to a subject of meaning [*sujet de sens*], to a subject that could bear [*supporter*] this sense [*sens*] and present it in a manner or another, to signify it, and more, demonstrate it" (113). Nancy goes on: "Instead of that which is to be discovered or supposed behind or in advance, [it] would be what singularly engages itself, guarantees itself, promises itself each time, at each moment, not behind or before, but precisely here, at the place of the exposition of a singularity" (113–14). It is this

unintelligible *sense* that Nancy's "who" or "some one" "is each time in an infinite newness [*nouveauté ou novation*] of sense" (114), that it is "inventing itself each time, interminably, or 'terminably,' as a new possibility of singular sense" (114).

36. My rhetoric here might appear to come close to Bataille's, especially when Bataille speaks of "inner experience" or "unproductive expenditure." However, as I will highlight in the section on friendship, love, and community, Bataille's extreme gestures veer dangerously too much toward nihilism. Nihilism, however, as mentioned earlier, is of the order of the *subject*, and from which a theory of the *reject* must refrain, given that it is of creative regeneration in general. In that regard, I would take some distance from Bataille in my notion of the *auto-reject*. In fact, I would say that my rhetoric is actually approaching that of Nancy here, since "abandonment" is a critical term for his philosophy. I return to Nancy's abandonment in the Conclusion of this work.

37. Nancy, "Ipso facto cogitans et demens" in *Derrida pour les temps à venir*, 130. Here, I follow Celine Surprenant's translation in "Mad Derrida," 26.

38. Derrida, "'Il faut bien manger,'" in *Points de suspension*, 275.

39. Ibid., 276.

40. I would like to highlight that to renounce proclaiming to give hospitality to the other is not contrary to Derrida's "unconditional hospitality," which is hospitality open to *anyone*, without any demand for any return from the other, without any demand either for the other to identify him- or herself. My rhetoric here is meant to prevent any subjective appropriation of "unconditional hospitality," any assuming of such hospitality as a property of any particular *subject*, as something that he or she alone has the power, right, authority, or even generosity to give to the other. Certainly, one must work toward a condition where "unconditional hospitality" can be put in place and maintained. However, one must also be vigilant to avoid making oneself the guardian of that hospitality, from which place he or she consciously, and therefore subjectively, summons or even makes the interpellation to the other to come.

41. See note 6, above.

42. Kristeva, *Pouvoirs de l'horreur*, 10.

43. See Žižek, *Violence*.

44. Critchley, *Faith of the Faithless*, 213, 219. I do think that the notion of "objective violence" is undeniably close to Derrida's argument of the irreducible violence of the trace, which precedes, inheres in, and exceeds writing or discourse, in "Violence et métaphysique," 117–228, not to mention that the respective arguments of Critchley and Derrida, and also of Butler, as we will see in a while, all have Lévinasian ethics as their point of departure. Lévinasian ethics undoubtedly has bearings for a theory of the *reject*. However, for reasons that I will spell out soon, Lévinas's philosophy lies outside the scope of this present work.

45. See Nancy, "L'Insacrifiable," in *Une Pensée finie*, 65–106.

46. Critchley, *Faith of the Faithless*, 208.

47. Žižek, *Violence*, 217.

48. Butler, *Precarious Life*, xi. See also Jean Furtos's *De la précarité à l'auto-exclusion*, in which he argues that the first sign of precarity is when one loses all sense of certitude or confidence, to the point where one starts to shut oneself out from everything and to view oneself abjectly.

49. Butler, *Precarious Life*, xii, xi, xii.

50. Ibid., xii.

51. Ibid., 137, xii.

52. See Antelme, *Vengeance?*

53. In a letter to Cixous, Derrida has written, "Even where there are dialogues, in Plato . . . these dialogues remain in the service of the monologic thesis" (Unpublished correspondence, quoted in Cixous, "Co-Responding Voix You," 50).

54. I note here that Foucault has even once raised the question if all philosophy after Plato is essentially a rejection of Platonic philosophy: "Are all philosophies individual species of the 'anti-Platonic' genre? Does each begin in articulating the grand refusal [*le grand refus*]?" ("Theatrum Philosophicum," in *Dits et écrits II: 1970–1975*, 75, my translation).

55. According to Ian James's account in *The New French Philosophy*, "postdeconstructive" thinkers such as Nancy, Badiou, Rancière, Bernard Stiegler, François Laruelle, and Catherine Malabou break with, or reject, the linguistic turn of 1960s French structuralism. John Mullarkey picks up the term "postcontinental philosophy" as used by Kevin Mulligan to signal the apparent end of contemporary French thought, but modulates it to mean it "as both an assessment of the current transitional state in which Continental thought finds itself with respect to its theorization of science in particular and immanence in general, as well as a caution against thinking that such an engagement could ever be a straightforward evolution" (*Post-Continental Philosophy*, 3). According to Mullarkey, Deleuze, Badiou, Laruelle, and Michel Henry would represent such "postcontinental" philosophers: "*Rejecting* both the phenomenological tradition of transcendence (of Consciousness, the Ego, Being, or Alterity), as well as the poststructuralist valorization of Language, they instead take the immanent categories of biology (Deleuze), mathematics (Badiou), affectivity (Henry), and science (Laruelle) as focal points for a renewal of philosophy" (2, my emphasis).

56. "Introduction" to Cadava, Connor, and Nancy, eds., *Who Comes After the Subject?*, 7.

57. On this point, I note that Nancy's original contributors to the initial collection published in *Topoi* and *Cahiers Confrontation* disturbingly do not include female thinkers. It is only when the collection appears as *Who Comes After the Subject?* that we see contributions from Sylviane Agacinski, Luce Irigaray, and Sarah Kofman. I thank Eduardo Cadava for reminding readers of this problematic difference between the initial and later publications.

58. Nancy, *Ego sum*, 126. Gérard Granel, for his part, takes Descartes's *ego sum* as a textual inscription. According to Granel then, "as *Ego cogito cogitata mea*, the subject *in his text* has never been someone"; instead, "it has always been a 'what'" ("Qui vient après le sujet?" in *Écrits logiques et politiques*, 327, my translation). Granel's response is also reproduced in Cadava, Connor, and Nancy, eds., *Who Comes After the Subject?*).

59. "Passage," in Jean-Luc Nancy and Jean-Claude Conésa, *Être, c'est être perçu*, 23, my translation.

60. Ibid., 20.

61. Nancy, *Ego sum*, 140, 139.

62. Ibid., 145–47.

63. Ibid., 124.

64. Ibid., 24.

65. See Nancy, "Ipso facto cogitans et demens," 119. Again, I follow Surprenant's translation in "Mad Derrida," 17.

66. Nancy, "Mad Derrida," 31, translation modified; Nancy, "Ipso facto cogitans et demens," 137.

67. Nancy, "Mad Derrida," 29, 30; Nancy, "Ipso facto cogitans et demens," 137.

68. Nancy, "Mad Derrida," 25; Nancy, "Ipso facto cogitans et demens," 130.

69. Intellectual histories of twentieth-century French thought would also suggest that the *reject* subtends its history; if not, its history is very much a history of *rejects*. That seems to be historical narrative that François Dosse constructs in his two-volume *Histoire du structuralisme*. He underscores how structuralism in the early 1960s began very much outside institutional walls, as structuralist thinkers such as Lévi-Strauss, Althusser, Barthes, and Lacan all faced initial rejections by established academic and psychoanalytic institutions. It did become an undeniable force in the times leading to the eventful date of May 1968, but fissures had begun to rupture among its leading thinkers as it started to lose its revolutionary trajectory and took on a staid disposition resembling a school of some sort. Post-1968 thinkers such as Derrida, Deleuze, and Foucault would try to revive its dynamic force, but the demise of the movement's main stars—Barthes, Lacan, Althusser, and Foucault—in the 1980s would signal its marginalization, or indeed its swansong according to Dosse, in France. Rejected in France, Foucault (until his death in 1984), Derrida, Deleuze, Baudrillard, Lyotard, Nancy, Lacoue-Labarthe, and Balibar will find more successes in the United States, and this adventure of French thought in the United States would be François Cusset's story in *French Theory*. Gary Gutting's *French Philosophy in the Twentieth Century* traces the intellectual history of the philosophers of the Third Republic up to Barthes and Foucault, ending with a less than favorable critique of Derrida and Deleuze. Gutting is interested in the question of freedom in twentieth-century French philosophy, or how it seeks to set itself free from the confines or limits of institutions and

disciplines. I mention Gutting's work here because of the numerous occurrences of the word "reject" in his narrative. That might be a trivial or banal point, but it is not insignificant in my view, and I would say that Gutting's account concerns very much the story of active *rejects* in French philosophy.

70. I am aware that *déclosion* has been recently translated as "dis-enclosure." However, as the question of the secret (or rather mystery as Nancy would say in "L'Évidence du mystère" in *Le Voyage initiatique*) is at stake not only in *déclosion* but also in the *reject* in all its engagements with ethics, religion, and politics, I have chosen to simply translate it as "dis-closure," which preserves the sense of the secret.

71. See especially Hardt and Negri, *Commonwealth*.

72. Bauman, *Wasted Lives*, 5.

73. Ibid., 12.

74. Ibid.

75. Rogozinski and Surya, "Présentation au collectif sur 'Le rebut humain'" in *Lignes 35*, 6. I note that this collection is also inspired by Bauman's work, and like Bauman, several of the contributors make reference to Agamben's *homo sacer*. Like Bauman again, most contributors consider *le rebut humain* or human trash as something produced. In Rogozinski's piece on the lepers of the Middle Ages, he argues, "In truth, there is *no* figure of the *rebut* that is ever originary [*originaire*]: all are constituted by a complex process where the rupture of an initial ambivalence [regarding what is pure or not, sacred or not] plays a decisive role" ("Pire que la mort," 27). Marc Nichanian, for his part, argues that the *rebut* is a conjuration of the humanist *subject*, that the construction of a *subject* in its unitary properness and sanctity "needed the *rebut*" ("Le Rebut du sujet," 40). But this only means that the *rebut* is in effect "the inverted image [of the humanist human *subject*] in the mirror" ("Le Rebut du sujet," 47). According to Jérôme Lèbre, "The human trash does not cease to be created, because it is humanity itself, expelled from itself" ("Les Failles du monde," 72).

76. Martin Crowley, in his contribution to the issue on "Le Rebut humain" of *Lignes* (see note above), argues that there is even life on the side of the *rebut*, on the side of those that are separated from the rest of the world: "Life [. . .] from the other side. At a distance" [*La vie (. . .) de l'autre côté. À l'écart*] ("Vivre à l'écart," 60). There are no doubt resonances between my *auto-reject* and Crowley's work, including his notion of "man without" in his *L'Homme sans*.

2. (AFTER) FRIENDSHIP, LOVE, AND COMMUNITY

1. This word is used by Blanchot in *La Communauté inavouable* to describe Bataille's engagement with the thought of community. It has been picked up again

recently by Andrew J. Mitchell and Jason Kemp Winfree in their edited volume of essays on Bataille and community, *The Obsessions of Georges Bataille*.

2. See Nancy's introduction to Cadava, Connor, and Nancy, eds., *Who Comes after the Subject?*, 8.

3. Bataille, *L'Expérience intérieure*, 74, my translation.

4. Ibid., 40.

5. See ibid., 74.

6. Ibid., 15.

7. Ibid., 40.

8. Ibid., 21.

9. See ibid., 28–29, on silence. In a later passage, Bataille also argues that "the refusal to communicate [that is, silence] is a more hostile means to communicate, and the most powerful" (64).

10. Ibid., 74.

11. Ibid., 115, 40.

12. Ibid., 24.

13. It is this affirmation that *there is* always already community that forms Nancy's critique of Bataille's community of lovers, which Bataille celebrates as standing opposed to all formations of community in society—communities that are constituted to be functional, purposeful, and productive. For Nancy, the community of lovers does not stand outside of community. Otherwise, there is the risk that the community of lovers become some sort of insular, subjective, communion, and hence antithetical to all thoughts of community. See Nancy, *La Communauté désœuvrée*, 90–98. See also 60–65 for Nancy's critique of Bataille in not going far enough with his critique of the *subject*, allowing a trace of the *subject* or subjectivity to remain in his thought. And on the difference of Nancy's *there is,* or *il y a,* of community with Lévinas's *il y a* and an ethical community based on the face-to-face instant, see 224.

14. Nancy, *La Communauté désœuvrée*, 152, 71.

15. Ibid., 22.

16. To return to the *there is* or *il y a* of community of Nancy, I refer here to Nancy's essay "Cum" (in *La Pensée dérobée*), where he gives the notion of *Mitdasein* a further analysis than Heidegger had done. For Nancy, *Mitdasein* must be rearticulated as *mit-da-sein* or "being-with-there" [*être là avec*] ("Cum," 120), where "with-there" points *being* to its fact as "being sharing or *sharing itself* according to the *there* [*da*], which strives to designate the 'opening'—the 'opening' of the exposed" (ibid., 120).

17. Nancy, *La Communauté désœuvrée*, 225.

18. See Nancy, *L'Adoration*, 2.

19. Nancy, *La Communauté désœuvrée*, 151.

20. Ibid., 198.

21. Ibid., 146.

22. Ibid., 87.

23. Ibid., 230, 226.

24. Ibid., 41.

25. Ibid., 260.

26. Agamben, *Coming Community*, 65. I note too that another Italian thinker, Roberto Esposito, has also taken the cue from Nancy to think about community with a critique of the *subject* as its point of departure. See especially his *Communitas*. I mention Agamben above in particular simply because *The Coming Community*, more than *Communitas* perhaps, posits a figure of thought otherwise of the *subject* in relation to the rethinking of community.

27. Agamben, *Coming Community*, 1.

28. Ibid.

29. Ibid., 2.

30. Ibid., 11.

31. Ibid.

32. Ibid.

33. Ibid.

34. Ibid.

35. Ibid., 86.

36. Ibid., 11.

37. Ibid., 86, 25.

38. Ibid., 86.

39. For a critique of these concepts, see especially Dominick LaCapra's "Approaching Limit Events: Siting Agamben," in *History in Transit*; and LaCapra's "Reopening the Question of the Human and the Animal," in *History and Its Limits*.

40. Derrida and Ferraris, *Taste for the Secret*, 25.

41. Derrida, *Politiques de l'amitié*, 338. I have consulted and used in large part George Collins's translation of this passage in *Politics of Friendship*, 304–5. This is also true for the other references to *Politiques de l'amitié*. Subsequent citations from this text will therefore be indicated by references to the French text first (to be marked as *PA*), followed by those to Collins's translation (henceforth marked as *PF*).

42. I also note that a critique of the withdrawal from the radical trajectory in relation to friendship in Derrida, and an inquiry into the question of community in Deleuze, are insufficiently dealt with in Derridean and Deleuzian scholarship. Hence, turning to Derrida and Deleuze here also fills certain gaps there.

43. I acknowledge too that our contemporary teletechnological world, especially its operative or operational aspect, forms the backdrop or point of departure for Nancy's critique of community as well. For a comprehensive study of that, I refer to Philip Armstrong's *Reticulations*, where he points out that Nancy's notion of

community or *being-with* [*être-avec*], *being-together* [*être-ensemble*], or *being-in-common* [*être-en-commun*] is anterior to all (tele)technology in the instrumental sense. I note too that Armstrong does an inimitable job as well in situating Nancy's philosophy, especially its political implications, within today's network culture, in order to critique the latter. I hence defer all considerations of Nancy's philosophy as critique of contemporary network-centric friendship, love, and community to Armstrong's book, and I will focus only on Derrida and Deleuze.

44. As Deleuze says in an interview, "Today, it is information technology, communication, and commercial advertising [*promotion commerciale*] that have appropriated the words 'concept' and 'creative,' and these 'conceptualists' form an arrogant race that expresses the activity of selling as capitalism's supreme thought, as the *cogito* of merchandising" (*Pourparlers*, 186; in translating this passage, I have consulted Martin Joughin's translation in *Negotiations*, 136). For Deleuze, the task of creating concepts does not lie with information and communications industries and advertising enterprises. Instead, it properly belongs to philosophy, and the true (philosophical) act of concept-creation has no time for, or has nothing to do with, communication, conversations, discussions, and exchange of views or opinions or gossips. (See also Deleuze and Guattari's *Qu'est-ce que la philosophie?* on this question of concept-creation.) In fact, according to Deleuze, things predicated on speech and communication are not only nonphilosophical or nonconceptual but also corrupt: "Maybe speech and communication have been corrupted. They're thoroughly permeated by money: not by accident but by nature" (*Pourparlers*, 238). It seems then that for Deleuze, speech and communication are intrinsically already inclined toward buying into, or even bought by, capitalist ideology, hence his distrust not only of them but also of any "concept" that they claim to articulate. Irigaray, in a less polemic way than Deleuze, has also expressed her mistrust of teletechnologies with regard to future relations in *Way of Love* and *Être deux*.

45. Deleuze, *Pourparlers*, 236–37.

46. Derrida, *Spectres de Marx*, 88.

47. Derrida, *L'Autre cap*, 54, 53, 57.

48. Ibid., 117.

49. Deleuze, *Pourparlers*, 236.

50. Derrida, *L'Autre cap*, 55. Here, I follow Pascale-Anne Brault and Michael B. Nass's translation in *The Other Heading*, 54.

51. Deleuze, *Pourparlers*, 238. Here, I have also consulted Martin Joughin's translation in *Negotiations*, 175.

52. See Stross, "When Everyone's a Friend, Is Anything Private?" I recall Deleuze here, who says that the true, philosophical task of concept-creation requires the commitment to the difficult endeavor "to understand the problem posed by someone and how the latter poses it," and "to enrich it, to vary the conditions, to add to it, [and] to relate it to something else" (*Pourparlers*, 191). The mere, or frivolous,

communicative gregariousness of network-centric friendship surely disqualifies it as a real concept, and hence one must refer to it only as a "concept."

53. Blanchot, *Pour l'amitié*, 7, my translation. The full passage goes like this: "Sait-on quand elle commence? Il n'y a pas de coup de foudre de l'amitié, plutôt un peu à peu, un lent travail du temps. On était amis et on ne le savait pas." [Does one know when [friendship] begins? There is no love at first sight of friendship. Rather, little by little, it is a slow work of time. One would be friends and one would not know it.]

54. The *New York Times* article cited in an earlier note also reports that people over thirty years of age have been resistant to the kind of friendship offered by digital social networks. However, as "each week, a million new members are added [on Facebook] in the United States and five million globally; the 30-and-older group is its fastest-growing demographic." It also notes an evolving "Law of Amiable Inclusiveness" among digital social network members, where they accept, without much if any thought, any request by anyone to be their friend just by a quick and simple digital function. See also CNN's September 16, 2009, report, "Facebook Nearly as Large as US Population," on Facebook crossing the 300 million users threshold, close to the 307 million people living in the United States, and that its "fastest growing demographic is people older than 35." The report also quotes Facebook CEO Mark Zuckerberg saying that Facebook is "just getting started on [their] goal of connecting everyone." The universalizing or universal dimension of network-centric friendship will give the Deleuzian perspective another occasion to point out that network-centric friendship does not constitute a real concept since, according to Deleuze, "a concept is not a universal [. . .]" (*Pourparlers*, 200).

55. Deleuze, *Pourparlers*, 186. See also note 44 above. It is even commonplace today for digital social networks to be a source of information to be commercially mined by telecommunications corporations for the development and sales of future products or objects of desire. Resistance is also almost futile against software that stealthily tracks consumption patterns of digital social media users, which then sells such information to enterprises that in turn send product advertisements to all the friends of those users to generate greater sales.

56. The phrase "ecstasy of hyper-gregariousness" is evidently informed by the works of Baudrillard. I use "hyper" in *hyper-gregariousness* on the one hand to refer to the virtual or electronic dimension (as in "hyperspace," "hyperlink," "hyper-reality," or "hypertext") where contemporary forms of friendship are developing. On the other hand, I also use it in the Baudrillardian sense, as in Baudrillard's notion of the "hyper-real" or the simulacrum, which refers to things more real than real or in excess of the real, yet at bottom are in fact empty or without truth (see Baudrillard, *Simulacres et simulation;* Baudrillard, *Amérique*). In that sense, the hyper-gregariousness of friendship proliferating in digital social networks is but a symptom of hyper-friendship—empty and without truth. The notion of "ecstasy"

is of course taken from Baudrillard's *Ecstasy of Communication*. Baudrillard there was writing mainly on television culture, and not on real-time digital connectivity, but his observation that "ecstasy is all functions abolished into one dimension, the dimension of communication" clearly is applicable to contemporary network culture (*Ecstasy of Communication*, 23–24). Predicating friendship on the incessant real-time exchange of messages in hyperspace, reporting on almost everything—from the extraordinary to the most mundane and banal—of one's everyday life, has certainly given network-centric friendship a quality of ecstatic "cool communicational obscenity" (*Ecstasy of Communication*, 24).

57. In invoking the idea of a network empire, I am here following a line of contemporary theorists such as Michael Hardt and Antonio Negri, Alexander Galloway and Eugene Thacker, Brian Massumi, and McKenzie Wark. Building on Deleuze's prophecy of "societies of control," these theorists identify the mode of "continuous control and instant communication" of such societies in the twenty-first century in the form of something like a network empire, which "has emerged as a dominant form describing the nature of control today" (Galloway and Thacker, *The Exploit*, 4), and which "not only regulates human interactions but also seeks directly to rule over human nature" or "social life in its entirety" (Hardt and Negri, *Empire*, xv). Pertinent to the point at hand, Hardt and Negri also argue that the network empire is the manifestation of "capitalism's colonization of communicative society" (*Empire*, 404). See also Brian Massumi's *Parables for the Virtual*, 87.

58. See note above.

59. Derrida, *L'Autre cap*, 53, my translation.

60. Cf. note 44, where I point to Deleuze's commitment to reclaim the task of concept-creation for philosophy, by revealing the false and ideological nature behind the "concepts" that information and communications industries and advertising enterprises claim to "create."

61. I note that while digital social networks allow one to count friends incredulously in the thousands, many of these "friends" are most likely people whom one would have merely exchanged a message or two in hyperspace. In other words, they are hardly those one would have met physically and interacted for a duration of time in real life. Again, the "slow work of time" of friendship according to Blanchot is clearly missing here.

62. *PA*, 90/ *PF*, 70–71.

63. Cf. Nietzsche: "The philosopher [. . .] has, in every age been and has *needed* to be at odds with his today: his enemy has always been the ideal of today" (*Beyond Good and Evil*, 106 §212). See also Agamben's "What Is the Contemporary?" in the collection *What Is an Apparatus?* The collection also includes Agamben's essay on friendship, where he draws an almost unfriendly distinction with Derrida. This is not the space to treat Agamben's thinking of friendship and its difference from

Derrida's. For that, see Weber, "'And When is Now?' (On Some Limits of Perfect Intelligibility)"; and Wortham, "Law of Friendship: Agamben and Derrida."

64. Derrida, *Spectres de Marx*, 16.

65. Derrida, *L'Autre cap*, 119.

66. Ibid.

67. Stiegler, *La Technie et le temps*, 1: 194. With regard to Epimetheus being rendered a *reject*, one also wonders if that is but a certain payback for his oversight while partitioning out survival skills among mortal creatures, forgetting about humans altogether in that process, making them some sort of unintended *rejects* in his thoughtlessness.

68. Stiegler, "Le Bien le plus précieux à l'époque des sociotechnologies," 18.

69. Ibid., 21.

70. Ibid., translation modified.

71. Ibid., 20.

72. Ibid., 23, translation modified.

73. Ibid., 26. This is also where the *subject*, more than the *reject* perhaps, inheres in Stiegler's thought. According to Stiegler, teletechnologies driven by a writing system or a technics of the trace or "traceability" (20) allow the inscription of the *I* or the *subject*, whose identity and individuation can be affirmed and disseminated in the "process of transindividuation" (see *La Télécratie contre la démocratie*, 31).

74. Stiegler, "Le Bien le plus précieux à l'époque des sociotechnologies," 29. Stiegler is clearly working from a Derridean logic of the trace, or else the pharmaco-logy of writing systems, through all this, and he does not fail to acknowledge that debt. According to that logic, which goes back to Plato, writing is akin to *pharmakos*, which is both poison and remedy. It is on that basis that Stiegler argues that digital social networks predicated on a writing system can, on the one hand, "aggravate dis-individuation by a control that is less policing than behavioral, and exercised by marketing [ideologies]" (30), "short-circuiting networks of [physical] proximity that has always supported the social" (14), and therefore lead to "the destruction of the social" (32). On the other hand, as noted in the main text, they are also, in Stiegler's view, "the only way to invent new forms of individuation" (32).

75. Stiegler, "Le Bien le plus précieux à l'époque des sociotechnologies," 30.

76. Stiegler, *La Télécratie contre la démocratie*, 134, 72. *Lien*, more traditionally, is translated as "tie," but I choose "link" over "tie" because, keeping in mind the background of digital social networks here, *lien*, when used in the context where digital interfaces are in question, also refers to hyperlinks.

77. Ibid., 30.

78. See ibid., 136–37, for Stiegler's critique of relations that are "ephemeral" or "unstable" and not enduring.

79. Nietzsche, *Beyond Good and Evil*, 41 §44.

80. In this respect, I depart from the horizons of contemporary theorists mentioned in note 57. I do think their theories trace a communitarian and even communicative outline. For example, in their resistance against global capital in its network-empire form, they would invoke the "common," which breaks away from the ideological capture and control of network empires and wrests back their rights to "free access to and control over knowledge, information, communication, and affects" (Casarino and Negri, *In Praise of the Common*, 82). They make it clear that the common is predicated on communication or conversation, but a mode of communication different from that which "has become the central element that establishes the relations of production, guiding capitalist development and also transforming productive forces" (Hardt and Negri, *Empire*, 347–48; see also *Multitudes*, 204; and Casarino and Negri, *In Praise of the Common*, 2). This also applies to Paolo Virno's "multitude," the communitarian basis of which, or "unity," comes from the ground, arising from "language, intellect, the communal faculties of the human race," including idle talk, in contrast to Heidegger's denigration of it (*Grammar of the Multitude*, 25, 89–90). These communitarian and communicative aspirations mark these theorists' distance not only from Deleuze, but also from Derrida, who, as mentioned in the text proper above, is not inclined toward the thought of the "common" either.

81. That is what Derrida says of the politics of his *Spectres de Marx*. In response to queries about the political dimension or responsibility of *Spectres de Marx*, Derrida will say, "The form of my gesture would seem to include, at a minimum, the demand that one *read*, a demand which remains, for its part, at once theoretical and practical: it asks that people take into account the nature and form [. . .] of this gesture, if only to criticize its utility, possibility, authenticity, or even sincerity" ("Marx & Sons," 200). Nancy, in speaking about the politics of Derrida's works, argues for a form of politics "on paper"—albeit a politics of writing or conceptualizing rather than reading—instead of concrete political action on the part of philosophers: "The political character of a work of thought is not to be measured only, indeed far from it, by the practical interventions of the man. [. . .]. The thinker [. . .] acts politically before all else by thinking the truth [. . .] of a world, of the situation of a world in which concepts like politics, as well as aesthetics or ethics, have to be put back in play, put to work, and elaborated. The first political duty of a philosopher is to philosophize, just as the first political duty of a musician is to compose" ("Philosophy as Chance," 216).

82. I certainly do not deny the importance of discussing the politics of friendship or politics of *Politiques de l'amitié* in terms of political acts that engage with political institutions. See especially A. J. P Thomson's *Deconstruction and Democracy* on that topic. Furthermore, the same digital social networks have already implicated themselves in American party politics in the 2008 US presidential campaign, wherein they created a hyperspace of political fraternity by disseminating

mutually shared hopes and ideologies precisely through their digital platforms (see Stelter, "Facebooker Who Friended Obama"). That is the kind of politics of friendship that Derrida critiques precisely. The interest of this section, however, is more inclined toward ethical and/or philosophical considerations, so I would like to limit any notion of politics of philosophical friendship and/or *Politiques de l'amitié* here to the question of reading as stated above. That also means that there will be no manifesto-like point-by-point application of my reading or argument for a possible political action against contemporary digital social networks. I leave that to activists who, if possible, have the will to reject friendship while striking out against social network apparatuses.

83. Just to cite two readings of Derrida's *Politiques de l'amitié*: John W Phillips writes that "what we learn about friendship in *Politiques de l'amitié* is, strictly speaking, unacceptable; friendship itself will turn out to be unacceptable" ("Loving Love," 166); and in the words of David Wills, "friendship [in *Politics of Friendship*] involves turning one's back" ("Full Dorsal," §8). Another notable reading of Derrida's text, which deals with the politics of friend/enemy, is Gregg Lambert's "Enemy (der Feind)." Lambert also has a reading of the politics of friendship in Deleuze, which resonates quite a bit with my discussion of Deleuze later (see Lambert's "Deleuze,"35–53).

84. I note here that the French original is "Rien peut-être de dicible."

85. In a text written in the wake of Bataille's passing, Blanchot critiques all spectacles of mourning, especially that which commemorates the dead friend by claiming not only to remember everything he or she has written but also to hold the key to the mystery of the personal pronouns in the friend's *œuvre*. According to Blanchot, thought forgets, and this thought "must accompany friendship into forgetfulness" ("L'Amitié," in *L'Amitié*, 330, my translation). In fact, friendship is hinged on "something in us that rejects all remembering" (326). Following the death of a friend, one must not, "through artifices, create semblances of continuing a dialogue" (329) with the friend. Instead, the death of the friend, Blanchot argues, should be the occasion where we accept "the infinite distance" or "fundamental separation" (328) in friendship, or that there is always a "faraway" [*lointain*] (326) at the heart of friendship, and which disappears with the passing of the friend.

86. In the French original: "Être aimé, qu'est-ce que cela veut dire? Rien, peut-être [. . .]." Compare the French original of "nothing sayable" quoted in note 84.

87. On the refrain also of contemporary theorists from breaking away from the thinking of community, see note 80 above.

88. One could also argue that Derrida's *reject* arrives by way of modulating Aristotle's oft-cited phrase, "O my friends, there is no friend." It is with this phrase, in its form of an address, that one can elicit too the sense that both the self and the other are *rejects* in or before friendship. On the one hand, the address rejects the other by structuring the latter's imminent disappearance: according to Derrida,

through Aristotle's phrase, "[friends] are summoned to be spoken to [. . .] then dismissed [. . .] saying to them, speaking *of them*, that they are no longer there. One speaks *of them* only in their absence, and *concerning* their absence" (*PA*, 197/ *PF*, 173). In other words, a certain dismissal of friends is at work in this phrase, rendering the friend a (passive) *reject*. On the other hand, the phrase also signals some form of refusal of the other to respond to the address. This is where the self is rendered a (targeted) *reject*, because "there is no friend" that has responded.

89. See Nietzsche, *Beyond Good and Evil*, 104 §210.

90. As Derrida observes too, "Nietzsche makes the call [. . .] to his addressee, asking him to join up with 'us,' with this 'us' which is being formed, to join us and to resemble us, to become the friends of the friends that we are!" (*PA*, 53/ *PF*, 35). I do think that Derrida also finds this Nietzschean "we" suspicious. When Derrida speaks of the "unheard-of" and "totally new" "arrivant" (*PA*, 46/ *PF*, 29) that is to come in or from the future, I do not think that he attributes it to Nietzsche's free spirits or new philosophers. Reading §214 of *Beyond Good and Evil*, Derrida underscores that in the "we" of Nietzsche and the new philosophers, Nietzsche also "declares his appurtenance *qua* heir who still believes in his own virtues" (*PA*, 51/ *PF*, 33), claiming an alliance to a no doubt rare but nonetheless existing or past spirit whose virtues are or have been to strike out against other past values (for example, Platonic philosophy and Christian religion). This only means that Nietzsche is always ineluctably tied to the past, and as such, the question of a "totally new" or "unheard-of" "arrivant" will be undeniably diluted in Nietzsche and also, by implication, in the new philosophers, by virtue of the "we" that Nietzsche addresses them with. Perhaps this is also why Derrida in *Politiques de l'amitié* says that "we will not follow Nietzsche" (*PA*, 51/ *PF*, 33)? I do agree with Derrida's reading. Nietzsche may indeed proclaim that he and the new philosophers are "not to be stuck to our virtues" (*Beyond Good and Evil*, 39 §41) but, "beyond what [Nietzsche] believes, what he thinks he believes" (*PA*, 52/ *PF*, 33) as Derrida says, there is always that *one* virtue that explicitly and forcefully remains, which is Nietzsche's will to demolish old values, morals, religions, and philosophies. In relation to Derrida's "arrivant" that rejects both setting a teleologic program for itself and all *a priori* or existing programs, Nietzsche's singular virtue is undeniably programmatic, which is perhaps betrayed in his following words on the new philosophers: "we do not want to fully reveal what a spirit might free himself *from* and what he will then perhaps be driven *towards*" (Nietzsche, *Beyond Good and Evil*, 41 §44).

91. Aristotle, *Nicomachean Ethics*, 205–6, 205.

92. Ibid., 197, 196. In Aristotle's words, "Young people are amorous too; for the greater part of the friendship of love [in contradistinction to the friendship of *l'aimance*] depends on emotion and aims at pleasure; this is why they fall in love and quickly fall out of love, changing often within a single day" (ibid., 196).

93. I emphasize that this radical Nietzschean *aimance* is a result or effect of Derrida's reading. I have already pointed out above that Nietzsche's *Beyond Good and Evil* in fact reveals the problematic of a possible rapprochement, on the part of Nietzsche, arising between Nietzsche and the new philosophers, rather than "disappropriation" or "infinite distance" as Derrida reads it.

94. "Entretien avec Robert Maggiori," *Libération*, November 24, 1994. Available at http://www.hydra.umn.edu/derrida/ami.html. My translation.

95. One could also add that Derrida is countersigning Aristotle's *aimance* in another way here. Aristotle's *aimance* only loops back to the self or the loving friend. In other words, it begins and ends where it starts in the Aristotelian perfect friendship. With Derrida, however, it is from a space outside of friendship, that is, love, where *l'aimance* begins, and it reaches something other than what it was before, which in this case would be friendship.

96. Let me say that I do not refute the ethics that arises from *not* walking away from friendship or from this waiting-without-expectation at the margins of friendship (and love). Contrary to Aristotle's *aimance*, which concedes to the insurmountable experience of chronological time and therefore sets up a practical limit as to the number of friends one can love, Derrida's *aimance* will not put arithmetic into operation. Waiting without expecting, Derrida's *aimance* is not averse to the imminence of whoever, whatever, or *anyone* (to follow Derrida's rhetoric in his texts on cosmopolitanism and the *voyou*) that arrives. Derrida's *aimance* does not count who or what can arrive. It looks toward a relation between singularities that do not add up, an *aimance* that opens up (to) a "singular world of singularities" that is "of non-appurtenance" (*PA*, 62/ *PF*, 42). There, one does not know, and one is not interested to know, how to begin counting the singularities within such a relation: "How many of us are there? Does that count? And how do you calculate?" (*PA*, 54/ *PF*, 35) There will be no quantifying of friends, nor delimiting the boundaries of friendship by predicating it on a recognition of similarities. In other words, Derrida's *aimance* is open to a noncounting multiplicity of singularities and their heterogeneity. It does not judge any of these singularities as good or evil, friend or enemy, and therefore also takes the audacious risk of welcoming even the figure that is, or potentially is, monstrous.

97. I note that Derrida is not forceful with the rejection of the term "friendship" as he is with regard to the term forgiveness. The rhetoric Derrida deploys in speaking of forgiveness is almost similar to the rhetoric in his instruction to the other to not pick up his call. In the latter, as seen, he warns that should the other pick up the call, friendship will be undone. With regard to forgiveness, he writes, "forgiving must [. . .] be impossible [. . .]. If when I forgive, the wrongdoing, the injury, the wound, the offense become forgivable because I've forgiven, *then it's over* [my emphases]" ("A Certain Impossible Possibility," 234). There, Derrida will repeatedly insist on an impossibility of forgiveness. One then wonders why

Derrida does not insist on the impossibility of friendship as thoroughly as he does with the term of forgiveness.

98. I note that dispersion also constitutes part of the theoretical strategies by the aforementioned thinkers such as Hardt and Negri, and Galloway and Thacker, against the network empire. Hardt and Negri put theirs in terms of desertion: the tactical position that is "most effective is an oblique or diagonal stance. Battles against the Empire might be won through subtraction and defection. This desertion does not have a place; it is the evacuation of the places of power" (*Empire*, 212). Galloway and Thacker also advocate this strategy, seeing desertion as a future "resistive act" (*The Exploit*, 101, 111). But once again, I differ from them on account that there is *no* "construction of a new society" (Hardt and Negri, *Empire*, 404) nor any opening into "the common" (Galloway and Thacker, *The Exploit*, 111) at the end of my dispersion.

99. "L'Aimance comme l'attirance de l'autre: Réponse à 'L'aimance et l'invention d'un idiome' d'Abdelkébir Khatibi." Unpublished address presented at the colloquium "Khatibi's Œuvre: Materiality and Writing," Northwestern University, April 12–17, 2007. I thank Samuel Weber for sending me his manuscript.

100. Clément, *La Syncope*, 189. Here, I follow Sally O'Driscoll and Deirdre M. Mahoney's translation in *Syncope*, 119.

101. Clément, *La Syncope*, 198, my translation.

102. Such syncopic love certainly will not be love according to Alain Badiou. In his *Éloge de l'amour*, which proceeds via a critique of contemporary love arranged by online sites for potentially compatible lovers to be paired up and meet, Badiou defines love as the chance or uncalculated encounter of difference. The subsequent test of this love is not just the declaration of fidelity to it, but the fidelity to make this encounter endure, to make it a work of lasting duration.

103. Clément, *La Syncope*, 202. Here, I follow the translation in *Syncope*, 128.

104. Ibid., 204–5. I follow once again the translation in *Syncope*, 130.

105. Ibid., 205, 200.

106. Of course, Nancy's more thorough engagement with syncope can already be found in his early *Le Discours de la syncope*. However, the context in which Nancy discusses syncope there, which has its basis Kant's philosophical discourse, is rather different from both Clément's and that of this chapter, and so I refrain from discussing that text here.

107. Nancy, "L'Amour en éclats," 247.

108. Ibid., 236. To be precise, Nancy does not say that the *subject* says *I love you*. Nancy argues that it is instead the heart that makes that declaration. The heart, according to Nancy, "is not a subject, even if it is the heart of a subject" (236). I leave aside all discussions of the heart according to Nancy here.

109. Ibid., 246.

110. Ibid., 246–47.

111. Nancy would say, "during the time of love, *I* is *constituted as broken*" ibid., 247).

112. Ibid., 236.

113. Ibid., 227.

114. Ibid., 249.

115. See ibid., 249–50.

116. Ibid., 242.

117. Ibid., 250.

118. I will just cite two examples here. Firstly, there will be the moment when Derrida speaks of the necessary faith in indecision or indetermination, or a "break with calculable reliability and with the assurance of certainty" in thinking about friendship, and Derrida will say, "the truth of friendship, if there is one, is found there, in darkness ["l'obscurité" as the French original goes]" (*PA*, 34/ *PF*, 16). Secondly, the imperative to refrain from any outward gesture to compel the friend to enter into a proximity with the self essentially "produces an event, sinking into the darkness [here, the French original says "pénombre," which could mean half-light or penumbra] of a friendship which is not yet" (*PA*, 63/ *PF*, 43).

119. "Entretien avec Robert Maggiori."

120. I note that Irigaray's "L'Amour entre nous" was included in Cadava, Connor, and Nancy, eds., *Who Comes After the Subject?* It subsequently appears as the introduction to her *J'aime à toi*.

121. Irigaray, *Sharing the World*, 20.

122. Ibid., 32.

123. Ibid., 20.

124. Ibid., 10.

125. Irigaray, *Way of Love*, 77.

126. Irigaray, *Sharing the World*, 43.

127. Irigaray, *Entre orient et occident*, 26, my translation.

128. Cf. "F as in Fidelity," in *L'Abécédaire de Gilles Deleuze*. Available at www.langlab.wayne.edu/CStivale/D-G/ABC1.html

129. Deleuze and Guattari, *Qu'est-ce que la philosophie?*, 9.

130. Deleuze, *Marcel Proust et les signes*, 25, my translation.

131. Deleuze and Guattari, *Qu'est-ce que la philosophie?*, 76.

132. "One morning he started thinking about a problem and stood there considering it, and when he didn't make progress with it he didn't give up but kept standing there examining it. When it got to midday, people noticed him and said to each other in amazement that Socrates had been standing there thinking about something since dawn. In the end, when it was evening, some of the Ionians, after they'd had dinner, brought their bedding outside (it was summer then), partly to sleep in the cool, and partly to keep an eye on Socrates to see if he would go on standing there through the night too. He stood there till it was

dawn and the sun came up; then he greeted the sun with a prayer and went away" (*Symposium*, 60).

133. Deleuze and Guattari, *Qu'est-ce que la philosophie?*, 33. I note here once again, as I did in the introduction, that Derrida draws a similar conclusion: "Even where there are dialogues, in Plato [. . .] these dialogues remain in the service of the monologic thesis" (Unpublished correspondence with Hélène Cixous, quoted in Cixous, "Co-Responding Voix You," 50).

134. Deleuze and Guattari, *Qu'est-ce que la philosophie?*, 32

135. Ibid., 33.

136. Ibid., 32.

137. Ibid., 104.

138. Ibid., 9.

139. Ibid. I note that Hugh Tomlinson and Graham Burchell translate *Objectité* as "Objectality" (see their translation of *What Is Philosophy?*, 3).

140. Deleuze and Guattari, *Qu'est-ce que la philosophie?*, 12. I have consulted Hugh Tomlinson and Graham Burchell's translation of the passage in *What Is Philosophy?*, 6.

141. Deleuze, *Marcel Proust et les signes*, 85.

142. Ibid., 25–26.

143. Ibid., 87, 85. In translating the line on p. 87 of the French text, I have consulted Richard Howards's translation in *Proust and Signs*, 163.

144. I note here that the critique of friendship in *Marcel Proust et les signes* has a corresponding critique of "philosophy." But this "philosophy" is Proust's idea of philosophy, which has no resonance with Deleuze and Guattari's notion of concept-creation. In Proust's view of the history of philosophy, according to Deleuze's reading, philosophy arrives by way of a genial love, which is an error for philosophy: "It is wrong of philosophy to presuppose within us a willingness [*une bonne volonté*] to think, or a desire or natural love for the true. In that case, philosophy arrives only at abstract truths that do not compromise anyone or shake things up [*bouleversent*]. [. . .] They remain gratuitous because they are born of intelligence, which only confers upon them only a possibility, and not an encounter or a violence that would guarantee their authenticity" (*Marcel Proust et les signes*, 13). Philosophy as such, benevolent in its trajectory, traces only a possibility among many; it lacks a force that would interest others as a contemporaneous critical necessity. In this case, "the truths of philosophy are lacking in necessity and the stamp [*griffe*] of necessity" (85). The truth that philosophy seeks never arrives congenially in fact. It arrives by way of a violent betrayal function, through a sign emitted by something or someone other than oneself: "There is always the violence of a sign that forces us to seek [the truth], that deprives [*ôte*] us of peace. The truth is not found by affinity, nor by good will [*une bonne volonté*], but is betrayed [. . .]" (13).

145. Deleuze and Guattari, *Qu'est-ce que la philosophie?*, 33.

146. Ibid., 26. Here, I follow Hugh Tomlinson and Graham Burchell's translation in *What Is Philosophy?*, 20, 21.

147. Deleuze and Guattari, *Qu'est-ce que la philosophie?*, 76.

148. "In any concept there are usually bits or components that come from other concepts [...]. This is inevitable because each concept carries out a new cutting-out, takes on new contours, and must be reactivated or recut" (Deleuze and Guattari, *Qu'est-ce que la philosophie?*, 23. Here, I follow Hugh Tomlinson and Graham Burchell's translation in *What Is Philosophy?*, 18).

149. Deleuze and Guattari, *Qu'est-ce que la philosophie?*, 24.

150. Ibid., 8.

151. Ibid., 11.

152. Ibid.

153. Ibid., 10.

154. Ibid., 9.

155. Ibid., 69.

156. Ibid., 52.

157. Ibid., 8.

158. Deleuze, "Statements and Profiles," 87.

159. Ibid.

160. Ibid.

161. Ibid.

162. Ibid., 90.

163. Ibid., 87.

164. Ibid.

165. Ibid.

166. Ibid.

167. Ibid., 88.

168. Ibid.

169. Ibid.

170. Ibid.

171. Ibid.

172. See translator's note in Deleuze, "Statements and Profiles," 93.

173. Ibid., 88.

174. Ibid.

175. Ibid., 88, 89, my emphasis.

176. Ibid., 89.

177. Ibid.

178. Ibid., 87.

179. See Bennington, "Forever Friends," 112.

180. Deleuze, *Marcel Proust et les signes*, 27. Deleuze's preference for love in relation to thought would find its echo in Nancy's "L'Amour en éclats," where Nancy would even go further to equate love to thought, so long as both are always open to, or welcome, that which is other than the present object of love or thought. In that regard, Nancy also considers love to be without end. As will be seen in a later note, Deleuze has a different take on the ends of love.

181. Ibid. 5.

182. Ibid.

183. Ibid., 5–6.

184. Ibid., 6.

185. Ibid.

186. Ibid., 7. I follow Richard Howard's translation of *destin* as "fate" here (see *Proust and Signs*, 9).

187. In a more apocalyptic tone, Deleuze's reading of Proust will also reveal that love only seeks its own end. Unlike Bennington's popular reading of love (in "Forever Friends") as the endeavor of lovers to construct a shared world that is eternal, Deleuze follows Proust to negate this sentiment. As Deleuze notes, the protestation for such eternal love is "not essential": it is "neither necessary nor desirable" (*Marcel Proust et les signes*, 27). Furthermore, "love unceasingly prepares its own disappearance, acting out its rupture" (15). In other words, there is neither forever love nor "forever friends" (to use Bennington's titular phrase) in *Marcel Proust et les signes*.

188. Deleuze, *Spinoza*, 175.

189. See Blanchot, *L'Entretien infini*.

190. I leave aside the problematic of invoking the name "Auschwitz," since that lies beyond the scope of both this section and this present work as a whole. For the understanding of that problematic, see especially LaCapra, *History and Memory;* and LaCapra, *Representing the Holocaust*.

191. Deleuze and Guattari, *Qu'est-ce que la philosophie?*, 69.

192. I am indebted to Jonathan Culler for the phrase that gestures toward the impossibility of friendship after Auschwitz.

193. Deleuze and Guattari, *Qu'est-ce que la philosophie?*, 102. I have consulted Tomlinson and Burchell's translation of this passage in *What Is Philosophy?*, 107.

194. The notion of fatigue in friendship is found especially in Blanchot's *L'Entretien infini*, which Blanchot draws from Antelme's *L'Espèce humaine*, as evident in the section "The Indestructible"; and distress in friendship is taken from Mascolo's *Autour d'un effort de mémoire*.

195. Deleuze and Guattari, *Qu'est-ce que la philosophie?*, 10.

196. Mascolo, *Autour d'un effort de mémoire*, 52, 51, 55. Antelme's notion of "original indetermination" is found in his letter to Mascolo, which is reproduced in *Autour d'un effort de mémoire*, 15, my translation.

197. Letter to Mascolo, dated August 6, 1988, reprinted in *Deux régimes de fous*, 307, my translation.

198. Deleuze and Guattari, *Qu'est-ce que la philosophie?*, 10.

199. Letter to Deleuze, dated September 28, 1988, reprinted in *Deux régimes de fous*, 309. Trans. modified.

200. Mascolo, *Autour d'un effort de mémoire*, 69.

201. I certainly am mindful that one can also read the *reject* in Primo Levi's writings, especially in the figure of the *Musulman*, not to mention that Deleuze and Guattari make references to Levi too, and I thank Daniel Heller-Roazen for reminding me of that. I confess, however, to a lack of expertise in the works of Levi, and the least I can do here is to refer to Agamben's analysis of the *Musulman* in *The Remanants of Auschwitz*.

202. Améry, *At the Mind's Limits*, 68. I am grateful to Dominick LaCapra for bringing to my attention the writings of Améry.

203. On *ressentiment* as a reactive force, see Deleuze's reading of Nietzsche in *Nietzsche et la philosophie*.

204. Nietzsche, *On the Genealogy of Morality*, 20 §10.

205. Ibid., 21 §10.

206. Ibid., 29 §15.

207. Deleuze, *Nietzsche et la philosophie*, 136, my translation. I acknowledge that Deleuze's association of *ressentiment* with something "feminine" here, which clearly deviates from his greater tendency to attribute positive implications to "feminine power" such as his notion of "becoming-woman," demands critique. Unfortunately, this is not the space to do so.

208. Ibid., 134.

209. Nietzsche, *On the Genealogy of Morality*, 56 §16.

210. Ibid., 57 §16.

211. See Deleuze, *Nietzsche et la philosophie*, 151.

212. Améry, *At the Mind's Limits*, 69.

213. Ibid.

214. Ibid., 79.

215. Levi, "Deportees. Anniversary," in *The Black Hole of Auschwitz*, 44.

216. Améry, *At the Mind's Limits*, 69, 77.

217. Ibid., 78.

218. Agamben, *Remnants of Auschwitz*, 104.

219. Caygill, "Shared World," 19.

220. Perhaps one should keep in mind here the Derridean logic of keeping things unforgivable and/or unforgettable. If something is (easily) forgivable or forgettable, there is no real need for forgiving or forgetting in the first place.

221. Améry, *At the Mind's Limits*, 72, 70. It is perhaps as such that Améry argues that "a forgiving and forgetting induced by social pressure is immoral. Whoever

lazily and cheaply forgives, subjugates himself to the social and biological time-sense, which is also called the 'natural' one. Natural consciousness of time actually is rooted in the physiological process of wound-healing and became part of the social concept of reality. But precisely for this reason it is not only extramoral, but also *anti*moral in character. Man has the right and the privilege to declare himself to be in disagreement with every natural occurrence, including the biological healing that time brings about" (72). Time is not on the side of *l'homme du ressentiment* after Auschwitz either. According to Améry, "All recognizable signs suggest that natural time will reject [*refüsieren*] the moral demands of our resentment and finally extinguish them" (79).

222. Sebald, "Against the Irreversible," in *On the Natural History of Destruction*, 158, 156. I agree with Sebald that Améry "believes as little in the possibility of revenge as in the idea of atonement" (157–58), but, as I have shown, that does not mean that Améry is completely free from all thoughts of revenge in his writings.

223. One might rightly think of Agamben's "messianic community" of remnants of "non-non-Jews" (a mode of being that Améry seems to occupy before and during the reign of Nazi rule) in *The Time that Remains* here.

224. I am also suggesting here that assuming the figure of the *reject* here would help in the letting-be of *l'homme du ressentiment*. Of course, it is not the active *reject* that must be projected here. Instead, it is the *auto-reject* that must be in place: the *auto-reject* that would not only be sensitive to the difficulties of *l'homme du ressentiment* in reconciling with society, but also allow *l'homme du ressentiment* to do so in his or her ways and in his or her time, rather than recommending what is supposedly best for him or her. On this note, I am disturbed by Blanchot's suggestion of a "Me-Subject" [*Moi-Sujet*] for the recuperation of the Nazi concentration camp victim. Blanchot would clarify that this "Me-Subject" is not a "dominating and oppressive power raised against others [*autrui*]" ("L'Indestructible," in *L'Entretien infini*, 197). Instead, it would be an "intermediary" and "exterior" *subject*, "representing a collective structure," through which the victim, as "the dispossessed," "is [. . .] welcomed as 'other' [*autrui*]" (197). I find this recourse to the *subject* problematic, given that Blanchot seeks its dissolution or "deconstruction" in his philosophy of writing (and which he makes clear in the opening note to *L'Entretien infini*, vii).

225. Nietzsche, *On the Genealogy of Morality*, 59 §18.

226. Ibid., 58, 59 §17.

227. Ibid., 66 §24.

228. Améry, *At the Mind's Limits*, 81.

229. Ibid.

230. I follow Susan Neiman here in her article, "Jean Améry Takes His Life," in refraining from making the banal deduction that Améry's writings led to his suicide in 1978.

231. Deleuze and Guattari, *Qu'est-ce que la philosophie?*, 103. To state the implication of Blanchotian fatigue here, I recall the dialogue between the two friends that opens Blanchot's *L'Entretien infini*. Fatigue between friends there proves to be more than an extinguishing element for friendship. Instead, it is that which motivates each friend to live on, to continue talking to the other, only because fatigue has rendered each one a stranger to the other.

232. One may compare this point to Judith Butler's take on posttraumatic communities in her afterword to the collection of essays *Loss: The Politics of Mourning*. There, she argues that something can survive, or to put it in a Derridean way, sur-vive, experiences of loss. Community is not impossible after the trauma or catastrophe such as the AIDS pandemic, the context upon which the book is set. In her words, "Loss becomes condition and necessity for a certain sense of community, where community does not overcome the loss, where community *cannot* overcome the loss without losing the very sense of itself as community" ("After Loss, What Then?", 468). Butler repeats this gesture with respect to 9/11, when she writes that "it was my sense in the fall of 2001 that the United States," "in response to the conditions of heightened vulnerability," "was missing an opportunity to redefine itself as part of a global community" (*Precarious Life*, xii). I am, however, somewhat skeptical of thinking or articulating community, if not a future community, in light of highly mediatized catastrophes. One recalls the expression coming from France in the wake of 9/11: the expression "we are Americans," in solidarity with America's mourning of the loss of lives during the attacks and the trauma of suffering such attacks. But what of the appeals to the so-called "international community" for military, medical, alimentary, and reconstruction aid in areas of the world that have not been picked up by the media? Furthermore, must the thought of (future) community arise only from trauma, mediatized or not?

233. Deleuze, *Marcel Proust et les signes*, 25.

234. I am certainly with O'Sullivan here in understanding the notion of encounter in Deleuze, an encounter that is essentially already secant. According to O'Sullivan: "The encounter [. . .] produces a cut, a crack. However this is not the end of the story, for the rupturing encounter also contains a moment of affirmation, the affirmation of a new world, in fact a way of seeing and thinking this world differently. This is the creative moment of the encounter that obliges us to think otherwise" (*Art Encounters Deleuze and Guattari*, 1).

235. Blanchot, *L'Entretien infini*, xiii.

236. Dickens, *Our Mutual Friend*, 439.

237. Deleuze, "L'Immanence," 361.

238. Deleuze and Guattari, *Qu'est-ce que la philosophie?*, 105.

239. Ibid., 69.

240. Ibid., 28. I follow Tomlinson and Burchell's translation here in *What Is Philosophy?*, 23.

241. Deleuze and Guattari, *Qu'est-ce que la philosophie?*, 28.

242. See ibid., 38.

243. Ibid., 191.

244. Ibid., 104.

245. Deleuze, *Proust et les signes*, 135, my translation. This is the second edition of Deleuze's work on Proust, which includes the chapter "Antilogos ou la machine littéraire."

246. Deleuze, "L'Immanence," 361–62.

247. Deleuze and Guattari, *Qu'est-ce que la philosophie?*, 192.

248. Ibid., 206.

249. Deleuze and Guattari, *Mille plateaux*, 278. I follow Brian Massumi's translation in *A Thousand Plateaus*, 228. Translations of passages from *Mille plateaux* here try to be as close to the original French text, while Massumi's translation is consulted at the same time. Subsequent references to this work of Deleuze and Guattari will be marked, in parentheses, by *MP* for the French version followed by page numbers, and also by *TP* for Massumi's translation followed by page numbers.

250. Bauman, *Community*, 11–12.

251. "We will certainly not say that discipline is proper to the war machine: discipline becomes the required characteristic of armies when the State appropriates them, but the war machine answers to other rules of which we are certainly not saying are better, but which animate a fundamental indiscipline of the warrior, a questioning of hierarchy, perpetual blackmail by abandonment and by *betrayal*, and a very volatile sense of honor, and which, once again, go against [*contrarie*] the formation of the State" (*MP*, 443/ *TP*, 358, my emphasis). Deleuze will return to this question of the betrayal in the set of interviews with Claire Parnet in *Dialogues*. Deleuze, on speaking of nomads "who have neither past nor future" will also reaffirm that in the trajectory of nomadic movement, "there is always betrayal in a line of flight" (*Dialogues*, 49, 52). Betrayal here is "not to trick in the manner of an orderly man who charts out [*ménage*] his future, but to betray in the fashion of a simple man who no longer has any past or future" (52).

252. Deleuze, *Dialogues*, 52.

253. Bauman, *Community*, 2.

254. Ibid.

255. Ibid., 15.

256. Bauman reminds us that a homogeneous community may be a mirror image of the consolidation of the State via the project of nationalistic nation-building that it implements; Deleuze and Guattari will also say that "the modern State defines itself in principle as 'the rational and reasonable organization of a community'" (*MP*, 465/ *TP*, 375).

257. See Derrida's discussion on "practical hospitality" in *De l'hospitalité*.

258. I note here too that for Deleuze and Guattari, the mass is not insistently or necessarily a numerous assemblage; it may be a "'mass' individual" (*MP*, 263/ *TP*, 215). In any case, it is inherently "neither attributable to individuals nor overcodable by collective signifiers" (*MP*, 267–68/ *TP*, 219). Individual or a multitude, the multiplicity of smooth space, or the smooth space of the mass, is already traversed by a sense of community.

3. THE REJECT AND THE "POSTSECULAR," OR WHO'S AFRAID OF RELIGION

1. In that case, this chapter leaves aside philosophers who remain explicitly and faithfully religious such as Emmanuel Lévinas and Jean-Luc Marion. With regard to the latter, Adam Miller has noted that critics "[have] often charged [Marion] with trying to sneak God back into philosophy through a phenomenological backdoor" (*Badiou, Marion and St Paul*, 17).

2. See Caputo, *Prayers and Tears of Jacques Derrida*, xviii.

3. On the complexity of atheism in French thought, especially its transition from humanist atheism, that is, the turn to the human after the nineteenth-century proclamation of the death of God, to one that is antihumanist from the 1930s to 1950s, see the nuanced study of Stephanos Geroulanos in *An Atheism that Is Not Humanist Emerges in French Thought*. With regard to more contemporary French thought, that is, post-1968 French thought, Christopher Watkin will argue that atheism is a "term too blunt an instrument with which to make sense of the diversity of current approaches to thinking in the wake of the death of God" (*Difficult Atheism*, 16).

As to "radical atheism," I am clearly referring to Martin Hägglund's book of the same title (see his *Radical Atheism*). Hägglund barely treats the complexity of the term "atheism." He is more concerned with opposing readings of a "religious turn" in Derrida. He argues, by reiterating Derrida's thesis of a structural iterability that gives every mortal mark (being, trace, writing, signature, voice, and so on) its quasi-immortal dimension precisely by its repeatability beyond its own time and space, that that thesis implies a secular gesture emptied of any religiosity. However, Hägglund cannot explain the religious references that nonetheless remain in Derrida's works. I will make note of Hägglund's work again in a later discussion of Derrida.

On another note, I am aware of the quarrel between Caputo and Hägglund, a quarrel that is not in the interest of this present work. However, let me say that Hägglund is not wrong in pointing out Caputo's misreading of Derrida in *The Prayers and Tears of Jacques Derrida* when Caputo posits peace as the horizon, if not telos, of Derrida's thought. Caputo there has clearly missed out the opening to the risk of "radical evil" in Derrida's "messianicity without messianism," something that I will discuss later in this chapter. Caputo, in a later piece in *After the Death of God*, seems to have revised his position, no longer insisting on peace as the endpoint of Derrida's deconstruction of religion, but shifting to the notion of the event in the Derridean sense, that is to say, something incalculable and unforeseeable, hence allowing the possibility of "radical evil." Hägglund does not take into account this later position of Caputo. Besides, Hägglund, in attempting to make a clear demarcation between the divine and atheism, commits no less a misreading of deconstruction itself. Deconstruction does not make arguments with conclusions of a binary sort (for example that Derrida is an atheist and not a religious thinker). Instead, it will demonstrate how each term, in a supposed binary opposition, is always already found in the other's domain and affecting that domain. For a more precise critique of Hägglund falling short of deconstruction, see Laclau's "Is Radical Atheism a Good Name for Deconstruction?"

4. Derrida, "Penser ce qui vient," 21, my translation.

5. Derrida, "Comment ne pas parler," 536, my translation.

6. See especially Nancy, *L'Adoration*, 48, my translation.

7. Nancy, *La Déclosion*, 29, my translation.

8. Nancy, *L'Adoration*, 43.

9. Ibid., 44, 45.

10. Ibid., 45.

11. I suspect that Christopher Watkin misreads this phrase of Nancy. Watkin reads it as Nancy deconstructing Christianity, and "in deconstructing Christianity Nancy imitates Christianity [. . .]" (*Difficult Atheism*, 39). However, Nancy has clarified elsewhere that this is hardly the case. The "auto" in "auto-deconstruction," according to Nancy, "should not be confused with autocritique or autogeneration. In effect, it does come from the 'self,' but it's Christianity that self-deconstructs. This movement, however, neither preserves nor retains more or less secretly the identity of this 'self'" ("Commerce of Plural Thinking," 229).

12. With regard to the notion of openness, Nancy will point once again to Christianity's "assurance of another life opened in the very [present] life" [*assurance de l'autre vie ouverte dans la vie même*] (*L'Adoration*, 40) as a derivative source.

13. Nancy, *La Déclosion*, 32.

14. Ibid., 205, 9.

15. Nancy, *L'Adoration*, 35.

16. Ibid., 42, 43.

17. Ibid., 58.

18. Nancy, *La Déclosion*, 54.

19. Nancy, *L'Adoration*, 58.

20. Nancy, *La Déclosion*, 32.

21. Ibid.

22. Ibid., 41

23. Ibid., 226, 43.

24. If Nancy is indeed suggesting an "auto-deconstruction" of thought or reason, he comes close to Derrida's claim in *Voyous* that reason reasons with itself. The proximity between Nancy and Derrida here can be further affirmed in Nancy's reading of the Kantian notion of "the critique of pure reason." According to Nancy, what the latter points to is that "a critique of reason, that is to say an exigent and non-complacent examination of reason by itself, renders unconditionally necessary, in reason itself, an opening and a leaping-outside [*ex-hauusement*] of reason. It is not a question of 'religion' here, but one well of 'faith' as reason's sign of fidelity to that which *from itself* exceeds the phantasm of completely explicating [*rendre raison*] oneself as much as the world and man" (Nancy, *La Déclosion*, 44–45).

25. Or, in Nancy's words: "Deconstructing itself, [Christianism] uncloses [*déclôt*] our thinking: where Enlightenment's reason, followed by the world of complete progress [*progrès intégral*], judged necessary to close itself off from every dimension of the 'outside' [for example, nonlogical or nonscientific spiritual, religious faith], it is necessary to break the closure in order to understand that the push, the drive [*la pulsion*] for a relation, at this very point here, with the infinite outside comes from reason itself. Deconstructing Christianity means: opening reason to its very reason, even to its unreason [*déraison*]" (*L'Adoration*, 39). See note above for reason reasoning with itself.

26. Taylor, *Secular Age*, 19.

27. Ibid., 21. In his brief debate with Jürgen Habermas in *The Power of Religion in the Public Sphere*, Taylor would also critique Habermas's argument for religious discourse to divest itself of all religious rhetoric before it can make any real intervention or have real impact in social issues. According to Taylor, there is an underlying targeting or discrimination of religion in that argument (see the dialogue between Taylor and Habermas in *The Power of Religion in the Public Sphere*, 60–69).

28. Taylor, "Why We Need a Radical Redefinition of Secularism," in *The Power of Religion*, 40.

29. Ibid., 35.

30. See especially Casanova, *Public Religions in the Modern World*; de Vries, *Religion and Violence*, and *Political Theologies*; Habermas, "Notes on Post-Secular Society," Habermas, *Awareness of What Is Missing*, and Habermas, *Between Naturalism and Religion*; and Abeysekara, *Politics of Postsecular Religion*.

31. As will be evident, the "postsecular" is not that distant from Taylor's "secularity." The difference between them, as I would argue, is the emphasis on violence by the former. In any case, if Taylor finds the term "postsecular" adding little to his study, it is because, according to him, we continue to live amid the secularity in which spiritual belief and unbelief intersect with each other. In other words,

we are *not* beyond that secularity, not beyond belief and unbelief, and hence have no need for the term "postsecular." For Nancy, the term would also be redundant because the contemporary world, as he argues, is but the opening up of the world beyond the horizons of a divine principle or of an all-powerful and singular God, an "absentheism" in other words as noted above earlier. Hence, Nancy will say that "there is no post-Christianism nor whatsoever 'revival' [*renouveau*]," "not even 'atheism'" (*L'Adoration*, 48).

32. *Difficult Atheism*, 117.

33. Ratti, *Postsecular Imagination*, xxv.

34. Ibid., xxi.

35. Ibid., 23, 21.

36. Taylor, *Secular Age*, 13.

37. Ratti, *Postsecular Imagination*, 21.

38. I am highlighting the "(post)structuralist" aspect of contemporary French thought here in view of my disagreement with Alain Badiou in this section. Badiou is no doubt a primary figure in contemporary French thought today, but he distances himself from all "(post)structuralist" leanings.

39. See especially de Vries, "Two Sources of the 'Theological Machine,'" 366–89.

40. Nancy, *L'Adoration*, 43.

41. Ibid.

42. Ibid.

43. Badiou, *Théorie du sujet*, 28, my translation.

44. Badiou, *Second manifeste pour la philosophie*,132, my translation.

45. Ibid., 131.

46. Ibid., 131–32.

47. Peter Hallward has also written, "Badiou [. . .] salvage[s] [. . .] the subject from deconstruction [. . .]" (*Badiou*, xxviii–xxix).

48. See especially *St. Paul Among the Philosophers*. See also the special issue of *South Atlantic Quarterly* on "Global Christianity, Global Critique" (109[4] [fall 2009]) on the influence or impact of Badiou's *Saint Paul* on contemporary debates on contemporary religion in the world.

49. Badiou, *Saint Paul*, 1.

50. Badiou, *Second manifeste pour la philosophie*, 149n4.

51. Bruno Bosteels has discerned that besides the four conditions of science, politics, art, and love that Badiou predicates as the sites through which the event will arise, there is also "the eternal shadow condition of religion" (*Badiou and Politics*, 104). And "the essence of the Badiouian event," in the eyes of Frédéric Neyrat, is "marked by a theological excess" (*Aux bords du vide*, 4), an excess that Neyrat will later consider a "strange religious supplement" (23, my translation). According to Amy Hollywood, there is a "turn to theology" in Badiou especially in *Saint Paul*, which "is an attempt to use theology as a political tool" ("St Paul and

the New Man," 869). Less critical of the religious trace is Adam Miller, who interprets the Badiouian event as grace, which Miller defines as "an immanent novelty that is actually infinite" (*Badiou, Marion and St Paul*, 16). On a different trajectory, Christopher Watkin has tried to argue that Badiou approaches the "posttheological," that is to say, "a new atheism" that "re-think[s] philosophy without God or the gods and without parasitising any assumptions dependent on them," and which "refus[es] ascetically to renounce the notions associated with such gods—namely, truth and justice" (*Difficult Atheism*, 12, 13).

52. As Watkin has noted, this fidelity, in Rancière's eyes, is ineluctably tied to the Christ event, which makes the political thought of Badiou to rest on a basis of Christianity (see *Difficult Atheism*, 192–93). Gregg Lambert, for his part, reads Badiou's fidelity in terms of conviction, specifically a "post-secular form of 'conviction,' which is not religious in principle" ("Unprecedented Return of Saint Paul in Contemporary Philosophy," 4).

53. One finds a more in-depth analysis or interpretation of faith as opening in Nancy. In *Noli me tangere* (2003), Nancy makes the distinction between faith and belief. The latter has a definitive object in mind (and belief as such is perhaps more in line with Badiou's fidelity), while faith is, to wit, somewhat blind. It is open to anyone, to anything. In other words, faith is a pure opening to others. In the later *L'Adoration* (2010), Nancy argues that the verb "to adore" [*adorer*] bears the trace of such a faith, given that "to adore," especially in the more archaic French, which is always *adorer à*, suggests a movement toward someone or something (a suggestion granted by the preposition *à*), and hence is always open to whoever, whatever. This archaic French would also say *aimer à*, which Irigaray deploys in her *J'aime à toi*. According to Irigaray, by saying *j'aime à toi*, rather than *je t'aime*, "I reserve a relation of indirection with respect to you [*je garde à toi un rapport d'indirection*]. I neither subjugate [*soumets*] you nor consume you. I respect you as irreducible" (*J'aime à toi*, 171, my translation). She goes to say that "the 'to' [*à*] is the guarantee of the indirection. The 'to' prevents the relation of transitivity without the irreducibility of the other"; "the 'to' is the sign of non-immediacy, of the mediation between us" (ibid., 171). And further on: "The 'to' is the place [*lieu*] of non-reduction of the person to an object" (ibid., 172).

54. Johnston, *Badiou, Žižek, and Political Transformations*, xviii.

55. Pluth, *Badiou: A Philosophy of the New*, 141.

56. Ibid., 141.

57. See Badiou, *Saint Paul*, 118. Here, I follow, with slight modifications, Ray Brassier's translation (*Saint Paul: The Foundation of Universalism*, 110).

58. See Badiou, *Saint Paul*, 105, 118.

59. Ibid., 107.

60. Ibid., 106.

61. Ibid. It is in *L'Éthique*, written in 1993, where Badiou's critique of any philosophy of difference(s) is more forceful, if not less tolerant. Badiou might be correct in saying that today's claims to "multiculturalism" or "the right to differences" are superficial, as they accept only "good" differences, that is to say, differences that are passive and integrate themselves into the perspective or ideology of the dominant group or majority. Pluth has also observed in Badiou that "behind calls to respect others, respect life, and respect difference, Badiou finds a basically de-humanizing tendency. [. . .] Significant here is Badiou's claim that this seemingly very humanistic ethics is actually a *practical anti-humanism*" (*Badiou: A Philosophy of the New*, 139). "Practical antihumanism" occurs when radical differences, or differences that apparently pose an affront to others, are repressed. Certainly, there are superficial claims to "multiculturalism" or to "the right to differences." However, that does not mean that there are no endeavors to affirm, accept, or let be the other who is not only different, but also disagrees with, or is incommensurable to oneself. The recent "postsecular" texts of Habermas, and also Derrida's *Foi et savoir*, are at least works that testify to that endeavor. Unconvinced by Badiou's claim and opposed to Badiou's critique of differences in both *L'Éthique* and *Saint Paul*, Hollywood marks her intellectual distance from Badiou based "on the critical difference that difference (religious, ethnic, and, most pointedly perhaps sexual) continues to make" ("St Paul and the New Man," 871) significant changes in one's relations with others. Neyrat, for his part, has noted that Badiou's indifference to differences especially in *Saint Paul* risks "troubling political consequences" (*Aux bords du vide*, 21). A critique of Badiou's criticism of a philosophy of ethics can also be found in Lambert's "Unprecedented Return to Saint Paul in Contemporary Philosophy."

62. Badiou, *Saint Paul*, 106.

63. Badiou, *Théorie du sujet*, 294.

64. "D'un sujet enfin sans objet," in *Cahiers confrontation* 20 (winter 1989), 13–22, trans. as "On a Finally Objectless Subject," in Cadava, Connor, and Nancy, eds., *Who Comes After the Subject?*, 25. As noted in the Introduction, I am using the translated version of this text since the French original is not that readily available.

65. I certainly keep in mind that Badiou gradually kept "truth" separate from "event." In an interview with Peter Hallward and Bruno Bosteels, Badiou will resist any "confusion between event and truth," a confusion that "reduces the considerable difficulties involved [in truth] in maintaining fidelity to an event to a matter of pure insurrection [in event]" ("Beyond Formalization," in Bosteels, *Badiou and Politics*, 323). In an earlier interview with Bosteels, Badiou also states that "truth, for me, is not the name of the event, even though that is how it is often interpreted. Truth is what unfolds as a system of consequences, secured by an unheard-of figure of the subject as consequence of the rupture of the event" ("Can Change Be Thought?" in Bosteels, *Badiou and Politics*, 307). In Bosteels's reading, "An event is

a sudden commencement, but only a recommencement produces the truth of this event" (*Badiou and Politics*, 173).

66. See Badiou, *Théorie du sujet*, 301–2.

67. Bosteels, "Beyond Formalization" in *Badiou and Politics*, 348.

68. According to Miller, "one never 'experiences' the event *per se*" (*Badiou, Marion and St Paul*, 134).

69. Badiou, *Saint Paul*, 96.

70. Badiou, *L'Être et l'événement*, 23, my translation.

71. "On a Finally Objectless Subject," in Cadava, Connor, and Nancy, eds., *Who Comes After the Subject?*, 31.

72. The quarrel between Althusser and Badiou has been well analyzed by Bruno Bosteels in his *Badiou and Politics*. In Bosteels's words, it is the delimiting conceptualization of the *subject* by Althusser as a subject of ideological interpellation that precludes any recognition of the appearance of the new in the world: "Because the efficacy of overdetermination in producing situations for a subject is now perceived to be profoundly ideological, Althusser's philosophy can no longer register any true historical event, not even in principle let alone in actual fact [. . .]. Conversely, we can surmise what will be needed to think through the possibility of a situation's becoming historicized by virtue of an event, namely, a theory of the subject that is no longer reduced to a strictly ideological function but accounts for the specificity of various subjective figures and different types of truth procedure. This is exactly the double task that Badiou ascribes to a formal theory of the subject in all his later philosophy" (*Badiou and Politics*, 65).

73. Badiou, *Saint Paul*, 15, 63.

74. Ibid., 63.

75. Ibid., 5, my emphasis.

76. "On a Finally Objectless Subject," in Cadava, Connor, and Nancy, eds., *Who Comes After the Subject?*, 30.

77. Badiou, *L'Être et l'événement*, 433.

78. "On a Finally Objectless Subject," in Cadava, Connor, and Nancy, eds., *Who Comes After the Subject?*, 30.

79. Badiou's rendering of the *subject* as a fragment sets up another counterpoint to Descartes's endeavor to construct a *subject* that is of a holistic constitution. As Badiou says in *L'Être et l'événement*, "We are [. . .] contemporaries of a *second epoch* of the doctrine of the Subject, which is no longer the centered, reflexive, founding subject," "not as support or origin, but as *fragment* of the process of a truth" (9, 22).

80. The "remnant" is of course Agamben's reading of Paul, a reading that, as Agamben declares, seeks "to restore Paul's Letters to the status of the fundamental messianic text for the Western tradition" (*The Time that Remains*, 1). According to Agamben, what is properly messianic, or what is proper to the "messianic

vocation" or calling [*klēsis*] is "the revocation of every vocation" (23). That is to say that the messianic calling calls for the rejection (or even auto-rejection) of the current state of affairs: "an urgency that works [the current vocation or 'factical condition'] from within and hollows it out, nullifying it in the very gesture of maintaining and dwelling in it" (24). The messianic "remnant" is therefore the "as not" (23) that remains, in relation to all existing vocations, after the revocation of the latter. As "as not," it will also always remain an "excess" (56) to every totalizing teleology: it is "neither the all, nor a part of the all but the impossibility for the part and the all to coincide with themselves or with each other" (55). It is through the messianic remnant's aspect of "as not," of that which never adds up, that Agamben disagrees with Badiou's reading of Paul as a thought of the universal. Beyond the Jews or the Greeks, there remains the "non non-Jews," who are "something like a remnant between every people and itself, between every identity and itself. At this point one can measure the distance that separates the Pauline operation from modern universalism—when something like the humanity of man, for example, is taken as the principle that abolishes all difference or as the ultimate difference, beyond which further division is impossible" (52). That "modern universalism," as Agamben does not fail to point out, is the universalism of Paul according to Badiou, one that traverses, or is indifferent to, all differences. Arguing against Badiou, Agamben says, "For Paul, it is not a matter of 'tolerating' or getting past differences in order to pinpoint a sameness or a universal lurking beyond. The universal is not a transcendent principle through which differences may be perceived—such a perspective of transcendence is not available to Paul. Rather, this 'transcendental' involves an operation that divides the divisions of law themselves and renders them inoperative, without ever reaching any final ground. No universal man, no Christian can be found in the depths of the Jew or the Greek, neither as a principle nor as an end; all that is left is a remnant and the impossibility of the Jew or the Greek to coincide with himself" (52–53). It is also through the fact that the messianic remnant does not add up that Agamben locates the "political legacy" of Paul with regard to the question of democracy and "a people": "It allows for a new perspective that dislodges our anticipated notions of a people and a democracy, however impossible it may be to completely renounce them. The people is neither the all nor the part, neither the majority nor the minority. Instead, it is that which can never coincide with itself, as all or as part, that which infinitely remains or resists in each division, and, with all due respect to those who govern us, never allows us to be reduced to a majority or a minority" (57).

81. On this point, see Badiou, *Logiques des mondes*, 75.

82. Ibid., 75, my translation.

83. Miller, *Badiou, Marion and St Paul*, 144.

84. Badiou, *Logiques des mondes*, 12, 13. In Peter Hallward's words: "Both truth and subject are occasional, exceptional" (*Badiou: A Subject to Truth*, xxv).

85. See "On a Finally Objectless Subject," in Cadava, Connor, and Nancy, eds., *Who Comes After the Subject?*, 27; and Badiou, *L'Être et l'événement*, 429.

86. As Miller has observed, "One must *decide* in favor of an event's occurrence because [. . .] an event's implications must be actively pursued, tested and extended in order for the event to have existed. Initially, an event 'is' only *for those who have decided* its existence" (*Badiou, Marion and St Paul*, 135, my emphasis).

87. Miller also argues that fidelity, as Badiou treats it, "like the state, has an institutional quality" (*Badiou, Marion and St Paul*, 140).

88. Badiou, *Saint Paul*, 45.

89. Ibid., 82.

90. Ibid., 6.

91. Ibid., 94, translation modified.

92. Ibid., 60.

93. I would argue that Badiou's rhetoric, in speaking of the Pauline Subject's rupture with worldly laws, in the sense of exposing "the law of the truth of the law" as nothing but a rupturing rather than an institutionalization of what has always existed, is not distant from Derrida's elucidation of the "auto-deconstruction" of laws as fiction, or predicated on mystical rather than substantive foundations, in "Préjugé—devant la loi" and *Force de loi*. See also Bosteels (*Badiou and Politics*, 95–100) for a comparison between Badiou and Derrida on this question of law. And while one may speak of a "deconstruction" of the law in Badiou's Pauline Subject, one finds something more excessive in Agamben's reading of Paul in relation to the law. For Agamben, "The messianic is not the destruction but the deactivation of the law, rendering the law inexecutable" (*Time that Remains*, 98). However, under the messianic logic of the revocation of all "juridical-factical" (26) condition, this would only open the way for another justice, if not a "messianic *plērōma* [overflowing] of the law" (108), which is neither appropriable by the whole nor reducible to parts of the whole. According to Agamben, "Justice without law is not the negation of the law, but the realization and fulfillment, the *plērōma*, of the law" (107).

94. I believe this is also Peter Hallward's suspicion in his "Sujet et volonté dans la philosophie d'Alain Badiou," in *Autour d'Alain Badiou*, 303–31.

95. Badiou, *Logiques des mondes*, 20.

96. Badiou, *Saint Paul*, 95, 105.

97. Ibid., 15.

98. Ibid., 81.

99. Badiou, *Théorie du sujet*, 158.

100. Ibid., 280.

101. See "Beyond Formalization," in Bosteels, *Badiou and Politics*, 346.

102. Pluth, *Badiou: A Philosophy of the New*, 7.

103. I have translated *le sujet obscur* as "obscurant subject" instead of "obscurantist subject" because the sense of "obscurantist" is somewhat too close to the

reactionary force that goes against the Enlightenment movement. As I highlight in the following note, Badiou's *sujet obscur* goes beyond such a context, as it manifests itself in fascist and/or Nazi regimes, which are distant from any movement against Enlightenment thought. I have also rejected the translation of "dark subject" ("dark" being the common translation of *obscur*). Translating *le sujet obscur* as such gives the term nothing but a mysterious aura. It also lacks the sense of preventing inquiry or of obscuring new knowledge, which Badiou attributes to *le sujet obscur*, and which is borne by the word "obscurant."

104. For Badiou's discussion of the obscurant *subject* as the fascist or Nazi *subject*, see *Second manifeste pour la philosophie*, 109–12.

105. Pluth elicits a higher degree of violence in Badiou's philosophy of the *subject*. Picking up on the notion of terror in Badiou's *Logiques des mondes*, Pluth identifies "a terroristic component" in this soldiering on by the faithful *subject*, or to put it in Badiou's rhetoric, in "pushing the 'decisive discontinuity' between the truth procedure and its world, such that the subject in question is fully 'achieved' and the truth procedure brought to completion quickly" (*Badiou: A Philosophy of the New*, 152). For Pluth, this implies that "any significant social movement," following Badiou's philosophy of the *subject*, "is going to have its hard edge" (152). Pluth certainly qualifies his observations by saying that such terror "is not necessarily a will-to-death" (152), but that does not eradicate the possibility of a violent, nihilistic trajectory or end in the *subject*'s fidelity to the event.

106. Badiou, *Logiques des mondes*, 75.

107. Ibid., 75.

108. Ibid., 78. Or as Pluth puts it: "The subject is not a thinking being, it is not identical to consciousness—it is not even identical to an individual or a group of individuals. Yet it does depend on the existence of human individuals in an important fashion" (*Badiou: A Philosophy of the New*, 120).

109. *Logiques des mondes*, 55. At work here, as I would read it, is another sacrificial logic regarding the corporeal body underlying Badiou's philosophy of the *subject*. The subordination of the corporeal body to the event and truth procedures to elucidate the event is also hinted at by Johnston: "A Badiouian body [. . .] is an 'agent' operating within a world *on behalf* of an eventual truth" (*Badiou, Žižek, and Political Transformations*, 64, my emphasis). Johnston will also underscore that "the body" in Badiou's philosophy has "no necessary relation to the common meaning of this word," but "Badiou might allow that the physical bodies of people, *insofar as they give themselves over to appropriation* by more-than-physical event-subject-truth sequences, can be transubstantiated from bodies as *mere organic entities* to bodies as material bearers of trans-world truths made immanent to worlds" (65, my emphases).

110. Badiou, *Logiques des mondes*, 57. One could say that there is a somewhat "posthuman" inclination in Badiou's move here. As he writes slightly further in

Logiques des mondes, and I quote here at length, "a procedure of truth has nothing to do with the limits of the human species, our 'consciousness,' our 'finitude,' our 'faculties' [. . .]. If one thinks of such a procedure according to solely formal determinations—as one thinks of the laws of the world according to mathematical formalism, one finds [. . .] [that] it is never necessary to pass through the 'real-life' human [*le "vécu" humain*]. In fact, a truth is that by which 'we,' humankind, are engaged in a trans-specific procedure, a procedure that opens us to the possibility of being Immortals, so that a truth is certainly an experience of the inhuman [*l'inhumain*]" (*Logiques des mondes*, 78–80). In a different vein, Neyrat has observed that "the Badiouian subject [. . .] is more and more like a humanist, if not over-humanist [*surhumaniste*], subject" (*Aux bords du vide*, 4). The humanist charge against Badiou certainly goes against Badiou's aversion toward all humanist modes of thinking. Pluth, in contrast to Neyrat, presents a more measured perspective with regard to the question of humanism in Badiou. He elicits the "presence of a philosophical and theoretical anti-humanism in Badiou's work" (*Badiou: A Philosophy of the New*, 104). This "theoretical anti-humanism," however, allows Badiou "to lead to, and to support, what is in effect his practical humanism" (105), that is to say, Badiou's faith in the human "as a practical possibility, as a possible way of living" (12), a way, to be more specific, yet unthought of.

111. Badiou, *Second manifeste pour la philosophie*, 144.

112. Johnston, *Badiou, Žižek, and Political Transformations*, 15.

113. Or as Pluth puts it: "Subjects may well be immortal, then, insofar as they are linked to the creation of eternal truths: sadly, we individuals who work on them remain mortal" (*Badiou: A Philosophy of the New*, 179).

114. According to Pluth's analysis of the *subject* deciding on its militant fidelity to the event and to the "truth procedures" to elucidate the latter, he says, "here we find Badiou using language according to which the subject is, precisely, deciding and forcing" (*Badiou: A Philosophy of the New*, 125).

115. Amy Hollywood also puts in question the veracity of the new in Badiou's Pauline Subject: "I see in [. . .] Badiou [. . .] the formation of a new (how new really?) counter-fantasy to global capitalism's endlessly desiring, consuming, and producing subject—that of a potent, active, implicitly male subject generated through an encounter with an unprecedented, absolutely singular Event" ("St Paul and the New Man," 870). In place of a not-so-new "new masculine subject" (870), Hollywood argues for "some new configuration of subjectivity in nonphallic, perhaps even, dare I say it, multiply sexed/ gendered or nonsexed/ gendered terms" (875).

116. Badiou, *Théorie du sujet*, 28.

117. Ibid., 107. On another note, that Paul is initially somewhat a *reject*, or *horlieu* in Badiou's rhetoric, to Jesus's other "original" apostles (that is, apostles who have been personally taught by Jesus), is not missed by Badiou. For Badiou,

Paul's anticipation that he will not be readily accepted by the other apostles probably motivated his sojourn in Arabia first rather than going to Jerusalem directly after his "subjectivation" by the Christ-event. See also Badiou, *Saint Paul*, 19–20, for Badiou's reading of the irreducible setting-apart of Paul from the rest of the apostles.

118. See chapter 5, "La Division du Sujet" of *Saint Paul* for Badiou's elaboration on the split between spirit and flesh in the *subject*.

119. Badiou, *Saint Paul*, 60. I note too that in the passage concerning both the real as "trash" and the corporeal body as embodying a "subjectivity of trash," Badiou also quotes from 1 Cor. 4:13: "We have become like the rubbish of the world, the dregs of all things, to this very day." Badiou, of course, seeks to lift the human condition out of this state of trash, if not the state of being a *reject*, through his theory of the *subject*. I further note that this verse from Corinthians is also taken up by Agamben in his reading of Paul. Once again, Agamben's reading takes on a different trajectory from Badiou's. As Agamben reads it, there is no lifting of oneself out of the state of trash, the state of being lost, abandoned, and forgotten. There is no movement from being a *reject* to becoming-*subject* here. In fact, Agamben even suggests that there is no more *subject* once the messianic calling is made, and especially when a response to that call is in place: "The messianic vocation dislocates and, above all, nullifies the entire subject" (*Time that Remains*, 41). The "as not" of the *reject* or trash here "has nothing to do with an ideal" (41). Paradoxically, according to Agamben, it is by remaining as *rejects*, as trash, as the lost or forgotten, that one's existence as such may be remembered: "The exigency of the lost does not entail being remembered and commemorated; rather, it entails remaining in us and with us as forgotten, and in this way and only in this way, remaining unforgettable" (40). I note here too that Simon Critchley has also read the verse from Corinthian as Paul's address to "a bunch of rejects" (*Faith of the Faithless*, 158).

120. Neyrat, *Aux bords du vide*, 29.

121. See note 53.

122. Neyrat, *Aux bords du vide*, 28.

123. Pluth has noted that Badiou, as he "persist[s] in using the term subject" (*Badiou: A Philosophy of the New*, 105), potentially runs the risk of developing a theory of a humanist subject, something that Badiou rejects. On that note, Pluth poses the question that I posed above, albeit in a different vein and with a different response in sight: "If Badiou is after a philosophy that contests the classical humanist subject's privilege, and if it is the case that the subject for him is not something or someone who knows the truth, or perhaps anything in particular, then why is one of Badiou's primary objectives nevertheless the development of a theory of the subject? Why not drop the topic altogether [. . .]?" (105).

124. Derrida, *Foi et savoir*, §29: 45/ §23: 33. Translations from this text are mine. Future references to this text will be indicated, in parentheses, by section number

followed by page number. I also note that Michael Nass has published an important text, *Miracle and Machine*, based on Derrida's *Foi et savoir*. Nass's text appeared at the time when the manuscript of this present text has just been completed, and I regret not being able to discuss his text here.

125. Habermas, "Awareness of What Is Missing," in his *Awareness of What Is Missing*, 19.

126. That something is missing also in the contemporary world of secularity as Taylor understands it is evident when Taylor writes, not so much in a negative or even frustrated sense as Habermas does, that this secularity "is a condition in which our experience of and search for fullness occurs; and this is something we all share, believers and unbelievers alike" (*Secular Age*, 19).

127. To return to Nancy a little here, what is shared in common between faith and reason, for Nancy, is the drive for the infinite. As Nancy argues, "All religion, to be sure, is traversed by a motion, a leap [*élan*]" under "the sign of the infinite [*l'infini*], itself infinite, spurred from itself [*s'envoie de lui-même*]." And not just all religion, but also, as Nancy goes on to say, "all types of knowledge [*savoir*], science or philosophy: for we will not even be in the movement of whatever knowledge [*connaissance*] if the desire for infinity [*le désir de l'infini*] did not [first] push us there" (*L'Adoration*, 61).

128. See Derrida, *Foi et savoir*, §29: 46.

129. Ibid., §37: 67n23.

130. Derrida, "Autoimmunity," 95.

131. See also *Foi et savoir*, §46: 87, where Derrida states that "religious reaction" is constituted by "rejection and assimilation, introjections and incorporation, indemnity and mourning [...]."

132. In the earlier section on Badiou, I have noted his critique in his *L'Éthique* of such superficial "right to difference" or claims to "multiculturalism."

133. Cf. Derrida, *Foi et savoir*, §34: 56: "The history of the word "religion" had to prohibit, in principle, all non-Christians to name "religion" [...]."

134. In Derrida's seminars collected as *La Bête et le souverain*, he argues that the supposed sovereign claim to speak for oneself, in one's own voice and in one's own name, in a language he or she determines to be the only authoritative means to address or respond to oneself, does not really establish the sovereign status of the human proper or what is proper to human. Instead, there is something *bête* about it, not just something stubborn or even stupid, but also something beastly or bestial. Following Deleuze, he would say that what follows from such sovereign claims would usually be tyranny and cruelty. This animal side of things, as will be seen later in this study, will have bearings for the relevance of Derrida's *Foi et savoir* to a "postsecular" future.

135. Call this "radical atheism" if you will, as Martin Hägglund has done, defining "radical atheism" as an "unconditional affirmation of survival," and arguing

that "the so-called desire for immortality [in conventional atheism] dissimulates a desire for survival that precedes it and contradicts from within" (*Radical Atheism*, 2, 1). Given such definition of "radical atheism," I do not think, however, that the definition exists outside of religion or the religious—as Hägglund apparently suggests, since he bases his argument about "radical atheism" on refuting any "religious 'turn' in Derrida's thinking" (1). In other words, his argument operates alongside religion or the religious, even if it is in order to negate it. In that sense, I ask if there can be atheism that is absolutely evacuated of the religious. In the opening of this chapter, I addressed Nancy's argument that any so-called atheism is but an extension of the "auto-deconstruction" of religion. I would think that Derrida would also agree that one cannot clearly define what is atheistic and what is religious. There is no clear frontier between the two, and each finds aspects of oneself in the other and vice versa. What is one to make of "radical atheism" then? Does one "save" Derrida from any "religious turn" by adding the adjective "radical" to "atheism"? Does the adjective really allow a reading of Derrida to go beyond religion or the religious? I doubt it (and so does Derrida, as noted earlier, who has said that any atheism on his part nonetheless involves a certain remembrance of God), since, as Hägglund's work itself makes evident too, there is no avoiding the irreducible religious references or traces of religious thinking in Derrida, which is not to deny Derrida's endeavor to prevent them from being regulating or determining horizons for a future thought of religion.

136. It loses too its claim to any spiritual organicity or organic spirituality, in contradistinction to all inorganic and mechanical aspects of the world of hard, technical sciences, as it proceeds almost automatically and mechanically with its autoimmune trajectory, according to Derrida (see *Foi et savoir*, especially §37 through §40).

137. See Derrida, *La Voix et le phénomène*, 92.

138. Derrida, "Autoimmunity," 108.

139. According to Derrida, too, it will be an "error" to think that one knows what religion "is" or to know much about religion (see *Foi et savoir*, §33: 53 and §35: 61).

140. See Derrida's *Donner la mort*, 92–93, for his take, following Kierkegaard's reading, on this particular chapter of Luke. In Derrida's reading, hating or rejecting one's loved ones is but the strongest proof of love. Or, as Derrida puts it, under the rubric of sacrifice—especially Abraham's sacrifice of Isaac—in obeisance to God: "If I put to death [*donne la mort*] what I hate, this is not a sacrifice. I must sacrifice what I love. I must come to hate what I love, in the very moment, at the instance of putting it to death [*donner la mort*]. I must hate and betray my own, that is to say, put them to death through sacrifice [*leur donner la mort dans le sacrifice*], not because I hate them—that would be too easy, but because I love them. I must hate them as I love them. Hate would not be hate—this would be too easy,

if it hates the hateful. It is necessary for hate to hate and betray the most loved. Hate can only be hate as the sacrifice of love to love [*La haine ne peut être la haine, ce ne peut être que le sacrifice de l'amour à l'amour*]. What one does not love, one has nothing to hate it for, to betray it in perjury, to put it to death [*à lui donner la mort*]" (*Donner la mort*, 92–93).

141. On the "weak force," that is, one without the militant, police, or legal force of the sovereign State and juridical institutions, but is nonetheless critical for providing a glimpse, or opening up all possibilities, to a future world of peace and justice according to all in their respective heterogeneity, see the concluding part of Derrida's interview with the BRussells Tribunal, "Pour une justice à venir," the foreword to *Voyous*, and more generally *Force de loi*.

142. I have italicized "just" in order to underscore a form of justice that is immanent and without delay, that is to say, the justice rendered to anyone or anything by the fact of its existence, regardless if it expresses itself or not through a rationalized *logos*. In other words, justice here is not dependent on the anthropocentric and anthropologic linguistic performativity that governs all present jurisprudence, and which only delays and sometimes denies justice to some, especially those who do not share or have access to that linguistic performativity. I say more of this *just* in the following chapter on politics.

143. That aspect of the event as coming from the future distinguishes the event according to Derrida from that of Badiou's, which, as mentioned in the previous section, bears aspects of the past or the present, aspects whose existences were previously refused but are now, as an event, undeniable.

144. In *Spectres de Marx*, Derrida will say further that this messianic figure will not "pre-determine, pre-figure, [and] pre-name" what or who arrives (266). On the impossibility of knowing or even speculating who or that which is to come, that is to say the rejection of all forms of knowledge granted to the messianic figure regarding the latter, see also Derrida's *Voyous*, 123.

145. One could perhaps say that this opening to "radical evil" in Derrida's event makes it more radical than Badiou's, which generally refuses to think the event, if it is an event, as evil. This refusal has been noted and critiqued by Mehdi Belhaj Kacem in his *Après Badiou*.

146. See *Foi et savoir*, §21: 30.

147. I refer to *Spectres de Marx* again, where Derrida explicates that the emphasis on the adjectival "messianic" is meant to "designate a structure of experience rather than a religion" (266). In an earlier passage there, Derrida would also link the "messianic" to "a certain emancipating affirmation [. . .], a certain experience of the promise that one can try to free it from all dogmatic and even all metaphysico-religious determination, from all *messianism*" (146–48).

148. At this point, I note that *khôra*, once again, finds its affinity with the messianic figure without messianicity, since, as Derrida says in the earlier *Khôra* text,

it takes on a contour of an abyssal "gaping opening" (*Khôra*, 45), which means that it willingly risks the arrival of something like "radical evil."

149. *Non-lieu*, as Derrida puts it in *Khôra*.

150. Derrida, *Khôra*, 57.

151. See ibid., 55–58. Michael Naas, not forgetting that *khôra* is a feminine maternal or nursing figure, has also noted that for Derrida in *Foi et savoir*, "*Khôra* is precisely that which or she who, while opening up the space for all phantasm, for the phenomena of the phantasm, constantly eludes and interrupts the phantasm of phenomena, including every anthropomorphic or theological phantasm" ("Comme si, comme ça," in *Derrida From Now On*, 202). Naas's study of *Foi et savoir* has also picked out the feminine figures of Gradiva and Persephone. In many ways, feminine figures are no doubt figures of the *reject*. As Derrida himself will note at the presentation of his text at Capri, not only are Muslim interveners absent, but female philosophers or intellectuals are also seemingly excluded from the discussion on religion. In Naas's reading, Gradiva and Persephone come to symbolize the rejection of any acknowledgment of the *real* lives of females by male figures, especially those who claim to a phantasmatic sovereign power over others, anxious at the same time to eradicate the *imaginary* threat posed by others, especially the symbolic threat of castration posed by feminine figures, an anxiety that precipitates too often into senseless violence against women.

152. Derrida, *Donner la mort*, 172.

153. See especially ibid., 165: "The secret of the secret [. . .] does not consist in hiding *something*, in revealing the truth, but to respect the absolute singularity, the infinite separation of what links me or exposes me to the unique, to the one as to the other, to *the One as to the Other*."

154. Ibid., 164.

155. On subjectivity that is given by God, or in assuming it through God, when one partakes in a secret pact with God, see ibid., 147. See also p. 126, on the difference of this subjectivity with "the (Kantian) autonomy of what I see myself do in complete freedom [*toute liberté*] and of a law that I give myself."

156. Ibid., 106.

157. Ibid.

158. Ibid., 105.

159. Ibid., 111.

160. On the sacrificial economy in response and responsibility, see especially ibid., 95–99.

161. See Josef Schmidt S.J., "Dialogue in Which There Can Only Be Winners," in Habermas, *Awareness of What Is Missing*, 60, 59.

162. The exclusion of animals in Habermas's communitarian theory for the "postsecular" persists even when he adds the "translation proviso," whereby religious communities, free to use religious language in the public sphere, nonetheless

"have to accept that the potential truth contents of religious utterances must be translated into generally accessible language before they can find their way into the agenda of parliaments, courts, or administrative bodies and influence their decisions" ("The Political," in *Power of Religion*, 25–26). I have already noted that Charles Taylor has critiqued this proviso, but the question of animals is equally absent in Taylor.

163. Can one say that Derrida here, in the anthropocentric ethical duty to mention non-Christian and female interlocutors, has sacrificed all consideration of animals in relation to the thinking of religion? I note however, that Derrida does bring up the issue of the treatment of animals in industrial farming and scientific experiment, and the related issue of vegetarianism (see *Foi et savoir*, §40: 78).

164. I note here that Derrida makes the explicit relation between *khôra* and animals only in a discussion with architects around the topic of "anyplace." It appears at the beginning of his intervention, titled "Faxitecture," where he reflects on the transhumance of translation and quotation, stating that it is a "*setting in motion* to transfer, deport, and export from one place to another" and "consists in migrating, changing land or terrain, going from one land to another, [. . .]—used primarily for a migrating animal population, more precisely, a herd accompanied or led by a shepherd" ("Faxitexture," 20). The proximity between transhumance and *khôra* becomes clear later when he speaks of the latter as a space that is "nothing other than the possibility, chance, or threat of replacement" (24). In the spacing between one place and another that is at stake in transhumance and/ or *khôra*, Derrida will also say that there lies "a certain relationship [. . .] to animality," since the movement or "organizing of man's habitat" is "regulated by the change of seasons, [. . .] [by] the life of nature, breeding, that is to say, the life and death of animals" (20). For Derrida, the question of animality in the between space of *khôra* and/ or transhumance is occasion to think what can be done for a hospitality to animals (20).

165. Derrida would also say, "If there is a question of religion, it must no longer be a 'question-of-religion.' Nor simply a response to this question" (*Foi et savoir*, §35: 61).

166. Derrida, *L'Animal*, 27.

167. I note here that this is also the case with Badiou's theory of the *subject*. As Badiou has remarked in several places, the *subject*, in his or her response to the event, by declaring its truth and by working out the conditions that maintain the existence of the event, not only lifts the *subject* from all normal human existence, but also marks his or her difference from animals. Animals are clearly subordinated in Badiou's philosophy. Or, as Neyrat has observed, "Badiouian morality is conditioned by a *principle of anthropological humanist distinction*, which passes [*transite*] without mediation to the great relegation of everything that is not human to the level of the sacrificeable" (*Aux bords du vide*, 33).

168. Derrida, *L'Animal*, 84.

169. Derrida, *Donner la mort*, 116.

170. Ibid., 98. This is also where everything turns around the phrase *tout autre est tout autre* as Derrida puts it, where every other is totally other, that is to say, the absolute singularity of each must not be privileged over that of the next. For the discussion of *tout autre est tout autre* in *Foi et savoir*, see §32: 52–53. This is not the space for a critique of the concept of the *tout autre*. For that, see especially Dominick LaCapra's critiques of Agamben and Derrida (in both *History and Its Limits* and *History in Transit*). LaCapra argues that the danger of the *tout autre* lies in leaving the other at such an extreme (unreachable) distance, and in a form that approaches the sublime to the point of emptiness, such that it becomes easy to either forget about the other or to negate or eliminate it as if without consequences. While I do maintain that a certain distance is necessary between one and the other, the ethics of which I have tried to elucidate in the previous chapter on friendship, love, and community, I would say, in light of LaCapra's precaution of the *tout autre*, that the *reject* is not an entity in some untouchable out-there existing as an empty category. I try to reduce any suggestion of the latter in the *reject* in the "posthuman" chapter, when I consider it in terms of *clinamen*, which is the communication of corporeal molecules between everything in the world, and which underscores the irreducible concrete contact between one being and another.

171. Derrida, *L'Animal*, 180.

172. Ibid.

173. Ibid., 181. I note here that this radical space will not only be one that is of a quasi-divine or quasi-religious trace, but also something of an animal-space. One can certainly recall *khôra* here as animal-space, which I have treated in the above note 164. But once again, Derrida does not develop this in either *Foi et savoir* or *L'Animal que donc je suis*.

174. See Cixous, "Conversation avec l'âne," in *L'Amour du loup*, which I will discuss below. But I will just note here first that a nonanthropocentric and nonanthropomorphic "messiniancity without messianism" plays out in that text, which is also the case of Cixous's *Messie*, where Cixous inscribes the messianic figure, which is always free to come and go, in a female cat [*la chatte*].

175. See especially the chapter "Reopening the Question of the Human and the Animal" in LaCapra's *History and Its Limits*.

176. Derrida, *L'Animal*, 82.

177. Ibid.

178. See the concluding chapter "The World Over" in Nass, *Derrida From Now On*, 229. According to the date of the original version of this chapter, Derrida's remark would have been made in spring of 2004. I note here that Derrida's elision of any discussion of the sacrificial ram in the Abraham story in *Donner la mort* is a point of critique for LaCapra in the chapter "Reopening the Question of the Human and the Animal" in his *History and Its Limits*. Derrida certainly does not

discuss that ram in *Donner la mort*, but the issue of animal sacrifice is nonetheless raised in that text (see *Donner la mort*, 99).

179. Caputo, *Prayers and Tears of Jacques Derrida*, xviii.

180. Pyper, "'Job the Dog,'" 83.

181. Renshaw, "Thealogy of Hélène Cixous," 173. See also Renshaw's *Subject of Love*.

182. Berkowitz, "Paradise Reconsidered," 176. In fact, Cixous would say in her own words, "I have never written without God," but "God is not that of religions" ("Conversation avec l'âne," 101, my translations). I will discuss this phrase much later in the main text.

183. Berkowitz, "Paradise Reconsidered," 177.

184. For example, in the almost blasphemous "The Whale of Jonas" (in *Le Prénom de Dieu*), there is not only the (feminine) disdain and doubt of the power and existence of a hidden god, but also the narrator's quest to place himself in the position of the "me" [*moi*] of the hidden god.

185. Cohen-Safir, "La Serpente et l'or," 361, my translation.

186. Ibid., 361.

187. Sellers, *Hélène Cixous*, 3.

188. Ibid.

189. See Sellars's *Hélène Cixous* and Renshaw's *Subject of Love*. I note, however, that with *Neutre*, one can already elicit in Cixous a deconstruction of the *subject*.

190. Cixous, "Birds, Women and Writing," 170.

191. Conley, *Hélène Cixous*, 130.

192. Beyond the texts of the 1990s, it will undoubtedly be interesting to pursue the inquiry into the extent of the turn toward being within religion in Cixous's more recent texts, which bear titles with religious overtones, such as *Ève s'évade*. These texts evidently lie outside the scope of this study (which is concerned with Cixous's works published in the 1990s), however, and therefore I will have to defer this inquiry to another occasion.

193. Cixous, "Without End, No, State of Drawingness, No, Rather," 29.

194. Ratti, *Postsecular Imagination*, xxv.

195. Derrida, "La Structure, le signe et le jeu," in *L'Écriture*, 412, 421–22, my translation.

196. Cixous, "Conversation avec l'âne," 95, 104. This translation and subsequent ones from this text are mine unless indicated. Subsequent citations from this text will also be indicated by page numbers from the French text in parentheses.

197. Such a move is surely in contradistinction to Christopher Watkin's quest for the "posttheological," which he takes it to be "a turn to religion in order to turn the page of religion" (*Difficult Atheism*, 13).

198. Cixous, "This Stranjew Body," in *Judeities*, 70.

199. As Derrida has noted in *L'Animal que donc je suis*, the "peculiarity of animals [...] is to be naked without knowing it," and the animal "does not feel itself nor see itself nude [*ni se sent ni se voit nu*]" (19, 20).

200. Cf. Gen 3: 6–9: "So when the woman saw that the tree was good for food, and that it was a delight to the eyes, and that the tree was to be desired to make one wise, she took its fruit and ate; and she also gave some to her husband, who was with her, and he ate. Then the eyes of both were opened, and they knew that they were naked [...]. They heard the sound of the Lord God walking in the garden at the time of the evening breeze, and the man and his wife hid themselves from the presence of the Lord God among the trees of the garden."

201. Cixous, "De la scène de l'Inconscient à la scène de l'Histoire," 22, my translation.

202. In *Messie*, Cixous will speak of the dog Uzi, which will guide, alongside the angel Raphael, Tobias to Media. However, as Cixous points out, "having made its appearance at the beginning of chapter six, one sees that the narrative will no longer give it attention" (*Messie*, 12. Translations from this text are mine). And in "Conversation avec l'âne," Cixous will speak of Abraham's donkey, without which, Cixous argues, Abraham's journey up to Mount Moriah in order to carry out God's commandment to sacrifice his son Isaac would have been "infernal." However, as Cixous chides, "The Bible does not recount the conversation Abraham had with the donkey" ("Conversation avec l'âne," 87).

203. Cixous, "Bathsheba or the Interior Bible," 14.

204. If, as I am arguing, an *other* Bible in Cixous's terms can be attained only via the movement from the rejection of human sight to an animal point of view, this movement is singularly found or completed in "Conversation" and not in "Savoir," *Messie*, or *Beethoven à jamais*, and hence my focus on "Conversation" here.

205. Cf. "Conversation": "a gift of the world [...] which is given to me" (83).

206. Cixous, "Savoir," 16. This translation and subsequent ones from this text are mine.

207. I follow Eric Prenowitz here to translate *entendre* as hearing.

208. Cixous, "Savoir," 18.

209. Ibid.

210. Ibid.

211. Ibid., 19, 17, 18. My reading of "Savoir" above certainly runs counter to Frédéric Regard's. Regard not only argues that "Savoir" is an unequivocal celebration of vision, but that as such, it also inscribes something like what Cohen-Safir calls a "counter-Bible," "another story or history [*histoire*], another genesis" in explicit opposition to the apocalyptic narrative of sight in Genesis 3 ("Faite d'yeux," 216, my translation). Evidently, I disagree with Regard's reading.

212. Cf. Cixous, "Conversation," 81.

213. Cixous, "Savoir," 14.

214. Besides an *other* Bible that is in the process of being inscribed here, perhaps what emerges in this traversing toward "the very interior of the body of words" is also what Cixous calls an "interior Bible." Cixous has regarded the "interior Bible" as a world where one disappears to by turning away from looking (as in the process of night-writing in "Conversation"). But this turning away from looking is put in place only in order to be attentive to living, and because of that, the "interior Bible" is a world of "immense limitless life" ("Bathsheba or the Interior Bible," 18).

215. Cixous, "Savoir," 18.

216. I refer to "Bathsheba or the Interior Bible" again to note that landscape is not something Cixous favors. Of her notion of "interior Bible," she will say, "it is a land *without landscape* [my emphasis], without monuments. But not without form and without inhabitants" ("Bathsheba or the Interior Bible," 5). As to what these "inhabitants" would be in this "interior Bible," I will soon argue that they are something other than human subjects.

217. Ian Blyth and Susan Sellers have noted that Cixous's early theoretical trajectory "stresses the need for writing to 'let go'" in order for the text to have "a sense of ease, assurance and open-handedness" (*Hélène Cixous*, 113, 114). As I will soon point out in the main text, I agree with Blyth and Sellers that letting-go is "to make room for the other" (ibid., 113). But I am suggesting here too that letting-go in the inscription of the *other* Bible or "interior Bible" would mean an indifference to Man's fallen state, an indifference to the anxious need to defend, justify, and even glorify Eve's eating from the Tree of Knowledge.

218. The question of forgetting or not holding on in "Conversation" provides an interesting counterpoint to "De la scène de l'Inconscient à la scène de l'Histoire." In the latter, there is the project similar to "Conversation" of writing a Paradise of the passage of living instants: "Paradise is this, it is to arrive at living the present. It is to accept the present that occurs [*advient*], in its mystery, in its fragility. It is to know that the present passes, and to accept not mastering it" ("De la scène de l'Inconscient à la scène de l'Histoire," 22, my translation). And yet, it will be said there too that writing essentially is an "anti-forgetfulness" [*anti-oubli*] (ibid.).

219. Cf. "Conversation," 81. Perhaps the term *animot* is more recognizable in Derrida's *L'Animal que donc je suis* (2006). The first time the term appears in Derrida's writing is in the summer of 1997—the same year when Cixous's "Conversation" was published—when Derrida presented his paper of the same title as the abovementioned book at the Cerisy-la-Salle colloquium on "Animal Autobiography." The published collection of papers from that colloquium does not feature any contribution from Cixous, and there is no certainty that she was present at Derrida's talk. On the term *animot*, Derrida does not make reference to Cixous, and neither does Cixous in "Conversation" make reference to Derrida. Based on the above information, it is difficult to attribute the first usage of *animot* to either Derrida or Cixous. In a 2000 colloquium, "Judeities: Questions for Jacques

Derrida," Cixous's contribution, "Ce orps étranjuif," interestingly would point to a knowledge of "L'Animal que donc je suis," when she writes of a scene of conversation with a cat, a clear reference to the opening of Derrida's text of 1997, where he speaks of the displacing situation where he sees himself being seen naked by his (naked) cat. This of course still does not resolve the problem of to whom the first use of *animot* can be attributed. In any case, Derrida's *animot* bears a very different sense from Cixous's. For Derrida in *L'Animal que donc je suis, animot* is deployed to counteract the phrase "the animal," which tends to reduce the multiplicity of animals into the singular. As Derrida will say, "There is no *the Animal* in the general singular, separated from Man by a sole indivisible limit" (*L'Animal*, 73). *Animot*, which is homophonous to *animaux* (the French word for animals in the plural), must then be allowed to resound, not only to (re)affirm "the plurality of animals in the singular" (ibid.), but also to undo the false anthropologic and anthropocentric opposition between humans and animals. In fact, as Derrida will continue to say, "the plurality [of the 'living' (*des 'vivants'*)] does not let itself be gathered into the sole figure of animality simply opposed to humanity" (ibid., 73). *Animot*, for Derrida, is "neither a species, nor a genre, nor an individual: it is an irreducible living multiplicity of mortals [*une irréductible multiplicité vivante de mortels*]" (ibid., 65).

220. *Le Grand Robert de la langue française* (2d ed., Paris: Parmentier, 1986) records that *passeur* can mean "a person who illegally crosses a frontier or a prohibited zone in order to get to someone or something."

221. I note that the passage here leads toward an animal condition as much as the animal condition, as discussed earlier, will later in (re)turn facilitate the movement toward the passage.

222. With reference to an earlier work of Cixous, this "paradisiacal nudity" can be said to be a post-Fall *jouissance.* In that earlier piece, Cixous speaks of a "second innocence," which is "the force of simplicity or of nudity," and which is also "that which no longer knows, that which knows not to know" ("Le Dernier tableau ou le portrait de Dieu," in *Entre l'écriture*, 182, my translation). I will discuss "second innocence" in the text proper soon. I will also argue that this "second innocence" is attained in "Conversation," when writing makes the passage toward the animal, and which takes nakedness simply, that is to say, without the human knowledge of shame. It is through the passage to the animal that one arrives at the condition of no longer knowing the human knowledge of shame, and of knowing better to renounce such human knowledge.

223. Cf. Cixous, "Conversation," 96.

224. Cf. ibid., 84.

225. See especially Cixous, "Grace and Innocence," in *Readings.* On the question of innocence, it would also be interesting to look at Cixous's *With ou l'art de l'innocence.* However, since innocence is not a primary focus here, and the

main concern is Cixous's works of the 1990s, I will leave aside any discussion of this text.

226. Cixous, "Grace and Innocence," 31.

227. Ibid., 68.

228. Ibid., 70.

229. Ibid., 67.

230. Ibid.

231. Ibid., 37.

232. Cixous, "Writing the Law: Blanchot, Joyce, Kafka, and Lispector," in *Readings*, 23.

233. See Cixous, "Grace and Innocence," 35–37.

234. Ibid., 57.

235. I note that Derrida also uses the phrase "passion of the animal" in *L'Animal*, which he uses to describe the "naked passivity" (*L'Animal*, 29) of an unclothed human standing before the gaze of the animal. As it will be explicated in the text proper, I am certainly *not* using "the passion of the animal" in this sense here.

236. Derrida, *Demeure*, 26, 28, my translation.

237. This is where grace is also at work in the *jouissance* of the passage to the animal condition in "Conversation." In contrast to "Grace and Innocence," grace here is not something to be worked for by the human alone. Instead, it is shared between humans and animals. This is another reason why I think *jouissance* in "Conversation" is beyond the "second innocence" Cixous talks about in "Grace and Innocence."

238. The negative association between God and the power of seeing is also evident in Cixous's *Beethoven à jamais* (following translations from this text are mine). Right at the beginning of that text, the narrator compares the respective points of view of mortals and of God on living. Mortals "live in the midst [*au milieu*] of life," while God looks at life from the sides. In terms of the mortal's point of view of life, "life appears to us without end and hence it is that" (*Beethoven à jamais*, 11). However, from God's point of view, a point of view akin to being "perched very high up on an ancient tree of the earth" (11), life is not only chaotic strife but deathly too. And this will lead the narrator to say it is "better to never arrive at the side" where God sees. But if it happens that one does arrive at such an apparently vantage point, it is "better to not look, better to close one's eyes" (11). To have had access to such a point of view, the text suggests that it would be better, to borrow a phrase that occurs just slightly later in the text, to blind oneself by having an "arrow in the eye" (15). Like "Conversation" then, the act of seeing, particularly the divine power of seeing, is renounced here. This motif of the arrow is worth taking up a little further here, since it turns up in "Conversation" too. In "Conversation," the passage toward writing the "interior body of words" will bear the image of the trajectory of an arrow, a sacred arrow, a "pfeilige" [a word which

combines the German word for arrow, *Pfeil*, and the German word for the sacred, *heilig*] (96), "an arrow [. . .] [that] is going to plant itself at the heart of internity [*l'internité*]" (94). To relate to what I have been trying to argue in the section on "Conversation," I would say that this "pfeilige" is shot through with the trajectory that first blinds human vision, which then traverses toward an animal vision whose perspective bears no traces of the "ancient tree" of knowledge, toward an animal that has its eyes closed to human knowledge and therefore is blind to a life that mourns the human *death by knowledge.*

239. See, for example, Derrida, *Spectres de Marx*, 148.

240. Ibid., 146.

241. Ibid., 266, 147.

242. Ibid., 266.

243. Ibid., 264, 148. The link between the messianic and religion will not be denied too when Derrida further writes that the "quasi atheistic dryness [*sécheresse*] of the messianic can be taken to be the condition of religions of the Book," or that one can "always recognize [in the messianic] the dry ground on which the living figures of every messiah, be they announced, recognized, or always expected, have emerged and passed" (267).

244. *Foi et savoir*, §21: 31, §38: 72.

245. Cf. Derrida, *Foi et savoir*, §21: 30. In *Foi et savoir*, Derrida would also say that the messianic is what makes such a future possible: "No to-come [*à-venir*] without [. . .] some messianic promise" (§38: 72).

246. *Foi et savoir*, §21: 30.

4. PROLEGOMENON TO REJECT POLITICS: FROM *VOYOUS* TO BECOMING-ANIMAL

1. Hardt and Negri, *Commonwealth*, 180.

2. Ibid., 181. As I have suggested in a note in the chapter on friendship, love, and community, I find such community-creation, driven by an "external cause" (181) such as Empire, or driven by a "common" deprivation of wealth and resources, too conditional. It is as if the thought of community is only a consequence of Empire (the global dissemination of which has left behind what Hardt and Negri call "a multitude of the poor") and not something worthy to think of in itself.

3. See Derrida, *Politique et amitié.*

4. See Nancy's "Surprise de l'événement," in *Être singulier pluriel.*

5. Derrida, *Voyous*, 126, 35, my translation.

6. Pheng Cheah and Suzanne Guerlac, in their introduction to *Derrida and the Time of the Political*, argue likewise that what is at stake in *démocratie à venir* is *not* the *subject*. They write: "[The] imminence [of *démocratie à venir*] is not something that can be predicted or anticipated precisely because the coming is that of

the other. Indeed, the other *is* this coming and *should therefore not be regarded as another subject* [my emphasis], substance, or presence" (14). In the same volume of essays, one will find Rancière's contribution, which critiques Derrida's *démocratie à venir* as too ethical and not political enough.

7. That is what I think the contributors, which include Nancy, Rancière, and Badiou, in *L'Idée de communisme*, attempt to do with the term "communism," after its disastrous perversion in the course of history, by Stalin in the ex-Soviet Union and by Mao in China, for example.

8. He reiterates this in *Voyous*, recalling what he has already said in *Politiques de l'amitié*, that there is always "the possibility, perhaps, one day, and the right, to abandon the heritage of the name [of democracy], of changing the name" (*Voyous*, 130). On an inquiry into Derrida's comparative ("better") or superlative ("the best") rhetoric surrounding democracy, and especially in relation to violence ("lesser" or "the least," which seems to be in question in "Violence and Metaphysics"), see Haddad, "Genealogy of Violence," 121–42.

9. Perhaps *auto-rejection* can be another way of saying "auto-critique" in the precise sense to which Derrida gives, which is close to autoimmunity: "The expression '*démocratie à venir*' takes into account the absolute and intrinsic historicity of the only system that welcomes in itself, in its concept, the formula of autoimmunity that one call the right to auto-critique or to perfectibility. Democracy is the only system, the only constitutional paradigm in which, in principle, one has or one exercises [*prend*] the right to publicly critique everything, including the idea of democracy, its concept, its history, and its name, including also the idea of the constitutional paradigm and the absolute authority of law" (*Voyous*, 126–27).

10. For the distinction that Nancy makes between affirmation as philosophical and politics as the creation of place or space for this affirmation, see especially *Vérité de la démocratie*, 46–50. The emphasis on politics as a question of place or space is also shared by other French thinkers. Thus, we find the notion of *khôra*, as place without fixed grounding or foundation, or spacing, so as to accommodate or welcome the other, in Derrida's discussion of politics in *Spectres de Marx* and *Voyous*. In Badiou, there is always the "evental site" [*site événementiel*] as a critical element, if not even necessary condition, for the political event. And in Rancière, we will find him saying, "Politics exists always as a repartition [*re-division*] of the policed space [*l'espace policier*] [which is the control by the State of the public sphere by determining and distributing those who have political voice and whose who do not], as a rethinking of the structuration of the space of community [...]" ("Politiques de la mésentente," in *Moments politiques*, 178, my translation).

11. See Nancy's interview with *Spriale*, "Politique tout court et très au-delà," 35, my translation.

12. Blanchot, *Michel Foucault*, 36, my translation.

13. Here, I am close to Nancy's thought on sovereignty when he says, in his contribution to the Cerisy-la-salle colloquium, *La Démocratie à venir*, that "sovereignty as a modern concept of politics is a concept of the subject" (, 348). I am aware of the "deconstructive" critique of sovereignty of the Schmittian form especially in the works of Bataille, Derrida, Agamben, Nancy, Bennington, and Sam Weber, among many others. This is, however, not the space to rehearse all those arguments.

14. In "De la souveraineté," Nancy would argue for a separation of politics from sovereignty. In this case, "politics" will no longer "designate the presumption of a subject or in a subject (be it an individual or a collective)" (*La Création*, 165, my translation). "The political order," Nancy continues, "would define its regulation by an equality and a justice that does not postulate a subjective presumption. In this case, politics would be without subject [...]" (165).

15. As Derrida states, "There is no sovereignty without force [...]" (*Voyous*, 144). And as he argues a little later, sovereignty secures itself through the exploitation of power: "The abuse of power is constitutive of sovereignty itself" (*Voyous*, 145). In other words, sovereignty is always nascent as long there is some manifestation of force, power, and affirmation. The form of sovereignty that results, whether it is imperialist, then depends on the degree and the manner of use of that force, power, and affirmation.

16. Nancy, *Le Sens du monde*, 143, my translation.

17. See Badiou's *Sarkozy*, for his total renunciation of electoral processes.

18. See especially Badiou's "La Figure du soldat," in *La Relation*.

19. This strict fidelity to the "Idea of communism" is another distinguishing feature that marks the distance between Badiou and other contemporary French thinkers such as Nancy, Rancière, and Derrida, this time with regard to political thought. In an earlier note, I have underscored that Nancy and Rancière in *L'Idée de communisme*, like Badiou, do not believe in any "end" of communism and are committed to rethink communism. However, unlike Badiou, they do not reject democratic thought tout court, even though, like Derrida, they critique existing forms of State democracies. They remain open to the thought of democracy that goes beyond the latter (beside their contributions in *Démocratie, dans quels états?*, see also Nancy's and Rancière's respective engagements with democracy as a problematic concept in *Vérite de la démocratie* and *La Haine de la démocratie*). Badiou's singular fidelity to a "communist hypothesis" as the only "politics of emancipation" would very much strike Derrida, in light of the latter's *Voyous*, as a Kantian monolithic, regulatory Idea, to which is opposed the thought of *démocratie à venir*, which is "a freedom of play [*une liberté de jeu*], an opening [*ouverture*] of indetermination and undecidability *in the very concept* of democracy, in the interpretation of democracy" (*Voyous*, 47). Contrary to Badiou's rather monolithic "Idea of communism" or "communist hypothesis," *démocratie à venir*, as already

mentioned in the main text, is also open to what is even contrary to existing democratic thought. I leave aside all discussions of communism in this work. For the question of communism in Nancy, see especially the chapter "Being Communist" in Philip Armstrong's *Reticulations* and Frédéric Neyrat's *Le Communisme existentiel de Jean-Luc Nancy*.

20. See especially Rancière, *La Mésentente*; Rancière, *Le Partage du sensible*; and Rancière, *Aux bords du politique*.

21. "Should Democracy Come?" in Cheah and Guerlac, *Derrida and the Time of the Political*, 278, my emphasis. Rancière's resistance to part with the category of the *subject* is consistent with his response to Nancy ("After What" in *Who Comes After the Subject?*). See also his essays, "Who Is the Subject of the Rights of Man?" 297–310, and "Work, Identity, Subject," in *Jacques Rancière and the Contemporary Scene*, 205–16.

22. See especially Balibar, "Civic Universalism and Its Internal Inclusions"; and the final section, Balibar, "Malêtre du sujet," in his *Citoyen sujet, et autres essais d'anthropologie philosophique*.

23. As Balibar explicates, *malêtre* concerns "a subject intrinsically affected by 'discontent' [*malaise*] or 'malformation' not in a moral or psychological interiority, but in the exteriority and the very immanence of the social relation that it entertains with all other subjects [...]" (*Citoyen sujet, et autres essais d'anthropologie philosophique*, 513).

24. See Foucault's "Les Hétérotopies," in *Le Corps*.

25. Balibar, *Citoyen sujet, et autres essais d'anthropologie philosophique*, 5.

26. Ibid., 2. Balibar's notion of liberty or freedom is surely different from Nancy's in the latter's *L'Expérience de la liberté*. A comparison between these two articulations of freedom, unfortunately, is beyond the scope of the present work.

27. Ibid., 6.

28. See especially the essay "'Droits de l'homme' et 'droits du citoyen,'" for Balibar's explication of *égaliberté*. I quote here a passage from that essay to recall that the affirmation of differences, if not the affirmation of both the liberty and equality of all differences, is at stake in *égaliberté*: "to seek [...] liberation as a 'right to difference in equality,' that is to say, not as the restoration of an original identity or as the neutralization of differences in the equality of rights, but as the production of an equality without precedent and model, which is difference itself, the complementarity and reciprocity of singularities. In a sense, one such reciprocity is already virtually included in the proposition of *égaliberté*, but it can – paradoxically – claim to it only on the condition of *reopening* the question of identity between 'man' and 'citizen': not to regress to the idea of a citizenship *subordinated to* anthropological differences (as in the understanding of citizenship in antiquity), but to progress toward a citizenship *overdetermined by* anthropological difference, explicitly drawn to its transformation, distinct simultaneously from institutional

naturalization and from a denial or formal neutralization (which functions in fact as a permanent means of its neutralization)" (*Les Frontières de la démocratie*, 145).

29. Balibar, *Citoyen sujet, et autres essais d'anthropologie philosophique*, 51.

30. Ibid., 52, 43.

31. Ibid., 52.

32. Ibid., 43.

33. Ibid., 64.

34. Ibid., 52.

35. Ibid., 52, 57.

36. See especially Balibar's "Sur la désobéissance civique," in *Droit de cité*, 17.

37. Balibar, *Droit de cité*, 18.

38. See Balibar, *Citoyen sujet, et autres essais d'anthropologie philosophique*, 61–64.

39. Ibid., 61.

40. Ibid., 63. Or, as Balibar says in the essay "Les Habits neufs de la citoyenneté," the concept of citizenship "has no definition that is fixed once and for all. It has always been the stake of struggles and the object of transformations" (*Les Frontières de la démocratie*, 100). Or further, in "Propositions sur la citoyenneté," he would attribute an "essential mobility" to the concept of citizenship, which is "the incessant transformation of its contents and its functions" (*Les Frontières de la démocratie*, 111).

41. Balibar, *Citoyen sujet, et autres essais d'anthropologie philosophique*, 65.

42. Ibid., 64.

43. Balibar, *La Proposition de l'égaliberté*, 24.

44. This is in the essay "L'Antinomie de la citoyenneté," in *La Proposition de l'égaliberté*, 14.

45. Balibar, *Les Frontières de la démocratie*, 66.

46. Ibid., 107.

47. Balibar, *Droit de cité*, 203.

48. See Balibar, *Les Frontières de la démocratie*, 100; Balibar, *Droit de cité*, 178.

49. I note here that Nancy, in the chapter "Politique II," in *Le Sens du monde*, has noted that the concept of the citizen or citizenship can take on a global dimension. According to Nancy, "The in-common of the city has no other identity except the space where citizens come together [*se croisent*], and it has no other unity except the exteriority of their relations. In a certain way, citizenship according to its pure concept is always virtually 'worldly' [*mondiale*]." He continues, "Therefore, the 'citizen' of the French Revolution was well founded to think itself [*se penser*], and to think, "France" or "the Republic" according to an international, European, and even cosmopolitan dimension" (*Le Sens du monde*, 165). I do not quite agree, evidently, with Nancy's view on "citizenship according to its pure concept." Having said that, I do not doubt that Nancy leaves this notion of citizenship without

deconstructing it, for the chapter will unfold toward a politics of linking-up [*une politique du nouage*] that is, contrary to what "citizenship according to its pure concept" allows, "nowhere founded and destined nowhere" (174, 175).

50. Balibar, *Citoyen sujet, et autres essais d'anthropologie philosophique*, 43.

51. Balibar, *La Proposition de l'égaliberté*, 18.

52. Balibar, *Citoyen sujet, et autres essais d'anthropologie philosophique*, 508.

53. Balibar, *Les Frontières de la démocratie*, 52.

54. Ibid. Yet, as Balibar suggests in "Sujets ou citoyens? (Pour l'égalité)" (also in *Les Frontières de la démocratie*), the distance between "citizen workers" and noncitizen immigrants, in times of economic crises, shows itself to be insignificant in effect. In other words, during such times, both groups face the similar situation of being at risk of unemployment as nationalistic companies try to *first* protect the livelihood of employees who are "native" citizens. In that case, one group is as much a *reject* as the other.

55. Balibar, *Les Frontières de la démocratie*, 52.

56. Balibar, *La Crainte des masses*, 375.

57. Ibid., 374. Balibar will go on to say that from there, "frontiers cease to be purely exterior realities, they also become, and perhaps before everything, what Fichte [...] had superbly called 'interior frontiers' [...], that is to say, [...] invisible, situated 'everywhere and nowhere'" (374).

58. Balibar, *Citoyen sujet, et autres essais d'anthropologie philosophique*, 43.

59. One must also pose to Balibar the question of what new frontiers must be in place in a "trans-national or post-national citizenship," for Balibar, through the thought of "extended citizenship," is not seeking a world without frontiers. As he says, "I would always hesitate [...] to identify a radical democracy [...] with the pursuit of a 'world without frontiers' in the juridico-political sense of the term. Such a 'world' would only risk to be a type of unchecked domination [*domination sauvage*] of private powers that monopolize capital, communication, and perhaps armaments [...]" (*La Crainte des masses*, 380). Keeping in mind that citizenship, for Balibar, is always the "antinomic" movement between its institutional constitution and its insurrection against institutions when the latter is inadequate to accommodate new forms of citizenship, one must also ask what institution, in a "trans-national or post-national" world, is "extended citizenship" in constant negotiation with. Where would this institution be situated? Why should it be located in that particular place? What right or privilege does that place have to warrant the establishment of the institution there? According to which laws, or whose laws, will this institution be subjected? Having posed these questions, I am not suggesting that one does away with institutions tout court. If I am arguing for a turn away from the figure of the "citizen subject" to the *reject*, and even if the *reject* is already there before institutions and across national frontiers and that one must try to address or respond to the *reject* in a way that goes beyond relying on

or waiting for institutional interventions that are usually regulated by national laws and restrictions, I do not mean that a theory of the *reject* envisions an institution-less world. Like Derrida's *démocratie à venir*, the *reject* can be assisted by institutions, but these institutions must be those that are not tied to any national sovereignty, and at the same time must have enough force to address in a timely manner and across national boundaries the injustices done to *rejects* everywhere. We have traces of such institutions in the UN or the BRussells Tribunal, but, as Derrida has observed, they are still limited in many ways to effectively address a *démocratie à venir* or, I would add, the *reject*. The *reject*, which does not need or seek institutional legitimation as the citizen or "citizen subject" does, is meant to orient thought to address such figures before institutions with adequate means to do so arrive. To be sure, I am not saying thought itself is an adequate measure, but at least there will be no delay, as the setting up of institutions undoubtedly has, in recognizing *rejects* and in thinking of ways to help affirm them and critique the forces that are negating them.

60. See especially Derrida, *Voyous*; Derrida and Dufourmantelle, *De l'hospitalité*; Derrida, *Cosmopolitiques de tous les pays.*Likewise in the interview in *Philosophy in a Time of Terror*, Derrida has also called for "the coming of a universal alliance or solidarity that extends beyond the internationality of nation-states and thus beyond citizenship" ("Autoimmunity," 124). As for the question of the impossible but necessary sharing of sovereignty, see *Voyous* again and Derrida's "Le Souverain bien – ou l'Europe en mal de souveraineté."

61. As Derrida acknowledges in the text, the engagement with *voyous* in fact derives from the proliferation in American politics, especially from the Clinton administration to the Bush administration that inaugurated the "war on terror," of the word "rogue" to label states that not only deviate from, but also go against, American political ideology. *Voyous* therefore is more properly the translation into French of "rogues."

62. Derrida, *Voyous*, 98.

63. Ibid., 96.

64. Ibid., 95.

65. Ibid., 100.

66. Hardt and Negri, *Commonwealth*, 39-40.

67. See Hardt and Negri, "Fight for 'Real Democracy.'"

68. Hardt and Negri, *Empire*, 203, 204.

69. Ibid., 204.

70. Ibid.

71. Ibid. Cf. also Derrida's reading of Bartleby in *Donner la mort*, even though Bartleby's solitariness is not Derrida's point of critique: "a sacrificial passion that led [Bartleby] to death, a death given by the law, by society that does not know why it acts as such" (*Donner la mort*, 107).

72. *Empire*, 204.

73. The invocation of Bartleby for Occupy Toronto appeared in a post dated October 19, 2011, on the movement's website (www.occupyto.org). The post has now strangely disappeared.

74. Melville, *Bartleby, the Scrivener*, 43, my emphases. ˙

75. Hardt and Negri, *Empire*, 203.

76. While Hardt and Negri have so far explicitly resisted identifying Bartleby as the political figure of the Occupy movement, that link is clearer in Žižek. For Žižek, what is of importance to the movement is their "first gesture," which is that of "pure negativity," and which consists in "occupying a place and displaying the firm conviction of remaining there" ("Žižek and the Occupy Wall Street Movement," my translation. In a later text, he will write, "The Wall Street protests were thus a beginning [...] with a formal gesture of rejection that is initially more important than any positive content – only such a gesture opens up the space for a new content" (*Year of Dreaming Dangerously*, 83). Politics as a question of place or space is once again at stake here, but what I would like to highlight here is "pure negativity," which resonates strongly with how Žižek describes Bartleby in another text. According to Žižek, Bartleby's *I would prefer not to* "is the gesture of subtraction at its purest" (*Parallax View*, 382). It is very probable then that Žižek would not hesitate to take Bartleby as the literary antecedent that prefigures the political figure of subtraction that the Occupy movement has seemed to embody in a collective dimension, or in a dimension of the multitude.

77. Melville, *Bartleby*, 27, my emphases.

78. Ibid., 31.

79. Ibid., 27.

80. Ibid., 42. In a way, I echo Deleuze's reading of Bartleby. According to Deleuze, Bartleby "can survive only in a swirling suspense that puts the world at a distance" ("Bartleby, ou la formule," in Deleuze, *Critique et clinique*, 92, my translation).

81. In Deleuze's terms, Bartleby "has nothing particular, nothing general either, about him: he is an Original" ("Bartleby, ou la formule," 106).

82. Melville, *Bartleby*, 44, my emphasis.

83. Ibid., 50.

84. Ibid., 24, 30–31, 31.

85. Ibid., 36.

86. I differ from Deleuze's reading here. In Deleuze's interpretation, work becomes impossible for Bartleby because – and this is what Deleuze argues as an essential point – of the effect the phrase *I would prefer not to* has on Bartleby too: "the moment he says I PREFER NOT TO (compare copies), he can no longer copy either" ("Bartleby, ou la formule," 91).

87. Melville, *Bartleby*, 36.

88. Ibid.

89. Ibid., 30.

90. Ibid., 24.

91. Ibid., 46.

92. Ibid., 32.

93. Ibid.

94. Ibid., 44.

95. Agamben, "Bartleby, or On Contingency," in *Potentialities*, 259.

96. Derrida, *Voyous*, 96.

97. Ibid., 99.

98. Ibid.

99. Ibid., 95.

100. See ibid., 101.

101. See ibid., 13.

102. See ibid.

103. Ibid., 101.

104. Ibid., 98, 100, 101.

105. Žižek, Transcript of "Žižek Speaks at Occupy Wall Street," October 25, 2011.

106. From the statement of the organizers of the Occupy Wall Street movement, "Occupy Together." http://www.occupytogether.org/occupy-wall-st/

107. Derrida, *Voyous*, 98.

108. Ibid.

109. Ibid.

110. Melville, *Bartleby*, 34.

111. On top of that, the narrator is not an employer who treats Bartleby unreasonably or unfairly. He is very patient with, and tolerant of, Bartleby's idiosyncrasies. And despite Bartleby's frequent refusals of his requests, the narrator-employer always has the intention to help Bartleby. In Deleuze's reading, he even seems to be a figure of "good fathers, of benevolent fathers or at least of protective elder brothers" ("Bartleby, ou la formule," 103–4). The main fault with him is that he is pressurized by the rest of Wall Street to not accept an uncommon figure such as Bartleby. He abandons Bartleby because the latter has become an anomalous sight or phenomenon, and he is afraid that this will result in him losing existing and potential clients. As Deleuze says, he is unable to protect the excluded, or what I would call the *reject*.

112. Derrida, *Voyous*, 99.

113. See the *New York Times* article, "For Annoyed Neighbors, the Beat Drags On," November 13, 2011.

114. See the *New York Times* article, "Dissenting, or Taking Shelter? Homeless Stake a Claim at Protests," October 31, 2011.

115. For a more sympathetic coverage of the movement, see *Occupy! Scenes from Occupied America*; the supplement issue of *Theory & Event* 14 (4), 2011; the final

chapter of Butler and Athanasiou, *Dispossession*; and Mitchell, Harcourt, and Taussig, *Occupy: Three Inquiries in Disobedience*.

116. I sense too that scholars sympathetic to the movement are not quite sure as to how to make sense of the ways the participants of the movement organized themselves. Sometimes, they choose to bracket out the organizational structures that Hardt and Negri have observed. For example, Mitchell prefers to focus on "the refusal of Occupy to designate leaders or representative spokespersons, its insistences on anonymity and equality, and its reluctance to issue a specific list of demands or policy recommendations" as "an effort to prolong [the] movement of rebirth and renewal of the political" (preface to *Occupy: Three Inquiries in Disobedience*, xi). Bernard E. Harcourt also seeks to make something out of the image of the movement being "leaderless." For him, it is a sign of the movement bearing the trace of what he calls "political disobedience," by which it "rejects conventional political rationality, discourse, and strategies," or else "politics *writ large*" ("Political Obedience," in *Occupy: Three Inquiries in Disobedience*, 47). Potentially, it could lead the movement "to rhizomic, nonhierarchical governing structures" (47). However, as Hardt and Negri's observation has shown, reality offers quite a different image, and Harcourt will also have to admit at the end of his essay that "an occupation requires discipline, and not just the kind of discipline that accompanies a protest or a march" and "committee structure – open to all, to be sure, but structured" (73). As we know from Deleuze and Guattari, the rhizomic, however, defies both discipline and structure.

I acknowledge here too that the Occupy movement might not have made explicit claims to sovereignty. However, I bring to mind that Derrida, in *Voyous*, has argued that when *voyous* take to the streets, occupying them with their numbers, they present themselves as some form of (counter)sovereign force. Nancy has also argued that any form of ordering, even if it is self-ordering, is a pre-figuration of a sovereign *subject* (see "Un sujet?," 61–62).

117. Žižek, *Parallax View*, 381, my emphasis.

118. The problematic raising of the *subject* in revolutionary movements perhaps recalls what Peter Starr has called the "logics of failed revolt." The failure arises from the "logic of recuperation," where "to oppose the Master (in specific ways) is merely to consolidate the Master's power," and the "logic of substitution," where "any figure that sets itself up as an alternative to the Master risks becoming a Master in its turn" (*Logics of Failed Revolt*, 15).

119. Deleuze has also said, Bartleby is "a pure excluded to which no social situation can any longer be attributed" ("Bartleby, or la formule," 95).

120. I note here that Hardt and Negri, following in some ways the nineteenth-century notion of multitude according to Adolphe Thiers, take movement as critical for the radical politics of the multitude: it is because the multitude "is so mobile and impossible to grasp as a unified object of rule" that it "is dangerous

and must be banished by law" (*Commonwealth*, 45). It is a little bewildering then that Hardt and Negri do not oppose the rather static occupational gesture of the Occupy movements, but still consider them to be constitutive of a "multitude form."

121. Žižek, *Parallax View*, 384.

122. Agamben, "Bartleby, or On Contingency," 253.

123. Ibid., 270.

124. Deleuze, "Bartleby, ou la formule," 93.

125. Melville, *Bartleby*, 44.

126. Agamben, "Bartleby, or On Contingency," 259.

127. Marcuse, *One-Dimensional Man*, 63.

128. Ibid., 252.

129. Ibid., 67.

130. Ibid., 142.

131. Ibid., 71.

132. Marcuse, "Beyond One-Dimensional Man," in *Collected Papers*, 115.

133. Ibid., 114.

134. "Žižek and the Occupy Wall Street Movement: 'That This Movement Has a Trace of Violence Is What I Approve Of.'"

135. Marcuse, "Beyond One-Dimensional Man," 117.

136. Marcuse, *One-Dimensional Man*, 77.

137. Derrida, *Voyous*, 13.

138. I note here that *rejects* are in fact no strangers to Marcuse's "Great Refusal," since he would speak of "outcasts and outsiders" (*One-Dimensional Man*, 256) with regard to that.

139. And if one wants to stay with Bartleby as perhaps the literary representation of the *reject*, it must no longer be a Bartleby with a "sacrificial passion" as Derrida calls it (see earlier note 71). A sacrificial logic can be found in Marcuse's theory too, since "it wants to remain loyal to those who, without hope, have given and give their life to the Great Refusal" (*One-Dimensional One*, 257). In my view, a "critical refusal," even though it must sacrifice its existing means and goals, must nonetheless try to be done with real sacrificial passions or logic, that is, sacrifices that involve the very lives of oneself and others.

140. Derrida, *Politique et amitié*, 116, my translation.

141. Derrida, *Voyous*, 102.

142. Ibid., 135.

143. Derrida, *L'Animal*, 12.

144. See, for example, Bruns, "Becoming-Animal (Some Simple Ways)"; Colebrook, *Deleuze and the Meaning of Life*; and Penny, "Parables and Politics."

145. See especially Bonta and Protevi, *Deleuze and Geophilosophy*; Buchanan and Thoburn, *Deleuze and Politics*; and Patton, *Deleuzian Concepts*.

146. I am referring to scholarship published in English so far. In terms of non-English scholarship, the collection of French essays in Antonioli, Chardel, and Regnauld's *Gilles Deleuze* must not be ignored. But suffice it to say that the question of becoming-animal and its political potentiality is not placed in the foreground there either. In another collection of French essays on the question of the animal, Paola Marrati's "L'Animal qui sait fuir" does explicitly deal with the politics of becoming-animal. Marrati focuses on the question of faciality, and she argues that the contest of faciality constitutes the transhistorical politics of becoming-animal. The transhistorical perspective is where I depart from her work, since I will seek to contextualize becoming-animal here within contemporary global politics.

147. Patton, "Becoming-Democratic," 190; Patton, "Utopian Political Philosophy,"

148. Patton's vision of politics in Deleuze and Guattari is undeniably anthropocentric. For Patton, that politics holds the promise "to achieve [...] improvements in the conditions of a given people," by extending rights and justices to people who are denied them, and through "a more just distribution of material social goods" ("Utopian Political Philosophy," 47, 51). This "given people" hardly includes animal beings, since the "political community" it forms is based on "rights [of this people] and duties [due them]," something to which animals are incommensurable ("Becoming-Democratic," 192). Becoming-animal does turn up in Patton's earlier *Deleuze & the Political*, but he does not explicitly suggest how becoming-animal can posit a potential political force, or how it can intervene or apply itself in a political context. In the more recent *Deleuzian Concepts*, Patton brings in becoming-animal in an essay on the *literary* treatment in J. M. Coetzee's *Disgrace* of the politics of colonization or postcolonization, but leaves it out in the section "Normative Political Philosophy."

149. Patton, "Utopian Political Philosophy," 49. I note too that such political thought is also a legacy of an anthropologic and/or anthropocentric reading of Aristotle's *Politics* throughout history. It reads in the latter a separation between humans and animals via the element of *logos* or rational speech, denying its presence in animals; consequently, deprived of *logos*, animals, unlike humans, are judged to be unable to organize their lives via the labor of jurisprudence, that is, to demand or to institutionalize a right to justice in the face of a wrong done to them. This canonized reading of the *Politics* has granted humans, and not animals, the category of "political animals." Bennington's deconstructive reading in his intervention in the special issue of *diacritics* on "negative politics" will show that in Aristotle, humans are only *more* political than animals, and that animals can have *logos*, except they cannot transform the latter into rhetoric. See Bennington, "Political Animals."

150. Deleuze and Guattari, *Mille plateaux*, 133. As in this present work's introduction, I am following Massumi's translation here. I note further that Deleuze

and Guattari identify this figure as underlying all existing political thought, and argue that it must be critiqued and combated. With regard to translating *Mille plateaux*, I am in large part in agreement with Massumi's translation, except in a few instances. In this case, as in the earlier section on friendship, love, and community, subsequent references to *Mille plateaux* will be made in parentheses, first indicating the pages in the French text (*MP*) then to those in the English version as translated by Massumi (*TP*).

151. Deleuze and Guattari, *Kafka*, 22. The translation here follows, with modifications, Dana Polan's in *Kafka*, 12.

152. Deleuze and Parnet, *Dialogues*, 168, my translation. The English translation of this text also exists, and the quote can be found in *Dialogues*, trans. Hugh Tomlinson and Barbara Habberham, 139.

153. Agamben, *State of Exception*, 18.

154. Obama's politics arguably participates in a post-9/11 worldview that is always predicated on a war "against terror," that is, a worldview that is always anxious to arm the State against all possible scenarios of threat. Obama's official campaign website has stated that his defense strategy will seek to further develop the "agility and lethality" of the American military complex, especially the "global reach in the air" by UAVs, in the face of conventional and nonconventional threats (see http://www.barackobama.com/issues/defense/index_campaign.php#invest-century-military). In a 2008 statement, Obama has also vowed to keep the US military "the strongest military on the planet" (see "Obama Vows US Will Maintain 'Strongest Military on the Planet," *Agence France Presse*, December 1, 2008). As State military and surveillance technics continue to be the condition or norm of contemporary American democratic geopolitics, Virilio's thesis that the militarization of the world by democratic powers such as the United States, regardless of which administration is in power, still holds true.

155. Marcuse, *One-Dimensional Man*, 71.

156. See Hardt and Negri, *Multitudes* and *Commonwealth*; Casarino and Negri, *In Praise of the Common*; and Virno, *Grammar of the Multitude*. Largely inspired by Deleuze's philosophy, the question of becoming-animal is interestingly absent as well in their works. For example, instead of becoming-animal, Hardt and Negri will speak instead of a "becoming-Prince," which is "the process of the multitude learning the art of self-rule and inventing lasting democratic forms of social organization" (*Commonwealth*, viii).

157. Galloway and Thacker, *The Exploit*, 135.

158. Deleuze and Guattari, *Qu'est-ce que la philosophie?*, 104.

159. This is where I deviate from Thacker's take on becoming-animal. Thacker argues that becoming-animal is a sort of swarming animality and suggests that its potential for radical politics lies precisely in the faceless dimension of its very entity as a swarm. Without a facial profile to identify itself as friend or foe,

becoming-animal as such unhinges the Schmittian definition of politics as the decisive determination of a friend-enemy distinction. In place is another politics, which poses "local actions and global patterns" and an "ambivalent, tensile topology" against sovereignty and control ("Swarming: Number versus Animal?", 181). In my view, such politics presents itself too hastily as a too explicit affront against State politics, which only invites the violent intervention of the State's surveillance and military apparatuses.

160. Three notes here: Firstly, I use *departure* because becoming or becoming-animal, according to Deleuze, is never a form of derivative politics, as if it needs to refer to existing norms or normativity of political thought (see Deleuze and Parnet, *Dialogues*, 152). Secondly, I share in many ways Matthew Calarco's vision of radical politics. Calarco has argued that it is "unrealistic and utopian" to continue looking to existing democratic politics for an ethicopolitical project that will take into consideration nonhuman animals. A "form of politics beyond the present humanist, democratic, and juridical orders" is necessary (*Zoographies*, 97–98). While Calarco discusses Deleuze and Guattari's becoming-animal (*Zoographies*, 41–43), I find the discussion too brief, not allowing him to elucidate becoming-animal's political potentialities, strategies, implications, and effects. Thirdly, I am using "striation" here in the Deleuzo-Guattarian sense, that is to say, the totalization of all thoughts and actions by the State, reducing or homogenizing them to State thought.

161. Recognizing that becoming-animal occurs via a time- and locale-specific chance encounter, Thacker calls becoming-animal a "topological temporality" ("Swarming," 173). On another note, becoming-animal, or even the politics of becoming-animal, as of a spatial dimension corresponds to the consideration of politics as space or place, as seen, according to other philosophers dealt with in this chapter: Nancy, Badiou, Derrida, and Rancière.

162. Marrati, "L'Animal qui sait fuir," 203.

163. See note 149 on "political animals."

164. The definition "political animal" would even suggest that such spaces are recoverable, since the term "animal" in the definition would seem to constantly retrace that which the definition, according to a long line of anthropologic and/or anthropocentric political thought, puts aside. An animal space can be recuperated by rethinking the term "political animal," by which the term must no longer be about the question of a human-animal separation or distinction, but how the human might cross over to the animal. For Bennington, the term "political animal" became anthropocentric through the exploitation of *logos* (which animals can have, in Bennington's reading, following Labarrière) into *rhetoric*, which is to say, deliberative phrases that decide, in human terms and language, what is good and evil, just and unjust. But Bennington also argues that something always remains (recoverable) that is shared between humans and animals, which he calls

"a residual *phonè*, a kind of persistent animality of language [...]" ("Political Animals," 34).

165. Here, I diverge from Laurent Dubreuil's call for an outside or to create "tears in the political fabric" ("Preamble to Apolitics," 7).

166. I am keeping in mind here Deleuze and Guattari's point that one must not delimit counterthought to the outside. When the outside is impossible, there is always the alternative to resist from within, and one can do that by creating an adjacent space. See *MP*, 437/ *TP*, 353.

167. I would not hesitate to say that there is something of "treason," if not a "treacherous" humor (see Deleuze and Parnet, *Dialogues*, 83), in the doubling effect of *I remain, I become* before the technics of identifiability. It makes light of the latter, and is therefore an unbearable humor for the political apparatuses that are putting in place such technics. On the element of humor in Deleuze and Guattari's philosophy as "a strategy of dissent," see also O'Sullivan's *Art Encounters Deleuze and Guattari*, 73.

168. It is in this way that becoming-animal, in the context of a militarized post-9/11 world, is the wiser strategy in relation to the tactics of current radical politics, such as the construction of a "multitude" or "common" via explicit "tactics of nonexistence."

169. Guattari, *La Révolution moléculaire*, 242, my translation.

170. Ibid., 245; Guattari, *Psychanalyse et transversalité*, 84, my translation. See also the section "Micropolitique et segmentarité" in Deleuze and Guattari, *Mille plateaux*.

171. See Sinclair's note 19 to *aisthēsis* in his translation of Aristotle's *Politics*. Daniel Heller-Roazen has also argued that the Aristotelian *aisthēsis* is that which reconnects the human and the animal, and that any endeavor to define, in sharp opposition to the animal, what is proper to the human (for example, the faculty of reason, as it has been claimed throughout history) always "produces a remainder, which cannot be attributed with any exclusivity to either human or inhuman beings" (*Inner Touch*, 93). Heller-Roazen goes on to say that this remainder "testifies to a dimension of the living being in which the distinction between the human and the inhuman simply has no pertinence: a region common, by definition, to all animal life," and this region is "sensation (*aisthēsis*)" (93). Bennington's "residual *phonè*" (see my note 164) is certainly close to Heller-Roazen's *aisthēsis* here.

172. I deliberately use the word "milieu" here in thinking the spatiality of the animal and/or of becoming-animal, avoiding the word "territory" because a territory always defines itself through several identifiable limits or boundaries. The point here is to think of a space that is unidentifiable, or escapes identifiability, and the term "milieu" would suit such a space. As Elizabeth Grosz puts it, and she will do it with reference to the animal and to a nonidentifiability, "a milieu [...] is not yet a territory. A milieu is what the fly inhabits, an indeterminable but limited

space" (*Chaos, Territory, Art*, 46). She also goes on to contrast the milieu to territory, which she defines as "the delimitation of a milieu" (47)

173. Such resensing of *aisthēsis* shared between humans and animals is largely at work too in Heller-Roazen's *Inner Touch* (see my note 171).

174. Aristotle, *Politics*, 60–61.

175. Deleuze and Guattari, *Qu'est-ce que la philosophie?*, 164.

176. For Bennington, following Lyotard, all these would be a question of the "vocalization or a vociferation" of the "quasi-animal affect-phrase" or *différend* that cannot be articulated or represented in anthropocentric rhetoric ("Political Animals," 9). As Bennington makes clear, the question of justice is also at stake with the Lyotardian *différend*, where justice is not decided on solely by the human and oftentimes manipulative rhetoric of institutional jurisprudence (see also Lyotard and Thébaud, *Au juste*).

On another note, I would like to say again that the departure from the patient faith in institutions does not mean the total rejection of institutions. The point is to respond to, or address, in a manner without unnecessary bureaucratic delays, the injustices done to others, and this is what I mean by "immanent response."

177. In this sense, becoming-animal perhaps goes further than the radical politics proposed by Hardt and Negri, Virno, and Cesarino, or even the "dissensus" politics of Rancière. Discourse- or "communication"-based counternetworks and "disagreements" not only risk being captured sooner or later by the *logos*-based State apparatuses, but also delimit the extension of the project of immanent justice without delay to those who do not share the capability to articulate a disagreement, or the idioms of the "multitude" or "common." I further note here that Rancière's political philosophy hardly takes into account animals or animal beings. Rancière's call for the exposition of political disagreements or "dissensus" especially from those who previously have not been counted or given the right to speak in the public sphere, remains predicated on some form of speech, and hardly considers animal silence or *phonè*. In an interview, Rancière extends his thesis on "dissensus" to state that politics proper must include the "struggle over words" (*Démocratie, dans quel état?* 97). Without "words" in the sense of those that are exchanged in present political domains, the animal or becoming-animal is once again rejected in this "struggle."

178. For a critique of the too hasty translation of the contemporary political situation in terms of biopolitics, and especially Agamben's hasty separation between *bios* and *zōē*, see Dubreuil's "Leaving Politics."

179. Biopolitics, for Agamben, is put in place by an "anthropological machine" that "functions by means of an exclusion" of those it deems unmanageable or unconceptualizable (for example, the animal) within its domain (*Open*, 37–38). To disrupt such biopolitics, in the sense of displacing its foundation built on making every of its subject knowable or a known subject, Agamben argues that one

must leap into a "zone of indeterminacy" where one enters into a relation with that which is unknowable (for example, the animal), rather than to exclude it. For a critique of Agamben's unconscious need to maintain the human-animal separation produced by the "anthropological machine" such that the leap into the "zone of indeterminacy" can take place, see once again Dominick LaCapra's chapter, "Reopening the Question of the Human and the Animal" in *History and Its Limits*.

180. See the opening of Derrida's *L'Animal*. Resonating with Derrida's and Deleuze and Guattari's discussions of the animal's secret, Agamben has written that there is in the animal a "zone of nonknowledge – or of a-knowledge – that [...] is beyond both knowing and not knowing [...]" (*Open*, 91). Despite my suggestion so far that Derrida and Deleuze and Guattari share a sense of the political potentiality of the secret of the animal, I note that Derrida disagrees with Deleuze's treatment of the animal, not so much with the question of becoming-animal, but with Deleuze's suggestion in *Différence et répétition* that *bêtise* or stupidity, or even *devenir-bête* or "becoming-stupid," is properly the essence of humans and not animals. See the January 30, 2002, seminar in *La Bête et le souverain*. I further note that the question of secrecy, for Derrida, is important for a thought of democracy or *démocratie à venir*. As he says in several places, there is no democracy without secrecy, or rather the right to secrecy. Derrida does not fail to recognize that there are state secrets or secret diplomacies and actions in democratic states, and such right to secrecy by the State will need to be deconstructed. That is not in the interest of this chapter, however. On the topic of secrecy, see especially Pheng Cheah's "The Untimely Secret of Democracy" in *Derrida and the Time of the Political*, and David Wills's "Passionate Secrets and Democratic Dissidence" in the "Derrida and Democracy" special issue of *diacritics*. To end this note, I add that the secret of the animal might also correspond to what Jonathan Culler calls "the right to absolute nonresponse," which I see it as another way of walking away (from the demand to respond). "The right to respond," Culler argues, following Derrida, "can be an essential feature of democracy, for it is totalitarian to *require* that one respond, to call one to answer for everything" ("Most Interesting Thing in the World," 8).

181. When I say that becoming-animal is beyond conceptualization or rationalization, I do not mean to place it in the domain of something like a hidden God, or to regard it as a totally blank category. I would say that becoming-animal is beyond conceptualization or rationalization because it escapes common or intelligible sense. But it still has *sense*, or that it *makes sense*, and we can *sense* it out there in the real world, except we do not have the rational or conceptual tools to logically articulate it.

182. Kant, General Remark Upon the Exposition of Aesthetic Reflective Judgment, *Critique of Judgment*, 128–29. Subsequent references in the essay proper to this edition of *The Critique of the Judgment* will be indicated by section number followed by page numbers in square brackets.

183. See Kant's preface to the 1790 first edition of *The Critique of Judgment*, 5; and the introduction, 36.

184. *The Critique of Judgment* §23 [90–91]. According to Kant, the formlessness of sublime things gives us a sensation of "negative pleasure" (§23 [91]) or "displeasure" (§27 [108]). Perhaps that is the pain of the sensation of becoming-animal that critics experience when they stand before it, not knowing how to conceptualize it within their political projects.

185. See my note 176 on what I mean by "immanent response."

186. General Remark on the Exposition of Aesthetic Reflective Judgment, *The Critique of Judgment*, 124.

187. See also General Remark on the First Section of the Analytic, 89.

188. On the importance of art in the philosophy and/or political thought of Deleuze and Guattari, see, for example, De Bloois et al., *Discern(e)ment*; Zepke, *Art as Abstract Machine*; O'Sullivan, *Art Encounters Deleuze and Guattari*; and Bogue, *Deleuze's Way*.

189. Deleuze and Guattari, *Qu'est-ce que la philosophie?*, 158.

190. In this case, aesthetic endeavors imminently face a similar fate as the *logos*-based radical politics of the "multitude" or the "common," where it is only a matter of time when the State captures these modes of expressions and neutralizes their radical political force. On the State appropriation of the cinematic arts, see Deleuze's *Cinéma 2*, 282.

191. "Ambient awareness" is a term social scientists have recently used to describe the phenomenon where a person claims to be able to sense the mood or feelings of another whom he or she is connected with via virtual- or tele-technology. I am borrowing the term here to articulate the sensitivity to surrounding elements or matter existing in a virtual state in the Bergsonian/ Deleuzian sense, which is to say, things that really exist but do not yet or do not need to assume a physical, concrete, actual form.

192. See Deleuze and Guattari, *Qu'est-ce que la philosophie?*, 161–62.

193. See note above.

194. See Deleuze, "Le Simulacre et philosophie antique," in *Logiques du sens*, 279, 298. It is at this point where one may note another difference between the sublime experience of Deleuze and Guattari's becoming-animal and that of Kantian aesthetics. Deleuze and Guattari maintain the unconceptualizable or unknowable sublime *out there*, in nature, while Kant will eventually give it an anthropomorphic and anthropocentric reduction by saying that "sublimity should, in strictness, be attributed merely to the attitude of thought" (*The Critique of Judgment* §30 [134]).

195. Deleuze and Guattari, *Qu'est-ce que la philosophie?*, 164–65. At this point, one may question the focus on the animal side of things in becoming-animal: what about becoming-vegetable, becoming-mineral, and becoming-woman? Thacker has even claimed that "becoming-animal has nothing to do with animals per se"

("Swarming," 172). That may be true to a certain extent. Deleuze and Guattari in *Mille plateaux* have at times also gravitated toward becoming-woman as the most critical term in becoming (*MP*, 338–40/ *TP*, 276–77). Yet, there are instances where animals seem to be of equal, critical significance for becoming as becoming-woman. Before turning to becoming-woman, they would in fact have already stated that "becoming can and *should be* [my emphases] qualified as becoming-animal [...]" (*MP*, 291/ *TP*, 238). It would also be becoming-animal that Deleuze would turn to when speaking about the sensation or affect of paintings in *Francis Bacon*, or about philosophy, as is the case in an interview in *Pourparlers*, where Deleuze associates the philosophical task of concept-creation with becoming-animal *first* before linking it to rhizomes. In that same interview, Deleuze goes as far to say too that becoming-animal is not so distinct from "relations with the animal" (*Pourparlers*, 197). The passage from *Mille plateaux* quoted earlier in the main text on *affect* as that which motivates becoming-animal has also shown that Deleuze and Guattari's preferred references are specifically animals: we scrape like "a rodent" or gaze with the yellow eyes of "a feline." And since the question of politics is at the center here, I recall the quote from Deleuze and Guattari's *Kakfa* and highlight that politics for Deleuze and Guattari proceeds via becoming-animal more than other becomings. In that quote, specific animals are again named: "a beetle," "a dog," "an ape." Thacker's caution about taking these animals as particularly specific is heeded, nonetheless, since Deleuze and Guattari will say that "every animal is fundamentally a band, a pack" (*MP*, 292/ *TP*, 239). The point might be about the multiplicity of a pack or a band, but I would argue that that multiplicity is invoked, if not is possible, only by passing through specific animals.

196. Deleuze and Guattari, *Qu'est-ce que la philosophie?*, 162.

197. Deleuze would say likewise of philosophical literature too. As in the essay "La Littérature et la vie" (in *Critique et clinique*) or in his interview with Claire Parnet in *Dialogues*, he would argue that if philosophical literature engages itself with politics, it would only be a militant commitment to liberate life where it is captured, striated, restricted, or delimited.

198. May, "Politics of Life in the Thought of Gilles Deleuze," 25.

199. Ibid., 28.

200. Deleuze and Guattari, *Qu'est-ce que la philosophie?*, 162.

201. Ibid.

202. I argue that there is nothing bourgeois or idealistic about the notion of life free(d) from politics. It is not an idle sitting back that lets political struggles be fought by others. In fact, as I have tried to demonstrate so far, a certain political battle would have already been fought along the trajectory of becoming-animal. The question of a life free(d) from politics concerns the aftermath of such a battle. Rather than being sucked into the temptation to extend or even reify one's political commitment into something of an eternal war, one must always keep in mind that there is life outside

all ideological struggles. Deleuze has in fact warned us of the danger of a life wholly absorbed by one's own politics, of not knowing how to depart from our politics: the danger of creating a personal "black hole" of "micro-fascisms," where "each sinks deeper [*s'enfonce*] in his black hole and becomes dangerous in that hole, dispensing an assurance about his case, his role and his mission, which is even more disturbing" (Deleuze and Parnet, *Dialogues*, 167).

203. Deleuze, "L'Immanence," 361. See also Colebrook, who writes, "Rather than turning back to life, [becoming-animal] is the course away from various processes of social organization toward the confrontation of the machine of the socius as such that is at once the trajectory of capitalism *and* the goal of Deleuze and Guattari's project" (*Deleuze and the Meaning of Life*, 152).

204. Philippe Mengue will argue against any politics of becoming-imperceptible, which can be considered the virtual in the Deleuzo-Guattarian sense. According to Mengue, what is virtual or what is not grounded in actuality only "misses the central and proper object of politics" ("People and Fabulation," 230). For Mengue, then, "Politics has to deal with a people that is other than virtual, potential or yet to come. A people that fears for its safety, that has borders to defend, that hopes to improve its well-being, a people that is territorialized, such a people is the proper object of politics" (231). Given Mengue's resistance to what can become-imperceptible, it is not surprising that becoming-animal barely counts in his study of Deleuzo-Guattarian politics.

205. This is in contrast to the highly militarized post-9/11 world, where the American State war machine is prepared to take out anything in the world at all cost, to obliterate the slightest sign of terror. It has put in place space-based imaging machines in communication with unmanned combat vehicles to identify and eliminate such signs. It has built stores of thermobaric armament that can hit subterranean bunkers, making sure that no life or living condition is possible in the depths of the earth. In 2005, Donald Rumsfeld, then US defense secretary, had even said that earth-penetrating nukes made all the sense in the world. In short, for the perfectibility of global security, it can be said that the militarized world is prepared to take the world out as its logical conclusion. This apocalyptic horizon had already been foreseen by Paul Virilio. According to Virilio, the perspective of militarized logic is that "everything just has to be uninhabitable. That way there's no more problem" (*Crepuscular Dawn*, 173). In a previous note, I have noted that the Obama administration, despite its promise of a radical change from the militant Bush administration, remains within a political worldview predicated on a post-9/11 sensitivity and therefore has not seen to any real deceleration of the militarization of the world.

206. Deleuze, *Spinoza*, 70.

207. The "transversal" may be said to be another form of *walking away*. As I have tried to suggest in the earlier section on *voyous* and Bartleby, this does not

necessarily entail the absolute renunciation of one's cause or objective. It might involve a change of strategies, when previous or existing ones become potentially nihilistic. The objective might change too, but that is because another trajectory toward different ends can negotiate with the former objective in better ways, or even surpass its limits.

5. *CLINAMEN,* OR THE AUTO-REJECT FOR "POSTHUMAN" FUTURES

1. After cyborgs, Haraway has also addressed the questions of animals, especially "companion animals [. . .] [like] horses, dogs, cats, or a range of other beings willing to make the leap to the biosociality of service dogs, family members, or team members in cross-species sports" (*Companion Species Manifesto,* 14.) I am suspicious, however, of Haraway's move to render animals as "companions," as members of human families, or else beings that serve humans (albeit not in any slavelike fashion, as Haraway would clarify). To me, such a move still remains within the order of the desire of the human to appropriate or domesticate the nonhuman other within his or her sphere of possession, to delimit the nonhuman other as something to call his or her own. Deleuze and Guattari have already warned us too that such a move only reduces animals to "individuated animals, sentimental and familial/ familiar [*familiers familiaux*] animals, and Oedipal animals of little histories [*petit histoire*]: 'my' cat, 'my' dog. All these invite and lead us to regress to a narcissistic contemplation, and psychoanalysis only understands these animals to better discover under them the image of a father, a mother, a little brother [. . .]" (*Mille plateaux,* 294).

2. Luhmann, "On the Concept of 'Subject' and 'Action,'" xlii, xl, xxxix.

3. Luhmann, *Social Systems,* xl. I note here too that we have seen this problem of the *subject* before, and it is in Sartre's *L'Être et le néant.* Sartre there will speak of the caress of a (male) subject, thanks to which, the caressed (female) body will assume the status of a (subjective) *being.*

4. Braidotti, *Posthuman,* 26.

5. Ibid., 86.

6. Ibid., 81.

7. Ibid., 26, 49.

8. Ibid., 49.

9. Ibid., 9.

10. I recall once again that a chapter of Wolfe's book bears the title "Learning from Temple Grandin: Animal Studies, Disability Studies, and Who Comes After the Subject" (in *What Is Posthumanism?*). Braidotti, for her part, refusing to think a figure of thought other than the *subject,* decidedly modifies the question of "who comes after the subject" to "what comes after the anthropocentric subject" (*Posthuman,* 58).

11. See Ivan Callus and Stefan Herbrechter's introduction, "Posthuman Subjectivities, or, Coming after the Subject . . . ". In their *Critical Posthumanism*, they give a further elucidation of the close link between "posthumanism" and "poststructuralism," and stress the import of "poststructuralism" in the form of the Derridean thesis on the (linguistic, or rhetorical, according to Callus and Herbrechter) reiterability of all things for their "critical posthumanism." In any case, the "poststructuralist" critique of the human *subject* is not missing in Callus and Herbrechter's "posthumanism," and neither is the question of the *reject*. With regard to the latter, they seek to think the "remainder" (*Critical Posthumanism*, 1) of "posthumanism," that is, a "posthuman" category that is left aside or left behind, which is not only "unthinkable" but unacceptably fatuous: "a posthumanism without technology" (3). This "posthumanism without technology" is surely in contradistinction to Wolfe's "posthumanism," which sees an intimate link with Luhmann's highly technological systems theory. Nonetheless, it shares with Wolfe's "posthumanism" the critique that puts in place "a negation of everything inherent to the potential of the human" (8).

12. While Braidotti also acknowledges her intellectual debt to "poststructuralist" thinkers such as Foucault, Deleuze, and Irigaray in her "posthuman" theory, especially in her development of notions such as nomadism, becoming, and the anomalous, and in her critique of the male *subject* indifferent to his ecological environment and nonsame others, she certainly takes distances from the "linguistic turn" of "poststructuralism," and from the latter's project to critique or deconstruct the *subject*. I believe that Braidotti's sympathy for the *subject* has its intellectual debt to Irigaray's philosophy, which calls for the articulation of a female *subject* in contradistinction to her male counterpart. I have shown how Irigaray's faith in the *subject* can be problematic in the earlier chapter on friendship, love, and community.

13. See again Callus and Herbrechter, "Posthuman Subjectivities, or, Coming after the Subject . . . "

14. Callus and Herbrechter's critical take on the apparent inheritance of "poststructuralism" by "posthumanism" can be found in "Posthuman Subjectivities, or, Coming after the Subject . . . "

15. Callus and Herbrechter, *Critical Posthumanism*, 1.

16. Braidotti, *Posthuman*, 11.

17. See especially Pearson, *Viroid Life*, 2

18. Braidotti, *Posthuman*, 89, 82, emphasis mine.

19. See note 1 to this chapter. This disregard is rather ironic, because Braidotti claims to be faithful to Deleuze's philosophy. This is not the first instance of Braidotti deviating from Deleuze's thought. As I have mentioned in another note to the Introduction of this present work, Braidotti's keeping with the term *subject* in her work in general, which would include her quest to inscribe a new, "posthuman"

subject, runs counter to Deleuze's philosophical endeavor to do without the *sub-ject*. Braidotti's take on becoming-animal in *The Posthuman* is also not true to Deleuze and Guattari's conceptualization. According to Braidotti, becoming-animal can aid "posthumanism" "to see the inter-*relation* human/ animal as constitutive of the identity of *each*" (*Posthuman*, 79). As I have tried to elucidate in the preceding chapter, becoming-animal according to Deleuze and Guattari does not have its sights on any identity-construction or serve any process of self-identification. Instead, it looks toward a becoming-imperceptible, where there is no longer any question or concern for identity. Braidotti's take on becoming-imperceptible constitutes yet another misreading of Deleuze. She reads it as one form of death, and celebrates it as "radical empirical immanence" that every "posthuman subject" shares, and therefore constitutes "another form of interconnectedness" (*Posthuman*, 136, 137). To my understanding, Deleuze and Guattari do not attach so much the notion of death to becoming-imperceptible, not to mention that it is life, and not death, that Deleuze advocates, at least philosophically.

20. Braidotti, *Posthuman*, 52.

21. Ibid., 82.

22. Ibid., 37. Braidotti's "posthumanism" in this case seems to echo Habermas's thought of the "postsecular," which, as seen in the chapter on the "postsecular," appears to seek understanding only by those who share human language.

23. Ibid., 53.

24. The question of secrets is certainly at stake here too. As noted in the preceding chapter on politics, for Derrida, there is no democracy without secrecy, be it State secrets or the secrets the individual reserves in and for him- or herself from the State. The demand for total disclosure of all secrets would only see to the institutionalization of a totalitarian state. The *auto-reject* then, which is the recognition, beginning from or with the self, that it has no right to demand the disclosure of the other, can make a critical intervention against the degenerative slide into a totalitarian manner of being-with others.

25. To reestablish the link between "posthumanism" and the Derridean strand of "poststructuralism" to which Callus and Herbrechter are faithful, I note that Derrida, in reflecting on the "Whither Marxism?" conference where he delivered the lecture that would eventually evolve into *Spectres de Marx*, also hears in the word "whither" a "withering away" ("Deconstruction of Actuality," in *Negotiations*, 109).

26. Braidotti, *Posthuman*, 50, my emphasis.

27. Ibid., 53. One can also add here that Braidotti's fidelity to the *subject* sees to the running aground of her declared allegiance to Foucault's thought. Braidotti clearly does not follow Foucault's lesson on the *subject* or *subject*-formation as the capture of individual beings within knowledge or discourse systems and technologies, such that every movement, location, behavior, and even thought of those

individuals are controllable or manageable by the apparatuses that govern them. And if Braidotti is critical of the biopolitical determination of life and death, the grounding of her "posthumanism" on a *subject*, which is also a "knowing subject" (*Posthuman*, 11), unconsciously reproduces the biopolitical anxiety to render even death knowable. There is nothing of a surprise, or an event, in the sense of something unknowable in advance, in death for the "posthuman subject": "Death is the becoming-imperceptible of the posthuman subject and as such it is part of the cycles of becoming, yet another form of interconnectedness, a vital relationship that links one with other, multiple forces" (*Posthuman*, 137). I have highlighted how this passage is problematic in relation to Deleuze's philosophy in note 19.

28. Ibid., 42.

29. On one system's rejection of another, see Luhmann, *Social Systems*, 27.

30. Ibid., 26. I say paradoxical, because the more sophisticated complexity that was generated to resolve existing complexities will only pose a greater complexity for other systems, which will itself generate a further complexity to negotiate with the new complexity, and so on. In other words, there is no real reduction of complexity in Luhmann's theory.

31. Ibid., 18.

32. I do not mean any negative or nihilistic sense of devolution here, however. Instead, I follow Nancy's suggestion that there is a close link between devolution and the perpetuation of the world, if not *worlding*: "Devolution is attribution, sharing [*le partage*], destination, contractual signings [*la passation*], transfer by progression [*déroulement*] (*devolvere*), unfolding, and disentangling [*désintrication*]. World, fragment: being devolved" (*Le Sens du monde*, 203).

The question of letting things devolve is also a question that I would pose to Henri Atlan (and also to Braidotti). Atlan speaks of an "auto-organization" that manifests itself through the emergence of complex structures and which functions within a system, or when systems encounter one another. It can be said that Atlan's "auto-organization" is without (human and/ or divine) *subject*, since it occurs "outside of all human organized intervention [*intervention planificatrice humaine*]" and "without [a] central generator [*générateur central*] organizing 'from above' [*d'en haut*] the behavior of individuals" (*Le Vivant post-génomique*, 8, 9, my translation). However, Atlan is also too quick to affirm an operativity for this "auto-organization." While speaking of the "hazardous perturbations" [*perturbations aléatoires*] between aspects of a system that bring about "disorganization," he would quickly add that they can also be sources "of reorganization at a level of greater complexity" (*Le Vivant post-génomique*, 33). Why not stay with "disorganization" a little more, and see what kind of structures emerge precisely from this "disorganization," and which might bear no semblance to any "reorganization"? It seems that we have not made much headway with Artaud's and/or Deleuze and Guattari's "body without organs," which is not a negation of the body, but a way to think of a body that does not demand that its organs serve some operative, organizational function.

33. Luhmann, *Social Systems*, 26.

34. Ibid., 32.

35. Ibid., 9, my emphases.

36. Derrida, *Foi et savoir*, §37: 67.

37. Derrida also suggests that the risk of autoimmunity in fact paves the way toward what he calls "unconditional hospitality" (see Derrida, "Autoimmunity," 133).

38. Ibid., 95.

39. Ibid., 109.

40. Ibid.

41. Ibid., 94.

42. Hird, *Origins of Sociable Life*, 36, 26.

43. See Wolfe-Simon et al., "Bacterium that Can Grow."At the time of completing this current work, two other articles refuting Wolfe-Simon's work have been published. See Reaves et al., "Absence of Detectable Arsenate"; Erb et al., "GFAJ-1 Is an Arsenate-Resistant." Based on the respective arguments laid out by these three reports, and not on my too limited scientific knowledge, I do think that the later two reports do not absolutely refute Wolfe-Simon's claim, that is, there remains aspects of Wolfe-Simon's findings that can counterargue the refutations. In any case, it remains to be seen what definitively turns up in this debate. Meanwhile, I do think that Wolfe-Simon's report nonetheless offers something interesting to think about autoimmunity and *auto-rejection*, and hence my reference to her work here.

44. See Overbye, "Microbe Finds Arsenic Tasty."

45. Felisa Wolfe-Simon, quoted in Overbye, "Microbe Finds Arsenic Tasty."

46. Hird, *Origins of Sociable Life*, 1.

47. Deleuze and Guattari, *Mille plateaux*, 294. See also p. 297.

48. Hird, *Origins of Sociable Life*, 56.

49. Given the possibility that "bacterial activities (bacterial doing) differentially sustain the greater survival of some organisms over others" (Hird, *Origins of Sociable Life*, 56), can we guarantee that we humans, all too human, restrain our desire to be those "some organisms," and that in our bid to be the latter, there will be no expedient appropriation and cultivation of bacterial life?

50. Ibid., 26.

51. See Wolfe, *Before the Law*.

52. Ibid., 10.

53. Shukin, *Animal Capital*, 42.

54. Ibid., 3.

55. Weil, *Thinking Animals*, 16.

56. Ibid., 17.

57. Ibid., 20.

58. Ibid., 27, 13.

59. I note here that there is even a reinvestment in *clinamen* in French academia today, arriving by way of a renewed interest in the work of Lucretius especially. The work of Élisabeth de Fontenay in promoting the latter's philosophy is significant. But see also the collection of essays in *La Renaissance de Lucrèce*. I also point to Neyrat's *Clinamen*.

60. Serres, *La Naissance de la physique*, 165, my translation.

61. Ibid., 165.

62. Ibid., 114.

63. See her introduction to Lucrèce, *De la nature*. On this note, I would express some caution in response to Callus and Herbrechter's "posthumanism without technology," which is heavily inclined toward rhetoric, as they acknowledge. Rhetoric, however, is very much a characteristic of the human, if not all too human. Geoffrey Bennington, in his article "Political Animals" in the special issue on "Negative Politics" of *diacritics*, has noted that rhetoric is in fact the humanization of *logos*, a process that would lead to the denial of *logos* to animals. My reservation here is that the emphasis on rhetoric in Callus and Herbrechter's posthumanism might lead to the rejection of animals, marginalizing animals once again as *reject*-others.

64. See Deleuze, "Simulacre et philosophie antique," in *Logique du sens*, 292–324.

65. See Nancy, ♪♪♪♪♪♪♪ in *La Démocratie à venir: Autour de Jacques Derrida*, 342.

66. Ibid., 346. Even though Nancy does not specifically speak of bacterial activity, he does nonetheless speak of "contagion."

67. Ibid., 346.

68. Ibid., 347. Or, as Nancy says elsewhere, *clinamen* "would not be chance [*le hasard*] [. . .] but the free opening [*le libre ouverture*] of the 'there is' [*il y a*] in general—which is never exactly general but always in the order of the 'each time' [*à chaque fois*]" (*L'Expérience de la liberté*, 202).

69. In this respect, the thought of *clinamen* resonates with Hird's "microontology," in the sense that the latter does away with the myth of a pure corporeal entity evacuated of all foreign elements, but situates the human body back into a bacterial milieu that already exists within and without that same body. It is also not distant from the project on deconstructing "bodily integrity," which has taken the form of a special issue of *Body & Society* (16[3] [2010]). Building on Aryn Martin's intervention in that issue on the nationalistic and frontier rhetoric surrounding "microchimersim," which is a phenomenon where fetal cells are found in the mother long after pregnancy, challenging therefore the position that a body's immune-system always destroys foreign cells, Lisa Blackman, in her introduction to the issue, will

say: "Microchimerism places the body back within its milieu, and it might be more aptly described as enacting human bodies as the very paradoxical beings that we are; rather than existing as bounded, autonomous subjects, we coexist in shared ecologies" ("Bodily Integrity," 4). In a supplemental introduction, Margrit Shildrick will add, "the body—my human body—is never self-complete and bounded against otherness, but is irreducibly caught up in a web of constitutive connections that disturb the very idea of human being" ("Some Reflections," 13). However, in sum, what I find still lacking in "microontology" and the deconstruction of "bodily integrity" is that aspect of *auto-rejection*, in the sense by which a body detaches part(s) of itself. To think the latter, *clinamen* seems to me a more adequate trajectory of thought.

70. According to Aryn Martin, "microchimersim," which proves that a body can be hospitable to a foreign body for a duration longer than expected, or that a foreign cell can live within another body without affecting it negatively, can help undo the prejudices typically associated with frontier-crossing especially by illegal immigrants. As Martin argues, "Microchimerism entails that borders of bodies (like nations) are blurry and change over time, and that individuals (like nations) are not discrete but constitutively intermingled" ("Microchimerism in the Mother(land)," 26).

On another note, and to return to the potential politics of *clinamen*, Neyrat has argued that *clinamen*, especially its aspect of (self-)subtraction, (self-)detachment, *auto-rejection*, or what Neyrat calls "dis-integration" [*dés-intégration*], can break the totalizing operation of capital to render everything become-fluid like capital, the operation of capital to hold everything within a controlled, absolute, and hence paradoxically immobile "integral flux" [*flux intégral*] (see *Clinamen*). "Dis-integration" in this sense is similar to a "withering" "posthumanism," which leaves bodies free to assemble with other bodies *and* to disassemble from existing assemblages, as they are wont to do naturally, rather than to order them to keep existing relations together superficially.

71. Hayles, *How We Became Posthuman*, 290.

72. Ibid., 5.

73. Ibid.

74. Ibid., 3.

75. Ibid., 290.

76. Ibid., 12.

77. Ibid., 5. I would like to quickly note here that one does not need to revert to the *subject* in order to keep in mind the body. As I have suggested above, thinking the *reject*, especially the *auto-reject* that is mindful of *clinamen*, is no less engaged with the question of the body.

78. The question of suturing in Hayles becomes more explicit in her reading of Shelley Jackson's *Patchwork Girl* in Hayle's *My Mother Was a Computer*.

79. Murray, *Digital Baroque*, 6.

80. See especially chapter 2 of Deleuze, *Le Pli*.

81. See chapter 1 of *Le Pli*.

82. Murray, *Digital Baroque*, 5.

83. Wolfe, *What Is Posthumanism?*, xv, xix.

6. CONCLUSION: INCOMPOSSIBILITY, BEING-IN-COMMON, ABANDONMENT, AND THE AUTO-REJECT

1. Deleuze, *Le Pli*, 188. See especially the final chapter of *Le Pli* on "the new harmony." I leave aside all specific discussions of the Baroque here. For that, I refer to Gregg Lambert's *On the (New) Baroque*, particularly the book's coda, where Lambert engages with "the new harmony."

2. Nancy, "Cosmos basileus," in *La Création*, 173, my translation with slight modifications.

3. Ibid., 175.

4. I note here that the *uncommon* is also what Judith Butler, in another context, would like to bring to the foreground, rather than any thought of the common. In a discussion that bears on the possibility of a "postsecular" coexistence of faith and knowledge, that is, the coexistence of secularity and the emergences of local religions, Butler says, "I'm not so much interested in the common." She continues, "I think maybe it's the uncommon, or what is not part of the common or what can never truly become common, which establishes really specific differences, and which also becomes the basis of an ethical relation that establishes alterity rather than the common as the basis of ethicality" (*Power of Religion*, 113).

5. The term "economies of abandonment" is Elizabeth Povinelli's, and it is taken up by Butler and Athanasiou in *Dispossession*, 31.

6. Butler and Athanasiou, *Dispossession*, 29. Bertrand Ogilvie also reminds us the insidious and terrible consequences if we allow such rendering of certain peoples as disposable beings by capital to go uncheck. He argues that the Nazi's extermination of Jews is "the development of an internal contradiction, a process of rejection, [...] the consequences of capitalism by capitalism itself" (*L'Homme jetable*, 110). In reading Antelme's *L'Espèce humaine*, Blanchot sees in the victim of Nazi concentration camps "the fact of being dispossessed [*être dépossédé*]" ("L'In-destructible," in *L'Entretien infini*, 197).

7. Butler and Athanasiou, *Dispossession*, 197, 196.

8. Deleuze, *Le Pli*, 81.

9. Ibid., 182.

10. Ibid., 81.

11. Ibid., 92, trans. modified.

12. See Nancy, *L'Impératif catégorique*, 20.

13. Derrida, "'Il faut bien manger,'" in *Points de suspension*, 270.

14. For this, see especially Derrida's "Préjugés, devant la loi," in Derrida, Descombes, et al., *La Faculté de juger*, 87–139 ; and Derrida, *Force de loi* .

15. Nancy, *L'Impératif catégorique*, 150.

16. Ibid., 25.

17. Ibid., 28.

18. Here, I refer readers to the collection of essays on law and justice in Nancy in *Jean-Luc Nancy: Justice, Legality and World*.

19. Nancy, "Dies Irae," in *La Faculté de juger*, 44.

20. Nancy, *L'Expérience de la liberté*, 14. Not unrelated to what has been said in the main text, Nancy here also says that freedom "takes place in the exposition of *being* in its own singularity that is always decidable anew, always newly surprised by its decision" (188).

21. Nancy, "Cosmos basileus," 173, 174.

22. Ibid., 174, 178, 175. In a more recent text, *nomos* and the "law of the law" seem to have found a new iteration in the name of "struction," which is that which precedes and exceeds all construction, destruction, and deconstruction. It is even "struction" that allow, if not in-struct, them to take place. "Struction," for Nancy, would be "the non-coordinated simultaneity of things and beings, the contingence of their co-belonging, the dispersion of profusions of appearances [*aspects*], species, forces, forms, tensions, and intentions (instincts, drives, projects, *élans*). In this profusion, no particular order is worthier than others [. . .]"; or, more simply, it would be "the state of the 'with' devoid of the value of partition [*partage*], involving [*mettant en jeu*] only the simple contiguity with its contingence" ("De la struction," in *Dans quels mondes vivons-nous ?*, 90, my translation).

23. Deleuze and Guattari, *Mille plateaux*, 459/ *A Thousand Plateaus*, 370–71, trans. modified. The work of Schmitt on *nomos* in *The Nomos of the Earth in the International Law of the Jus Publicum Europaeum* is no doubt important, but this is not the space to compare Schmitt's work with those of Nancy and Deleuze and Guattari.

24. Deleuze and Guattari, *Mille plateaux*, 459–60/ *A Thousand Plateaus*, 371, trans. modified.

25. That is also why Deleuze and Guattari regard *nomos* as distinct from law. See Deleuze and Guattari, *Mille plateaux*, 459.

26. Nancy, *L'Impératif catégorique*, 16.

27. Ibid., 22, 18.

28. Nancy, "Dies Irae," in *La Faculté de juger*, 40.

29. Nancy, *L'Impératif catégorique*, 20.

30. Nancy, "Dies Irae," in *La Faculté de juger*, 45. I note here that the question of justice is all at stake in Nancy's consideration of "law of the law," which, stated as *without force*, marks perhaps the difference with Derrida's thinking of justice.

Derrida has said, "I want [. . .] to insist on reserving the possibility of a justice, even a law [*loi*], which not only exceeds or contradicts right [*le droit*] but also perhaps has no relation with right," which Derrida observes as "always an authorized force, a force that justifies itself or is justified in its application" (*Force de loi*, 17). However, in following Kant to a certain extent in understanding that there is no effective law [which can be *loi* or *droit*] and/ or justice without force, Derrida will qualify his statement to say that his notion of justice, which is also a justice "to-come" (60), if not an "infinite justice always addressed to singularities, to the singularity of the other" (44), would, with regard to right [*droit*], nonetheless "entertain [. . .] a relation so strange that it can demand for it as well as to exclude it" (17).

31. Nancy, *L'Impératif catégorique*, 20.

32. Ibid.

33. Nancy, "Dies Irae," in *La Faculté de juger*, 48.

34. Nancy, *L'Expérience de la liberté*, 132. In this text, Nancy would even go as far to say that as long as we keep in mind the "law of the law," "there is no need for us to think of new laws" (206). However, Nancy is well aware that reality is such that we ignore the "law of the law." As Nancy suggests, for example in "Dies Irae," where he states that "all autonomous representation, issued from its autonomy, lacks the faculty of desire from which a series of events must begin" (29), the self-representing *subject* that claims to be autonomous belies that disregard for the "law of the law." That is why we still "have to decide on the contents and the norms of the [freedom]. We have to decide on laws, exceptions, cases, and negotiations" (*L'Expérience de la liberté*, 206).

35. Nancy, *La Possibilité d'un monde*, 117.

36. Nancy, *L'Impératif catégorique*, 150. I acknowledge here that there is the interesting question regarding which of our senses guide Nancy's notion of respect. Even though, as evident from this very quote from Nancy, sight or vision is not the critical sense for respect, Nancy later would still elucidate the declaration or constative "*ecce homo*," which he argues to be sufficient to demand respect, in terms of "here." Nancy deploys the French "voici" at this point, and rereads it as "vois ici" or "look here" (151), returning us to the question of vision or sight, therefore. One could argue, however, that there is already a shift to the sense of hearing, since any respect for the constative "*ecce homo*" would need to be heard first, and this would play to Nancy's inclination toward listening in *À l'écoute*. Yet, Nancy would deploy the term *esteem*, which he would say in *La Possibilité d'un monde* and *L'Équivalence des catastrophes* to involve not just the sense of sight and hearing, but also of smell, and of touch, in its sensitivity to moods, atmospheres, and corporeal and temporal rhythms. To prevent any privileging of a single sense, as Derrida warns in *Le Toucher, Jean-Luc Nancy*, I would prefer to follow Nancy in *Corpus* to say that respect or consideration of other existents takes place via that "one gram of

thought" (101) that every body emits and transmits to other bodies via *clinamen*, which is a way of sensing the world that goes beyond any singular operation of sight, hearing, taste, smell, or even touch.

On another note: supposing that the world of incompossibility is a Baroque world, I keep in mind here that Baroque perception, as noted at the end of the previous chapter, is not determined or conditioned by subjective vision but is constituted by an entity other than the *subject* and which subsequently allows the *subject* to form itself as such.

37. Nancy, *L'Impératif catégorique*, 150.

38. Ibid.

39. Nancy, "Cosmos basileus," 176–77.

40. See Nancy, *L'Équivalence des catastrophes*, 65–66. That is perhaps why Nancy will also say, "respect is the very alteration of the position and the structure of the subject" (*L'Impératif catégorique*, 25).

41. Butler and Athanasiou put this subjective abandonment in terms of dispossession. See especially the first two chapters of their *Dispossession*.

42. Nancy, *L'Impératif catégorique*, 142.

43. Ibid., 141.

44. Ibid.

45. Ibid., 144.

46. See especially the chapter "Irreparable" and the appendix in Agamben's *Coming Community*. It would also be interesting to compare this to Agamben's *Highest Poverty*, but this is not the space to do so, and hence I leave it for another occasion.

47. Nancy, *L'Impératif catégorique*, 142.

48. Ibid.

49. Ibid., 145.

50. Ibid., 144, 148. And as if to ensure that abandonment is void of all subjectivity or subjective control, Nancy will also add that it is always impossible "to fixate abandonment and to impute [*installer*] to it what renews and revives it" (148).

51. "Décision d'existence," in *Pensée finie*, 143. In this same essay, Nancy would also argue that such an opening "is not an auto-opening but an onto-opening" (135).

52. Nancy, *L'Impératif catégorique*, 144.

53. On abandonment and its relation to incommensurability, see Nancy, *L'Impératif catégorique*, 29.

54. See ibid., 149–50.

55. Ibid., 144.

56. On the question of forgetfulness and abandonment, see ibid., 144–45.

57. Nancy, *L'Expérience de la liberté*, 16.

58. Nancy, *L'Impératif catégorique*, 145.

59. On this point, see especially Nancy, *La Création du monde;* and also Nancy, *L'Impératif catégorique*, 28.

60. See Nancy's "L'Insacrifiable" (in *Une Pensée finie*, 65–106). Very briefly, Nancy there argues that "existence cannot be sacrificed [*l'existence n'est pas sacrifiable*]," because existence "is already, by itself, not sacrificed, but offered, to the world" (101). There is but "the event of existence," whose *there is* [*il y a*] "means that they is *none other* [*rien d'autre*]," which in turn means that there was nothing to sacrifice, or nothing of sacrifice, for that existence, and there is nothing other for which that existence must be sacrificed (103).

61. According to Nancy, "In respecting the law [of the law], abandonment respects itself [. . .]" (*L'Impératif catégorique*, 150).

62. At the time of writing this Conclusion, Nancy tells me that he is working on a book titled *Abandoned Community* [*La Communuaté abandonnée*]. Regrettably, that book, not even its draft, does not arrive in time for the completion of this present work.

WORKS CITED

Abeysekara, Ananda. *The Politics of Postsecular Religion: Mourning Secular Futures.* New York: Columbia University Press, 2008.

Agamben, Giorgio. "Bataille et le paradoxe de la souveraineté." Italian trans. Dominique Garand. *Liberté* 38(3) (1996): 87–95.

———. *The Coming Community.* Trans. Michael Hardt. Minneapolis and London: University of Minnesota Press, 1991.

———. "Friendship." Trans. Joseph Falsone. *Contretemps* 5 (December 2004): 2–7.

———. *The Highest Poverty: Monastic Rules and Form-of-Life.* Trans. Adam Kotsko. Stanford: Stanford University Press, 2013.

———. *Homo Sacer: Sovereign Power and Bare Life.* Trans. Daniel Holler-Roazen. Stanford: Stanford University Press, 1998.

———. *Means Without End: Notes on Politics.* Trans. Vincenzo Binetti and Cesare Casarino. Minneapolis and London: University of Minnesota Press, 2000.

———. *The Open: Man and Animal.* Trans. Kevin Attell. Stanford: Stanford University Press, 2004.

———. *Potentialities: Collected Essays in Philosophy.* Ed., trans., and intro. Daniel Heller-Roazen. Stanford: Stanford University Press, 1999.

———. *Qu'est-ce que le contemporain?* Italian trans. Maxime Rovere. Paris: Payrot & Rivages, 2008. English edition: *What Is an Apparatus? And Other Essays,* trans. David Kishik and Stefan Pedatella. Stanford: Stanford University Press, 2009.

———. *Remnants of Auschwitz: The Witness and the Archive.* Trans. Daniel Heller-Roazen. New York: Zone, 1999.

———. *State of Exception.* Trans. Kevin Attell. Stanford: Stanford University Press, 2005.

———. *The Time that Remains: A Commentary on the Letter to the Romans.* Trans. Patricia Dailey. Stanford: Stanford University Press, 2005.

———. "We Refugees." Trans. Michael Rocke. *Symposium* 49(2) (summer 1994): 114–19.

Agamben, Giorgio, Alain Badiou, et al. *Démocratie, dans quel état?* Paris: La Fabrique, 2009.

Alexandrova, Alena, Ignaas Devisch, Laurens ten Kate, and Aukje van Rooden, eds. *Re-treating Religion: Deconstructing Christianity with Jean-Luc Nancy.* With a Preamble and Concluding Dialogue by Jean-Luc Nancy. New York: Fordham University Press, 2012.

Améry, Jean. *Jenseits von Schuld und Sühne: Bewältigungsversuche eines Überwältigten.* Berlin: Szczesny Verlag, 1966. Reprint, Stuttgart: Ernst Klett, 1977. English edition: *At the Mind's Limits: Contemplations by a Survivor on Auschwitz and Its Realities,* trans. Sidney Rosenfeld and Stella P. Rosenfeld. Bloomington and Indianapolis: Indiana University Press, 1980.

———. *Radical Humanism: Selected Essays.* Ed. and trans. Sidney Rosenfeld and Stella P. Rosenfeld. Bloomington: Indiana University Press, 1984.

Antelme, Robert. *L'Espèce humaine.* Paris: Gallimard, 1957.

———. *Vengeance?* 1946. Reprinted with a postface by Jean-Luc Nancy. Paris: Hermann, 2010.

Antonioli, Manola, Pierre-Antoine Chardel, and Hervé Regnauld, eds. *Gilles Deleuze, Félix Guattari et le politique.* Paris: Sandre, 2006.

Aristotle. *The Nicomachean Ethics.* Trans. and intro. David Ross. Oxford: Oxford University Press, 1925.

———. *The Politics.* Trans. T. A. Sinclair. London: Penguin, 1981.

Armstrong, Philip. *Reticulations: Jean-Luc Nancy and the Networks of the Political.* Minneapolis: University of Minnesota Press, 2009.

Atlan, Henri. *Le Vivant post-génomique, ou Qu'est-ce que l'auto-organisation?* Paris: Odile Jacob, 2011.

Attridge, Derek, Geoff Bennington, and Robert Young, eds. *Post-structuralism and the Question of History.* Cambridge: Cambridge University Press, 1987.

Badiou, Alain. *De quoi Sarkozy est-il le nom?* Paris: Lignes, 2007.

———. *Deleuze: "la clameur de l'Être."* Paris: Hachette, 1997.

———. *L'Éthique: essai sur la conscience du mal.* Paris: Nous, 2009. English edition: *Ethics: An Essay on the Understanding of Evil,* trans. and intro. Peter Hallward. London and New York: Verso, 2001.

———. *L'Être et l'événement.* Paris: Seuil, 1988.

———. *Logiques des mondes.* Paris: Seuil, 2006.

———. *Petit panthéon portatif.* Paris: Fabrique, 2008.

———. *La Relation énigmatique entre philosophie et politique.* Paris: Germina, 2011.

———. *Le Réveil de l'histoire.* Paris: Lignes, 2011.

———. *Saint Paul: La fondation de l'universalisme.* Paris: Presses Universitaires de

France, 1997. English edition: *Saint Paul: The Foundation of Universalism*, trans. Ray Brassier, Stanford: Stanford University Press, 2003.

———. *Sarkozy: Pire que prévu; Les autres: prévoir le pire*. Paris: Lignes, 2012.

———. *Second manifeste pour la philosophie*. Paris: Fayard, 2009.

———. *Le Siècle*. Paris: Seuil, 2005.

———. *Théorie du sujet*. Paris: Seuil, 1982.

Badiou, Alain, and Nicolas Truong. *Éloge de l'amour*. Paris: Flammarion, 2009.

Badiou, Alain, and Slavoj Žižek. *Philosophy in the Present*. Ed. Peter Engelmann. Trans. Peter Thomas and Alberto Toscano. Cambridge: Polity, 2009.

———, eds. *L'Idée de communisme*. Paris: Lignes, 2010.

Balibar, Étienne. *Citoyen sujet, et autres essais d'anthropologie philosophique*. Paris: Presses Universitaires de France, 2011.

———. *La Crainte des masses: politique et philosophie avant et après Marx*. Paris: Galilée, 1997.

———. *Droit de cité*. Paris: PUF, 2002.

———. *Europe Constitution Frontière*. Paris: Passant, 2005.

———. *Les Frontières de la démocratie*. Paris: La Découverte, 1992.

———. *La Proposition de l'égaliberté: essais politiques 1989–2009*. Paris: PUF, 2010.

———. "Le Structuralisme, la destitution du sujet?" 2001. Available at http://ciepfc. fr/spip.php?article35. Accessed on June 1, 2012.

———. *Violence et civilité: Welleck Library Lectures et autres essais de philosophie politique*. Paris: Galilée, 2010.

Balibar, Étienne, John Rajchman, and Anne Boyman, eds. *French Philosophy Since 1945: Problems, Concepts, Inventions*. Postwar French Thought, Vol. IV. New York and London: The New Press, 2011.

Barrau, Aurélein, and Jean-Luc Nancy. *Dans quels mondes vivons-nous?* Paris: Galilée, 2011.

Bataille, Georges. *L'Expérience intérieure*. Paris: Gallimard, 1943.

———. *La Part maudite*. Paris: Minuit, 1967.

———. *La Souveraineté*. Paris: Ligne, 2012.

Baudrillard, Jean. *Amérique*. Paris: Grasset, 1986.

———. *The Ecstasy of Communication*. Trans. Bernard and Caroline Schutze. Ed. Sylvère Lotringer. New York: Semiotext(e), 1988.

———. *Simulacres et simulation*. Paris: Galilée, 1981.

Bauman, Zygmunt. *Community: Seeking Safety in an Insecure World*. Oxford: Polity, 2001.

———. *Wasted Lives: Modernity and its Outcasts*. Oxford: Polity, 2004.

Bennington, Geoffrey. "Forever Friends." In *Interrupting Derrida*, 110–27. London and New York: Routledge, 2000.

———. "Political Animals." *diacritics* 39(2) (summer 2009): 21–35.

Berkman, Gisèle. *L'Effet Bartleby: Philosophes lecteurs*. Paris: Hermann, 2011.

Berkowitz, Charlotte A. "Paradise Reconsidered: Hélène Cixous and the Bible's Other Voice." *Religion in French Feminist Thought: Critical Perspectives*, ed. Morny Joy, Kathleen O'Grady, and Judith L. Poxon, intro. Luce Irigary, 176–88. London and New York: Routledge, 2003.

Blackman, Lisa. "Bodily Integrity." *Body & Society* 16(3) (2010): 1–9.

Blanchot, Maurice. *L'Amitié*. Paris: Gallimard, 1971.

———. *La Communauté inavouable*. Paris: Minuit, 1983.

———. *L'Entretien infini*. Paris: Gallimard, 1969.

———. *Michel Foucault tel que je l'imagine*. Paris: Fata Morgana, 1986.

———. *Le Pas au-delà*. Paris: Gallimard, 1973.

———. *Pour l'amitié*. Tours: Farrago, 2000.

Blond, Phillip, ed. *Post-Secular Philosophy: Between Philosophy and Theology*. London and New York: Routledge, 1998.

Blyth, Ian, and Susan Sellers. *Hélène Cixous: Live Theory*. New York: Continuum, 2004.

Bogue, Ronald. *Deleuze's Way: Essays on Transverse Ethics and Aesthetics*. Hampshire, UK: Ashgate, 2007.

Bonta, Mark, and John Protevi. *Deleuze and Geophilosophy: A Guide and Glossary*. Edinburgh: Edinburgh University Press, 2004.

Bosteels, Bruno. *Alain Badiou, une trajectoire polémique*. Paris: La fabrique, 2009.

———. *Badiou and Politics*. Durham, NC, and London: Duke University Press, 2011.

Bracher, Mark, Marshall W. Alcorn Jr., et al., eds. *Lacanian Theory of Discourse: Subject, Structure, and Society*. New York and London: New York University Press, 1994.

Braidotti, Rosi. "The Ethics of Becoming-Imperceptible." In *Deleuze and Philosophy*, ed. Constantin V. Boundas, 133–59. Edinburgh: Edinburgh University Press, 2006.

———. *Nomadic Subjects: Embodiment and Sexual Difference in Contemporary Feminist Theory*. 2d edition. New York: Columbia University Press, 2011.

———. *The Posthuman*. Cambridge: Polity, 2013.

Bruns, Gerald. "Becoming-Animal (Some Simple Ways)." *New Literary History* 38 (2007): 703–20.

———. *Maurice Blanchot: The Refusal of Philosophy*. Baltimore, MD: Johns Hopkins University Press, 1997.

Buchanan, Ian, and Nicholas Thoburn. *Deleuze and Politics*. Edinburgh: Edinburgh University Press, 2008.

Butler, Judith. "Afterword: After Loss, What Then?" In *Loss: The Politics of Mourning*, ed. David Eng, David Kazanjian, and Judith Butler, 467–74. Berkeley: University of California Press, 2003.

———. *Precarious Life: The Powers of Mourning and Violence*. London: Verso, 2004.

————. *Subjects of Desire: Hegelian Reflections in Twentieth Century France.* New York: Columbia University Press, 1987.

Butler, Judith, and Athena Athanasiou. *Dispossession: The Performative in the Political.* Cambridge: Polity, 2013.

Butler, Judith, Jürgen Habermas, Charles Taylor, and Cornel West. *The Power of Religion in the Public Sphere.* Ed. and intro. Eduardo Mendieta and Jonathan VanAntwerpen. Afterword by Craig Calhoun. New York: Columbia University Press, 2011.

Cadava, Eduardo, Peter Connor, and Jean-Luc Nancy, eds. *Who Comes After the Subject?* New York and London: Routledge, 1991.

Cahiers Confrontation 20 (winter). "Après le sujet qui vient." Paris: Aubier, 1989

Calarco, Matthew. *Zoographies: The Question of the Animal from Heidegger to Derrida.* New York: Columbia University Press, 2008.

Calarco, Matthew, and Peter Atterton, eds. *Animal Philosophy: Essential Readings in Continental Thought.* London: Continuum, 2004.

Calle-Gruber, Mireille. *Du café à l'éternité.* Paris: Galilée, 2002.

————, ed. *Hélène Cixous: croisées d'une œuvre.* Paris: Galilée, 2000.

Calle-Gruber, Mireille, and Marie Odile Germain, eds. *Genèses Généalogies Genres: Autour de l'œuvre de Hélène Cixous.* Paris: Galilée, 2006.

Callus, Ivan, and Stefan Herbrechter. "Introduction: Posthumanist Subjectivities, or Coming after the Subject . . . " *Subjectivity* 5(3) (2012): 241–64.

Camon, Ferdinando. *Conversations with Primo Levi.* Trans. John Shepley. Marlboro, VT: Marlboro Press, 1989.

Caputo, John D. *On Religion.* London and New York: Routledge, 2001.

————. *The Prayers and Tears of Jacques Derrida: Religion Without Religion.* Bloomington: Indiana University Press, 1997.

————. "Spectral Hermeneutics: On the Weakness of God and the Theology of the Event." In *After the Death of God*, by John D. Caputo and Gianni Vattimo, ed. Jeffrey W. Robbins, afterword by Gabriel Vahanian, 47–88. New York: Columbia University Press, 2007.

Caputo, John D., and Linda Martin Alcoff, eds. *St. Paul Among the Philosophers.* Bloomington: Indiana University Press, 2009.

Carroll, David, ed. and intro. *The States of 'Theory': History, Art, and Critical Discourse.* New York: Columbia University Press, 1990.

Casanova, José. *Public Religions in the Modern World.* Chicago: University of Chicago Press, 1994.

Casarino, Cesare, and Antonio Negri. *In Praise of the Common: A Conversation in Philosophy and Politics.* Minneapolis: University of Minnesota Press, 2008.

Castells, Manuel, ed. *The Network Society: A Cross-Cultural Perspective.* Cheltenham, UK: Edward Elgar, 2004.

————. *The Rise of the Network Society.* 2d ed. Oxford: Blackwell, 1996.

Castells, Manuel, Mireia Fernández-Ardèvol, Jack Linchuan Qin, and Araha Sey. *Mobile Communication and Society: A Cultural Perspective.* Cambridge, MA, and London: MIT Press, 2007.

Cavell, Marcia. *Becoming a Subject: Reflections in Philosophy and Psychoanalysis.* Oxford: Clarendon, 2006.

Caygill, Howard. "The Shared World—Philosophy, Violence, Freedom." In *On Jean-Luc Nancy: The Sense of Philosophy,* ed. Darren Sheppard, Simon Sparks, and Colin Thomas, 19–31. London and New York: Routledge, 1997.

Cheah, Pheng, and Suzanne Guerlac, eds. *Derrida and the Time of the Political.* Durham, NC, and London: Duke University Press, 2009.

Cixous, Hélène. *L'Amour du loup et autres remords.* Paris: Galilée, 2003.

———. "Bathsheba or the Interior Bible." 1993. Reprinted, trans. Catherine A. F. MacGillivray. In *Stigmata: Escaping Texts,* 3–19. London and New York: Routledge, 1998.

———. *Beethoven à jamais ou l'existence de Dieu.* Paris: Des femmes, 1993.

———. "Birds, Women and Writing." In *Animal Philosophy,* ed. Matthew Calarco and Peter Atterton, 167–73. London: Continuum, 2004.

———. "Ce corps étranjuif." In *Judéités: Questions pour Jacques Derrida,* ed. Joseph Cohen and Raphael Zagury-Orly, 11–42. Paris: Galilée, 2003. English edition: "This Stranjew Body," trans. Bettina Bergo and Gabriel Malenfant, in *Judeities: Questions for Jacques Derrida,* ed. Bettina Bergo, Joseph Cohen, and Raphael Zagury-Orly, 52–77. New York: Fordham University Press, 2007.

———. "Le Dernier tableau ou le portrait de Dieu." 1983. Reprinted in *Entre l'écriture.* Paris: Des femmes, 1986.

———. *Entre l'écriture.* Paris: Des femmes, 1986.

———. *Ève s'évade: la Ruine et la Vie.* Paris: Galilée, 2009.

———. *Insister à Jacques Derrida.* Paris: Galilée, 2006.

———. *Le Jour où je n'étais pas là.* Paris: Galilée, 2000.

———. *Messie.* Paris: Des femmes, 1996.

———. *Neutre.* Paris: Grasset, 1972.

———. *Portrait de Jacques Derrida en jeune saint juif.* Paris: Galilée, 2001.

———. *Le Prénom de Dieu.* Paris: Grasset, 1967.

———. "Promised Belief." In *Feminism, Sexuality, and the Return of Religion,* ed. Linda Martín Alcoff and John D. Caputo, 130–59. Bloomington and Indianapolis: Indiana University Press, 2011.

———. *Readings: The Poetics of Blanchot, Joyce, Kafka, Kleist, Lispector, and Tsvetayeva.* Ed., trans., and intro. Verena Andermatt Conley. Minneapolis: University of Minnesota Press, 1991.

———. *Les Rêveries de la femme sauvage.* Paris: Galilée, 2000.

———. "De la scène de l'Inconscient à la scène de l'Histoire: Chemin d'une écriture." In *Hélène Cixous, chemins d'une écriture,* ed. Françoise van Rossum-Guyon and Myriam Diaz-Diocaretz, 15–34. Saint-Denis, France: Presses Universitaires de Vincennes; Amsterdam: Rodopi, 1990. English edition: "From the Scene of the Unconscious to the Scene of History," trans. Deborah W. Carpenter, in *The Future of Literary Theory*, ed. Ralph Cohen, 1–18. New York and London: Routledge, 1989.

———. *Tours promises*. Paris: Galilée, 2004.

———. *Le Vrai jardin*. 1971. Reprinted, Paris: Des femmes, 1998.

———. "Without End, No, State of Drawingness, No, Rather: The Executioner's Taking Off." Trans. Catherine A. F. MacGillivray. In *Stigmata: Escaping Texts*, 20–32. London and New York: Routledge, 1998.

Cixous, Hélène, and Catherine Clément. *La Jeune née*. Paris: Union générale, 1975.

Cixous, Hélène, and Jacques Derrida. *Voiles*. Paris: Galilée, 1998.

Clément, Catherine. *La Syncope: philosophie du ravissement*. Paris: Grasset, 1990. English edition: *Syncope: The Philosophy of Rapture*, foreword Verena Andermatt Conley, trans. Sally O'Driscoll and Deidre M Mahoney. Minneapolis: University of Minnesota Press, 1994.

Cohen, Adam. "One Friend Facebook Hasn't Made Yet: Privacy Rights." *New York Times*. February 18, 2008.

Cohen-Safir, Claude. "La Serpente et l'or: bible et contre-bible dans l'œuvre d'Hélène Cixous." In *Hélène Cixous: croisées d'une œuvre*, ed. Mireille Calle-Gruber, 361–66. Paris: Galilée, 2000.

Colebrook, Claire. *Deleuze and the Meaning of Life*. London: Continuum, 2010.

Conley, Verena Andermatt. *Hélène Cixous*. Toronto: University of Toronto Press, 1992.

———. *Hélène Cixous: Writing the Feminine*. Lincoln and London: University of Nebraska Press, 1984.

Copjec, Joan, ed. *Supposing the Subject*. London: Verso, 1994.

Cornell, Sarah. "Hélène Cixous' *Le Livre de Promethea:* Paradise refound." In *Writing Differences: Readings from the Seminar of Hélène Cixous*, ed. Susan Sellers, 127–40. New York: St. Martin's Press, 1988.

Critchley, Simon. *The Faith of the Faithless: Experiments in Political Theology*. London and New York: Verso, 2012.

Critchley, Simon, and Peter Dews, eds. *Deconstructive Subjectivities*. Albany: State University of New York Press, 1996.

Crowley, Martin. *L'Homme sans: Politiques de la finitude*. Postface by Jean-Luc Nancy. Paris: Lignes, 2009.

Culler, Jonathan. "The Most Interesting Thing in the World." *diacritics* 38(1–2) (spring–summer 2008): 7–16.

Culler, Jonathan, and Phillip E. Lewis, eds. "Derrida and Democracy." *diacritics* 38(1–2) (spring–summer 2008).

Cusset, François. *French Theory: Foucault, Derrida, Deleuze & Cie et les mutations de la vie intellectuelle aux États-Unis*. Paris: La Découverte, 2003.

Dallmayr, Fred. "An 'Inoperative' Global Community? Reflections on Nancy." In *On Jean-Luc Nancy: The Sense of Philosophy*, 174–96.

Davies, Paul Sheldon. *Subjects of the World: Darwin's Rhetoric and the Study of Agency in Nature*. Chicago and London: University of Chicago Press, 2009.

Davis, Creston, John Milbank, and Slavoj Žižek, eds. *Theology and the Political: The New Debate*, intro. Rowan Williams. Durham, NC, and London: Duke University Press, 2005.

De Bloois, Joost, Sjef Houppermans, and Frans-Willem Korsten, eds. *Discern(e) ments: Deleuzian Aesthetics/ Esthétiques deleuziennes*. Amsterdam and New York: Rodopi, 2004.

De Fontenay, Elisabeth. *Le Silence des bêtes: la philosophie à l'épreuve de l'animalité*. Paris: Fayard, 1998.

De Vries, Hent. *Religion and Violence: Philosophical Perspectives from Kant to Derrida*. Baltimore, MD, and London: Johns Hopkins University Press, 2002.

———. "The Two Sources of the 'Theological Machine': Jacques Derrida and Henri Bergson on Religion, Technicity, War, and Terror." In *Theology and the Political: The New Debate*, ed. Creston Davis, John Milbank, and Slavoj Žižek, 366–89. Durham, NC, and London: Duke University Press, 2005.

De Vries, Hent, and Lawrence E. Sullivan. *Political Theologies: Public Religion in a Post-Secular World*. New York: Fordham University Press, 2006.

Deleuze, Gilles. *Le Bergsonisme*. Paris: Presses Universitaires de France, 1966.

———. *Cinéma 2: L'image-temps*. Paris: Minuit. 1985.

———. *Critique et clinique*. Paris: Minuit, 1993.

———. "Description of Woman: For a Philosophy of the Sexed Other." Trans. Keith W Faulkner. *Angelaki* 7(3) (2002): 17–24.

———. *Deux régimes de fous: textes et entretiens 1975–1995*. Edition prepared by David Lapoujade. Paris: Minuit, 2003.

———. *Différence et répétition*. Paris: Presses Universitaire de France, 1968.

———. *Foucault*. Paris: Minuit, 1986.

———. *Francis Bacon: Logique de la sensation*. Paris: Seuil, 2002.

———. *L'Île déserte et autres textes: textes et entretiens 1953–1974*. Edition prepared by David Lapoujade. Paris: Minuit, 2002.

———. *La Philosophie critique de Kant*. Paris: Press Universitaires de France, 1963.

———. *Le Pli: Leibniz et le baroque*. Paris: Minuit, 1988.

———. *Logique du sens*. Paris: Minuit, 1969.

———. *Marcel Proust et les signes*. Paris: Presses Universitaires de France, 1964. English edition: *Proust and Signs*, trans. Richard Howard. New York: Braziller, 1972.

———. *Nietzsche et la philosophie*. Paris: Presses Universitaires de France, 1962.

———. *Pourparlers: 1972–1990*. Paris: Minuit, 1990. English edition: *Negotiations: 1972–1990*, trans. Martin Joughin. New York: Columbia University Press, 1995.

———. *Proust et les signes*. 2d ed. Paris: Presses Universitaires de France, 1971.

———. "Le Simulacre et philosophie antique." In *Logique du sens*, 292–324. Paris: Minuit, 1969.

———. *Spinoza: philosophie pratique*. Paris: Minuit, 1981.

———. "Statements and Profiles." Trans. Keith W Faulkner. *Angelaki* 8(3) (2003): 85–93.

Deleuze, Gilles, and Claire Parnet. *L'Abécédaire de Gilles Deleuze*. Dir. Pierre-André Boutang. 1996. Text transcribed and translated by Charles Stivale. Available at www.langlab.wayne.edu/CStivale/D-G/ABC1.html.

———. *Dialogues*. Paris: Flammarion, 1977. English edition: *Dialogues*, trans. Hugh Tomlinson and Barbara Habberham. London: Athlone, 1987.

Deleuze, Gilles, and Félix Guattari. *Kafka: pour une littérature mineure*. Paris: Minuit, 1975. English edition: *Kafka: Toward a Minor Literature*, trans. Dana Polan. Minneapolis: University of Minnesota Press, 1986.

———. *Mille plateaux: capitalisme et schizophrénie 2*. Paris: Minuit, 1980. English edition: *A Thousand Plateaus*, trans. Brian Massumi. Minneapolis: University of Minnesota Press, 1987.

———. *Qu'est-ce que la philosophie ?* Paris: Minuit, 1991. English edition: *What Is Philosophy?*, trans. Hugh Tomlinson and Graham Burchell. New York: Columbia University Press, 1994.

Derrida, Jacques. *L'Animal que donc je suis*. Paris: Galilée, 2006.

———. "Autoimmunity: Real and Symbolic Suicides." An interview with Giovanna Borradori. Trans. Pascale-Anne Brault and Michael Nass. In *Philosophy in a Time of Terror: Dialogues with Jürgen Habermas and Jacques Derrida*, 85–136. Chicago and London: University of Chicago Press, 2003.

———. *L'Autre cap*. Paris: Minuit, 1991. English edition: *The Other Heading: Reflections on Today's Europe*, trans. Pascale-Anne Brault and Michael B. Nass, intro. Michael B. Nass. Bloomington and Indianapolis: Indiana University Press, 1992.

———. "A Certain Impossible Possibility of Saying the Event," trans. Gila Walker, 2003. Reprinted in *The Late Derrida*, ed. W. J. T Mitchell and Arnold I. Davidson, 223–43. Chicago: University of Chicago Press, 2007.

———. "Comment ne pas parler : Dénégations." 1986. Reprinted in *Psyché: inventions de l'autre*, 535–96. Paris: Galilée, 1987.

———. *Cosmopolitiques de tous les pays: encore un effort!* Paris: Galilée, 1997.

———. *De la grammatologie*. Paris: Minuit, 1967.

———. "The Deconstruction of Actuality." In *Negotiations: Interventions and Interviews, 1971–2001*, ed., trans., and intro. Elizabeth Rottenberg, 81–116. Stanford: Stanford University Press, 2002.

———. *Demeure: Maurice Blanchot*. Paris: Galilée, 1998.

———. *La Dissémination*. Paris: Seuil, 1972.

———. *Donner la mort*. Paris: Galilée, 1999.

———. *L'Écriture et la différence*. Paris: Seuil, 1967.

———. "Entretien avec Robert Maggiori." *Libération*. November 24, 1994. Available at http://www.hydra.umn.edu/derrida/ami.html.

———. "'Il faut bien manger' ou le calcul du sujet." Interview with Jean-Luc Nancy. In *Points de suspension: entretiens*, ed. Elisabeth Weber, 269–302. Paris: Galilée, 1992.

———. "Faxitexture." Trans. Laura Bourland. In *Anywhere*, ed. Cynthia C. Davidson, 20–33. New York: Rizzoli, 1992.

———. *Foi et savoir: les deux sources de la "religion" aux limites de la simple raison*, suivi de *Le siécle et le Pardon*. Paris: Seuil, 1996.

———. *Force de loi: le "fondement mystique de l'autorité."* 1994. Reprint, Paris: Galilée, 2005.

———. *Khôra*. Paris: Galilée, 1993.

———. "Marx & Sons." Trans. G. M. Goshgarian. In *Ghostly Demarcations: A Symposium on Jacques Derrida's Specters of Marx*, Jacques Derrida et al., ed. Michael Sprinker, 213–69. London : Verso, 1999.

———. *Mémoires d'aveugle: l'autoportrait et autres ruines*. Paris: Editions de la Réunion des musées nationaux, 1990.

———. "Others Are Secret Because They Are Other." In *Paper Machine*, trans. Rachel Bowlby, 136–63. Stanford: Stanford University Press, 2004.

———. "Otobiographie de Nietzsche." In *L'oreille de l'autre: otobiographies, tranferts, traductions. Textes et débats avec Jacques Derrida*, ed. Claude Lévesque and Christie V. McDonald. Québec: VLB Éditeur, 1982.

———. "Penser ce qui vient." In *Derrida pour les temps à venir*, ed. René Major, 17–62. Paris: Stock, 2007.

———. *Politique et amitié: entretiens avec Michael Sprinker sur Marx et Althusser*. Paris: Galilée, 2011.

———. *Politiques de l'amitié*. Paris: Galilée, 1994. English edition: *Politics of Friendship*, trans. George Collins. London: Verso, 1997.

———. "Pour une justice à venir." Interview with Lieven De Cauter, ed. Maïwenn Furic. Available at http://www.brussellstribunal.org/pdf/Derrida_FR.pdf. February 19, 2004. Accessed on April 15, 2011.

———. "Le Souverain bien—ou l'Europe en mal de souveraineté." Lecture delivered at Strasbourg. June 8, 2004. In "Derrida politique: la déconstruction de la souveraineté (puissance et droit)," ed. Yves Charles Zarka. *Cités* 30 (2007): 103–40.

———. *Séminaire: la bête et le souverain*. Vol. 1 (2001–2), ed. Michel Lisse, Marie-Louise Mallet, and Ginette Michaud. Paris: Galilée, 2008.

———. *Séminaire: la bête et le souverain.* Vol. 2 (2002–3), ed. Michel Lisse, Marie-Louise Mallet, and Ginette Michaud. Paris: Galilée, 2010.

———. *Spectres de Marx: l'état de la dette, le travail du deuil et la nouvelle Internationale.* Paris: Galilée, 1993. English edition: *Specters of Marx: The State of Debt, the Work of Mourning & the New International,* trans. Peggy Kamuf, intro. Bernd Magnus and Stephen Cullenberg. New York and London: Routledge, 1994.

———. *Le Toucher, Jean-Luc Nancy.* Paris: Galilée, 2000.

———. *La Voix et le phénomène.* Paris: Presses Universitaires de France, 1967.

———. *Voyous: deux essais sur la raison.* Paris: Galilée, 2003.

Derrida Jacques, Vincent Descombes, et al. *La Faculté de juger.* Paris: Minuit, 1985.

Derrida, Jacques, and Anne Dufourmantelle. *De l'hospitalité: Anne Dufourmantelle invite Jacques Derrida à répondre.* Paris: Calmann-Levy, 1997.

Derrida, Jacques, and Maurizio Ferraris. *A Taste for the Secret.* Trans. Giacomo Donis. Ed. Giacomo Donis and David Webb. Cambridge: Polity, 2001.

Derrida, Jacques, and Elisabeth Roudinesco. *De quoi demain . . . Dialogue.* Paris: Fayard et Galilée, 2001.

Descartes, René. *Selected Philosophical Writings.* Trans. John Cottingham, Robert Stoothoff, and Dugald Murdoch. Cambridge: Cambridge University Press, 1988.

Dickens, Charles. *Our Mutual Friend.* Ed. and intro. Adrian Poole. London: Penguin, 1997.

Dosse, François. *Histoire du structuralisme I: le champ du signe, 1945–1966.* Paris: La Découverte, 1991.

———. *Histoire du structuralisme II: le chant du cygne, 1967 à nos jours.* Paris: La Découverte, 1992.

Dubreuil, Laurent. "Leaving Politics: *Bios, zōē,* Life." *diacritics* 36(2) (summer 2006): 83–98.

———. "Preamble to Apolitics." *diacritics* 39(2) (summer 2009): 5–20.

———. *Le Refus de la politique.* Paris: Hermann, 2012.

Erb, Tobias J., Patrick Kiefer, Bodo Hattendorf, Detlef Günther, and Julia A. Vorholt. "GFAJ-1 Is an Arsenate-Resistant, Phosphate-Dependent Organism." *Sciencexpress.* Published online, July 8, 2012.

Esposito, Roberto. *Communitas: The Origin and Destiny of Community.* Trans. Timothy Campbell. Stanford: Stanford University Press, 2010.

Finkielkraut, Alain, and Elisabeth de Fontenay. *Des hommes et des bêtes.* Genève: Tricorne, 2000.

Flaxman, Gregory. *Gilles Deleuze and the Fabulation of Philosophy.* Minneapolis and London: University of Minnesota Press, 2012.

Foucault, Michel. *Les Anormaux: Cours au Collège de France 1974–1975.* Paris: Seuil, Gallimard, 1999.

———. *Le Corps utopique suivi de Les Hétérotopies*, ed. and postface by Daniel Defert. Paris: Lignes, 2009.

———. *Dits et écrits II: 1970–1975*, ed. Daniel Defert and François Ewald. Paris: Gallimard, 1994.

———. *L'Herméneutique du sujet: Cours au Collège de France 1981–1982*. Paris: Seuil/ Gallimard, 2001.

———. *La Naissance de la biopolitique: Cours au Collège de France 1978–1979*. Paris: Seuil/ Gallimard, 2004.

Furtos, Jean. *De la précarité à l'auto-exclusion*. Paris: Rue d'Ulm, 2009.

Galloway, Alexander R., and Eugene Thacker. *The Exploit: A Theory of Networks*. Minneapolis: University of Minnesota Press, 2007.

Genosko, Gary. "A Bestiary of Territoriality and Expression: Poster Fish, Bower Birds, and Spring Lobsters." In *A Shock to Thought: Expressions after Deleuze and Guattari*, ed. Brian Massumi, 47–59. London and New York: Routledge, 2002.

———, ed. *The Guattari Reader*. Oxford: Blackwell, 1996.

Geroulanos, Stefanos. *An Atheism that Is Not Humanist Emerges in French Thought*. Stanford: Stanford University Press, 2010.

Goddard, Jean-Christophe. *Violence et subjectivité: Derrida, Deleuze, Maldiney*. Paris: Vrin, 2008.

Granel, Gérard. "Qui vient après le sujet?" In *Écrits logiques et politiques*, 327–40. Paris: Galilée, 1990.

Grosz, Elizabeth. *Chaos, Territory, Art: Deleuze and the Framing of the Earth*. New York: Columbia University Press, 2008.

Guattari, Félix. *Psychanalyse et transversalité: essais d'analyse institutionnelle*. Preface by Gilles Deleuze. Paris: François Maspero, 1972.

———. *La Révolution moléculaire*. Fontenay-sous-Bois, France: Recherches, 1977.

Guénoun-Marrati, Paola. "L'Animal qui sait fuir. G. Deleuze: Politique de devenir, ontologie de l'immanence." In *L'Animal autobiographique: Autour de Jacques Derrida*, ed. Marie-Louise Mallet, 197–214. Paris: Galilée, 1999.

Gutting, Gary. *French Philosophy in the Twentieth Century*. Cambridge: Cambridge University Press, 2001.

———. *Thinking the Impossible: French Philosophy Since 1960*. Oxford: Oxford University Press, 2011.

Habermas, Jürgen. "The Boundary Between Faith and Knowledge." In *Between Naturalism and Religion: Philosophical Essays*, trans. Ciaran Cronin, 209–48. Cambridge: Polity, 2008.

———. "Notes on Post-Secular Society." *NPQ* 25 (fall 2008): 17–29.

Habermas, Jürgen, et al. *An Awareness of What Is Missing: Faith and Reason in a Post-Secular Age*. Trans. Ciaran Cronin. Cambridge: Polity, 2010.

Haddad, Samir. "Genealogy of Violence: From Light to the Autoimmune." *diacritics* 38(1–2) (spring–summer 2008): 121–42.

Hägglund, Martin. *Radical Atheism: Derrida and the Time of Life*. Stanford: Stanford University Press, 2008.

———. "The Radical Evil of Deconstruction: A Reply to John Caputo." *Journal for Cultural and Religious Theory* 11(2) (2011): 126–50.

Hallward, Peter. *Badiou: A Subject to Truth*. Foreword by Slavoj Žižek. Minneapolis: University of Minnesota Press, 2003.

———, ed. *Think Again: Alain Badiou and the Future of Philosophy*. London and New York: Continuum, 2004.

Haraway, Donna. *The Companion Species Manifesto: Dogs, People, and Significant Otherness*. Chicago: Prickly Paradigm, 2003.

———. *Simians, Cyborgs, and Women: The Reinvention of Nature*. New York: Routledge, 1991.

Hardt, Michael. "The Withering of Civil Society" 1995. Reprinted in *Deleuze & Guattari: New Mappings in Politics, Philosophy, and Culture*, ed. Eleanor Kaufman and Kevin Jon Heller, 23–29. Minneapolis: University of Minnesota Press, 1988.

Hardt, Michael, and Antonio Negri. *Commonwealth*. Cambridge, MA: Belknap Press of Harvard University Press, 2009.

———. *Empire*. Cambridge, MA : Harvard University Press, 2000.

———. "The Fight for 'Real Democracy' at the Heart of Occupy Wall Street: The Encampment in Lower Manhattan Speaks to a Failure of Representation." *Foreign Affairs*. October 11, 2011. Available at http://www.foreignaffairs.com/articles/136399/michael-hardt-and-antonio-negri/the-fight-for-real-democracy-at-the-heart-of-occupy-wall-street?page=show

———. *Multitudes: War and Democracy in the Age of Empire*. New York: Penguin, 2004.

Hayles, N. Katherine. *How We Became Posthuman: Virtual Bodies in Cybernetics, Literature, and Informatics*. Chicago and London: University of Chicago Press, 1999.

———. *My Mother Was a Computer: Digital Subjects and Literary Texts*. Chicago and London: University of Chicago Press, 2005.

Hegel, G. W. F. *Phenomenology of Spirit*. Trans. A. V. Miller. Oxford: Oxford University Press, 1977.

Heller-Roazen, Daniel. *The Inner Touch: Archaeology of a Sensation*. New York: Zone, 2007.

Herbrechter, Stefan, and Ivan Callus. *Critical Posthumanism*. Amsterdam: Rodopi, forthcoming.

Hird, Myra J. "Chimerism, Mosaicism and the Cultural Construction of Kinship." *Sexualities* 7(2) (2004): 217–32.

———. "The Corporeal Generosity of Maternity." *Body & Society* 13(1) (2007): 1–20.

———. *The Origins of Sociable Life: Evolution After Science Studies*. Hampshire, UK: Palgrave Macmillan, 2009.

Hollywood, Amy. "St Paul and the New Man." *Critical Inquiry* 35(4) (summer 2009): 865–76.

Howells, Christina. *Mortal Subjects: Passions of the Soul in Late Twentieth-Century French Thought*. Cambridge: Polity, 2011.

Hutchens, B. C. *Jean-Luc Nancy and the Future of Philosophy*. Chesham, UK: Acumen, 2005.

Hutchens, Benjamin, ed. *Jean-Luc Nancy: Justice, Legality and World*. London: Continuum, 2012.

Irigaray, Luce. *Entre orient et occident: de la singularité de la communauté*. Paris: Grasset, 1999.

———. *Éthique de la différence sexuelle*. Paris: Minuit, 1984.

———. *Être deux*. Paris: Grasset, 1997.

———. *J'aime à toi: esquisse d'une félicité dans l'histoire*. Paris: Grasset, 1992.

———. *L'Oubli de l'air chez Martin Heidegger*. Paris: Minuit, 1983.

———. *Sharing the World*. London: Continuum, 2008.

———. *The Way of Love*. Trans. Heidi Bostic and Stephen Pluhá ek. London and New York: Continuum, 2002.

Irigaray, Luce, and Sylvère Lotringer, eds. *Why Different? A Culture of Two Subjects: Interviews with Luce Irigaray*. Trans. Camille Collins. New York: Semiotext(e), 2000.

Irigaray, Luce, Stephen Pluhá ek, and Heidi Bostic, et al. *Conversations*. London: Continuum, 2008.

James, Ian. *The Fragmentary Demand: An Introduction to the Philosophy of Jean-Luc Nancy*. Stanford: Stanford University Press, 2006.

———. *The New French Philosophy*. Cambridge: Polity, 2012.

———. "The Persistence of the Subject: Jean-Luc Nancy." *Paragraph* 25(1) (2002): 125–41.

Johnston, Adrian. *Badiou, Žižek, and Political Transformations: The Cadence of Change*. Evanston, IL: Northwestern University Press, 2009.

Kacem, Mehdi Belhaj. *Après Badiou*. Paris: Grasset, 2011.

Kant, Immanuel. *The Critique of Judgment*. Trans. James Creed Meredith. Oxford: Clarendon, 1952.

Khatibi, Abdelkébir. *Aimance*. Neuilly-sur-Seine: Al Manar, 2003.

———. *Jacques Derrida, en effet*. Neuilly-sur-Seine: Al Manar, 2007.

Kristeva, Julia. *Pouvoirs de l'horreur: essais sur l'abjection*. Paris: Seuil, 1980.

———. *La Révolution du langage poétique*. Paris: Seuil, 1974.

Lacan, Jacques. *Écrits I*. Paris: Seuil, 1966.

———. *Écrits II*. Paris: Seuil, 1966.

———. *L'Éthique de la psychanalyse 1959–1960*. Paris: Seuil, 1986.

LaCapra, Dominick. *History and Its Limits: Human, Animal, Violence*. Ithaca, NY, and London: Cornell University Press, 2009.

———. *History and Memory After Auschwitz*. Ithaca, NY, and London: Cornell University Press, 1998.

———. *History in Transit: Experience, Identity, Critical Theory*. Ithaca, NY, and London: Cornell University Press, 2004.

———. *Representing the Holocaust: History, Theory, Trauma*. Ithaca, NY, and London: Cornell University Press, 1994.

Laclau, Ernesto. "Is Radical Atheism a Good Name for Deconstruction?" *diacritics* 38(1–2) (spring–summer 2008): 180–89.

Lacoue-Labarthe, Philippe. *Le Sujet de la philosophie: typographies 1*. Paris: Flammarion, 1979.

Lacoue-Labarthe, Philippe, and Jean-Luc Nancy. *Le Titre de la lettre (une lecture de Lacan)*. Paris: Galilée, 1973.

———, eds. *Rejouer le politique*. Paris: Galilée, 1981.

———, eds. *Le Retrait du politique*. Paris: Galilée, 1983.

Lambert, Gregg. "Deleuze and the Political Ontology of 'The Friend.'" In *Deleuze and Politics*, 35–53.

———. "Enemy (der Feind)." *Angelaki* 12(3) (2007): 115–25.

———. "French Theory: The Movie." *symplokē* 18(1–2) (2010): 293–303.

———. *On the (New) Baroque*. Aurora: Davies, 2009.

———. *In Search of a New Image of Thought: Gilles Deleuze and Philosophical Expression*. Minneapolis and London: University of Minnesota Press, 2012.

———. "The Unprecedented Return of Saint Paul in Continental Philosophy." *Transformations of Religion and the Public Sphere: Postsecular Publics*. Eds. Rosi Braidotti, Bolette Blaagaard, Tobijn de Graauw, and Eva Midden. New York: Palgrave Macmillan, 2014.

Lawlor, Leonard. "Following the Rats: Becoming-Animal in Deleuze and Guattari." *SubStance* #117. 37(3) (2008): 169–87.

Leitch, Vincent B. "Late Derrida: The Politics of Sovereignty." In *The Late Derrida*, 11–29.

Lestel, Dominique. *Les Origines animales de la culture*. Paris: Flammarion, 2001.

Levi, Primo. *The Black Hole of Auschwitz*. Ed. Marco Belpoliti. Trans. Sharon Wood. Cambridge: Polity, 2005.

———. *The Drowned and the Saved*. Trans. Raymond Rosenthal. New York: Vintage, 1989.

———. *If This Is a Man: The Truce*. Trans. Stuart Woolf. Intro. Paul Bailey. London: Vintage, 1996.

———. *The Voice of Memory: Interviews 1961–1987*. Ed. Marco Belpoliti and Robert Gordon. Trans. Robert Gordon. Cambridge: Polity, 2001.

Lingis, Alphonso. *The Community of Those Who Have Nothing in Common*. Bloomington and Indiana: Indiana University Press, 1994.

Lucrèce. *De la nature*. Livres I-VI, ed., trans., and annotated by Alfred Ernout, intro. and notes by Élisabeth de Fontenay. Paris: Les belles lettres, 2009.

Luhmann, Niklas. *Social Systems*. Trans. John Bednarz Jr. and Dirk Baecker. Foreword Eva M. Knodt. Stanford: Stanford University Press, 1995.

Luhmann, Niklas, N. Katherine Hayles, William Rasch, Eva Knodt, and Cary Wolfe. "Theory of a Different Order: A Conversation with Katherine Hayles and Niklas Luhmann." In *Observing Complexity: Systems Theory and Postmodernity*, 111–36. Minneapolis and London: University of Minnesota Press, 2000.

Lyotard, Jean-François. *La Condition postmoderne: rapport sur le savoir*. Paris: Minuit, 1979.

———. *Discours, figure*. Paris: Klincksieck, 1985.

———. *L'Inhumain: causeries sur le temps*. Paris: Galilée, 1988.

Lyotard, Jean-François, and Jean-Loup Thébaud. *Au juste: conversations*. Paris: Christian Bourgois, 1979.

Macksey, Richard, and Eugenio Donato, eds. *The Structuralist Controversy: The Languages of Criticism and the Sciences of Man*. Baltimore, MD, and London: Johns Hopkins University Press, 1970.

Major, René, ed. *Derrida pour les temps à venir*. Paris: Stock, 2007.

Mallet, Marie-Louise, ed. *L'Animal autobiographique: Autour de Jacques Derrida*. Paris: Galilée, 1999.

———, ed. *La Démocratie à venir: Autour de Jacques Derrida*. Paris: Galilée, 2004.

Marcuse, Herbert. *An Essay on Liberation*. Boston: Beacon, 1969.

———. *One-Dimensional Man*. Intro. Douglas Kellner. London: Routledge, 1991.

———. "The Problem of Violence and the Radical Opposition." *Collected Papers of Herbert Marcuse: Vol. 3: The New Left and the 1960s*. Ed. Douglas Kellner. London and New York: Routledge, 2005.

———. "Repressive Tolerance." In *A Critique of Pure Tolerance*, ed. Robert Paul Wolff, Barrington Moore Jr., and Herbert Marcuse, 81–118. Boston: Beacon, 1965.

Martin, Aryn. "Microchimerism in the Mother(land): Blurring the Borders of Body and Nation." *Body & Society* 16(3) (2010): 23–50.

Martin, Jean-Clet. *Figures des temps contemporaines*. Paris: Kimé, 2001.

———. *Variations: la philosophie de Gilles Deleuze*. Preface by Gilles Deleuze. Paris: Payot et Rivages, 1993.

Martis, John. *Philippe Lacoue-Labarthe: Representation and the Loss of the Subject*. New York: Fordham University Press, 2005.

Massumi, Brian. "The Autonomy of Affect." In *Deleuze: A Critical Reader*, ed. Paul Patton, 217–39. Oxford: Blackwell, 1996.

———. *Parables for the Virtual: Movement, Affect, Sensation*. Durham, NC: Duke University Press, 2002.

———. "Requiem for Our Prospective Dead (Towards a Participatory Critique of Capitalist Power)." In *Deleuze & Guattari: New Mappings in Politics, Philosophy, and Culture*, 40–64.

May, Todd G. *The Political Thought of Jacques Rancière: Creating Equality*. University Park: Pennsylvania State University Press, 2008.

———. "The Politics of Life in the Thought of Gilles Deleuze." *SubStance* 20(3) (1991): 24–35.

Melville, Herman. *Bartleby, the Scrivener: A Story of Wall-Street*. 1853. Reprinted in *The Complete Shorter Fiction*, intro. John Updike, 18–51. New York: Alfred A. Knopf, 1997.

Mengue, Philippe. *Gilles Deleuze ou le système du multiple*. Paris: Kimé, 1994.

———. "People and Fabulation." Trans. Anna Bostock. In *Deleuze and Politics*, 218–39.

———. "Le Peuple qui manque et le trou de la démocratie." In *Gilles Deleuze, Félix Guattari et le politique*, 17–33.

Miami Theory Collective, ed. *Community at Loose Ends*. Minneapolis: University of Minnesota Press, 1991.

Miller, Adam. *Badiou, Marion and St Paul: Immanent Grace*. London: Continuum, 2008.

Mitchell, Andrew J., and Jason Kemp Winfree, eds. *The Obsessions of Georges Bataille: Community and Communication*. Albany: State University of New York Press, 2009.

Mitchell, W. J. T., Bernard E. Harcourt, and Michael Taussig. *Occupy: Three Inquiries in Disobedience*. Chicago and London: University of Chicago Press, 2013.

Mullarkey, John. *Post-Continental Philosophy: An Outline*. London and New York: Continuum, 2006.

Murray, Timothy. *Digital Baroque: New Media Art and Cinematic Folds*. Minneapolis and London: University of Minnesota Press, 2008.

———, ed. *Mimesis, Masochism, & Mime: The Politics of Theatricality in Contemporary French Thought*. Ann Arbor: University of Michigan Press, 1997.

Nancy, Jean-Luc. *L'Adoration: Déconstruction du christianisme, 2*. Paris: Galilée, 2010.

———, ed. *L'Art et la mémoire des camps: représenter exterminer*. Paris: Seuil, 2001.

———. "Church, State, Resistance." Trans. Véronique Voruz. In *Political Theologies*, 102–12.

———. "The Commerce of Plural Thinking." Interview with Marie-Eve Morin and Peter Gratton. In *Jean-Luc Nancy and Plural Thinking: Expositions of World, Ontology, Politics, and Sense*, ed. Peter Gratton and Marie-Eve Morin, 229–39. Albany: State University of New York Press, 2011.

———. *La Communauté affrontée*. Paris: Galilée, 2001.

———. *La Communauté désœuvrée*. Paris: Christian Bourgois, 1986.

———. *Corpus*. Paris: Métailié, 1992.

———. *La Création du monde* ou *la mondialisation*. Paris: Galilée, 2002.

———. *La Déclosion: La déconstruction du christianimse, 1*. Paris: Galilée, 2005.

———. ♪ [musical notation] . In *La Démocratie à venir*, 341–59.

———. *Le Discours de la syncope 1: Logodaedalus*. Paris: Flammarion, 1976.

———. *À l'écoute*. Paris: Galilée, 2002.

———. *Ego sum*. Paris: Flammarion, 1979.

———. "Entretien: Politique tout court et très au-delà." Interview with Ginette Michaud. In *Spirale: Arts, Lettres, Sciences humaines* 239 (2012): 33–36.

———. *Être singulier pluriel*. Paris: Galilée, 1996.

———. *L'Équivalence des catastrophes (après Fukushima)*. Paris: Galilée, 2012.

———. "L'Évidence du mystère." In *Le Voyage initiatique*, 85–98. Collectif. Paris: Albin Michel, 2011.

———. *L'Expérience de la liberté*. Paris: Galilée, 1988.

———. *L'Impératif catégorique*. Paris: Flammarion, 1983.

———. "Ipso facto cogitans et demens." In *Derrida pour les temps à venir*, ed. René Major, 118–39. English edition: "Mad Derrida: *Ipso facto cogitans ac demens*," trans. Celine Surprenant, in *Adieu Derrida*, ed. Costas Douzinas, 17–33. Basingstoke, UK, and New York: Palgrave, 2007.

———. *L'Intrus*. Paris: Galilée, 2000.

———. *Noli me tangere: essai sur la levée du corps*. Paris: Bayard, 2003.

———. "Passage." In Jean-Luc Nancy and Jean-Claude Conésa, *Être, c'est être perçu*, 13–31. Saint-Just-la-Pendue, France: Éditions des Cahiers intempestifs, 1999.

———. *La Pensée dérobée*. Accompanied by "L'Échappée d'elle" by François Martin. Paris: Galilée, 2001.

———. *Une Pensée finie*. Paris: Galilée, 1990.

———. "Philosophy as Chance." Interview with Lorenzo Fabbri. Trans. Pascale-Anne Brault and Michael Naas. In *The Late Derrida*, 209–22.

———. *À plus d'un titre: Jacques Derrida. Sur un portrait de Valerio Adami*. Paris: Galilée, 2007.

———. *Politique et au-delà: entretien avec Philip Armstrong et Jason E. Smith*. Paris: Galilée, 2011.

———. *La Possibilité d'un monde*. Dialogue with Pierre-Philippe Jandin. Paris: Les petits Platons, 2013.

———. *Le Sens du monde*. Paris: Galilée, 1993.

———. "Shattered Love." Trans. Lisa Garbus and Simona Sawhney. In *A Finite Thinking*, ed. Simon Sparks, 245–74. Stanford: Stanford University Press, 2003.

———. "Un sujet?" In *Homme et sujet: la subjectivité en question dans les sciences humaines*. Lectures of the Centre d'Études Pluridisciplinaires on Subjectivity, ed. Dominique Weil, 47–114. Paris: L'Harmattan, 1992.

———. *Tombe de sommeil*. Paris: Galilée, 2007.

———. *Vérité de la démocratie*. Paris: Galilée, 2008.

Nass, Michael B. *Derrida From Now On*. New York: Fordham University Press, 2008.

———. *Miracle and Machine: Jacques Derrida and the Two Sources of Religion, Science, and the Media*. New York: Fordham University Press, 2012.

Negri, Antonio. "The Political Subject and Absolute Immanence." In *Theology and the Political*, 231–39.

Neyrat, Frédéric. *Aux bords du vide: événement et sujet dans la philosophie d'Alain Badiou*. Paris: Éditions è®e numérique, 2011.

———. *Clinamen: Flux, absolu et loi spirale*. Paris: Éditions è®e, 2011.

———. *Le Communisme existentiel de Jean-Luc Nancy*. Paris: Lignes, 2013.

Nieman, Susan. "Jean Améry Takes His Life." In *Yale Companion to Jewish Writing and Thought in German Culture, 1096-1996*, ed. Sander L. Gilman and Jack Zipes, 775–82. New Haven, CT, and London: Yale University Press, 2007.

Nietzsche, Friedrich. *Beyond Good and Evil: Prelude to a Philosophy of the Future*. Ed. Rolf-Peter Horstmann and Judith Norman. Trans. Judith Norman. Cambridge: Cambridge University Press, 2002.

———. *Human, All Too Human: A Book for Free Spirits*. Trans. R. J. Hollingdale. Intro. Erich Heller. Cambridge: Cambridge University Press, 1986.

———. *On the Genealogy of Morality*. Ed. Keith Ansell-Pearson. Trans. Carol Diethe. Revised ed. Cambridge: Cambridge University Press, 2007.

———. *Thus Spoke Zarathustra: A Book for Everyone and No One*. Trans. and intro. R. J. Hollingdale. London: Penguin, 1961.

———. *The Will to Power*. Trans. Walter Kaufmann and R. J. Hollingdale. Ed. Walter Kaufmann. New York: Vintage, 1968.

O'Sullivan, Simon. *Art Encounters Deleuze and Guattari: Thought Beyond Representation*. Basingstoke, UK: Palgrave, 2006.

Ogilvie, Bertrand. *L'Homme jetable: essai sur l'exterminisme et la violence extrême*. Paris: Éditions Amsterdam, 2012.

Overbye, Dennis. "Microbe Finds Arsenic Tasty; Redefines Life." *New York Times*. December 2, 2010.

Patton, Paul. "Becoming-Democratic." In *Deleuze and Politics*, 178–95.

———. "Deleuze and Democracy." *Contemporary Political Theory* 4(4) (2005): 400–13.

———. "Deleuze et la démocratie." In *Gilles Deleuze, Félix Guattari et le politique*, 35–47.

———. *Deleuze & the Political*. London and New York: Routledge, 2000.

———. *Deleuzian Concepts: Philosophy, Colonization, Politics*. Stanford: Stanford University Press, 2010.

———. "Future Politics." In *Between Deleuze and Derrida*, ed. Paul Patton and John Protevi, 15–29. London and New York: Continuum, 2003.

———. "Utopian Political Philosophy: Deleuze and Rawls." *Deleuze Studies* 1(1) (2007): 41–59.

Pearson, Keith Ansell. "Viroid Life: On Machines, Technics and Evolution." In *Deleuze and Philosophy: The Difference Engineer*, ed. Keith Ansell Pearson, 180–210. London and New York: Routledge, 1997.

———. *Viroid Life: Perspectives on Nietzsche and the Transhuman Condition*. New York: Routledge, 1997.

Penny, Laura. "Parables and Politics: How Benjamin and Deleuze & Guattari Read Kafka." *Theory & Event* 12, no. 3 (2009).

Phillips, John W. "Loving Love or Ethics as Natural Philosophy in Jacques Derrida's *Politiques de l'amitié*." *Angelaki* 12(3) (2007): 155–70.

Plato. *Symposium*. Trans. and intro. Christopher Gill. London: Penguin, 1999.

Pluth, Ed. *Badiou: A Philosophy of the New*. Cambridge: Polity, 2010.

Pollock, Mary Sanders, and Catherine Rainwater, eds. *Figuring Animals: Essays on Animal Images in Art, Literature, Philosophy, and Popular Culture*. New York: Palgrave, 2005.

Protevi, John. "Love." In *Between Derrida and Deleuze*, ed. Paul Patton and John Protevi, 183–94. London: Athlone Press, 2002.

Pyper, Hugh S. "'Job the Dog': Wounds, Scars, and the Biblical Text." *parallax* 3(13) (2007): 83–93.

La Renaissance de Lucrèce. Paris: Presse Universitaires de Paris-Sorbonne, 2010.

Rancière, Jacques. "The Aesthetic Revolution and Its Outcomes: Emplotments of Autonomy and Heteronomy." *New Left Review* 14 (2002): 133–51.

———. "Aesthetic Separation, Aesthetic Community." In *The Emancipated Spectator*, trans. Gregory Elliott, 51–82. London and New York: Verso, 2009.

———. *Aux bords du politique*. Paris: La Fabrique, 1998.

———. *La Haine de la démocratie*. Paris: La Fabrique, 2005.

———. *Malaise dans l'esthétique*. Paris: Galilée, 2004.

———. *La Mésentente: politique et philosophie*. Paris: Galilée, 1995.

———. *Moments politiques: interventions 1977–2009*. Paris: La Fabriques, 2009.

———. *La Nuit de prolétaires*. Paris: Fayard, 1981.

———. *Le Partage du sensible: esthétique et politique*. Paris: La Fabrique, 2000.

———. *Le Spectateur émancipé*. Paris: La Fabrique, 2008.

———. "Who Is the Subject of the Rights of Man?" In *South Atlantic Quarterly* 103(2/3) (spring–summer 2004): 297–310.

————. "Work, Identity, Subject." In *Jacques Rancière and the Contemporary Scene: The Philosophy of Radical Equality*, ed. Jean-Philippe Deranty and Alison Ross, 205–16. London: Continuum, 2012.

Ramond, Charles, ed. *Alain Badiou: Penser le multiple*. Actes du Colloque de Bordeaux, October 21–23, 1999. Paris: L'Harmattan, 2002.

Ratti, Manav. *The Postsecular Imagination: Postcolonialism, Religion, and Literature*. New York and London: Routledge, 2013.

Reaves, Marshall Louis, Sunita Sinha, Joshua D. Rabinowitz, Leonid Kruglyak, and Rosemary J. Redfield. "Absence of Detectable Arsenate in DNA from Arsenate-Grown GFAJ-1 Cells." *Sciencexpress*. Published online on July 8, 2012.

Regard, Frédéric. "Faite d'yeux : genèse sans généalogie." In *Genèses Généalogies Genres: Autour de l'œuvre de Hélène Cixous*, 215–27.

Renshaw, Sal. *The Subject of Love: Hélène Cixous and the Feminine Divine*. Manchester, UK, and New York: Manchester University Press, 2009.

————. "The Thealogy of Hélène Cixous." In *Religion in French Feminist Thought: Critical Perspectives*, ed. Morny Joy, Kathleen O'Grady, and Judith L. Poxon, intro. Luce Irigary, 162–75. London and New York: Routledge, 2003.

Rogozinski, Jacob, and Michel Surya, eds. *Lignes 35*. "Le Rebut humain." Paris: Lignes, 2011.

Rothenberg, Molly Anne. *The Excessive Subject: A New Theory of Social Change*. Cambridge: Polity, 2010.

Schmitt, Carl. *The Nomos of the Earth in the International Law of the Jus Publicum Europaeum*. Trans. G. L. Ulmen. New York: Telos, 2003.

Schrift, Alan D. *Twentieth-Century French Philosophy: Key Themes and Thinkers*. Malden, UK: Blackwell, 2006.

Sebald, W. G. *On the Natural History of Destruction*. Trans. Anthea Bell. New York: Random House, 2003.

Sellers, Susan. *Hélène Cixous: Authorship, Autobiography and Love*. Cambridge: Polity, 1996.

Serres, Michel. *La Naissance de la physique dans le texte de Lucrèce: fleuves et turbulences*. Paris: Minuit, 1977.

Sheppard, Darren, Simon Sparks, and Colin Thomas, eds. *On Jean-Luc Nancy: The Sense of Philosophy*. London and New York: Routledge, 1997.

Shildrick, Margrit. "Some Reflections on the Socio-cultural and Bioscientific Limits of Bodily Integrity." *Body & Society* 16(3) (2010): 11–22.

Shukin, Nicole. *Animal Capital: Rendering Life in Biopolitical Times*. Minneapolis and London: University of Minnesota Press, 2009.

Smith, Paul. *Discerning the Subject*. Foreword John Mowitt. Minneapolis: University of Minnesota Press, 1988.

Starr, Peter. *Logics of Failed Revolt: French Theory After May '68*. Stanford: Stanford University Press, 1995.

Stelter, Brian. "The Facebooker Who Friended Obama." *New York Times*. July 7, 2008.

Stiegler, Bernard. "Le Bien le plus précieux à l'époque des sociotechnologies." In *Réseaux sociaux: Culture politique et ingénierie des réseaux sociaux*, ed. Bernard Stiegler, 13–36. Paris: FYP, 2012.

———. *La Technie et le temps. 1. La Faute d'Épiméthée*. Paris: Galilée, 1994.

———. *La Télécratie contre la démocratie*. Paris: Flammarion, 2008.

Stivale, Charles. "The Folds of Friendship: Derrida-Deleuze-Foucault." *Angelaki* 5(2) (2000): 3–15.

Stross, Randall. "When Everyone's a Friend, Is Anything Private?" *New York Times*, March 8, 2009.

Surin, Kenneth. "Rewriting the Ontological Script of Liberation: On the Question of Finding a New Kind of Political Subject." In *Theology and the Political*, 240–66.

Surya, Michel. "Figures du rebut humain." In *Humanimalités: Matériologies, 3*. Preceded by *L'idiotie de Bataille*, 189–208. Paris: Léo Scheer, 2004.

Taylor, Astra, Keith Gessen, and editors from *n+1, Dissent, Triple Canopy* and *The New Inquiry. Occupy! Scenes from Occupied America*. London and New York: Verso, 2011.

Taylor, Charles. *A Secular Age*. Cambridge, MA: Belknap, 2007.

Thacker, Eugene. "Networks, Swarms, Multitudes: Part 1." *CTheory*. Article 142a. May 18, 2004.

———. "Networks, Swarms, Multitudes: Part 2." *CTheory*. Article 142b. May 18, 2004.

———. "Swarming: Number versus Animal?" In *Deleuze and New Technology*, ed. Mark Poster and David Savat, 161–84. Edinburgh: Edinburgh University Press, 2009.

Thomson, Alexander J. P. *Deconstruction and Democracy: Derrida's Politics of Friendship*. London: Continuum, 2005.

Tully, James. "Communication and Imperialism." *CTheory*. td 035. February 22, 2006.

Valentin, Jérémie. "Gilles Deleuze's Political Posture." Trans. Constantin V. Boundas and Sarah Camble. *Deleuze and Philosophy*, ed. Constantin V. Boundas, 185–201. Edinburgh: Edinburgh University Press, 2006.

Van Den Abbeele, Georges. "Lost Horizons and Uncommon Grounds: For a Poetics of Finitude in the Work of Jean-Luc Nancy." In *On Jean-Luc Nancy: The Sense of Philosophy*, 12–18.

Virilio, Paul, and Sylvere Lotringer. *Crepuscular Dawn*. Trans. M. Taormina. New York: Semiotext(e), 2002.

Virno, Paolo. *A Grammar of the Multitude: For an Analysis of Contemporary Forms of Life*. Trans. Isabella Bertoletti, James Cascaito, and Andrea Casson. Foreword Sylvère Lotringer. New York: Semiotext(e), 2004.

Vodoz, Isabelle, and Fabien Tarby, eds. *Autour d'Alain Badiou*. Paris: Germina, 2011.

Wark, McKenzie. *A Hacker Manifesto*. Cambridge, MA, and London: Harvard University Press, 2004.

Watkin, Christopher. *Difficult Atheism: Post-Theological Thinking in Alain Badiou, Jean-Luc Nancy and Quentin Meillassoux*. Edinburgh: Edinburgh University Press, 2011.

Weber, Samuel. "'And When is Now?' (On Some Limits of Perfect Intelligibility)." *MLN* 122 (2007): 1028–49.

———. *Targets of Opportunity: On the Militarization of Thinking*. New York: Fordham University Press, 2005.

Weil, Kari. *Thinking Animals: Why Animal Studies Now?* New York: Columbia University Press, 2012.

Wills, David. "Full Dorsal: Derrida's *Politics of Friendship*." *Postmodern Culture* 15 (2005): 3.

Wolfe, Cary. *Animal Rites: American Culture, the Discourse of Species, and Posthumanist Theory*. Foreword by W. J. T Mitchell. Chicago and London: University of Chicago Press, 2003.

———. *Before the Law: Humans and Other Animals in a Biopolitical Frame*. Chicago and London: University of Chicago Press, 2013.

———. *What Is Posthumanism?* Minneapolis: University of Minnesota Press, 2010.

———, ed. *Zoontologies: The Question of the Animal*. Minneapolis: University of Minnesota Press, 2003.

Wolfe-Simon, Felisa, Jodi Switzer Blum, Thomas R. Kulp, Gwyneth W. Gordon, Shelley E. Hoeft, Jennifer Pett-Ridge, John F. Stolz, Samuel M. Webb, Peter K. Weber, Paul C. W. Davies, Ariel D. Anbar, and Ronald S. Oremland. "A Bacterium that Can Grow by Using Arsenic Instead of Phosphorous." *Sciencexpress*. Published online, December 2, 2010.

Wortham, Simon Morgan. "Law of Friendship: Agamben and Derrida." *New Formations* 62 (autumn 2007): 89–105.

Wurzer, Wilhem S. "Nancy and the Political Imaginary After Nature." In *On Jean-Luc Nancy: The Sense of Philosophy*, 91–102.

Zepke, Stephen. *Art as Abstract Machine: Ontology and Aesthetics in Deleuze and Guattari*. New York and London: Routledge, 2005.

Žižek, Slavoj. "On Alain Badiou and *Logiques de mondes*." Available at http://www.lacan.com/zizbadman.htm

———. *The Parallax View*. Cambridge, MA, and London: MIT Press, 2006.

———. *The Sublime Object of Ideology*. London and New York: Verso, 1989.

———. "The Thrilling Romance of Orthodoxy." In *Theology and the Political*, 52–71.

————. *The Ticklish Subject: The Absent Centre of Political Ontology*. London and New York: Verso, 1999.

————. "Žižek et les Indignés de Wall Street: 'ce mouvement a trait à la violence, ce que j'approuve.'" Interview with Julien Charnay. *Philosophie Magazine* (October 18, 2011). Available at http://www.philomag.com/fiche-philinfo.php?id=275

————. "Žižek Speaks at Occupy Wall Street." Transcript. October 25, 2011. Available at http://www.imposemagazine.com/bytes/slavoj-zizek-at-occupy-wall-street-transcript

————. *Violence: Six Sideways Reflections*. New York: Picador, 2008.

————. *The Year of Dreaming Dangerously*. London and New York: Verso, 2012.

INDEX

Heidegger, Martin, 20, 26, 161, 267n80
Heller-Roazen, Daniel, 317n171
Herbrechter, Stefan, 221, 225, 324n11, 328n63
Hird, Myra, 228, 230
Hollywood, Amy, 283n51, 285n61, 290n115

Irigaray, Luce, 9, 57–60, 258n57, 284n53

Jabès, Edmond, 81
James, Ian, 258n55
Johnston, Adrian, 107, 289n109

Kafka, Franz, xii, 198–99, 209
Kant, Immanuel, 14, 20, 127, 208, 246, 271n106, 320n194
Kierkegaard, Søren, 131, 132
Kleist, Heinrich von, 154
Kofman, Sarah, 258n57
Kristeva, Julia, 9, 10, 18

Lacan, Jacques, 2–3, 254n7, 259n69
LaCapra, Dominick, 136, 297n170
Lacoue-Labarthe, Philippe, 106, 259n69
Lambert, Gregg, 268n83, 284n52
Leibniz, 238, 239
Levi, Primo, 80, 276n201
Lévinas, Emmanuel, 15, 16, 257n44, 280n1
Lévi-Strauss, Claude, 254n7, 259n69
Lispector, Clarice, 154
Lucretius, 233
Luhmann, Niklas, 218, 219, 221, 226–27, 229
Lyotard, Jean-François, 15, 16, 106, 259n69

Malabou, Catherine, xi
Mann, Thomas, 80
Marcuse, Herbert, 193–95, 201

Marion, Jean-Luc, 280n1
Marrati, Paola, 314n146
Martyn, Arun, 328n69, 329n70
Marx, Karl, 164, 173
Mascolo, Dionys, 76, 77–78, 83
Massumi, Brian, 253n5, 265n57, 279n249
May, Todd, 214
Melville, Herman, xii, 132, 183–87, 189, 190, 191–94, 195, 209, 251
Mengue, Philippe, 322n204
Mikkel, Borch-Jacobsen, 3
Miller, Adam, 113, 280n1, 284n51, 288n86,87
Mullarkey, John, 258n55
Mulligan, Kevin, 258n55
Murray, Timothy, 237, 238

Naas, Michael, 292n124, 295n151, 297n178
Nancy, Jean-Luc, 1–2, 3, 4, 5, 6, 12, 14, 15, 16–18, 19, 20, 26, 27–30, 46, 54–55, 56, 95, 97, 98–100, 103, 105, 106, 110, 121, 133, 140, 163, 165–66, 172, 174, 214, 221, 224, 233, 234–35, 238, 240–41, 244–48, 292n127, 305n19
Negri, Antonio, 21, 163, 182–83, 184, 185, 190, 191, 194, 201, 241, 265n57, 271n98
Neyrat, Frédéric, xi, 121, 283n51, 285n61, 296n167, 329n70
Nichanian, Marc, 260n75
Nietzsche, Friedrich, xiii, 39, 41, 43, 44–45, 46–47, 48, 49, 50, 56, 78–79, 80–81, 82, 269n90, 270n93
Nisard, Charles, 196

Obama, Barack, 200, 315n154
Ogilvie, Bertrand, 330n6
O'Sullivan, Simon, 278n234

Parnet, Claire, 61, 88, 279n251
Patton, Paul, 213, 314n148
Paul, St., 105–19

COMMONALITIES

Timothy C. Campbell, series editor

Roberto Esposito, *Terms of the Political: Community, Immunity, Biopolitics.* Translated by Rhiannon Noel Welch. Introduction by Vanessa Lemm.

Maurizio Ferraris, *Documentality: Why It Is Necessary to Leave Traces.* Translated by Richard Davies.

Dimitris Vardoulakis, *Sovereignty and Its Other: Toward the Dejustification of Violence.*

Anne Emmanuelle Berger, *The Queer Turn in Feminism: Identities, Sexualities, and the Theater of Gender.* Translated by Catherine Porter.

James D. Lilley, *Common Things: Romance and the Aesthetics of Belonging in Atlantic Modernity.*

Jean-Luc Nancy, *Identity: Fragments, Frankness.* Translated by François Raffoul.

Miguel Vatter, *Between Form and Event: Machiavelli's Theory of Political Freedom.*

Miguel Vatter, *The Republic of the Living: Biopolitics and the Critique of Civil Society.*

Maurizio Ferraris, *Where Are You? An Ontology of the Cell Phone.* Translated by Sarah De Sanctis.

Irving Goh, *The Reject: Community, Politics, and Religion After the Subject.*

Kevin Attell, *Giorgio Agamben: Beyond the Threshold of Deconstruction.*

J. Hillis Miller, *Communities in Fiction*